THE TEACHER IN CURRICULUM MAKING

EDUCATION FOR LIVING SERIES

Under the editorship

of

H. H. REMMERS

The Teacher
in Curriculum Making

JOSEPH LEESE
KENNETH FRASURE
College of Education at Albany
State University of New York

and

MAURITZ JOHNSON, Jr.
School of Education
Cornell University

HARPER & ROW, PUBLISHERS, NEW YORK AND EVANSTON

43855

The Teacher in Curriculum Making

Copyright © 1961 by Harper & Brothers

Printed in the United States of America

E-M

Library of Congress catalog card number: 61–6283

CONTENTS

FOREWORD   vii

PREFACE   ix

Part I. Perspective for the Teacher
    1. *The Study of the Curriculum*   3
    2. *The Curriculum Problem*   14
    3. *The Teacher as Key Factor*   39

Part II. Providing the Bases for Revisions
    4. *Personal Development of the Teacher*   63
    5. *Building the Foundations for Choice*   95
    6. *Working on the Broad Framework*   129

Part III. Individual Action for Better Experience
    7. *Planning Learning Experiences*   167
    8. *Production and Use of Resource Units*   206
    9. *Selection and Development of Instructional Materials*   230
    10. *Toward Improved Experience in the Subjects*   268
    11. *Developing and Working with the Core Curriculum*   305
    12. *Improving the Extraclass Program*   338

Part IV. Working with Others for Improvement
    13. *Organization for Curriculum Change*   369
    14. *Cooperative Procedures with the Staff*   398
    15. *Community Participation*   429
    16. *The Teacher and Curriculum Research*   463

INDEX   491

FOREWORD

....

Our founding fathers believed it to be essential that, in order to preserve our freedom and our republican form of government, every citizen should receive an education suited to his capacities. This education would prepare him first of all to become an intelligent participant in the process of decision-making, which in America has, since our independence was first won, been broadly diffused among the citizenry.

Over the years our country has gradually adopted the Jeffersonian principle of local control and applied it to our education. We have believed that authority should be placed as close as possible to the scene of action, in the interest of efficiency and creativeness.

A teacher in today's schools, educated in this philosophy of local control and widely diffused education, is confused by many voices, as were the workers on the biblical Tower of Babel.

In the face of great international crisis it is logical to anticipate that some leading voices will call for greater centralization of authority over education. These leaders present a highly logical case, for local control is not quickly responsive to national purpose in an emergency.

Other voices, activated by the fear that our nation will not be able to muster quickly the scientific and technical talent necessary to assure our defense, are understandably calling for greater and greater emphasis on the education of the gifted and talented, sometimes appearing to lose sight of the long-range purpose of education: to produce a generally enlightened electorate.

Today's teacher has been taught that his key role in education is to adapt a suitable curriculum to the needs of growing, individual children. In the absence of these adaptations, the curriculum is "as sounding brass and tinkling cymbals."

The purpose of *The Teacher in Curriculum Making* is to clarify for today's teacher in a clear, scientific manner, the techniques and procedures by means of which this traditional role may most effectively be carried out.

The Teacher in Curriculum Making is an excellent tool for this purpose. Teachers making careful use of this document as a guide to their day-to-day adaptation of today's curriculum will not only find their professional growth stimulated; by their efforts they will serve

to strengthen that local control and broadly diffused education to
which our founding fathers were dedicated.

This document should prove also to be a useful dimension of
teacher-preparation curricula.

WALTER CREWSON
Associate Commissioner
New York State Education Department

PREFACE

....

Most of the literature on the improvement of the curriculum stresses the need for the participation of a variety of contributors in these efforts. Among those usually identified, the classroom teacher is often referred to as the most important participant. He, it is held, makes the really important decisions that in the long run determine the quality of experience pupils will have in school.

Despite the assertions of the curriculum specialists it is not uncommon for the teacher to question what part he can and should take in curriculum work. Moreover, it is quite natural for the teacher to wonder how he can really exercise much influence on the extent and course of curriculum improvement. Since this is so, we believe the classroom teacher should have more opportunities and resources to study directly his various individual and group roles in curriculum improvement efforts. This book has been written to examine what the teacher can and should do in behalf of curriculum revisions.

In each of the four parts of the book an attempt has been made to be realistic about what this teacher participation means and about how teachers may go about making an impact. It is freely admitted, however, that broader tasks and responsibilities have been proposed for teachers than have been customary even in the recent past. It is not unlikely that some will despair of time or of capacity for executing well what is recommended. On the other hand we are sure that it will seem only proper to most teachers that now our profession has matured to the point where each teacher must interest himself actively in all the dimensions of school keeping that lead to better education. We do seem to be justified in setting our goals at our furthest reach.

Part I seeks to set the stage for this broader and more intimate involvement of the teacher. Against an analysis of some of the numerous problems confronting those who would improve the school program, the critical roles of the classroom teacher are emphasized. In Part II attention has been directed to the self-examination and basic preparation appropriate for some and necessary for many more to promote positive and effective effort.

The teacher's most important contribution, of course, must lie in the steps he takes to develop the richest possible experiences for the pupils with whom he meets daily. Part III is thus focused on those aspects of preparation and planning which are most directly related to the face-to-face relationships of pupil and teacher. Inasmuch as many of the changes and adaptations required to improve program are beyond the individual choice of the teacher and depend on general understanding and support and on broad policy change, the last part of the volume has been given over to consideration of how teachers can and should work together and with others outside the school staff.

Needless to say, much more might have been covered than is now contained in this book. Curriculum-making is a complex and difficult task that involves not only the development of a broad and extensive background and insight but also the exploration and attainment of many technical skills. Neither of these has been neglected in this volume. On the other hand the volume is not focused upon curriculum philosophers and theoreticians nor upon curriculum directors and specialists. It should, we believe, be useful to both these groups but its most pertinent contribution should be to the thousands of teachers upon whom curriculum quality depends. The book should be most helpful to those in service. At the same time it has been written to provide appropriate reading for the many classroom teachers who regularly make up the greatest portion of those registered in curriculum courses.

We are obviously indebted to just this latter group for the emphasis in the book. Both colleagues in the field and preservice teachers have contributed much in their suggestions, comments, and innumerable problem censuses. Further encouragement to make this approach to curriculum improvement has come from our immediate colleagues and from specialists in the New York State Education Department who have recognized the special function of the teacher in curriculum development. To Associate Commissioner Walter Crewson we are grateful for continuing stimulation and support, for his suggestions, and for the Foreword which expresses so vigorously our faith in the "grass roots." Particular appreciation is due Professor Hugh Smith of the College of Education at Albany who read the entire manuscript and made invaluable criticisms and suggestions.

JOSEPH LEESE
KENNETH FRASURE
MAURITZ JOHNSON, JR.

December 1960

PERSPECTIVE FOR THE TEACHER

CHAPTER 1

....

The Study of the Curriculum

"Curriculum: What Happens in our Schools—and Why," was the title of an issue of a newsletter published by the board of education of a certain school district to keep citizens informed about their schools. What happens in our schools—what teachers teach and what pupils learn—is the main concern of boards of education and should be a matter of great interest to all citizens. To those who are professionally engaged in education the question is of overwhelming significance.

School administrators are employed primarily to assure that the right things do happen in schools. Some people devote their lives to being curriculum specialists so that they may offer suggestions as to the aims of the curriculum and method of approach. But in the final analysis the key people in determining what does happen to pupils are the teachers. More than any other group they are the real curriculum makers and with them rests the responsibility for some of the most important and far-reaching decisions a society requires.

If these decisions are to be wise ones, teachers must be students— students of the curriculum and of the processes by which it may be improved. They must clarify for themselves their roles in these processes and how they may fit themselves for these roles. But first it is important to understand the nature of the curriculum.

THE CURRICULUM AS PLANNED LEARNING EXPERIENCES

The curriculum has been defined by specialists in very broad terms. Once thought of as a list of subjects taught in any school, it is now described as all the experiences children have as a result of their attendance in school. Others more modestly consider the curriculum as all the plans for learning, developed and organized by those responsible in school. Whichever recent definition one chooses, he must realize that curriculum study has been given a very broad scope. The student

3

of curriculum finds himself faced with a crushing burden of problems. In pursuit of improved experience, the student and his professor can range from discipline to promotion policy. Examination of possible plans may include methods of teaching and evaluation. In some colleges the course in curriculum is so closely tied to the way growth and development take place that the course of study is entitled, "Child and the Curriculum."

So far no one seems to have been concerned with setting sharp limits on what should be covered in the study of the curriculum. Since it is a relatively new title or subject, any such effort may be premature. Subjects apparently have a way of coming into focus over the years. In time, a separate, fairly discrete and precise area emerges from many related disciplines or one broad category.

Maturity of this kind has not come to this study known as curriculum. As yet there is no group of scholars who are prepared to lay down explicitly the proper dimensions of curriculum study. Thus, finding a locus and the points related to it depends very much upon those who teach and who would and should learn as much as possible about the curriculum.

The central goal of curriculum study, however, should not be difficult to determine. It must be obvious that what everyone wants, adults and children alike, is better experiences for those who go to school. Children want to have satisfaction and stimulation and to obtain the most useful and appropriate learning possible. Adults want their offspring to know more and to direct their own behavior ever more maturely. Professional educators want to discover what can be done; what adjustments, additions or eliminations, will raise the quality of experience in school. The goal of curriculum study is the improvement of the plans and the actual happenings we call experience.

The term *experience* needs some explanation at this point. Essentially it involves situations in which a person and his environment interact. From experience and only from experience comes learning. Not every such interaction, however, is productive of learning. If a previously established habitual pattern of response is adequate in a situation, little if any learning results. Learning ensues only when the pattern is modified or a new one is employed. The term *learning experience* is used, then, to denote one which produces a change in behavior, and those which are deliberately designed to do so constitute the curriculum.

Most teachers know the broad outlines of the usual over-all plan for children in school. It encompasses formal and informal activities under the direction of the school staff and includes for the most part an organized series of time allotments proposed for the learning of a selected variety of facts, skills, and attitudes. In some schools this program of more formal studies, flexible and elective activities, and special services is much more comprehensive than in others. In one school it may be so broad as to include quite different plans and arrangements for different pupils, while in another all pupils may be limited to a rather narrow set of exposures. Sometimes the different subplans are specially designated as the "college entrance curriculum" or the "vocational curriculum," or even at times the plan for teaching a subject may be called the "history curriculum" or the "science curriculum." This variety of usage may be somewhat disturbing, particularly if one prefers to be quite precise and detailed. For those who would make the word curriculum and experience synonymous, it is hardly satisfactory at all. It will not contribute much, however, to argue this point. We can proceed without too much difficulty if we keep in mind that all schools have plans for students and students have reactions. The combination makes for good education or poor education: it is the curriculum.

The plans schools do have at present have evolved over many years and represent the evaluations and efforts of many people. Location, size, finance, philosophy, and apparently a multitude of factors near at hand and far away also influence what the program of studies and the other provisions for learning will be. The maintenance of the local school system preserves the power of communities to pass on extensions and retractions. At the same time, we know that, throughout the country, state regulation, the interests of colleges, and the recommendations of school leaders have led to a widespread similarity in basic offerings and provisions. We can not tell with any degree of accuracy the quality of the experience pupils have as a result of these plans, but we do know the common structure and practice.

VARIETY OF PLACES FOR BEGINNING

Regardless of this devotion to formulating better plans, there is considerable evidence that the level to which teachers, parents, and pupils aspire with respect to school programs and results has not been achieved. Pupils drop out of school disgruntled; teachers know that pupils graduate much less well educated than they would like; patrons do not see the behavior change they anticipate. Improvement seems either too elusive a quarry, or is so complex that great effort yields but minor reward. Actually, effort has not failed to be productive. A great deal has been accomplished, particularly in the years following intensive examination of the curriculum. More can be done and more will need to be done each succeeding year. The rapidity of social change and the increases in knowledge about human behavior, to mention but two factors, will not relieve us of the necessity of giving continuous attention to curriculum adaptation.

What to study and where to initiate that study in pursuit of improvement depends, of course, on time and breadth of purpose. To be most efficient in one sense, we should be orderly and should move from simple and obvious questions to those more complex and involved. On the other hand, contributions to improvement may be secured by quite instrumental choice of issues to be resolved or problems to be solved. The alternatives may well be selected on the basis of whether one proposes to be a curriculum scholar or a curriculum worker, or both. Some would argue that examination of the curriculum begins most appropriately with a list of the personal concerns a teacher has to face. Others would start with a study of the purposes of schools. At least one author would begin with a thorough review of what the schools of the past offered and an investigation of those they served and how they operated.

To contribute much to the improvement of the curriculum, though, it is clear that the curriculum worker must deal with a large number of related areas. Even on the most practical and immediate matters, choices grow from insights and commitments drawn from many fields and disciplines. One actually initiates curriculum study when he seeks to understand what motivates interest in and desire for knowledge. He takes a major step when he undertakes to acquire mastery of an academic discipline. Registration in an undergraduate methods course leads to consideration of appropriate assignments, techniques of guidance and control, and other elements in the teaching process. This means that all teachers begin to study the curriculum when they set out on teaching preparation. It is only proper that this point be recognized and that those who plan to improve the curriculum or to pursue any formal course of study on the curriculum recognize that what must be considered can not be completely novel and discrete.

CRITICISMS AS A STARTING POINT

In Chapter 2 there is a short review of the deficiencies and limitations in the present school program. The complaints voiced by a number of educators and noneducators have been listed and described.

Claims and counterclaims about the same procedures, outcomes, and offerings reveal the confusion and complexity of the situation. We find those who disavow and want to dispense with a large portion of the reform which has taken place; some want to move vigorously ahead, replacing traditional courses with new ones, instituting more liberal methods in the classroom, expanding and extending the scope of the tasks given the school. Apparently the majority of citizens and a very large portion of teachers are uncertain as to what they can accept as the truth of the matter and as to where they stand. The student of the curriculum, then, can well afford to attend carefully at an early point to the actual state of affairs. No one can decide for him now and there is little chance that anyone will decide for him in the future.

VALUES INVOLVED

The disconcerting aspect of improvement and change is of course the determination of what ought to be changed. If there were clear direction and overwhelming support for that direction, some would be relieved. They would know what the majority supported and that would be enough. But most of us reserve the right to think for ourselves and to vote independently for what we believe to be proper. Even many of those who want to know what the experts believe hold dear the prerogative to pass personal judgment and to campaign for the right as they see it.

Part of curriculum study, then, is philosophy. Each person needs to decide for himself what he values, what is important to him, what he believes about the process of education. He will then find some with whom he agrees and many with whom he is in disagreement.

To anticipate, however, that one can come soon or firmly to positions on what is right for all times about the goals and processes of education would be too optimistic. Most of the values one develops never become completely fixed. They are always subject to review and revision.

KNOWLEDGE OF APPROACHES

Extremely important in the life and development of any institution are the values and opinions maintained by particular members. In the family, if the father believes prompt and precise obedience is important, children are likely to toe the mark and do as the father says.

Even if the children do not value obedience and are disinclined to obey, the odds are that they will sit at the table until excused and report home when the curfew hour arrives. It is obvious that the plan can be laid out by those who have authority and control. The power to discipline restricts subordinates who have different values.

The school program is subject to similar controls. There are those who have power and authority to decide much of the over-all structure and educative process in the school. There is the possibility also that subordinates who have different values may rebel and disobey in one form or another.

Change or improvement in the curriculum plan may come about through the vigorous effort of those who can make major and sweeping decisions. At the same time it may be the product of intimate and personal action on the part of a teacher who, valuing something strongly, exercises influence within the general controls laid down by others.

Curriculum study, then, must include search into the ways by which each participant can bring about those situations and conditions he values. For some changes he must win the approval and support of colleagues near and far. For many which are extremely important, he must have the personal conviction, the skill, and the courage to make substantial changes in his own method.

MANY WAYS TO IMPROVE THE CURRICULUM

Real and significant changes do not come about all at once or all by the same means. Proverbially, "there is more than one way to skin a cat." Too, there are many channels by which the deficiencies and limitations in the curriculum may be removed. Many of the channels are already represented in the plethora of courses offered in colleges for the preparation of teachers. Among them we all recognize easily those courses in evaluation, methods of teaching, mental hygiene, guidance, reading, directing pupil study, educational sociology, and so on. Few catalogs call these curriculum courses, but in effect most of them are. They help the teacher contribute more to the quality of pupil experience. They also help develop broad concepts of what a school should do.

Throughout this book, therefore, we have discussed topics similar to some found in courses such as those mentioned. In addition we have devoted attention to how the teacher may work cooperatively with colleagues upon a number of tasks, including building morale, clarifying position and attitude, informing and advising the public. Through research, through participation in workshops, through experimentation in his own classroom, the teacher may introduce new ideas and challenge old ones. In professional associations and through service on official district committees, he can exert influence far beyond the immediate situation in which he works. Above all, the teacher can make his contribution through a thorough examination of his own professional and personal responsibilities.

It is probable that so far the greatest amount of time in the curriculum improvement movement has gone into talking about what ought to be done. This, perhaps, is quite defensible, because, through extensive interchange of opinion, we clarify our own ideas and help others more fully explore theirs. On the other hand, there are many who are inclined to think that there has been far too much talk and too little action. The changes that should have come about have not. Apparently, failure to get things down on paper and failure to get specific decisions about details out of broad oral generalizations and agreements have resulted in much too much inaction.

The obverse of talk and exploration in a number of places has been precipitant action in getting curriculum guides and courses of study written. Filled with enthusiasm to prepare their very own materials, led to believe it almost sinful to use texts and workbooks, faculty groups have exhausted themselves in producing guides and bulletins, only to discover that subsequent administrators and supervisors have not been impressed.

DETERMINATION OF PURPOSE PARAMOUNT

The goals and purposes of the program of education must be clearly understood; agreement has to be reached as to the most important requirements. If we do not have clear direction, we can not make the basic choices about major or minor details on school regulations. Some critics have already thrown us into great confusion with unrestrained attacks. That their mischief misleads the public is understandable. But widespread uneasiness and self-doubt on the part of teachers and their leaders is all but unforgivable. A profession should know what it stands for, what it fervently believes. That a few leaders, a few commission members, a few philosophy professors give vigorous support to something called education for democracy is not enough. The rank and file must know all the practical intricacies and byways of the argument. Otherwise they engage in veritable sabotage. At not too great a risk, it may be said that this gap between those who have a carefully examined position and commitment and those who play by ear is enormous. And those who play by ear are great in number, their usual response being that deciding major alternatives is for the giants of thought. Not so! The giants may propose; but they must neither impose nor depose.

ORGANIZATION AND STRUCTURE NEED ATTENTION

Once agreed on the objectives, any group has only begun its job, although it has accomplished a most critical step. The question of how to achieve them (what broad arrangements or plans will permit and facilitate progress) has to be faced. Few school districts start from scratch on this. They inherit a great deal.

Upon first view, the existence of so much tradition, prior decision, and external control in the form of rules and regulations by state boards, legislatures, and accrediting agencies may suggest that the local district and the teacher have no prerogative or responsibility. Neither is the case. Although state agencies do have the power to provide the outlines for a program, the freedom granted local faculties to plan what should be included and how it should be managed is great. Needless to say, nobody has *carte blanche*. Too much is at stake. Nevertheless, the cooperative nature of program planning is clear. Which subjects to offer, whether to provide an elective system, what definition and form to give guidance and counseling, how important extra-class activities should be made, what to include in the common experience program—all these questions must be considered.

IMPROVING TEACHING OF PRIMARY IMPORTANCE

The whole of the effort devoted to analyzing the needs of society and of the individuals who comprise it, to specifying purposes, to identifying what is to be learned, and to producing textbooks and units is of no avail unless it results in worthwhile education for children. The crux of the whole process is what happens to and in a child. Regardless of the brilliance of remote plans and the wisdom demonstrated in adding new subjects and maintaining old ones, little is accomplished if the child is not influenced, if his behavior does not move to a higher and more mature level as a result of his experience.

The tragedy of much curriculum improvement activity is that it has not substantially affected the quality of the learning situation or the quantity learned. Prodigious efforts by study committees, intensive workshops, and numerous conferences have had limited influence because they often have not been effective in changing what goes on within the classroom; in altering what happens in the relationship between child and teacher—the relationship that leads to learning.

In the classroom the teacher is, in effect, master. Once the door is closed, it is upon the teacher that students depend for knowledge, for insight, for stimulation. The teacher has it in his power to determine whether a student will increase or decrease his interest. In the end, the choice of tasks, the nature of assignments, and the pace of learning rest upon the guidance provided. If rich and exciting stories are suggested and quick insight is obtained through the consideration of problems that can be managed, the student usually finds the further pursuit of knowledge and skill worthy of time and effort. On the other hand, if learning is made tedious, if there seems to be no purpose in the acquisition of facts, if the excuse for study is some vague future application, we may anticipate that respect for, and satisfaction with, school will diminish. The student will evade his responsibility and default on his opportunity. The experience the student has under school auspices will be unrewarding.

There is, then, no good curriculum, regardless of the organization, the subjects offered, or the content selected, until what the pupil does with and under the direction of the teacher results in positive, practical, and permanent learning. Curriculum improvement must be improvement in the classroom. This means simply that the teacher must play a continuous and critical role. His examination of his own procedures, of his values, of his approaches to learning, of his personal resources is absolutely necessary if progress is to be recorded.

We may have national studies; we may have testimony on the value of traditional subjects; we may have careful counting of Carnegie units and an increase in the number required for high school graduation; we may move areas of study up or down in the program sequence. These may look like important curriculum decisions and they may make some contributions quantitatively and administratively. But we must not be misled; the essence of the curriculum will always be in the learning transaction, in the impact of teacher and situation upon pupil.

CURRICULUM AS A COMPREHENSIVE AND COOPERATIVE EFFORT

We can easily see that no individual or small group can determine all the curriculum or all the plans for experiences children have in school. Schools have been a long time in developing. What they are expected to do is expressed in the law; it is impressed in the memories of those who have attended and approve or disapprove; it is condensed in the broad outcome anticipated from pupils. Top officers in state education departments have great power to direct and decide. But their decisions can be no better than the willingness and capacity of their colleagues in the classroom to implement them. The best resources and materials, developed by experts, will be drab trappings indeed, and ineffectual, in the hands of dull and dispirited mechanics.

Improvements in plans which guarantee richer and more rewarding experiences for children must grow from the combined efforts of many. Much will have to be coordinated and planned and directed by those invested with leadership responsibility. A great deal more will have to be done independently, on the basis of personal commitment and perception, by those who work intimately with children.

In the next chapter attention is focused on the nature and scope of the problems of improving the curriculum. It will be soon made clear, if the reader is not already convinced, that the development of a program for the schools that our people want is a complex and involved matter. We can not expect much progress by simple tinkering at one spot or by working along without grasp of what needs to be done to relate the near and the remote. Each participant needs to see the broad issues and their counterparts in immediate matters to which he can make his own unique contribution. Both molar and molecular views are necessary for the teacher as well as the director of the curriculum.

Questions for Discussion

1. The curriculum has become a professional subject in colleges of education since World War I. Why? Does it seem necessary to you to have a curriculum specialist in a school system?
2. What do you think should appropriately be considered in a curriculum course? Could you establish any logical hierarchy in a curriculum course and in curriculum course content?
3. Do the program of studies and the curriculum differ?
4. What areas of the curriculum should be studied and by whom?
5. Who should decide the relative merits of the curriculum?
6. Why are you engaged in curriculum study? What can it do for you? What are your expectations?

Selected Bibliography

Association for Supervision and Curriculum Development, *What Should the High School Teach?* The Association, 1956, chap. 3.

Hopkins, L. Thomas, "Overview," *Interaction: The Democratic Process,* Heath, 1941.

Krug, Edward, *Curriculum Planning,* rev. ed., Harper, 1957, chap. 1.

Romine, Stephen, *Building the High School Curriculum,* Ronald, 1954, chap. 2.

Saylor, J. Galen, and William Alexander, *Curriculum Planning,* Rinehart, 1954, chap. 1, 2.

Stratemeyer, Florence, *et al., Developing a Curriculum for Modern Living,* Bureau of Publications, Teachers College, 1957, chap. 1.

CHAPTER 2

....

The Curriculum Problem

With as many stockholders and consumers as there are in the public school enterprise, it is little wonder that the secondary school curriculum is not free from criticism and debate. Now grown to unexpected proportions, the school serves the young and old alike, and in its program pursues goals far beyond the dreams of its founders. To it, in peace and war, in depression and prosperity, parents, businessmen, and youth turn in the hope that it will fulfill so many varied expectations, simple and complex, similar and different as nearly to stun the imagination. Some know exactly what they want; others are vague and uncertain in their demands. In similar vein, the results are viewed at some points with alarm and at some points with gratification. If a business man who wants a typist is satisfied, a college professor who requires special competence in exposition and description is not. If there is one group of students which is enthusiastic about reading *The Tempest* and learning about the Pendleton Act, there is certainly a group which objects to these or similar assignments with vigor and with distaste. While there are patrons who want swimming pools and practical arts courses, there are other citizens who decry the indulgence of youth and call for a return to traditional methods and recapture of the old virtues.

So turbulent a state of affairs can not be anything but disturbing to some. It would be much better for them if there were no controversy, no sharp difference of opinion, no anguished doubts. Many more would be happier with a somewhat less aggressive contention, particularly about minor matters. The great majority seems relatively satisfied with continuous and periodically more enthusiastic debate. For them, apparently, out of vigorous difference of opinion come growth and progress, new direction, new faith. In the tradition of

America every man has not only the right, but the responsibility, to speak up!

A quick review of our educational history over the last fifty years will reveal almost continuous discussion, evaluation, and criticism of the schools. Throughout the 1930's and 1940's the tempo increased with numerous committee reports, investigations, and surveys adding volumes of ideas and proposals. In the decade following World War II the vigor of the critics created a furor which promises to continue for some time to come. The issues have been taken up by journalists and commentators who use the mass media to reach the lay public, and doubtless more citizens are being informed, advised, and invited to think about their schools than has been the case at any previous time. Problems heretofore discussed only in academic circles, in professional meetings, and in school board sessions are being presented in the lay journals, for the most part by articulate critics of modern developments in education.

In some ways it appears that more confusion than clarity is produced. Certainly plenty of heat has been generated. Yet out of the welter of assertion, claim, denial, proposal and counterproposal, as has been the case before, there will and must emerge a program best suited to the time and place in which we live. Obviously, now, the decisions both large and small will not come easily nor will those who make them prevail easily. Obtaining sufficient, if not a full, grasp of the details presents both a tedious and time-consuming task.

Many Advocates Involved in Resolution of the Problems

The number of people who need to have clear understanding of the problems and issues at stake and who require knowledge, insights, and skills to help improve the situation is great. Nearly everybody can vote and express himself on the school program and its quality in one way or another. The forceful citizen influences the board member on everything from cafeteria accounting to the extent of intramural sports activity. The unhappy college professor affects the textbook writer or writes the high school texts himself. The administrator sets restrictions or liberties that determine program offerings. The teacher raises or lowers his standards in the light of the circumstances surrounding his work.

The influence of a single chief school administrator, textbook writer, or professor of pedagogy is generally of greater impact, and more easily brought to bear, than is the influence of a parent, social critic, or self-appointed reformer. There is indeed a hierarchy of those who can affect more quickly and more widely what is done in and by the school. On the other hand, in recent years there has been constant pressure to increase the number of those who can affect the program and its development and to focus more effectively their ideas and desires. Leadership in this direction has been taken by the schools' administrators and supervisors. The fruits are the wider public interest noted above and more active participation by large groups, specialized and nonspecialized.

What each of these potential advocates and participants knows and believes and how he acts upon that knowledge and conviction will have appreciable influence on the work of others upon whom improvement depends. The remote participant will have to act upon little specific information, only broad generalizations. He has neither the time nor the interest to become a student of curriculum problems, particularly those pertaining to the selection of specific learning experiences and to the motivation and guidance of learning activity. At times he may act upon little knowledge in ways that actually hamper and handicap, but that is the price that must be paid for wider participation. On the other hand, the closely and intimately involved professional needs to know the whole state of affairs, to be informed of the antecedents, to know the present position and the alternatives, and to have reasoned, deliberate proposals for improvement. Against such a full background, the administrator, the supervisor, the staff person, or the teacher must play out his role with poise and finesse if the educational program is really to move forward.

With so many observing the program of the schools and evaluating the products, opinions as to the deficiencies and requisites of the program are almost as varied as the observers. At many points there are direct contradictions regarding the situation and directly opposing ideas about what needs be done to improve it. Those who would develop a better curriculum, then, regardless of their role, are faced with the difficult job of separating truth from fiction, the defensible from the unacceptable. Their job is further compounded by the fact that the so-called curriculum experts themselves disagree sharply at many points.

LAY CRITICISMS

There is little evidence that the majority of the public is personally very concerned about the curriculum. Most are willing to rely upon the educators to work out a stimulating and rewarding set of experiences for their children. When the randomly selected adult is asked how satisfied he is with what is being taught in the schools, the most common response is likely to be, "O.K., I guess." If pushed further, he may express some discomfort with vaguely defined "progressive stuff" which he "does not go for," but he is hard put to be explicit. Many of those who once attended the secondary school wonder if any progress is being made toward dropping out "some of the stuff you can't use," and adding "more practical things."

Those who had real difficulty doing the work of the school are reminded of their discomforts when asked what they think. For the most part their questions are directed toward the inappropriateness of the curriculum. They wonder if it is right to keep young people in school when they can not or do not want to learn, and they object to the academic and verbal nature of the subjects. A few among them repent their earlier failure to apply themselves as well as they think they might have and hope teachers are being more insistent on harder study even if pupils resist. They have begun to think it is a good thing to be required to do hard tasks.

Most of the opinions the usual layman has about the program in the schools appear to be related to the financial burdens involved or to feelings and attitudes expressed by his children who go to school. The man in the street wonders if it all ought to cost so much and if "some of those things they do" could not just as well be eliminated. He repeats his son's objections that "they make you study a lot of stuff you'll never use," and he shares with his daughter her interest in having some more studies that will help her get and do well on future jobs. Primarily, his concerns are with the personal and what is near at hand. His major general observation is that the schools do not change as quickly as they ought to in the face of the way "things are happening these days." Most likely he knows there are lots of things wrong in the schools, as there are everywhere, in government, in business, in labor activity, but he can not itemize very much.

Small but Vigorous Protest Groups

However, what the usual layman lacks in specific and critical reaction is compensated for by a few scholars, authors, and magazine and newspaper writers. In the books and articles of these critics there are full accounts, truths, half-truths, and completely misleading statements about the curriculum problem. Several summaries and analyses of the evaluations made by these articulate laymen have been made. In general their criticisms fall into a fairly common pattern.

FUNDAMENTALS POORLY TAUGHT

The most often repeated claim is that the schools are inefficient with respect to achievement in both the simple and complex goals. It is asserted that the fundamental skills are inadequately learned, that students can not write meaningfully, legibly, nor correctly, that they can not read understandingly or appreciatively, and that they have no power to work effectively with mathematical symbols.

The complex goals said to be neglected are the powers to reason and to think through problems, to exercise imagination and creativity, to manifest high levels of insight and appreciation. To these are added attributes of character which it is held the traditional school produced in abundance.

INTELLECTUALISM ABANDONED

The second weakness emphasized by this group is the departure of the school from serious intellectual pursuit. The introduction of courses of study to accommodate the needs and interests of nonacademic pupils is viewed with alarm as a planned effort to reduce the schools to practicalism and vocationalism.

The counterproposal is to "restore" the five intellectual disciplines —mathematics, foreign languages, history, English, and science—to a commanding place in the curriculum, to fortify them with stiff examinations, and to urge, if not impose, them upon all pupils.

PROPER SCOPE OF SCHOOLS OUTGROWN

A third target is the redefinition and extension of purposes of the high school and the consequent change in its offerings. The opinion is expressed that youths now study in school a multitude of matters which are better left to the church, the home, the community, and other agencies of society. The well-developed and expanded extracurricular program is seen as a drain on pupil time which would be better spent on academic study, and as an indulgence of interests better kept outside the school.

SERIOUS SCARS LEFT BY PROGRESSIVISM

Soft pedagogy, defined as lowering of standards of accomplishment, reduced competition, continuous promotion, and increased involvement of pupils in selecting what to study, constitutes another discouraging area. Recognizing that the broader definition of the curriculum is the kind of experiences which youth can obtain in school, the dismayed critic asserts, conversely, that what the young are really learning from the schools is to search for "pie-in-the-sky," to get by with nothing, to be disrespectful of true accomplishment.

MORAL AND SPIRITUAL VALUES NEGLECTED

A sizable segment of the articulate discontents belabor the absence in the curriculum of any adequate approach to or treatment of religion. The claim is made that if the schools are not already antireligious in applying a Deweyan philosophy, they are at best ineffectual because they ignore religion. Most of the emphasis in these complaints is on the asserted failure of the schools to attend to the development of moral and spiritual values.

QUESTIONABLE PRACTICES INTRODUCED

The sixth major objection is that the curriculum makers are confused about values and are pursuing ends and purposes of questionable validity for America. The de-emphasis on examinations and report cards, the attention given to cooperative and group work, and the reorganization of history into social studies are seen all as one piece—a compromise with, if not a direct assault upon, the American system of free enterprise and competitive effort.

With the publication of *The Lonely Crowd* by David Riesman there was a vigorous revival of attacks upon the "adjustment" orientation of the curriculum. Quick to accept the viewpoint that Americans are becoming much less independent in thought and action and much more inclined to set their course by sensing the direction of the group, many have expressed hope that the schools will shift sharply away from cultivation of the power to "group-think." The "desperate conformity" of the adolescent, fostered by the schools as much as anything, is sure to carry the common man further into commonness, they say. In "Is the Common Man Too Common?" Krutch writes

Unfortunately, the fanatical exaltation of the common denominator has been taken up not only by the common man himself and by those who profit by his exploitation but also and increasingly by those who are supposed to be educators and intellectual leaders. Instead of asking "What should a good education consist of?" many professors of education are asking "What do most college students want?"; instead of asking "What books are wisest and best and most beautiful?" they conduct polls to determine which the largest number of students have read.[1]

The feeling is that the curriculum makers are more concerned with pleasing than with setting standards of excellence and are more con-

[1] Joseph Wood Krutch, "Is the Common Man Too Common?" in Blaine Mercer and Edwin Carr, *Education and the Social Order*, Rinehart, 1957, p. 194.

cerned with seeing that the student does not get off the beaten track and become "inner directed," than they are that he develop his uncommon excellence.

SOCIAL ILLS AND INEFFICIENCY OF THE SCHOOLS

In addition to these six rather commonly and persistently alleged shortages, there are many other more specific items selected as illustrations of the inadequate and unsatisfactory curriculum of the secondary schools. Any number of social ills are considered to be in large part products of the inefficiency of the school program. Poor taste in literature, naiveté about the wild promises of advertisers, rampaging installment debt, juvenile delinquency, rejections for physical and health deficiency of those conscripted for military service, the paucity of engineering manpower, ignorance of international events, nonparticipation in voting, and a host of others, are held to result from the lack of unity and stability in the school curriculum, the excess of so-called functional courses, and the license given the pupil to fritter away his time on unimportant and frivolous undertakings which do not train his mind. The elective system is bemoaned; the decreasing registration in foreign languages is decried; and the lack of interest and dedication of students is emphasized.

More Balanced View of Deliberative Groups

The general survey in the preceding paragraphs has reported in the main the expressed opinions of a number of vigorous individual contributors to journals and the ideas of several of a limited group of dissatisfied and determined college professors. The justice and fairness of their evaluations are not to be examined here. The appropriate comment may be that much fault has been found with their sweeping generalizations, particularly as they imply incompetence and irrationality on the part of professional educators. Well-documented, scholarly replies have been written. A collection of these may be found in *Public Education Under Criticism.*[2]

A much more restrained and rational kind of lay statement of the curriculum problem can be found in a number of reports presented by citizens to boards of education. As a result of the exchange of opinion about the educational program since World War II, several states commissioned groups of laymen to examine the work of the schools and make recommendations for improvement. One of the most

[2] C. Winfield Scott and Clyde Hill, *Public Education Under Criticism*, Prentice-Hall, 1954.

complete of these surveys and deliberations was that undertaken in New York State by the Regents Council on Readjustment of High School Education—a group of twenty prominent representatives of industry, labor, commerce, agriculture, etc. Working, studying, and deliberating for nearly five years these citizens reported their conclusions in *The Schools We Need,* written by the committee chairwoman, a housewife. Concluding that "Our schools have made mistakes, including occasional glaring misapplications of new teaching methods and instances of shortsighted planning, they are far better on the whole than most people realize," the Council proposed the following credo to the Board of Regents which was adopted by that body in 1954.

EDUCATION—AN AMERICAN HERITAGE

We, the people of New York State, believing in the equality of opportunity for all and realizing that education is fundamental to our democratic way of life, do hereby recognize and accept these basic premises:
—that every youth should be afforded the opportunity to obtain at least a high school education;
—that every youth shall have the fullest opportunity for moral and ethical development in keeping with our American heritage;
—that every youth has certain needs and responsibilities that are common to all youth and to the perpetuation of our democratic society;
—that every youth, as a person of inherent worth, differs from every other young person in respect to health, mental ability, interests and background.
Since these premises are self-evident to those who have faith in our democracy, it becomes necessary that our high schools provide:
—a program of studies in general education that will insure the unity of our people for the common good;
—diversified experiences and educational services that will meet the educational, vocational and avocational needs of our youth;
—counseling that will help young people make intelligent choices beneficial to self and society;
—those services that will assist youth to be physically and mentally healthy;
—qualified teachers, extended research and expanded facilities to meet more effectively the changing demands on education
Recognizing that the school is but one segment of our complex society requiring the full support of the community, we conceive it our duty as citizens of New York State to provide for the full support of these schools to guarantee each youth his American heritage.[3]

To implement that credo and to carry forward to an improved curriculum for New York State the Council presented sixteen specific recommendations. Like other lay critics they called for higher standards,

---

[3] Isabel Kideney (ed.), *The Schools We Need,* New York State Education Department, 1954, p. 13.

but to them, "The highest standard of education a school can aim at is the development of every one of its students to his *maximum potential*. A school with this aim is setting its sights much higher than a school that tries mainly to fit as many pupils as possible into a uniform pattern of courses."[4]

The study conducted in Connecticut at the behest of Governor Bowles was even more extensive in its involvement of laymen. The conclusions there grew from intensive investigations by hundreds of people in eighty-five towns. The lengthy synthesis of their research and reactions, *Do Citizens and Education Mix?*, includes recommendations on critical factors relating to the improvement of education. Admonishing the elementary schools to provide better preparation for and articulation with the high schools, most of the subgroups throughout the state called for more intensive work upon the fundamental skills. They saw for the high schools the obligation to provide better preparation for earning a living, going to college, and being a citizen. The latter goal, it was felt, could be achieved more satisfactorily if all Connecticut students learned from their high school programs to

Get along with others—respect others
Know what is going on in the world
Understand how democracy works and what their role in it is
Be able to assume responsibility—to lead and to follow
To behave as a part of a group, to win and lose gracefully, to cooperate, to be a good sport
To be critical, to be able to analyze, to locate and evaluate sources of information, to be able to express themselves coherently and convincingly
To apply what they have learned to actual practice
To know how to use leisure time, to enjoy themselves[5]

The work of the Ohio School Survey[6] conducted in sixty-six of the eighty-eight counties of that state reveals comparable observations, if not discomforts and dissatisfactions with the school program. Offering 107 recommendations, as a result of intensive study by 100 subcommittee members of the opinions of more than 40,000 respondents, *What Faces Ohio's Public Schools* focuses attention on what Ohio citizens believe the schools ought to be doing for their children. The report spells out the need for a broader, more effective program for

---

[4] *Ibid.*, p. 29.

[5] Governor's Fact Finding Commission on Education, *Do Citizens and Education Mix?* The Commission, 1951, p. 146.

[6] Ohio School Survey Committee, *What Faces Ohio's Public Schools?*, The Committee, 1954, p. 10.

health protection and physical development, for a more adequately stated and more widely understood specification of objectives, for more and higher quality vocational education, for a richer general education supplemented or extended by opportunity for courses in home arts, business, and consumership, as well as in art, music, and other aesthetic activity. The failure of many Ohio schools to assure an adequate range of offerings of the essential subjects is noted with dismay, particularly when the cumulated evidence demonstrates that programs of extraclass activity are very likely overemphasized. The need for greatly extended library resources and services is added as especially important, among a considerable number of other recommendations.

Probably the most discussed report about the program of the secondary school is that submitted to the American public by James B. Conant. Through the efforts of the Carnegie Corporation and through the paperback edition published by McGraw-Hill, *The American High School Today* has found its way to a very large number of people. The twenty-one recommendations for improving the program in the comprehensive high school propose that

1. The counseling system be extended and expanded
2. Student programs be individually adapted
3. There be a required general education provision with four years of English and at least three years of social studies
4. Ability groups be provided for
5. The high school diploma be supplemented with an academic record
6. One-half the time of English teaching be devoted to composition
7. A diversified arrangement be provided for teaching marketable skills
8. Special consideration be given very slow readers
9. Offerings for the academically talented include the five traditional high-school subjects, supported by homework, characterized by hard study, and supplemented by additional academic opportunity
10. Very special provision be made for the gifted, including as possibilities, special tutors, advanced placement courses, and other benefits
11. A yearly academic inventory be undertaken
12. The number of periods of instruction in the school day be increased
13. A well-understood prerequisites regulation be established to protect advanced study
14. Class rank not be related to pupils' grades in all subjects
15. Academic accomplishment be particularly and publicly noted
16. There be provided a developmental reading program
17. A tuition-free summer school be operated
18. Foreign language instruction be extended and improved
19. Science offerings be increased and divided between consumer and producer courses
20. Homerooms be organized to become significant social units in a school

21. A twelfth-grade course in the social studies with cross-sectional membership be installed[7]

It can be seen quickly from these proposals and from a reading of
Conant's concise volume that the report is more concerned with structure and organization and with the administrative aspects of the program than it is with the dynamics and details that produce quality
education. Even so, it is obvious to anyone that Conant's ideas touch
on extremely important aspects of the job of improving the curriculum. Convinced that the comprehensive high school is the most
appropriate means to secure the broad objectives of American education, he has laid out one format which indicates where many important
adaptations need to be made.

OPINIONS OF YOUTH

Obviously it is just as hard to satisfy all the adolescents in the
secondary schools as it is to satisfy the adults who pay for the schools.
The range of approval and disapproval is great, but for the most part
youth is not in revolt. The school is a must. In the main, young
people have faith in their teachers; they think things are about as good
as they could be. However, from a number of surveys of youth opinion
it is possible to draw some generalizations regarding the curriculum
problem as seen from the youth point of view.

Drop-outs and Criticism of School

The number of youth who drop out of school before graduation
indicates a broad and basic weakness in the school curriculum. When
asked their reasons for failure to continue in school, a sizable percentage cited their discomfort with the offerings, regarding them to be too
difficult, too impractical, too lacking in interest for them. Suggestions
offered by the drop-out for improving matters usually included better
understanding, more sympathy, and respect from teachers, more time
devoted to practical arts, more counseling and guidance, reduction of
verbal and book learning with emphasis on making things interesting,
more time devoted to business training and getting ready for a variety
of jobs, providing opportunity to earn while going to school, and
making available a greater number of varied offerings.[8]

[7] James Conant, *The American High School Today,* McGraw-Hill, 1959,
pp. 44–76.
[8] A study by Henry in Arkansas revealed that the percentage of withdrawals
decreased as the number of curriculum offerings increased. See J. D. Henry, "A

Unfulfilled Requirements

Perhaps the objection repeated most often by those who have completed school is that it does not provide them with a salable skill. Despite the argument that the school should not provide apprentice training or involve itself extensively in vocationalism, there is widespread expectancy among youth that the school will give them specific practical training in earning a living. The fact, regularly repeated by high school counselors, that the greatest proportion of jobs require no special in-school preparation, really has little effect on the expectancy. Few youths appear willing to think of themselves as bound for or limited to unskilled or semiskilled jobs.

A large number of surveys, opinion inventories, and studies have been conducted over the last quarter of a century to find out what students want and what they think they get. A good review was prepared by Doane[9] in his *Needs of Youth,* and a more recent summary has been included in the Fifty-second Yearbook[10] of the National Society for the Study of Education. No study has been comprehensive enough to provide anything like a national picture of the adequacy of the curriculum with respect to what youth expects of the school, but many of the studies indicate adolescents are unhappy that the school does not help them understand themselves, does not provide them with sufficient skills to get along well and comfortably with others their own age, does not give them a philosophy of life, and does not satisfactorily help them with problems of sex adjustment, in addition to failing to help them select and prepare for a vocation.

One item of discontent is that, although they are often asked about the failure of the school, students seldom, if ever, have a real opportunity to bring about any changes. Only occasionally does the student have a real opportunity to participate effectively in determining how his time will be used and how his program will be managed. Proposals for greater participation by youth in curriculum planning have been made in many of the writings on curriculum improvement. To date the suggestions have been mainly concerned with the way teacher and pupil can plan together to develop experiences for

---

Study of Some Factors Associated with the Withdrawal of Students from the Secondary Schools of Arkansas," Ph.D. Thesis, University of Arkansas, Fayetteville, 1953.

[9] Donald Doane, *The Needs of Youth,* Bureau of Publication, Teachers College, 1942, Contributions to Education, No. 848.

[10] Nelson Henry, ed., *Adapting the Secondary School Program to the Needs of Youth,* National Society for the Study of Education, 1953.

the class unit, but the implication that students should have a wider role has been clear. The point has been argued effectively in a number of books and articles.[11]

EVALUATIONS BY PROFESSIONAL EDUCATORS

It may be fair to say that the educators themselves are the source of the greatest portion of criticism expressed about the school curriculum. Thousands of classroom lectures and discussions have been devoted to evaluation, suggestions, and proposals. The number of magazines serving the teaching profession has grown rapidly, and they are regularly filled with articles identifying deficiencies and limitations in the profession and exhorting it to higher goals and to more efficiency in obtaining them. In-service training programs and faculty meetings are constantly focused on improvement of program. The research undertaken to assess the effect of the teaching, the attitudes of pupils, the validity of content, and the motivation of students has reached astonishing proportions—too much for any person to acquaint himself with even during five years of preparation for teaching.

The upshot of all this is a mass of data, opinion, and suggestion which both the interested layman and the student of education have come to know in some or great amount, depending on interest and purpose. After exposure to it, many an exasperated teacher has concluded that there are many more questions than answers and much more that is wrong than is right. A greater portion of those who are not so overwhelmed recognizes that a great deal needs to be done to bring practice into line with theory and to approximate in reality the ideals to which educators often are dedicated but quite unable to spell out.

Curriculum Improvement Wanted by Teachers

Classroom teachers in general seem to support the contention that the curriculum as a whole is still too much oriented to the college-bound student, satisfying his need for verbal and academic education, but neglecting a vast number of pupils who need training in the practical arts, work experience, knowledge, and skill for adequate solution of everyday problems of living. They would increase the courses offered, substitute in many places less rigorous programs of study, and minimize the importance of, or eliminate, selected traditional courses

[11] H. L. Caswell, *Democracy in the Curriculum,* Appleton-Century, 1939; L. T. Hopkins, *Interaction: The Democratic Process,* Heath, 1941, chap. IX.

which have been proposed to "train the mind" in order to provide for the 60 percent now claimed to be unserved.

LOW MOTIVATION BLAMED

Students who are uninterested in what the program has to offer magnify the need for curriculum revision. Difficulty in motivating pupils keeps teachers constantly agitated and irritated. They are now keenly aware of the superficiality of grades, marks, and threats as a source of pupil application yet disconcerted with pupils' lack of enthusiasm for their offering. This problem is more pronounced for the teachers of traditional subjects, particularly in small schools where there is limited opportunity for so-called homogeneous grouping. On the other hand, it is not appreciably avoided by the teachers of either the prevocational commercial and shop subjects or general so-called practical subjects. These courses are often considered by instructors to be "dumping grounds" for the less intellectually able, who are resented because radical adaptations have to be made for them, lowering the standards desired by the teacher.

TEACHERS' FEELING OF HELPLESSNESS

Restrictions actually imposed by higher authority or defensively imagined by teachers to exist are regularly identified by school staffs as a serious curriculum problem to them. The patterns of courses still required by many colleges, the syllabi imposed from central offices, and end examinations such as those in New York State, threaten the instructor, discourage experimentation, and handicap cooperative improvement programs. Despite exhortation from curriculum specialists to do something to improve the program, the teacher says, "They will not let me." Afraid to venture, actually desirous of outside provision and direction, but dissatisfied with it, the teacher is inclined to say, "You can not do anything about it."

UNEASINESS CREATED BY CURRICULUM ISSUES

There is considerable confusion among teachers as to what guiding principles for the secondary curriculum should be. The majority would still organize the curriculum around the traditional subjects and seek to teach in logical sequence the appropriate content selected from the organized disciplines. A gradually increasing number believe the subjects to be inadequate instruments for helping youth to acquire knowledge and skill for more effective living. They would organize a large portion, perhaps half, of the pupil's time in school around a variety of personal and social problems arrived at by a continuing kind of cooperative planning.

Whether the program of the secondary school should focus on general education and vocational education equally, or whether the balance should favor one or the other remains an unresolved question. Conversation among teachers quickly centers on the real advantages to motivation in work education which establishes an easy and immediate relationship between what is to be learned and how it is to be used. Despite strong statements about the inadvisability of training specialists in the secondary school, many teachers see no alternative to full-scale vocational education as the answer to the curriculum problem.

The widespread philosophy practiced in the elementary school with respect to promotion is still discomfiting to secondary teachers. That a pupil should be accepted where he is and taken forward as far as he can go, seems more than impractical in the existent framework. To a great many, the high school diploma "should represent something," and there is pervasive uneasiness with what is felt to be an indefensible compromise in having multiple standards, not explained and seemingly unexplainable to the public.

Another frustration of teachers with the curriculum is the threat presented by learning theory and explanations of how children should be taught. Over the last two decades psychologists have been more and more insistent that learning tasks be set on a basis of felt and developed need, and that methods, materials, and situations used should produce meaning. On the face of things, to create a real need and to insure meaning, although difficult, are such admirable goals that teachers can not reject them. On the other hand, they do not have great assurance that they can do either, particularly in the ways in which the psychologists claim the job must be done. Constantly reminded they do not "meet youth needs" and that there is poor retention because youth have not had "meaningful experience," teachers are inclined to see the curriculum problem as one to be solved only by unusually bright and creative people. Meaningful learning activity as described by the curriculum specialist would require extensive changes in the way teachers work with pupils. Teachers are tempted, but do not see how the structure can be changed, the public relations accomplished, the evaluation devices replaced, and the materials developed to make these new arrangements possible.

To teachers, perhaps the most bothersome aspect of the curriculum problem is the issue regarding the most worthwhile content. Each person has his own prejudice and pride about what he knows and has found useful. Even so, most teachers are somewhat reluctant to say that one set of items is more important than another. Thus, they have traditionally depended upon the expert to select topics and information and to identify skills that are important. But since they often find that content to be uninteresting to pupils and since they observe adults who are successful despite the lack of all or part of that content, teachers wonder how much confidence they should have in the selection. The need is great for criteria, widely accepted and understood, by which to determine what to teach.

Variety of Obstacles Seen by Administrators

As the on-the-spot leaders responsible for organizing resources to bring about curriculum improvement, school administrators have many misgivings similar to those of parents, pupils, and teachers. Of paramount concern to the administrators is the question of *how* to provide more adequate scope for the program, surer attainment of the broader objectives such as learning to think and reason, character, respect for authority, and student enthusiasm. They usually see so many things to be done that they do not know where to start.

More often than not, administrators feel that the curriculum problem is really the teachers'. It is they who are with the students daily and it is their responsibility to select tasks that are inviting and stimulating to children and youth. This can be done and is done by persons who are willing to apply themselves, to use their imaginations, and to become intimately and extensively acquainted with their students. The first item in the curriculum problem, then, is one of motivating and encouraging teachers to work more diligently and actively, both independently and on the various committees set up to consider and recommend additions, variations, and changes in policy and program. Out of their deliberation and with their support, administrators feel they may be able to develop a case for large-scale or limited changes acceptable to the local board of control.

BETTER PREPARED STAFF NEEDED

Allied with this are the problems of not having, not being able to develop, and not being able to locate teachers prepared to undertake and carry out variations considered by curriculum specialists to be panaceas. The common protest among administrators is that they can not make theory work because there is no one to do what the experts say should be done. They say that if only the training colleges would provide the right people, perhaps the curriculum problem could be quickly solved.

PUBLIC UNDERSTANDING ESSENTIAL

Informing and convincing the public of the changes that ought to be made can not be separated from curriculum development. In recent years a number of imaginative adaptations in traditional curriculum practices have been scotched because they had become unacceptable to the public. Several prominent and respected superintendents have been the unfortunate victims for having sponsored comprehensive curriculum study programs and subsequent revisions. Despite real and concerted effort, public understanding and the attendant approval of proposals for change have not been widely forthcoming. The public prefers to be conservative and to be comfortable with schooling that resembles in large degree that to which they were exposed.

MODELS SOUGHT

It is well known that administrators pride themselves on being realistic and practical. One soon learns from them that they seldom try something that does not have a pretty good chance of working out favorably. A clear and present curriculum problem for many of them is the lack of complete and refined detail in the curriculum literature on how to implement what is recommended for the schools. Since few examples exist of the actual functioning of a highly satisfactory curriculum, ambitious and cautious administrators have little to give them confidence that they can reproduce the concrete from the verbal model. There is considerable testimony from this group, too, that when they have visited situations referred to and described in the curriculum literature as examples of "best" practice, they have come away with something less than clear demonstrations. A common finding is that the described school was doing something similar several years before, but has given it up or found it necessary to draw back a little. Even some widely acclaimed schools beg to have it recognized that the way the curriculum "has been written up makes it look quite a bit different from what it really is."

Faults Indicated by Curriculum Specialists

It is not easy to say what constitutes a curriculum specialist or expert. In recent years there seems to have been a frantic effort among those who write and teach about the curriculum to prove that no one ought to consider himself an expert in this area. The burden of what follows in the succeeding chapters supports this trend by emphasizing the unique and critical role of the classroom teacher and others in curriculum making. However, there are scholars, research specialists, and philosophers who have made and continue to make it their business to appraise the program of the schools, over-all and in particular, and to propose changes in purpose, in structure and organization, and in methods of teaching. For the most part, what they have offered is well supported by careful research and reasonable argument. There is agreement with a fairly large area of their reaction, but sharp differences of opinion do exist. Some are alarmed, while others anticipate and encourage slow change. A few would literally tear the present curriculum apart. A much larger group would make important but not devastating alterations. A review of what the various spokesmen have to say, whether they be cautious or reckless, yields an impressive list of dissatisfactions. For the purpose of some order, seven categories are set out below.

IMMEDIATE CONCERN FOR RESULTS

Consideration of the outcomes or results of the educational program seems to be a common starting point for many evaluations by the expert. As can be imagined, there are extremely varied ideas of what to expect from the school process. Generally, the idea the specialist has of what the school can and should do is more extensive than what the school actually attempts to do. Yet schools do seek in some way or another most of the goals felt by the experts to be legitimate pursuits. Their success and failure are the expert's reference points for telling a large part of the story about what the curriculum problem is.

One of the studies usually quoted as evidence of curricular failure is the New York Regents Survey.[12] Although made back in 1937, it is still generally felt by curriculum specialists to characterize outcomes from secondary education. In many surveys conducted by institutions of higher learning for school systems throughout the country over the last twenty years similar conclusions have been drawn. Comprehensive examination of the schools in St. Louis[13] led the staff of Teachers College to observe that extensive instruction in the social sciences contributed practically nothing more to understanding of social-civic problems than did a minor program requiring half that time. Knowl-

[12] Francis Spaulding, *High School and Life,* McGraw-Hill, 1938.
[13] *Report of a Survey of the Public Schools of St. Louis, Missouri,* Bureau of Publications, Teachers College, 1939, p. 44.

edge of health was shown to be little affected by courses in general science and biology. Critical thinking apparently had no demonstrable relationship to the number or kind of science courses taken.

In Newark[14] a similarly complete evaluation resulted in comparable conclusions, and the combined group that investigated the schools of Buffalo in 1951 found itself in general agreement. Reviewing the common subject offerings in the Buffalo schools, the group observed that "the rigidity with which this core of required work is administered in Buffalo makes it ineffective for a large percentage of pupils. Because of the uniformity in content and method and the uniformity of the examination requirements for pupil success, instruction tends to be stereotyped and textbookish. For large numbers of pupils it is totally unrelated to their abilities and interests. For all such pupils it fails to achieve either the goals of citizenship or personal development."[15]

Opinion polls, such as the Purdue University Opinion Poll, often reveal startling kinds of failure in our product. Among other findings reported in a recent survey:[16] 25 percent of the teenagers answering the questions in the poll would prohibit the right of the people to assemble peaceably, limiting the exercise of that right to certain approved organizations. Twenty-six percent believed the police should be allowed in some cases to search a person or his home without a warrant. Fifteen percent would deny to some criminals the right to have a lawyer. Fifty-eight percent agreed that the police may be justified in giving a man the "third degree" in order to make him talk; and only 45 percent believed newspapers should be allowed to print anything they want except military secrets. This kind of denial of rights guaranteed to all by the Constitution indeed raises questions about the effectiveness of our curriculum.

It is seen that there are many more deficiencies than have been pointed out here. This summary was not intended to be complete; the purpose rather has been to show the kinds of outcome about which many curriculum students are disturbed.

PURPOSES AND SCOPE BELABORED

It has already been pointed out that much of the dissatisfaction of the experts is with the school's failure to produce knowledge and skills

---

[14] *Report of a Survey of the Public Schools of Newark, New Jersey,* Bureau of Publications, Teachers College, 1942, p. 379.

[15] *Buffalo Public Schools in the Mid-Twentieth Century,* New York State Education Department, 1951, p. 109.

[16] Jean Barge *et al.,* "Do Teenagers Reject the Freedoms?" *New York State Education,* February, 1954, pp. 369–371.

for a wide variety of life activities. A very large portion of American youth, by choice or because they live in communities where subject additions have not caught on, still focus on a very limited kind of goal—that of obtaining information about a few subjects. A major cause for this resides in the failure of many school authorities to accept broader purposes and goals for the schools. In other cases broader goals have been accepted on paper, but little or nothing has been done to adapt the program to permit activities likely to bring about such achievement.

Recent arguments that the way out of the present profound social crisis and disintegration is through a curriculum geared to critical evaluation and positive action for societal reconstruction still appear to have minimal effect on school programs. Controversial issues, vigorous contention with the status quo, and courageous exploration of social, political, and moral ills are generally avoided in communities, large and small.

Widespread opinion among the experts, then, is that despite efforts to extend both purpose and scope, the curriculum is still too academic, too narrow, and too unrelated to life. The late wave of national commissions and some truly valuable spadework here and there have done little to move matters very far. As Harold Spears[17] observes about the report on the *Functions of Secondary Education,* the educators gorge themselves on their documents, but the boys and girls continue on their starvation diet.

CONTENT CONSIDERED INAPPROPRIATE

Study of the indexes of curriculum books for a direct reference to the term *content* will reveal that the word is seldom found there. In only one out of ten published since 1950 was the word used and then as a part of a phrase about outlines to be used in subjects. Yet, the content of the curriculum or the learning to be acquired—the facts, skills, appreciations, and meanings—is actually the item about which curriculum specialists are most disturbed. Constantly, the inadequacy of the program is illustrated by examples of what pupils learn or try to learn that is useless to them. Spears,[18] in asking the question "Useful or ornamental?" suggests by means of a list of choices that little relationship exists between what is required in a subject and what is needed to get along and to solve life's problems. Determining the size of inside angles formed by a secant's intersection with two radii extending beyond the circumference of a circle makes little difference to

---

[17] Harold Spears, *The High School for Today,* American Book, 1950, p. 27.
[18] Spears, *op. cit.,* pp. 57–58.

the gas station attendant. Similarly, there is felt to be no need for knowledge of the special meanings of either the vocabulary of Shakespeare or Chaucer. Such words are not to be found in the magazines read or heard on favorite television shows.

Much of the reaction, of course, results from the fact that unused as they are, except for further study at institutions of higher learning, these items of knowledge, skills, and generalizations are forgotten. They can not be recalled, even when required for a quiz program prize, and the realization swiftly comes that they actually are not very important parts of everyday experience. Many times, too, it seems that the adult whose head has been filled with the content of the traditional curriculum is extremely inept in practical situations.

As a consequence, curriculum specialists react approvingly and sympathetically to a piece like Harold Benjamin's trenchant satire[19] on the anachronisms in the present program. They agree that a good housecleaning is necessary, that whole courses of study could well be removed from the program, and that far-reaching and radical revisions should be made in the content requirements or electives now so well fixed as to be likely to remain for a long time to come.

ORGANIZATION A CONTINUING ISSUE

When all the knowledge considered worth knowing could be subsumed easily under mathematics, science, history, foreign languages, and English, there arose no question about the arrangement for transmitting it. The child was sent to school and specialists in a few areas told him what to learn. What the specialist knew was a subject and what he taught was the matter of that subject. As knowledge has increased and new disciplines have emerged, as the wealth of information has resulted in finer classifications of knowledge, the struggle for acknowledgement and allocation of time and place to all the differing categories has waxed heavy. Critical studies of how learning takes place appear to support the contention that insight is obtained more easily and kept longer when knowledge is sought as required for the solution of problems of more general and natural form, more intimately related to the normal, rather than the school-contrived, experiences of the child's living. Thus for the last twenty-five years there has been insistence among curriculum experts on a radical change in organization.

The advantages of the subject order are held to be outweighed by

[19] Harold Benjamin, *The Saber-Tooth Curriculum*, McGraw-Hill, 1939.

the disadvantages. The subject organization is assailed for being psychologically unsound, for fractionating the student's knowledge, for hampering application and extension of good guidance, and for hamstringing approved teacher-pupil planning, wider use of resources, and pursuit of social objectives. No amount of tinkering or patching up will make it adequate, say the critics.

OVERHAUL OF TEACHING PROCEDURES NEEDED

However, many who discuss the curriculum are likely to think almost completely in terms of an outline of facts and skills to be taught. They do not go beyond the outline to consider the way the subject can best be taught and learned, nor do they take into consideration the total products of the learning situation. To them, the curriculum is an organized list existing in advance of any face-to-face relationship between pupil and teacher. They have no concept of the curriculum as embracing the quality of experience the pupil has.

Over the last two decades, however, the broader definition has emerged as a criterion for most of those who concern themselves with improving the curriculum. Curriculum directors, professors, and school supervisors see the curriculum in large part as the quality of the experience the child has in situations created by pupils and teachers. In this view, where there is poor teaching, there is a poor curriculum, regardless of the variety of subjects offered, the breadth and balance of objectives posed, or the way in which the blocks of time for pupils in school are arranged. The focus of attention, the curriculum problem, for them, then, is improving the teaching-learning process. One of the foremost specialists who has worked extensively in state programs of curriculum improvement has concluded after years of experience that this is the central activity in reform.[20]

Defense for this significant shift exists largely in the researches of the educational psychologists whose findings have not, according to curriculum workers, been given sufficient recognition. In a later chapter attention is given to the basic ideas about learning which should guide the teacher in seeking high quality experience with pupils. The important point is that much pioneer study has fallen on deaf ears. In the face of consistent and overwhelming evidence claims continue to be made about the superiority of traditional methods of teaching, and the adoption of procedures consistent with research is vigorously resisted. Motivation is still largely a matter of threat; the goals of pupils

[20] Edward Krug, *Curriculum Planning,* rev. ed., Harper, 1957, p. 6.

in schools are grades and marks rather than understandings and skills known to be important; a sizable portion of what is taught is not related in any significant or meaningful way to the present or future needs of youth; drill is employed regularly in hopes of fixing skills and knowledge before wide and proper exploration and application have established an insight into process or relationship.

INADEQUACY OF THE CURRICULUM IMPROVEMENT PROCESS

Extensive and involved examination as to how the curriculum may be improved has grown with the development of education as an area to study. According to Caswell,[21] Franklin Bobbit gave the first comprehensive treatment of curriculum problems in 1918 and served during the early 1920's as one of the first curriculum specialists. From the time of the publication of his book, *The Curriculum,* increasing attention was given to changing the curriculum. The National Society for Study of Education Yearbook for 1926 was devoted to a discussion of *Foundations of Curriculum Making;* curriculum resource libraries and laboratories were developed by 1930; and in a number of large cities and states, comprehensive programs were undertaken to establish the rationale for school offerings and a more defensible relationship of all parts to purpose. Early exception was taken to the movement and sharp criticism was directed against those who promoted and led reform effort, and against the methods used. Expressed distrust and disagreement did little to stem the tide. The 1930's proved to be a period of almost feverish activity; curriculum study reached into state, city, and small schools. Departments of curriculum sprang up in a number of large universities; and curriculum leaders, directors, and supervisors appeared in ever-increasing numbers. World War II slowed the forward momentum, but efforts to improve the curriculum have achieved even greater dimensions since.

Despite the enthusiasm and the attention given to curriculum improvement, change has been neither as widespread nor as far reaching as many would desire. In fact, to some the limited amount of revision has been distressing. Too many of the ills long ago identified remain,[22] and now the likelihood of their disappearing soon seems even smaller. One with a more balanced view, however, can detect many marks of progress over these years. There are better and more helpful materials;

[21] Hollis Caswell, *Curriculum Improvement in Public School Systems,* Bureau of Publications, Teachers College, 1950, p. 43.
[22] See Calvin O. Davis, *Our Evolving High School Curriculum,* World, 1927, chap. 4.

programs are broader and better adapted to the spread of ability and interest in school; learning tasks are more appropriately placed and better related—to mention but a few changes.

DIFFICULTY OF REMOVING OBSTACLES

If merely willing a change in the organization of the curriculum, the outcomes sought, or methods of teaching were to bring it about, all would be well. Unfortunately so much bears upon every other matter that adaptation and adjustment are extremely complex operations and usually must wait upon changes in somewhat remote places. A decision to discontinue the use of textbooks can not be made if relatively rich resources do not exist in the available written materials, in community resources, in teachers. It is impossible to deny youngsters the opportunity to learn special mathematical skills or the names of certain treaties if scholarships and university admissions depend upon that knowledge. It is useless for a local school committee to encourage vigorous treatment of controversial issues if powerful interests in the community or the state will not tolerate anything but the "right" approach.

Among those related influences that slow curriculum progress appreciably, one of the foremost is probably the widespread lethargy in the profession. The majority of teachers have survived a long exposure to courses of study in which they were told what to do, when to do it, and how to do it. Although at times the compulsions of the academic lockstep have rankled, educators have been unable for the most part to take any initiative in bringing about a different approach. They have "learned a method which they have lived" and had little opportunity to try another, even if they have had exhortations to do so from teacher-training professors. The pattern is for the college graduate to go back into the classroom to do pretty largely what was done for him. When that does not work too well, he is likely to complain and to seek more exhortations from the professors, but will be more or less satisfied to continue as before.

Questions for Discussion

1. A great portion of the curriculum problem seems to center around whether the school is of help in dealing with a variety of cultural difficulties. These include broken homes, lowered general moral tone, slums and poor public health facilities, seeming disrespect of adolescents for authority, apparent unreadiness of some young people to accept job responsibility. What should be the school's role in handling these problems? To what degree is the school supplemental?

2. It is claimed that in the attempt to adjust school offerings to adolescent interest and ability, the curriculum has been "watered down," and American children are being deprived of their birthright to quality education. What is your version?

3. Much of the difficulty said to exist in the curriculum is attributed to the irresponsibility, if not the insensibility, of "educationists" who have allegedly set up a powerful bureaucracy and keep out the scholars who could make tratitional courses valuable and meaningful. What logic and what emotion are there in these claims? What credence shall we attach to the accusations? Can we resolve the issues?

4. Some people feel that our curriculum problem is mainly that the "dish has run away with the spoon." The professional educators have engaged in lengthy and able discussion of goals and purposes of schools, and issued well-reasoned books and pamphlets. But the ideas of those professional educators really have not permeated very deeply, and the public has not accepted the ideas on a meaningful basis, thus being essentially lost as supporters. What do you think?

5. The subjects and the subject-organized curriculum have been special targets of curriculum reformers for years. Review your experiences with the subject curriculum. Do you agree that it has all the reported weaknesses and limitations? (See L. T. Hopkins, *Interaction, the Democratic Process,* chap. 21, and J. Galen Saylor and W. Alexander, *Curriculum Planning,* chap. 8.)

Selected Bibliography

Alberty, Harold, *Reorganizing the High School Curriculum,* rev. ed., Macmillan, 1953, chap. 1.

Association for Supervision and Curriculum Development, *Forces Affecting American Education,* The Association, 1953.

Bestor, Arthur, *Educational Wastelands,* University of Illinois Press, 1953.

Bestor, Arthur, *The Restoration of Learning,* Knopf, 1955.

Caswell, H. L., ed., *The American High School,* Harper, 1946, chaps. 1, 6.

Leonard, J. Paul, *Developing the Secondary School Curriculum,* rev. ed., Rinehart, 1953, chap. 8.

Lynd, Albert, *Quackery in the Public School,* Little, Brown, 1952.

Romine, Stephen, *Building the High School Curriculum,* Ronald, 1954, chap. 1.

Saylor, J. Galen, and William Alexander, *Curriculum Planning,* Rinehart, 1954, chap. 1.

Scott, C. Winfield, and Clyde Hill, *Public Education Under Criticism,* Prentice-Hall, 1954.

Woodring, Paul, *Let's Talk Sense About Our Schools,* McGraw-Hill, 1955.

....

The Teacher as Key Factor

Many criticize the curriculum and many influence it. Requirements for high school diplomas and college entrance are specified by policy groups remote from the classroom. Deciding the over-all purposes of the schools remains the prerogative of deliberative groups of laymen. Legal authority over the curriculum rests with boards of education. The general scope and structure of the program is determined by administrators whose decisions affect many schools.

From time to time, teachers have been called upon to advise on these and similar matters or they have taken the initiative to do so through resolutions and proposals from their voluntary professional organizations. Until recently, however, the greater portion of decisions affecting school programs was made without benefit of any real participation by teachers, invited or volunteered. Mandates were imposed and proposals were accepted without review.

INCREASE IN TEACHERS' ROLES

Recognition of the contributions teachers could make in various kinds of decision-making has come only in the last several decades. The conviction that little real progress could be made without teacher involvement was expressed by several leaders during the early depression years after numerous failures in curriculum revision. Attempts were made then to get extensive committee participation prior to remote decision-making. Planning and action by teacher groups was promoted. Since then, dependence upon individual and cooperative effort by teachers to decide when, how, and what to teach, to revise courses and offerings, to select content and plan experiences, and to produce aids to teaching has become much more common practice. Reliance upon textbooks and restrictive state courses of study has waned. In 1940 Saylor[1] showed in the Virginia program section of his curriculum development study that in the counties where participation was more inclusive and where more teachers were engaged in deliberative meetings and in production of materials, there was more genuine adaptation in the program, and significant changes took place in the classrooms and in the teaching process. Thus Krug concluded in 1957, "Teacher participation in curriculum planning today is to be regarded not as a pleasant gesture to the teachers, but rather as an indispensable part of the process."[2]

This conclusion has not grown from the idea that teachers are needed because they have made good and workable suggestions, had bright new ideas, and added balance to policy decisions. Rather, it has stemmed from the conviction that in the end the major measure of curriculum growth is demonstrable improvement in the quality of experience youth has in the schools, especially in the classroom. In this view the crux of curriculum work or development is the active effort of the teacher to bring about in the pupil more insight, greater knowledge, increased enthusiasm for learning, and added skills. When the teacher is probing to find the most pronounced needs of youth, seeking to work out a variety of activities to make learning possible through several media, finding ways to fix knowledge and skills through practical applications and helping solve the problems of youth, the most vital part of curriculum planning is being performed. New objectives can be stated, different scope and structure evolved, new courses added, new learning tasks suggested, traditional goals re-emphasized, and new readings suggested, but these will not in themselves improve the curriculum. Perhaps they will make it look better on paper, or even make it possible for youth to have a wider scope of experience or training, particularly when a new subject, like consumership, is added. However, their potential can be realized only through the planning and action of the teachers and pupils who manage the learning situations in school. In the teacher's sensitivity to youth needs, in his method of focusing learning power upon tasks, in his utilization of interest, in his illustration and use of situations to attain meaning, and in his procedure to fix knowledge and skill, the teacher plays the prepotent part in setting the quality of pupil experience.

When teachers are not in sympathy with proposed revisions, threatened by the different ways in which they are expected to behave,

---

[1] J. Galen Saylor, *Factors Associated with Participation in Cooperative Programs of Curriculum Development*, Bureau of Publications, Teachers College, 1941.

[2] Edward Krug, *Administering Curriculum Planning*, Harper, 1957, p. 13.

or required to expend extra energy and effort to acquire additional knowledge and skills, they are inclined to resist or to be uninterested in carrying out the details necessary to achieve the broad goals set by others. The early attempts at curriculum reform demonstrated this conclusively. When a few administrators and carefully appointed representatives proposed and installed program changes, children's experiences remained about the same as they had always been. Good testimony on this kind of gap can be obtained from the many who have visited the "pioneering" states and schools after reading the reports and the manuals produced by curriculum committees. To their chagrin, they found that programs, activities, classroom procedures, and the kind and quality of experience provided were not noticeably different from those in their own "traditional" schools. There was evidence of much activity in certain quarters, but little real variation where the important elements of education take place.

There are other important roles which the teacher can perform beyond those of spelling out or putting to work the general ideas as to what in the face-to-face relationship will improve educative experience. In each of these, the failure of the teacher to carry on efficiently may not prove as serious as would his ineptitude in the classroom, but it has become clear that the rate of curriculum improvement is surely dependent on how active and interested the teacher is in adding his contribution and sharing in responsibility at these other stages. In the sections which follow, the primary functions of the teacher in the solution of curriculum problems such as those identified in Chapter 2 are examined, and a number of the other responsibilities that make him a key factor in curriculum improvement are discussed.

THE TEACHER AND PLANS OF OTHERS

A wealth of proposals in regard to what should guide him in his work with children is now available to the teacher. Out of philosophy and the work of deliberative committees have come broad generalizations about the school, its purpose, program and operation. Yearbooks and reports propose principles and criteria by which to judge the school's objectives and activities. Planning groups at the national, state, and local level have decided on major goals, proposed variations in the broad curriculum framework, spelled out objectives for limited areas of study, identified content, and suggested approaches. From among these suggestions the teacher is almost always at least free to emphasize, if not actually empowered to select, and thus determine daily and weekly what children may be expected to learn. In a number of places local committees, after extensive study and review, may have agreed upon certain beliefs and principles to which the teacher is expected to give his assent and adherence. Occasionally all the teachers, after study and discussion, express support for a certain set of ideas.

Yet, however extensive deliberation or prolonged discussion of general principles or guides is, it is almost impossible to spell out completely what a statement means for the continuous, daily interaction in the classroom. Consequently, many specific decisions must always be left to the classroom teacher. Here some help has been given through the efforts of course-of-study committees, commissions of voluntary professional organizations, and publishing firms. Publications of these groups contain numerous illustrations of exactly how teachers and classes work to exemplify a better curriculum. But even so, they seldom give more than an idea of what could be done; they are limited in circulation; and in the end each teacher must himself come to understand these ideas and principles sufficiently to continue in the pattern suggested. The great gap in curriculum improvement is in the translation of high-sounding phrases and convincing abstractions into positive first-hand experiences.

Priority of Objectives

Few courses of study issued by states or cities and prepared by statewide representative committees or by local unit, community or single school committees do not contain statements of goals and objectives. The common practice is to list general objectives at the beginning of a publication and include more specific objectives by grade or unit, depending upon the nature and scope of the courses of study. It is assumed that the statement of objectives will provide the definition of breadth for the teacher's work with pupils as well as a checking device to guarantee balance in pupil purpose and activity.

There seems to be little disagreement on a number of very noble and abstract objectives such as those listed by the Educational Policies Commission, the Russell Sage Foundation, and the National Council for the Teachers of English. These include thinking clearly, respecting the rights of others, appreciating good music and art, and functioning effectively as a citizen.

However, as is regularly asserted, these statements of objectives are very often just window dressing. Even when they have been derived from genuine soul-searching, and when they have been finally stated and neatly arranged at the beginning of courses of study or at the outset of units, they have little effect on what happens thereafter. Probably this is most true in schools where the teacher's sole purpose is to teach the facts in a textbook. Depending on recitation as the major means of acquisition of learning, the teacher may actually disregard almost all of the suggested activities found in a fine modern book. He may further dominate and direct the class even at the expense of such a vaunted goal as that of learning how to work democratically, and commonly he may be satisfied to seek as evidence of school success the ability of pupils to recall isolated items of information, paying little or no attention to the extent of changed attitudes and appreciation.

Pursuing the more abstract and complex goals usually requires a disruption of the traditional framework for teaching, forces the teacher to develop unique methods of appraisal, and too often leaves the teacher without very tangible or immediate results. Therefore, he concentrates instead on what has fairly neat dimensions and can be treated numerically and objectively, and limits himself to the so-called content of a subject: names, places, lists, and dates.

On the other hand, the teacher may accept the whole of a carefully spelled-out set of objectives as the guiding force in his work with pupils, with the idea of giving them all real attention. He must recognize at the outset that no outsider, no committee, no teacher can really decide upon goals for any learner. Actually, the teacher can only suggest possible outcomes and encourage his pupils' acceptance of them. But when he focuses attention upon all the objectives, keeps them in the forefront of pupil thinking, and actively seeks to promote, develop, and bring about experiences that will lead to such outcomes, he is able to make the kind of contribution sought by those who are striving to improve the curriculum.

The decision whether to make this kind of adjustment seldom rests with anyone but the teacher. Most schools are lacking in sufficient supervisory personnel to encourage and provide motivation for teachers to experiment. Where there are sizable supervisory forces, the theory of supervisor-teacher relationship is commonly one of requiring the teacher to take the initiative, using the supervisor as a resource person in developing projects, units, and culminating experiences. The classroom teacher thus decides what to "set his cap for," what to emphasize, and what to set store by.

Difficulty of Implementation

There are, of course, good reasons why teachers do not try to achieve the full order of objectives to which they have been committed or to which they may have committed themselves in an enthusiastic reading or production of a course of study. All too often their competence is judged on the basis of standardized tests which emphasize specific facts and skills. Then, too, broader objectives often require adaptations with which the patrons of the school are unfamiliar. Rather than risk severe criticism, teachers find it safer to stick within narrow confines and to use procedures to which parents were once exposed and with which they feel more comfortable.

Actually, ideas about what schools can and should be have now reached astounding proportions. Teachers often find there is just not enough time in the school year to do all the things they see as desirable. In some cases, of course, they are handicapped by lack of resources and of equipment. Even the more commonly agreed upon objectives are frequently not pursued most meaningfully for some children because quite different settings are required if much is to be accomplished.

Most important, perhaps, achieving certain types of objectives greatly taxes a teacher's imagination and ingenuity. In addition to being exceedingly demanding of already hard-pressed time and energy, it can be threatening to the ego. Hence, when conventional methods do not result in the attainment of the anticipated goals, the goals are casually abandoned or it is unrealistically hoped that somehow they will succeed later.

It can not be hoped that the individual teacher alone has the power to overcome each of these obstacles and others of a similar nature. Yet, as the teacher agrees, it is his personal obligation to seek more comprehensive objectives and to set stiff standards for himself. He will be required to find ways to attack these barriers. Until the teacher clearly indicates how he has been handicapped, and until he both insists upon help and agrees to help in the gradual elimination of adverse conditions, it is almost certain that they will continue to exist.

THE TEACHER AND CONTENT

The increasing freedom of the teacher to elect how he will work in the classroom and to determine what he will work toward has been alluded to several times above. In nearly all the curriculum bulletins released in recent years this freedom for the teacher to "call his own shots" has been emphasized. Likewise, the literature dealing with methods of teaching is filled with encouraging and practical suggestions as to how the teacher can exercise his independence in determining the subject and method. The syllabus and "prescribed" course-of-study bulletin have given way to Handbooks, Guides, Suggestions, and Resources for teaching. In an early bulletin of the Kansas Improvement Program this point was made explicitly in introducing the units thought appropriate for general education in that state:

> These guidance materials are planned to help teachers of the state keep a common direction while they develop local school programs in terms of community needs and pupil characteristics. They offer aid to the teacher in developing a school program that will use to the optimum the opportunities the school offers for giving practice in living democratically . . .
>
> Each teacher is confronted with the immediate task of planning instruction for a particular group of children with distinctive characteristics in a community with particularized needs and resources. These suggestive guidance materials aid the teacher in selecting and directing experinces for growing children in the important areas of contemporary living. . . . They present materials of three kinds which she can use in organizing instruction. Some of these materials are comprehensive and from them she can gain detailed information for developing a unit of work. Some of the materials suggest sources that she may consult and others merely suggest a lead to a unit of work that she might develop. In each case the materials are *flexible, merely suggestive, and the plans for using them* must be made by an individual teacher of a special group of children.[3]

Similar conviction is expressed in a publication of the New York State Education Department, where the following advice is given with respect to use of the bulletin:

> The ideal general science program is custom-built. It should meet the interests and needs of pupils to the fullest extent possible in view of the local resources available for instruction. It should be planned as an integral part of the school curriculum and should make its own unique contribution to the total educational program. Since teaching conditions differ from school to school as well as from year to year, the course of study needs to be flexible and so organized that it lends itself to continuous improvement.
>
> The materials outlined in this section present several alternative plans upon which a good general science program can be built. . . .
>
> The following outline lists significant science topics and understandings which can serve as a kind of check list for developing an instructional program for the early secondary grades. This outline, organized in terms of 10 major areas, is not intended as a course of study but as a suggested scope of content and learning outcomes upon which a variety of courses of study can be built.[4]

With this kind of support teachers can hardly argue that they do not have the prerogative to determine the content sought, the topics, or

[3] Kansas State Education Department, *Suggestive Guidance Materials for Teachers in Developing a Core Program,* The Department, 1941.

[4] New York State Education Department, *Science 7–8–9,* The Department, 1956, p. 21.

the problems for study. Obviously they will be left increasingly to their own initiative. Most curriculum theorists seem convinced that few, if any, requirements should be given to the teacher and that sharply defined specifics should be kept to an absolute minimum, and only broad expectancies identified. Standardized tests and state-wide examinations may continue to interfere to some extent, and so will the policies of some communities and states where the adoption of certain texts is required and where appropriations for libraries and supplementary materials are kept low. However, decided effort is being made to liberalize examinations to diminish specific content required, and real progress is being made nearly everywhere to increase budgets for supplementary or alternative materials.

Despite these encouragements and changes, the teacher can choose to limit his expectancies and his materials to the minimum, to the stereotyped, to the traditional. The most common conservative pattern has been to depend upon the material found in only one textbook. This has been particularly easy to do in traditional subjects in which texts have been developed by the scholars and purport to contain the best. Exactly this happened in one state curriculum revision program wherein a most appealing paper plan was worked out, with widespread teacher preparation, to include themes, suggested broad areas for concentration, and extensive suggestions for activities. Teachers continued to use the texts for the traditional subjects and to require of pupils the mastery of the facts and skills selected by these text authors from the massed material in the subject field. Everywhere they ignored the themes and goals, the synthesis of subject matter around problems, and the activities suggested in the state-adopted curriculum guide.

Opportunity Provided by Improvements in Texts

In recent years, cognizant of this continuing teacher need for and dependence upon authoritative and well-organized materials, textbook publishers have made a decided contribution by increasing the flexibility of texts to encourage teacher initiative. Actually, many of the better books are now set up as initial and basic resource tools containing extensive and appropriate suggestions for the development of a variety of learning activities. Portions of the content organized around persisting personal and social problems, themes, or generalizations set the stage for accompanying ideas about group activity and individual projects for further study and research. Teachers' guides and teaching aids contain ideas for planning with pupils, for motivation, for correlation or application to other areas and for evaluation. Extended bibliographies are included for stimulating student understanding and appreciation.

The teacher can capitalize on this progress if he wishes or he can ignore these valuable additions, usually the result of careful attention by experts in teaching who have been employed to make a volume a good competitor because of its practicality.[5] He may ignore it because somehow he has been convinced that use of a textbook is a pedagogical sin, since it can not help but interfere with teacher and pupil freedom. On the other hand he may conceive of teaching as a daily recitation matter and look with jaundiced eye on the extraneous dressing included in the text to please the progressive.

The numbers of teachers at either extreme is not overwhelming, but there are many more who ally themselves with the extremes than is good for curriculum improvement. There is of course some justification for both positions, but the most practical and promising solution lies somewhere in between. With teachers rests the choice whether to work out that compromise and thus to affect significantly the content of the educational program.

Resource Units and Choice of Varied Content

Another helping tool provided for and more often worked out by teachers in recent years is the resource unit. This aid to teacher planning has become popular since the Progressive Education Association experiment placed its emphasis on adapting programs to student needs and interests. A number of such units are now available from professional organizations and publishing agencies. The largest production has taken place in local school programs and as a part of several state programs. Over the last several years, staff of the Garrett County, Maryland, schools have developed units for each of the problem areas in the core program. Similar work has been done in other Maryland counties; in Dade County, Florida; in Wisconsin; and elsewhere.

The purposes of these resource units as analyzed by Leonard are:

1. To furnish suggestions for materials, methods, activities, teaching aids, and evaluative procedures for building a learning unit
2. To provide a means for helping the teacher to organize materials so that he can depart from the traditional use of the textbook as a guide in curriculum development
3. To provide suggestions for the teacher for translating an education philosophy into practice

[5] For careful discussion of the textbook, its limitations, uses, and improvement, see Lee Cronbach, *Text Materials in Modern Education,* University of Illinois Press, 1955.

4. To serve as a guide in helping the teacher to include in the learning unit certain important values basic to education in a democracy
5. To sensitize the teacher to all of the significant problems and issues that have a bearing on an area of living
6. To utilize the personnel resources of the school appropriate to the cooperative preplanning of a particular unit
7. To conserve the time of the teacher
8. To make it possible to have teaching materials available when needed[6]

If it is used properly, the resource unit may lead to rich, varied, and extensive experiences for pupils. The facts learned, the skills developed, the attitudes built depend on the choices teacher and pupils make together, on the emphasis given in individual and group experience as objectives, ideas, problems, and activities are drawn from this compendium. However, no matter how complete the resource, if the teacher does not know how, or does not care, to use it, it can not be really effective.

THE TEACHER AND QUALITY OF EXPERIENCE

The improvement of the curriculum is no longer limited to defining the subjects to be offered and the facts to be learned. Rather, it includes the examination of the total effect of the school on the child, and consideration of what situations and conditions lead to what results. Both the tangibles and the intangibles must be weighed, and the processes of teaching and learning that contribute to the outcome must be given equal, if not greater consideration. What the teacher proposes to be learned, what the pupil even may set out to learn, actually may prove to be only a minor outcome, and other concomitant effects may not only be more quickly assimilated into behavior but retained over a longer period of time.

For instance, the stated goals may be to acquire knowledge of early efforts to conserve our natural resources, and to realize the need for active participation now in behalf of our original bounty. The course of study may call for a few days' classwork and the adopted text may contain some few pages on various aspects of the topic. The pupil may be desirous of knowing more about action by Roosevelt and Pinchot, about the laws that have been evolved, about the work of the soil conservation service, and about protection against erosion on his own farm.

However, knowledge, understanding, and insight can not come

[6] J. Paul Leonard, *Developing The Secondary School Curriculum*, Rinehart, pp. 477–478.

automatically, so the pupil must apply himself independently and perhaps with others in activities ranging from reading to observation on the land and to actual conservation practices. If what he does increases his knowledge and his enthusiasm and if he feels positive about what he does, the curriculum at this point includes building a desirable attitude toward schooling as well as toward conservation. If he is required to take stiff and unreasonable examinations, whereupon he plans to cheat more effectively, and succeeds; if he is allowed no freedom to seek answers of interest to himself, whereupon he conceives of himself only as doing what he is told to do; if he is not permitted to plan his own ways to learn and determine his progress, whereupon he thinks little or not at all how to tackle problems, and learns to depend always on the letter of rules and regulations—his curriculum includes aspects of experience which were not intended. Quality of experience can thus become exceedingly unsatisfactory. What actually happens to students under the guidance and direction of the school is much greater than the curriculum that is outlined.

The most common situation for learning about conservation or about most things is one in which the teacher establishes the need for the pupils to know the facts and builds the attitudes. Many of the pupils have no real interest in conservation and are little concerned with contour plowing, hedgerow planting, and crop rotation. Their desire is to avoid as much as possible the displeasure of the teacher, to complete as early as possible the task required by him so to have the minimum interruption possible with their own on-going activities. Consequently, little real change takes place in them as a result of their exposure, except increasing dislike for this kind of experience. Their curriculum has been largely composed of ways to cut corners to get by, to manage the teacher to obtain a mark from him, or to collaborate with others in deluding the teacher into thinking that fine independent work is being done. They have learned that the teacher sets the goals and gives the tasks; they have learned to arouse themselves to act only under threat or drive from the teacher; they have learned to look upon school as a place to go to acquire knowledge or skill for retention only until the marks have been determined.

This kind of experience obviously grows more from the teacher's conceptions of how learning is accomplished, and of the conditions and arrangements which contribute to pupil reaction and participation, than from any other source. No matter how logically organized the items to be learned or the tools provided, the outline can not determine the quality or fix the quantity of learning that takes place. In the classroom, capitalizing on pupil interest and need, the teacher must find the incentives to valuable attitudes, skills, and knowledge. Thus the teacher determines the quality of learning.

More of the recent curriculum texts therefore contain extensive sections on the teaching-learning process, on the management and operation of the classroom learning situation. The bulk of the production of the National Association for Supervision and Curriculum Development since the inception of that organization in 1946 has been devoted to this problem.

THE TEACHER AND EXPERIMENTATION

Nearly all proposals for curriculum changes mean doing things differently. The "doing" may range from scheduling pupils for different subjects and periods, changing the requirements for graduation, or restricting participation in extraclass activities to using a new organization of topics in a subject, setting up procedures for pupil evaluation rather than end-point testing, or dispensing with a prepared spelling list administered weekly. For instance, the proposal to discontinue the diagramming of sentences as a means of learning how words function in sentences as parts of speech, and removal from the teacher guide for Grade 8 of the suggestions to use this method, encourages the teacher to seek other ways to obtain understanding of word use in parts of a sentence. It may have been all the teachers involved who made such a proposal or a representative committee. But when this crutch is no longer recommended, the teacher is presented with the problem of getting proper pronoun and adverb use without it. How shall he do it? Alternative ways will likely be proposed and probably some opportunity made available to check and discuss with colleagues different ways of approaching the teaching. Nevertheless, the classroom teacher is the one who must try to make the "new" way work. It is he who must plan the steps, discover the limitations, and make the adaptations. He must undertake to develop skill, master the alternative approach, and, more than is usually felt to be the case, bear the discomforts of failure or anxious anticipation of the outcome.

All curriculum change proposals do not, by any means, require exploration or experimentation by teachers, but perhaps the most significant and more liberal ones do. Probably the best illustration of this is the idea that teachers actively include pupils in planning what to study. The exhortations with respect to this adaptation are many and vigorous. Some help is given with lists of possible topics and some rather highly abstract statements about needs and characteristics of pupils at certain age levels. Several volumes have been devoted to rather detailed and explicit descriptions of how the teacher did or would work in developing the curriculum with learners, and the steps in cooperative planning have been recently treated in a book on principles of teaching.[7] But exhortation and description can give the teacher neither the skill nor the experience. He must find his own way to work with pupils while maintaining his self-confidence and security in the process. A teacher who is timid, who is uncertain of himself, and who does not have consistent and warm support from administration and colleagues will seldom venture. Yet if he does not, the dreams of the professors will stay suspended and little progress will be made on the multitude of limitations our programs and their products now possess.

THE TEACHER AND PUBLIC RELATIONS

Throughout the curriculum literature one finds reiterated the statement that appreciable curriculum change can be obtained only with the understanding, consent, and support of the public. Much progress is now being made through citizens' committees with professional staff consultants to describe the present program—what its content is, as well as why it is effective. Many systems are distributing more regular and extensive reports on goals, methods, and outcomes. Use is being made of the varied channels available to schools for enlightening and informing the public: newspaper releases, civic group meetings, parent association programs, radio, and television.

Despite this increase in informing citizen representatives and involving them in some over-all planning, the most influential public-opinion-forming agent is doubtless the pupil who attends the school. He regularly carries home a fairly well-defined attitude about his school experiences and rather pronounced prejudices about what appeals to him and what does not. He is at the same time a vivid, present example of the results of the school's effort, and therefore of what it teaches.

If the child is pleased with what he experiences and learns in school and if the parents approve, continued adaptation and experimentation are possible and usually encouraged. However, if the parents seriously question the progress their child is making and become annoyed at the child's attitude toward activities in school, they are quick

---

[7] William Alexander and Paul Halverson, *Effective Teaching in Secondary Schools*, Rinehart, 1957.

to insist on less attention to the new and on a hurried return to the scope of program and the practices and procedures with which they are familiar. Just a few teachers who fail to establish a good learning situation with children because of misinterpretation, overenthusiasm, or ineptness can set curriculum progress back years. Failure to give proper attention to the teaching of phonics in the grades and default in getting an adequate command of grammar in the secondary schools exemplify this. Much of the excitement among patrons today grows from excessive teacher compromise on seeking these goals that parents, and the children, when really given a chance, support.

Those who propose and suggest variations can often escape with the excuse that they "did not mean all that" or that teachers did not really understand and use good judgment in carrying out their ideas. The teacher can not and knows he can not. He is aware that what he does with the children daily builds up confidence or spreads doubt in the mind of the parents. If he is willing to accept the charge of the curriculum reformer and idealist, and if he can balance his revisions artfully enough to manage real growth in the child in areas familiar to parents and to promote growth in areas, and by ways, new to the parents, the teacher can speed curriculum progress through the public support and confidence he establishes. On the other hand, if he sends children home exasperated with his inability to set tasks for them, if his methods are so radical and foreign to them that he leaves them panicky and confused, he will frustrate the best laid plans of those who would improve the curriculum through public support of different methods.

THE TEACHER AND BROADER PLANS

Earlier discussion in this chapter has dealt with some roles of the teacher in the classroom or in face-to-face relationship with pupils. Emphasis was put first on this aspect of his over-all curriculum function to emphasize the position that the quality of a teacher's daily activity with pupils is really the crux of curriculum improvement. However, it is a simple fact that what pupils and teachers do in the classroom fits into more comprehensive plans and organization, and that guidance is given each teacher through policy, material, general objectives statements, definition of scope, and so on. The anticipation of certain outcomes, the planning of a variety of methods, and the creation of particular kinds of organization are also done by groups, sometimes less intimately and directly connected with specific classroom activity than the teacher and often remote from any school. Through such remote groups, broad structure for pupil experiencing is set up. Teacher-learning situations develop as they do in part because these groups, vested with authority, have determined that certain activities are necessary for obtaining the results thought desirable.

It might be said that anything done to make the experiences of children in school more worthwhile is part of curriculum improvement. With such a definition, it is possible to go pretty far afield, for it can be shown easily that most decisions made with respect to buildings, teacher preparation, teacher employment, teacher evaluation, financing schools, or bus transportation do have some effect on the kinds and quality of school offerings. A more manageable classification of activities to be considered as curriculum planning is given, however, by Krug.[8] In his view the variety of important and most pertinent activities can be thought of as (1) identifying and stating educational objectives, (2) developing the all-school program, (3) improving teaching and learning procedures and processes, (4) providing curriculum guides, (5) providing instructional aids and materials.

Clearly, teachers perform many of these activities in their individual roles as planners and managers of the teaching-learning situation. But some, it will be noted, are more appropriately done at levels more or less remote from that situation, and indeed contributions can be made to all of them at these other levels. Officially, the hierarchy ranges in remoteness from the grade or department, the school and the system to the state, with intermediate positions. Unofficially, professional and lay organizations at various levels are concerned and make their influence felt.

Other Teacher Roles

At each of these levels the teacher has been called upon increasingly in recent years to participate, to make suggestions, and to take major responsibility for the production of ideas, for the clarification and meaningful delineation of concepts, and for the creation of resources. This development has resulted from the vigorous emphasis on cooperative democratic action in planning almost everything in education. It has derived (1) from the agitation of conscience on the part of of those who preach "education for democracy," (2) from greater insight into what democratic relationship means (3) from clear evidence that those who are involved in the development of plans have a much greater commitment to see them work, and (4) from the theory that out of effectively organized groups can come a greater number of more

[8] Edward Krug, *Curriculum Planning*, rev. ed., Harper, 1957, p. 4.

significant and valuable contributions. The faith of curriculum experts now rests on the thesis that, given the responsibility for improving the experiences of children in school, classroom teachers working together will produce far more than could be obtained by leaving the obligation solely or mainly with the supervisors and directors of instruction. Furthermore, the practitioner is a hard taskmaster and is "down to earth." He is soon exasperated with verbalism and abstraction. Very intimate with the day-to-day, minute-by-minute difficulties of working with children, he focuses on the manufacture of tools that will work for him and those who are like him.

With this viewpoint, the work of curriculum directors or co-ordinators has become largely that of managing teacher groups, acting as a resource to them, encouraging and stimulating them to develop better meanings, convictions, and motives through their efforts to define and solve a variety of problems. The supervisor of instruction has thus become more a catalyst and facilitator whose major skill now is that of knowing how to work effectively with groups to get the members to change their commitments, their personal goals, and their styles of behaving. The following functions of a leader, identified in one analysis illustrate this

1. Cooperating with others in the identification of mutually acceptable goals
2. Stimulating individual and cooperative decision, action, and evaluation
3. Developing a favorable climate for individual and group effort
4. Guiding individuals and groups toward greater self-direction and competence
5. Helping individuals and groups to maintain perspective regarding immediate and long-range activities
6. Providing individuals and groups with needed guidance and resources at appropriate times
7. Coordinating the efforts of others
8. Carrying out effectively any responsibilities for action that have been accepted[9]

Consistent with this definition, objectives for a school program in a city are selected by teachers through representative city-wide committees; courses of study, resource units, and supplementary materials are prepared by groups appointed from the total staff; specific problems felt and listed by teachers—such as providing for individual differences, relating achievement to mental ability, and diagnosing pupils' personal needs, are investigated by teachers who have been helped to identify them by their status leader.

[9] Gordon Mackenzie and Stephen Corey, *Instructional Leadership,* Bureau of Publications, Teachers College, 1954.

Even in New York, which more than most states has relied upon centralized direction, "the local development of courses of study, within a state framework, is recommended" and school systems are ". . . encouraged to engage in cooperative curriculum study." The State Education Department explains its position thus:

In New York State at the present time there is wide variation in the amount and equality of supervision. It is the policy to encourage the introduction and expansion of that type of supervision which recognizes the cooperative nature of the undertaking and includes democratic participation of teachers in the development of instructional programs and in the determination of educational policies. Supervision of this type encourages teachers to be more self-directive and to evaluate their own services much as they in turn encourage children to use their own initiative and to evaluate their activities.[10]

A number of approaches to such teacher participation have been described by Caswell and his associates. In Denver, for example,

the Senior High School Committee on Instruction consists of the principal, the coordinator, and two elected teachers from each of the six senior high schools in the city. To this group are added representatives of each of the instructional departments plus the assistant superintendent in charge of secondary and adult education.

The development of the program of instruction for the senior high schools of the city is the responsibility of this committee. Policies adopted by this group are regarded as mandates by the schools and the supervisory officers of the district when approved by the administration. . . .

Subject-matter committees on the various levels are subcommittees of the Committees of Instruction. Activities of curriculum committees consist of recommending textbooks, achieving integration between schools, recommending new courses or changes in existing courses, developing in-service education programs, and bringing subject-matter instruction in harmony with the general objectives of the school. . . .[11]

It is not likely that there will be a reversal of this trend toward more widespread participation and use of teacher group study, research, and analysis. In fact, it is almost certain that it will continue apace. The teacher will not only work daily face to face with an assigned group of pupils, but increasingly as:

1. A deliberate social analyst
2. A student of adolescent growth and development characteristics and needs so to advise on what to offer in and how to manage schools
3. A value judge determining what priority to place on various goals and content

[10] New York State Education Department, *Objectives of Elementary Education,* The Department, 1955, p. 13.

[11] H. L. Caswell, ed., *Curriculum Improvement in Public School Systems,* Bureau of Publications, Teachers College, 1950, pp. 155 and 157.

4. A policy-maker on organization and structure of the educational program
5. A research planner and manager, testing out the appropriateness of plans and procedures
6. A critic and supporter of the ideas and proposals of peers and superiors
7. A public relations participant both explaining and seeking reaction and suggestion from patrons

Success of Cooperative Programs and Teacher Competence

When appointing special project groups or committees to evaluate, prepare, and revise guides for teaching or to propose solutions for specific local problems, it has been customary for leaders to seek out the members of the staff who have the greatest competence and the greatest amount of energy. These people are rich in ideas and insight, fluent with innovations, artful, and their resultant efforts are usually approved by the colleagues for whom they have worked.

But in the true democratic spirit, all the work upon guides, problems, issues, ideas or methods can not be done by representatives. Many, perhaps most, of the problems can be wrestled with successfully only through full understanding, genuine commitment, and positive action by large portions of the staff. All teachers can work on ways of making youngsters happier in school, on methods of arousing sensitivity to the rights of others, on means of developing more persistent behavior in the pursuit of health. The extent of their contributions of course will depend in part upon their sheer intellectual power. But personality, conditions of work, and types of preparation are also important and can affect how much is accomplished.

Inadequate Training for Group Work

Despite the extensive discussion in curriculum journals and books about the need for widespread teacher participation and the methods by which to acquire it, on the whole, teachers have had little training in cooperative curriculum work. Within the last five years several books on the improvement of teaching and on teaching methods have included portions on how the teacher should work with his colleagues, the types of problems he will encounter, and the kinds of skills he will need to develop. Some attention is given in preservice training to methods of group study and committee production of units, and much discussion is precipitated on what ought to be done in the schools to improve programs. But, for the most part, the new teacher has not been required to explore widely the dynamics connected with professional group solutions to persisting and annoying conditions in the curriculum. In view of this fact, the last sections of this volume are devoted to examining the way the teacher may best contribute as a curriculum improvement participant outside his classroom.

READINESS AND WILLINGNESS REQUIRED

Although many do lack training, steady progress is being made through in-service programs, the work of professional organizations, and slow adaptations at the college level. But know-how is not alone the crux of the matter. The teacher who "knows how" can participate wholeheartedly or can hang back and withhold his ideas and his capacity to develop conviction and new modes of behavior. He may doubt any real need for getting exercised over matters. He may beg that he has neither time nor energy. He may argue that he does not have the responsibility or the pay for making administrative and supervisory decisions and therefore he should not be expected to do such work. If a teacher be of such a mind, it is obvious that he can stall any program or process dependent upon his cooperation. Therefore, the teacher must be in accord with the principle that the teaching assignment includes working with colleagues on problems related to curriculum improvement. Little progress will be made otherwise.

REALISM ABOUT ASSIGNMENTS NECESSARY

The pressure upon teachers to act as adjuncts in administration—to cooperate with and report extensively and personally to parents, to study pupils more thoroughly, and to make reports on everything from absence to incidents involving conflicting emotions—nearly drives them into a frenzy and regularly leaves them exhausted at the end of the day. Cognizance of this has led many administrators to make committee work, specially assigned individual studies and research, workshops, and the like a regular part of the school day.

Arrangements are often made to release teachers from other duties, to provide substitutes for class work, to schedule workshops before or after the regular school year, and to pay teachers for their participation during this extra time. With this kind of accommodation, it is likely that participating teachers will drop their defensive behavior and respond optimistically and positively to suggestions of consultants, colleagues, pupils, and parents. There will be some possibility that teachers will fulfill the expectations of the curriculum experts that in them are the resources to make the present plans for improvement work and in them are the creative powers to evolve even better plans.

More Extensive Knowledge and Broader Insight Needed

The important task of deciding the knowledge that is of most worth or problems and concerns of man and society that should be identified for school study obviously can not be delegated to the superficially or shallowly informed. Since the stakes are high, those who make the choices need be sharply aware of the deficiencies and limitations of man in our time, well fortified about the values generally supported, and of the point at which specific knowledge, skills, and approaches will contribute to societal-personal growth. On the whole the equipment of teachers is less adequate than it should be in this respect. For many, exposure to the liberal arts and social sciences has been limited.

The teacher's judgment, though, is critical in the many communities where there is appreciable dependence upon him to determine objectives, scope, and content of the school program. Especially is this so in determining a program for the "non-college-bound" who now constitute a large majority of the high school population. With no well-tried pattern to serve as a guide and with no standards set by college entrance examinations in familiar subjects, the teacher must call upon local studies of needs in the community and in youth, and interpret significant and complex social problems sufficiently well to determine goals and plan valid experiences for this group. Important social issues, bodies of knowledge, purposes, and goals can easily be overlooked by those whose view is unbalanced because of narrow interest and concentration.

Questions for Discussion

1. If final decision-making bodies—such as boards of control or administrators with the power to determine the offerings in a school—include the teaching of Russian and Chinese and rule that French and Latin are to be dropped, in what respect will the teacher be a key factor in curriculum change? If it is preferred to call such a substitution an improvement, rather than a change, could this be judged as such by teachers?
2. Do you think what a pupil learns is very often defined by the content of a textbook? What threat to good education do you see in limiting a pupil to the text? What threat do you see in encouraging teachers to depart from the text?
3. Should an ordinary teacher take the time to study a great variety of societal problems in order to plan for a balance of experiences with pupils?
4. In what way would changing the marking system, setting up a detention program, and dispensing with home study be curriculum problems?
5. A class in English comes directly from a preceding period in geometry. They are overexcited, contentious, noisy, and reluctant to settle down. They

literally exhaust the English teacher with near explosions resulting from their tension. Could this be a curriculum problem? Explain.

6. Should teachers be expected to plan and produce materials for teaching and also set up the kinds of problems youth are to study?

7. What proposal would you make for curriculum improvement as a member of the faculty in the school best known to you? What do you see as factors which would prevent their acceptance?

8. One author would re-establish and insure high standards of achievement in school by putting "real teeth" in examinations, thus putting curriculum making more in the hands of outside agents. Would you approve of this?

Selected Bibliography

Anderson, Vernon, Paul R. Grim, and William Gruhn, *Principles and Practices of Secondary Education,* Ronald, 1951, chap. 5.

Association for Supervision and Curriculum Development, *Action for Curriculum Improvement,* The Association, 1951, chap. 3.

Association for Supervision and Curriculum Development, *Group Planning in Education,* The Association, 1954.

Douglass, Harl R., ed., *The High School Curriculum,* Ronald, 1956, chap. 17.

Krug, Edward, *et al., Administering Curriculum Planning,* Harper, 1957, chap. 5.

Krug, Edward, *Curriculum Planning,* rev. ed., Harper, 1957, chap. 5.

Miel, Alice, *et al., Cooperative Procedures in Learning,* Bureau of Publications, Teachers College, 1952, chap. 18.

Spears, Harold, *The Teacher and Curriculum Planning,* Prentice-Hall, 1951.

Wynne, John P., *The Teacher and the Curriculum,* Prentice-Hall, 1937 chaps. 1, 2.

PART II

PROVIDING THE BASES
FOR REVISION

CHAPTER 4

....

Personal Development of the Teacher

Although the curriculum literature is extensive with respect to what the curriculum should include in scope and how it should be organized, there has been little comparable attention to what is involved personally and psychologically for the teacher in promoting curriculum adaptations, individually or with colleagues. Several years ago one volume[1] treated broadly the problem of change and concluded that only minor amounts of progress could be accomplished without bringing about basic changes in people. The Illinois bulletin,[2] *Human Relations in Curriculum Change,* which followed a few years later, encouraged the administrators and teachers who desired school program improvement to seek the development of new and different perceptions through the process of common and group problem-solving. It also pointed up some of the techniques for more effective group interaction and for group contribution to personal growth. A study by Sharp[3] analyzed what is involved in re-educating the teacher and then discussed how the supervisor can aid in the process. A more recent volume[4] by Mackenzie and Corey reviews a number of critical elements in leadership for curriculum change. However, there is a paucity of published material on what the teacher may need to consider in regard to his own personality as he takes the position of a key factor in curriculum improvement. In this chapter our discussion turns to what the classroom teacher may well attend to in himself. Here we have attempted to discuss why teachers resist or reject experimentation and

----

[1] Alice Miel, *Changing the Curriculum,* Appleton-Century, 1946.

[2] Kenneth Benne and Bozidar Muntyan, *Human Relations in Curriculum Change,* Dryden, 1950.

[3] George Sharp, *Curriculum Development as Re-education of the Teacher,* Bureau of Publications, Teachers College, 1951.

[4] Gordon Mackenzie and Stephen Corey, *Instructional Leadership,* Bureau of Publications, Teachers College, 1954.

active participation in the curriculum development process and what is involved in personal adaptation and restructuring of attitudes toward curriculum work.

A CONTRAST IN TYPES

Despite the enthusiastic support given to modern concepts of the teacher's role in the classroom and elsewhere by professors in teachers colleges, by authors of books on teaching method, and by professional groups, a very large number of teachers have continued to resist adaptations. They adhere to practices common several decades ago and resist not only new instructional techniques and approaches, but also seriously question policies and procedures recommended for improvement of the total educational program. By contrast there are in the profession those who are much more inclined to give serious consideration to educational research, to entertain more optimistically ideas about substantial changes in curriculum organization and teaching method, and to engage more actively in a searching evaluation of the status quo.

Obviously it is impossible and probably unfair to attach a label to any one teacher who resists some of this or some of that. Likewise one should be hard put to find a completely accurate and correct designation for those who more often respond to or seize avidly upon ideas for change. Labels may cover up as much as they reveal and exceptions are always to be found. However, to provide a departure point for our discussion here, we have characterized two types of teachers as traditional and modern.

In our view the traditional teacher is one who conceives of himself as an informer or teller. He decides what is to be learned and he accepts largely without question the choices made by his superiors or by scholarly authorities. He uses recitation as the basic method. His major source for information and explanation is the textbook, and only rarely does he depart from that order of logical presentation of facts, principles, and ideas. He looks upon adaptation to promote social, physical, and emotional development as of minor importance. His concern for the effect of personal problems, the impact of out-of-school pressures, the influence of factors infringing on interest and attention is decidedly limited, and he usually resists the idea of intensive personal study of the individual child. Although occasionally motivated to set up special tasks for the more able, he is fundamentally committed to teach or to tell or to demand the same things from all students at the same time and to the same extent. From time to time he may present reasons for learning and try to show the relationship of required knowledge and skill to probable future uses, but for the most part this occurs only when students do not seem willing to accept on faith his claim that they need to and ought to know, or when threats of lowered marks and grades are inadequate to obtain interest and application.

Although the traditionalist teacher may at first be thought of as one devoted only to academic areas of study, such is not the case. Even in the practical subjects, there are traditionalists. Individual differences are seldom provided for; the facts set out for acquisition are unrelated to immediate problems or concerns; the major classroom procedure is telling by the teacher and continual repetition by the students to insure as exact a re-presentation as possible. In general, little sympathy is afforded the child who does not intensely want to secure what the teacher knows. Clearly manifest is the conviction that school is a privilege. Dependence on competition as motivation is a natural outgrowth of this privilege concept and a corollary of the inadequately examined idea that schools exist to give the individual a chance to develop himself almost completely for his own personal profit.

Further, the traditional teacher may be described as one who resists the idea of flexible standards and who protests the introduction into the program of new and varied activities and experiences calculated to provide rewarding and satisfying schooling for the less able. In fact he is often inclined to doubt the reliability of tests of ability and to suggest rather that higher level performance could be secured merely by insistence upon it. The evidence that certain subjects neither train the mind nor teach how to think better seems to have little effect upon either his attitude or his practice. His general outlook rather is to scoff at the educational research specialists and the psychologists who have thoroughly analyzed a multitude of claims and found them wanting. Since the traditionalist is unwilling to accept the results of studies of physical growth and development, of how learning takes place, of measures of appraisal, transfer, and application, he rejects the proposals for program, policy, and teaching method based on these careful investigations.

The contrast of this model is what we would call the "modern" teacher who seeks critically and constantly to review his attitudes, his methods, and his influence. This teacher sees the learning situation as one in which the purposes of children are of paramount importance. He constantly seeks to adapt his materials to the interests and aptitudes of his pupils and views their lack of interest or their failure to acquire and retain as his responsibility. Working with his group as a collection of individuals, he plans with them around goals and expectations to help them acquire the mastery over areas of knowledge and over the kinds of skills possessed by the mature and scholarly. Convinced that school is an investment for the purpose of developing all children for the benefit of society, this teacher views each child as an opportunity and recognizes the need for finding ways to capture his interest and his effort.

. This teacher sees himself as the major factor in selecting learning opportunities and experiences of high quality for children. He accepts the challenge to have a larger view of program and to study what the role of schools as a whole is and how it may be accomplished. He knows adaptations are the inevitable products and requisites of the changing environment. The need to dispense with the no longer appropriate and useful, the obligation to pay heed to demonstrated fallacies in unexamined beliefs, the advantage of working with the support of others in reorganizing are all obvious. He seeks no escape either through denial of change or through disavowal of responsibility.

REORIENTATION IS DIFFICULT

In most of us, whether we fit a traditional model or not, resistance to change is strong. The image of the "modern" teacher is different from what many know from past experience and from exposure to their own teachers. Now there is demand for one thoroughly informed about evolving research on learning, for one whose reference is children as well as subjects, for one who enjoys independence, exploration, and novelty. Here is a discomfiting picture of a teacher who no longer occupies a pedestal, who no longer knows the answer to everything.

Yet we know many teachers have accepted the modern role for themselves. It is our conviction that these teachers have fortunately been able to accomplish some or all of the following:

1. They have come to see that half a century of tinkering by "specialists," half a century of rearrangement of subject-matter in limited academic areas by those remote from the classroom, and prodigious production of teaching suggestions have resulted only in very minor improvement in the experiences children have. They are in agreement with the argument presented in Chapter 3 that the critical factor in curriculum improvement is the imagination and ingenuity of the

teacher in the classroom situation, and his willingness to implement what is appropriate for him.

2. They have come to accept the fact that subject-centered teaching, telling, and reciting have proved to be inadequate and they can not be content with the results. The numerous studies showing insufficient retention, lack of power to use presumed learnings in practical situations, as well as pupil dissatisfaction with school have served to develop the conviction that more of the same will bear no better fruit. They have examined carefully the procedure and method used in obtaining these data, recognized their scientific defensibility, and accepted the results as a challenge to alter or adapt or revise the procedures that lead to such poor outcomes.

3. They have become convinced that real learning takes place only when there is purpose and that purpose can not be forced on the child. Rather they have come to see clearly that purpose in learning develops slowly from the rich environment of proper and effective use of the present experience, first-hand acquaintance, and the imagination of the learner. Respect for the rights of the child as an individual is seen as critically related to his enthusiasm and application.

4. They have thoroughly examined their own purposes in teaching and have come to understand what real professionalism requires. They know that teaching is more than a job or a sinecure or an opportunity to satisfy one's own personal interest in a subject field. It has ceased to be or never has been for them a temporary insurance policy, a waiting station where one does as little as possible to earn a salary. Also, teaching is not seen as an opportunity to exercise power and control over others and to obtain satisfaction from holding youth at their mercy. They do not see their task as a mechanical one, tediously using the same inadequate tools, hearing lessons, going through a series of paces. Teaching rather is an opportunity for the master technician who sees his group as an inspiring combination of urges, arts, and aptitudes and who is constantly in search of the key that will release a rush of ambitions, ideas, and skills. They have come to value most the teacher's power to open vistas, to raise sights, to introduce the exciting as well as the rewarding, and to help create those concepts of self in each child that focus energy and release effort.

5. They have welcomed the point of view that has created for the school a broader responsibility and function. To make the most possible of all children has become their fulcrum for action, and they are constantly alert to detect immediately those compromises

that will promote fractionization, elitism, and unnecessary categorization. For them the school's purpose is to encourage creativity, to extend imagination, and to promote acting on thinking. They know that this can be accomplished only when children can be independent, when they have freedom for action, when they are respected for their power to judge and make decisions, when they are given opportunity to contemplate and to choose, when they are free to seek what they need to accomplish what can become important to them. In this kind of setting the modern teacher is fully convinced that interest in, respect for, and love of learning will develop.

6. They have acquired confidence in their own ability to act independently, to draw on personal resources, and to find unique and creative ways of solving problems. They attempt to try things out differently, and submit to honest self-evaluation and self-criticism that prevent complacency and facilitate adaptation and experimentation. They happily entertain suggestions from others and actively search in books, in visits, in professional meetings, in the comments of fellow teachers and in the advice of experts for more appropriate and interesting content, for high yield activities, and for ways of diagnosing, motivating, and presenting. But they are not solely or even for the most part dependent on these outside resources and they find solutions to their problems independently. Evidence of such independence is to be found in the production of teaching materials locally, in taking the opportunity to plan with pupils, in the development of personal courses of study.

7. They have developed a healthy but not submissive attitude toward specialists, experts, and authorities. Mindful of the attributes of scholarship, their urge has been to relate knowledge and skill to need and to natural condition and situation and to exercise the prerogative and responsibility to prune, to add, and to allocate differently. Working daily with children, particularly in the humanities and in the social sciences, these teachers have grown to respect their own judgment about what is important, what counts, and what is worth knowing, and out of their familiarity with and study of child, community, and society, they have come to have more than a few convictions about how and in what areas competence and wisdom can and should be wisely sought. They are almost exact opposites of what Wilhelms has noted in those who lacked power and interest to do. He said of them

They all knew their stuff. But a good many of them seemed to know it in only one order, one pattern—roughly the order and pattern in which it had been taught to them, the order and pattern (and scope) of the traditional high school presentation. They couldn't play around with their stuff in the deft, nonchalant manner of the real master. They wouldn't shuffle the deck, cut it any old way, and be comfortable playing the cards as they came up. They couldn't reach across big spaces and weave relationships, and they weren't relaxed when perfectly new material showed up in a new synthesis.[5]

8. They have above all developed a mind open for challenge. With new ideas, with contentions about the status quo, with exhortations to get on the move they are pleased and comfortable. In fact, the absence of wholesome doubting creates depression and unfulfillment. To these teachers we have just begun on the exhilarating task of building a great education and to be anywhere except on the frontier, staking out new areas and personally doing the prospecting would be to sacrifice the very heart of their prerogatives. Their own education has caused them to feel adequate only when they are busy at searching inquiry, when they are free to balance and weigh, and when they are entitled to engage in the steps that may lead to ever more fruitful results. They must then never be the passive assimilators of the efforts of others.

GROWTH AND ACTIVE EFFORT

Obviously teachers who are resistant to change can make contributions to curriculum improvement, but the position taken here is that their efforts will be hampered without the above attributes. The major concern of most teachers and certainly of supervisors who complain about teacher inactivity, unreadiness, and unwillingness is to find ways to develop these qualities. In this section several suggestions are given on some matters the teacher may well consider in building toward these goals.

Informed Choice-Making

It is not possible to review here the vast amount of literature in psychology and philosophy that can serve to develop the teacher's outlook. It is obvious though that it has now reached such proportions that a teacher may reasonably expect to sample only a limited part. The problem no longer is whether or not to seek direction from these materials, but what and how much to choose.

The teacher should be conversant with and know the implications of the research of the psychologists on motivation, on emotion in learn-

[5] Fred T. Wilhelms, "The Importance of People," *Educational Leadership,* October, 1958, p. 39.

ing, on effect of school practice on attitudes, maturation, and transfer, and similar topics. He should know the experiments of the methodologists on group process, on project approaches, on the interest and use value of selected content, and on the sequence and placement of that content. He should know the convictions of the philosophers on who should go to school for what, on what is of most value to a society whose faith rests on the use and the extension of practical intelligence, on the role of school as related to the future, on the rights and wisely determined privileges and responsibilities of children, and on varied other questions that can provide the measurements for practice.

Interaction

Some people can achieve nearly all they need by independent study and cogitation. More, however, must check their reactions constantly and widely against the opinions of others. Through thorough examination and quest for further information understanding is advanced.

Usually there are opportunities to test ideas, to get clearer meanings, to reinforce thinking. The faculty meeting, in-service courses, casual conferences and relaxation periods, sessions on policy and program are common ground for the interchange of opinion, for the presentation of reasons underlying attitudes, for requests for clarification. Still too many of these and similar situations are not used for such good purpose and are rather devoted to announcements, to listening, to idle chitchat, and to not very constructive complaint.

Problems Presented by Change

Few people have not at some time or other "got themselves into something they would rather have avoided." Their regret regularly is a result of the discovery that their assent or compliance has led to long hours of work or to denying themselves something which is more pleasurable. Very often the discomfort results not only from the nature of the actual work but also from the compulsion to go along after having started.

Change of viewpoint, attitudes, and ways of doing frequently lead one to identify with new people, new groups, and their convictions. Birds of a feather apparently do flock together and demand loyalties. When anyone entertains a new set of ideas or permits himself to be exposed to media which may bring new ideas, invariably he takes risks. Examination of the novel and the different can easily lead to a dislocation in customary human relationships. Espousal of the new

thus usually requires careful consideration of what effect such behavior will have on those the individual admires and is admired by.

We may illustrate this in a number of ways; two examples
should be sufficient.

Garth Walsh was a second-year teacher who elected to take some courses
at a nearby university. On several occasions he took the required books for the
course to his school to read in spare moments. On each of these occasions one
of the staff whom he admired kidded him about the volumes, scoffed at their
content, and suggested that his effort was not very sensible. Several other times
Garth found that arguments or points that he introduced into conversation and
which came from his courses and his books were received with some hurt
surprise and even ridiculed. In the faculty room, at private social gatherings,
in casual meetings he came to feel that his old friends seemed a little distant
or to be less enthusiastic about him. Gradually Garth found himself developing
a cynical attitude toward his university program and covering up increasingly
his tottering sympathy for ideas he had begun to give more recognition. He
found that faced with the choice of departing from old friends or of identifying with several others who were taking a different position, he preferred to
maintain the approval, in this case, of the more numerous and powerful.
Within two years he was effectively lost to those activities and experiences by
which he might in time have come to develop the attributes above considered
important to curriculum improvement.

David Eglund thought he was convinced the school faculty should work
together to improve local program. He had studied carefully the literature on
the way groups ought to work together and how they should and could analyze
their own process. As a result, after there had been some difficulty in communication and interpretation at a meeting over school policy and after the observation had been made that the group did not know how to work together, he prepared for the faculty both a reaction form and a subsequent summary of what
some factors were that might be interfering with smooth operation. Walter
Evans was attracted by the form and the summary and became fairly interested
in what the next steps might be. He offered to help in David's plans to move
the faculty to a maturer level and he obtained some books and materials on
the theory of group dynamics and on techniques useful to good group development and performance. In time despite David's good sense and good leadership,
the faculty split into at least two camps, one of which abruptly turned its back
on group process. Walter Evans, although he had some greater faith by then
in David, discovered that at least for some good time he would have to forego
the respect of an appreciable number of those who had considered him a man
of good sense. At best he saw David's chances of success as slim and obviously
demanding of great time and effort. He capitulated and now easily reminds
others that "Well, we tried that once, and you know, it didn't really work."

Sources of Anxiety Under Examination

More extensive in most of us than reluctance to establish or to re-
pattern friendships is general insecurity and anxiety about exploring

uncharted areas. Habit is indeed a compelling influence in the lives of all of us. Unfortunately, improving the curriculum requires adaptation, if not radical adjustment in habitual patterns; the literature is vigorous in attack on sacred cows; the proposals made stretch the imagination and clearly demand ingenuity, intellectual stamina, and courage to probe well beyond the known, the safe, and the secure. How one may cope with this generalized insecurity and its accompanying anxiety is not a simple matter. We can not explore the problem very much here, for it is involved and not without the requirements of very special knowledge and insight. But the books listed below do provide lengthy treatment.[6] From them we know several simple rules for dealing with security needs include (1) retraining oneself by trying out new procedures on a very limited scale, (2) reviewing one's early experiences to locate and understand events that led to and fixed retiring attitudes and stubborn inaccessibility, (3) identifying with some one who can accept, understand, and reflect one's expressions of apprehension and excuses and explanations of self-effacement and self-protection, and (4) finding situations where others similarly afflicted are reworking their outlooks and sharing their experiences in obtaining altered perceptions of self and environment.

Recognition of the Need for Change

Getting to "see" things in a different way is for most of us a personal matter. Until the will has emerged to view conditions, environment, and stimuli in another way, and until the decision is made to react to that environment in some alternative fashion as suggested by others, we can expect no real progress. Obviously a person can be forced to act as if he agreed and he can get to the point where he says that the "moon is made of green cheese," but this does not guarantee or prove that he either willingly accepts or believes what he says.

The resistant teacher would perhaps change then if he would read books, listen to arguments, study the extent of his own effectiveness, become dissatisfied with what he is doing or with what is being done. However, the problem is that he does not "see" the usual "growth" helps or facilitators as something he wants or requires to relieve his present needs or to change his outlook. Rather he looks upon the authors as inadequate, their ideas as impractical, "re-search" in education as incomplete and unconvincing, the proponents as strident noise

[6] Karen Horney, *The Neurotic Personality of Our Time,* Norton, 1937; P. M. Symonds, *The Dynamics of Human Adjustment,* Appleton-Century, 1946; H. A. Overstreet, *The Mature Mind,* Norton, 1949.

makers and their proposals as ill-considered and irresponsible. He also considers leaders who have been appointed to promote curriculum improvement or those teachers who have elected to encourage and support efforts to change outlook as unnecessary meddlers who both annoy and threaten.

Individual Value Systems

Another area of inaccessibility is the depth and rigidity of the individual's value system. Although one may not be able to see differently because he does not want to, he more likely does not because he has so effectively crystallized his version and view out of past experience. Literally he is so set in his ways that even if he actively engaged in trying to look from another angle he could not see differently. Enforced by personal satisfaction and gratification and by status figures more often past than present, his outlook is fixed. With his mind made up about intelligence and its sources, about competition, about what schools should do, about who should receive schooling, this person is thoroughly trapped by the strength of his convictions.

We need then to ask ourselves constantly are we too sure of too many things and are we using our intelligence to defend what we believe, squirming and dodging, rather than applying ourselves most positively to weighing one value against another. Common sense requires us to be cautious about those who seek to prevail upon us, but it also dictates that we constantly search our reasons, and check our proper doubts as well as convictions.

Clarification of Ideas About Status and Power

We have already shown that there is a trend to involve teachers in program-planning and in policy making. However, active as the trend is, it has not appreciably affected many teachers.

Probably the preservice teacher is most likely to have the idea that a teacher really has little to say about what is taught, and should have little to say. This attitude doubtless comes more from his youthful lack of knowledge of what to teach than from anything else. And surely it is normal to think that the established personnel can make better decisions.

But the mature teacher should want to voice his opinion and to exercise his influence. He should know when and how much he can help in recommending courses to be added and dropped, content to be included or replaced, experiences to be required, and teaching methods to be approved and encouraged. He should know his responsibility in preparing resource units, teaching suggestions, diagnostic materials, guides for teacher-pupil planning. He should take the initiative in clarifying for himself and others what he is to do in setting up and carrying out research and in preparing explanations for the board of education and the community.

But having important role and accepting that role are not at all easy to do. That the theorists have said curriculum-making is a teacher's responsibility and that some school systems employ teachers as curriculum workers are not in themselves convincing. The fact that there are problems in carrying out the role only serves to spread the news that the theorists do not really mean it, and are a little unreasonable if not "wacky."

It does take time to bring about change in an institution, and what is done at one moment or instance may not bear fruit for a very long time. The strategic time to seek a new policy, new personnel, better materials, and schedule changes in most school districts is related to a constellation of factors often beyond the immediate view of the teacher and the control of the administrators. Therefore the teacher participant in curriculum change needs to appreciate how slowly adaptation may take place and overcome the impatience and normal agitation at waiting which encourage one to deny his own importance.

The deliberative process too takes time and requires compromises at numerous junction points. No matter how pressingly obvious a proposal may be there are always people whose status, welfare, security, comfort, even complacency, can be affected by change.

This is particularly so when those slow to convince or to respond are status personnel whose position of legal authority requires their personal decision and their sole acceptance of responsibility. In all of our schools the democratic and deliberative process functions in an advisory sense. The power to make a final choice is retained somewhere by a higher authority. Usually such an authority, despite faith in the good sense and intelligence of a qualified subordinate group, is sensitive to the designated burden he or it, if a committee, carries.

A clear task of every teacher is to come to grips himself with this problem of subordination and to see that a "staff" member must include in his role the obligation to study, to examine, to advise, and to recommend. He must act on faith that his best thoughts and considered judgments will have every proper chance of direct translation. And in this of course he must realize that his own effort and action must be at least informed and prudent.

Broader Concept of the Profession

Finally, coming to the view that a teacher does have a significant place depends on our growth in understanding the proper dimensions of professional activity. Some of the problems of creating this broader vision we have mentioned before. There are rather convincing arguments that a teacher's primary and only job is to teach, to talk with children, to hold conferences, to contemplate his students, and that additional tasks ought to be rejected because they distract attention, drain energy, and dissipate the focus and concentration which are so essential to effective teaching. Yet it behooves us to ask if we will ever have a true profession and with it personal self-respect until we get away from being underlings, employees, retiring craftsmen in cubicles. There are those who believe we shall never have democracy in school administration until we accept the challenge to select our own goals and manage our own experiences. We very probably will have no true respect from the public until we come to believe in ourselves, to act as masters of our own fate, and to seek the total impact which both a true liberal education and an adequate professional training prepare us to exercise.

ADAPTATIONS IN PERSONALITY

The personal attributes a teacher ought to have to get along well in his work have often been studied. On the whole the results indicate a list of characteristics that teachers want from fellow teachers, that administrators seek in teachers, that curriculum directors and supervisors feel are essential. There is also wide agreement on personal limitations.

We find that attributes teachers ought to have, among others at least, are

1. To have initiative, self-motivation, drive
2. To be responsive to opportunities and to invitations to study, to research, to self-evaluate, to compare notes, to participate in planning policy, etc.
3. To be alert to educational trends and aware and informed about educational issues
4. To be able and willing to experiment sensibly, independently and with others, and to be tactful about and sympathetic with colleagues
5. To have sufficient self-control and enough information and ideas as well as interactive skill to engage in intensive work with others
6. To be widely trained and broadly informed in areas beyond their subject and particularly about research on children and learning

7. To be independent and wholesomely self-directed yet comfortable with subordination and with compromises
8. To be emotionally stable and mentally healthy

Some of the personality weaknesses identified are

1. Excessive dependence, need for direction and extensive assistance from others
2. Defensiveness at suggestions, self-protectiveness, easily hurt feelings
3. Low energy and stamina level, quickness to surrender when tasks are difficult, annoyance at problems not easily resolved
4. Low level of self-esteem, doubt of self-worth, retiring and apologetic about importance and intelligence
5. Over-aggressive, dominative, urgent, excessively persistent in having things their own way
6. Overly idealistic about goals, unrealistic in ambition and in perception of conditions
7. Anxious, hostile, accusatory and blame-oriented
8. Impatient, precipitant, incautious
9. Subjective, prejudicial, and stereotyped, unable to read the behavior of others objectively
10. Distrustful, suspicious, fearful, and faithless
11. Antagonistic to the theoretical, the different, and the new out of habit, insecurity, competitiveness
12. Overly intensive in focus, ego-oriented, and uninterested in others and their problems

It would be an unusual teacher, a paragon, who would possess all the traits in the first list and none in the second. Doubtless none such exists. Most or all teachers have some of each of the attributes. Even so it is often difficult for one to recognize his own minor limitations and certainly it is extremely difficult for an individual to accept the more serious ones as persistent or permanent handicaps. In fact most of us have handy and wonderful ways of allaying our own suspicions and of turning aside the honest and correct assessments of both friendly counselors and exasperated or boldly objective enemies.

Regardless of how we handle the limitations in ourselves, it hardly seems possible to argue very effectively and without some transparent display of special pleading against the ideal model in the first list. In fact the most common reaction of teachers is to agree heartily that the model is good and to resolve to be like that. The trouble is that reading the lists and accepting the format does not build into many the "motoric" action Sharp[7] writes about in his volume on re-education of the teacher. We know and accept what we *should* be like, yet we go on being or slip back into being, after a short try, what

[7] Sharp, *op. cit.,* p. 23 ff.

we have been. The model and the product do not get to look alike. There is obviously no sure way to overcome the limitations set out here, but it does help to recognize their existence and to know what situations and conditions tend to reveal and release them.

A Review of Self-Helps

Critical self-appraisal and introspection, despite the tricks the mind may use, are by far the most appropriate ways in which we may rate ourselves. If the teacher can take a trait list[8] and check himself honestly against it, trying to compare his behavior with that of a sizable number of others whom he knows, he may be able to see himself as others see him, even without their judgments. A step beyond this personal relating is self-testing on one of the numerous personality or personal adjustment inventories. Many of these are not sufficiently oriented to teaching, but on the whole they do give respectable evidence of rather general categories of behavior. At least when one is as objective as one can be in responding to the items there is a chance there will be a reasonable amount of reliability.

Obtaining the judgments of others or taking advantage of their willingness to provide reactions or of their responsibility to render analyses (the supervisory conference) is an easy extension of the self-trait study. In some situations the judgment checking process is a yearly step in employee counseling and stimulation. When one is positively inclined, the procedure can be particularly useful in helping one gauge his level of growth.

Although these steps seem obvious and simple, they appear to be practiced far less often than would be salutary for any teacher. When 150 teachers were asked if they had rated themselves within the last five years on teaching practices and procedures in a formal way, 90 percent said they had not. Over 60 percent had not even discussed their teaching or their faculty participation as rated or appraised by any supervisor or colleague. And none had tried himself out on a mental health inventory, a personality test, or a personal adjustment scale. In fact 50 percent had never examined or discussed their responses on any form of personality inventory they had had to take and 20 percent did not recall ever having taken one. Interviews subsequent to this simple survey both with some of the teachers and their administrative officers revealed that a surprising number of those considered difficult,

[8] See checklist for "Professional Qualifications," *Evaluative Criteria; Cooperative Study of Secondary School Standards,* Washington, 1950, p. 282. See also check list on pp. 81–82.

obstructive, hostile, uncooperative, and ineffectual actually were the people who had had little or no exposure to any systematic analysis. As might be expected a few who had had the "works" or used one or more of the steps reviewed here still remained unaffected. Some apparently did not believe or would not; others believed but just could not change, and were, it seems, truly sorry. Far deeper exploration and the help of a competent therapist were indicated, and the teachers did not have the stomach or the resources for it. And their school systems neither required treatment nor facilitated it.

We do not see this as the place to review the mental mechanisms nor their development over long periods in the growing stages precedent to the entrance of adults upon teaching. Likewise it is out of place at this point to examine the conditions and interactions which produce pervading needs for nurturance, for self-abasement, for infavoidance,[9] for defensiveness, for aggression, or for dominance. It is enough here to say that these needs are what determine perception and action. A person will have constant trouble with himself until these needs are in balance.

Better Outlook Toward Authority

A perennial problem among teachers, young and old, is their view of supervisors and administrators as untouchables, threats, enemies, incompetents, father figures, and so forth. Quite fairly some may be accurately classified as vindictive, egoists, charlatans, and excess baggage, but anyone who would attempt to be objective surely would have to contend that for the most part those who move to supervisory and administrative roles have demonstrated skill, knowledge, good attitudes, and general competence. Some lack the knack for good human relations and insight into leadership. Their problem, however, is more often need for training in skills rather than a thorough housecleaning in their personal and emotional makeup.

It is important that each teacher develop his ideas about what a modern supervisor is and should be and that he help his supervisors to fit the model. Through intensive self-study supervisors and administrators have been changing their models, to a very large extent in the direction indicated by teachers as desirable both for them and for good education. In much of what they now wish to become or have been

---

[9] Term used by Murray to include need "to avoid failure, shame, humiliation, ridicule. To refrain from attempting to do something that is beyond one's power. To conceal disfigurement." Henry A. Murray, *Explorations in Personality*, Oxford University Press, 1938, p. 81.

told they ought to become, they need the cooperation of teachers. Part of their difficulty in changing, however, is generally held to be the nature of the concept too many teachers still have of them and too often prefer in order to excuse their own behavior and to retain a convenient target for frustration.

The proper supervisor today is held to be one who helps in and participates in bringing about a better education for children through his skill in leadership, in group process, in personnel administration, and in evaluation. He no longer is a director, task-setter, and boss, but rather a co-worker whose time and special resources are at the disposal of the willing teacher who wishes and is encouraged to improve his teaching.

Such a supervisor then should focus his effort on the areas where the classroom teacher needs help. According to Replogle who asked over 300 teachers in the Middle West what their needs are, the supervisor should help them in

1. Improving teaching techniques and methods
2. Utilizing some of the newly discovered principles of group dynamics
3. Locating and utilizing community resources
4. Providing for individual differences
5. Handling pupil behavior, discipline cases
6. Meeting needs of atypical pupils
7. Caring for the needs of the emotionally maladjusted
8. Enabling teachers to evaluate their own teaching competency
9. Using art and music to better advantage in the regular classroom situation
10. Relating the on-going activity (unit, center-of-experience, project) to the problems, concerns, and tensions of pupils
11. Using the current teaching situation to make understandable the contemporary social realities
12. Making better use of visual aids
13. Locating and making available resources personnel as special problems arise
14. Identifying and utilizing the possibilities of the current classroom for deeper democratic values
15. Constructing and building teaching units on problems and topics not found in basic textbooks[10]

In his conclusion to his study Replogle emphasizes particularly that these areas of need should give direction to the supervisor's efforts. He writes

Supervision which takes into account human relationships and total growth can never be standardized in terms of graphs, charts, lesson plans,

[10] Vernon L. Replogle, "What Help Do Teachers Want?" *Educational Leadership,* April, 1950, pp. 445–449.

gadgets, and tricky techniques; effective supervision can take place only after we have gained the confidence, respect, and faith of those whom we wish to help. Supervisors need to become better students of the human side of teachers; they had better throw away the gold braid authority usually attached to supervision and establish rapport on a person-to-person basis. . . . Teachers . . . want a kind of supervisor that permits them to remain captains of their own souls, that makes it possible for them to respect themselves thoroughly, and gives them a feeling that they are in business for themselves—not for the supervisors.[11]

Every teacher must accept the fact that the supervisors who perform these roles properly and adequately are essential to his profession. When one crosses this bridge and is no longer reluctant to recognize that in a profession all can use help, that organization and system make help possible, that a guide to conscience is useful to most men and can really raise both sight and action levels, that there is an advantage in having some one with time to study, to appraise, to promote, there will be real possibility that forward motion will develop.

Insight into Relationships

Although a teacher may close his door, escape almost completely from his colleagues and proceed vigorously against the problem of improving quality alone for one or several fifty-minute periods each day, he can not avoid his colleagues forever and he can not avoid affecting their effort nor avoid having even his independent effort affected by theirs. The importance then of knowing how to create in self-defense a mutually permissive and supportive atmosphere, if not a cooperative one, is very great.

We may see our colleagues as stuffy, conservative, and impervious to and incapable of growth. We can conclude they are low in professional morale, interested only in the almighty dollar, time-clock punchers who aspire to no reaches of inspiration in teaching.

Or we can view them as really wholesome people with convictions. They may seem to be fairly secure but normally threatened by change and naturally upset by sharp appraisals. And although reasonably self-critical, they may be honestly defensive against provocative ideas about themselves presented by others. We can look upon them as intuitively practical-minded, quite responsive to relatively concrete and well-defined projects and tasks.

Only naïveté would lead us to include everyone in the latter category, and nothing but stupidity would permit the conclusion that

[11] *Ibid.,* pp. 448–449.

Interpersonal matters:

1. Are you aware of and do you help other teachers with their problems?
2. Do you encourage others to tell of their difficulties?
3. Can you make your position clear without expression of emotion or feeling?
4. Are you constantly asking yourself how others view your behavior?
5. Are you able to focus your attention fully on and react to the ideas of others?
6. Do you look for the attributes or strong points in your colleagues and seek ways to have use made of them?
7. Are you known by your colleagues as one who is enthusiastic about other people?
8. Do you like to work on projects with people less able than yourself?
9. Do you regularly attempt to settle differences by finding middle ground?
10. Are you quite willing to postpone your own concerns to attend to other people?
11. Do you remember easily the specific problems and interests of people whom you meet after a lapse of time?
12. Can you handle the opposition of others gracefully?

Personal matters:

1. Do you see yourself as significant contributor and act as one?
2. Do you work actively at trying to see things differently through exploring why you feel and respond as you do?
3. Have you honestly examined how thoroughly you enjoy teaching and what you seek from it?
4. Are you able to dissociate reactions and responses from feelings toward those who have them?
5. Are you willing to give great amounts of time and energy to add to the quality of your work and do you?
6. Do you resent suggestion, are you fearful of correction, do you dislike those who encourage you to action or to greater effort?

7. Do you find yourself regularly at odds with superiors and highly critical of those who take leadership and reveal enthusiasm?

8. Do you spend much time complaining, telling what you could have done?

9. Are you ambitious to find out what can and should be done?

10. Are you uncomfortable in new situations with relaxed controls where you have less directive power?

11. Is your appetite for recognition, attention, and approval high?

12. Do you lack staying power, do you sag or lose drive and interest easily when returns are not forthcoming rapidly?

Professional matters:

1. Are you interested in and want to cope with issues and problems?

2. Do you inform yourself regularly and specifically through study of professional literature?

3. Do you actively seek out opportunities to test out your thought and extend your ideas, even at expense of time and money?

4. Can you look upon university people as provocateurs whose proper role includes analysis, criticism, and proposal?

5. Do you permit good sound research to have impact on your thinking and to affect your plans and practices?

---

all fit the first description. Some may be found at either extreme; most, doubtless between. Our behavior then, it would seem, ought to be governed to fit a generally wholesome situation.

Colleagues who need help are indeed the proper targets of administrators and supervisors, but certainly not the sole obligation of that group. Inasmuch as we as teachers are constantly interacting with these unhappy people it is our responsibility to make those contributions we can in behalf of their welfare and, in effect, of our own. For not only can they lower our morale but also they can actually undermine our own efforts to obtain better learning and happier children.

An uncooperative and antagonistic colleague then should be a challenge to all of us. The causes for his low-level function may be, however, far beyond our reach and in such a case our normal and limited aid is ineffectual. Yet with many, enthusiasm itself is catching; true willingness to work on another's problem may be a first start and a subtle way of building up reciprocity; understanding for and sympathy for past difficulties will reveal a sense of balance and fair play. We can establish sound out-of-school personal relations as a first step, looking for the attributes and gifts that will serve as even a small basis for respect. Reaction and reluctance can be seen more often than we think as caution, desire for assurance, need for specific and manageable suggestions. Our job is to find out casually, indirectly, by conversation and common observation what our antagonistic colleagues want to obtain.

We would be unwise, however, if we failed to anticipate that active pursuit of self-improvement or of improvement in the attitudes and work of others could not have some implications not only for negative-minded but for certain positively inclined colleagues. The influence we exert surely depends upon the views others hold of our prerogatives and responsibilities and of our motives and methods. The state of our own morale and self-esteem and of individual self-involvement are similarly related to the reactions and responses of those with whom we work. Efforts can be seriously hampered and deflected by others who perceive our personal action as threatening, blaming, professionally unwise, or perhaps unethical. It is not at all uncommon to hear from the disillusioned "eager beaver" that he has been maligned, mistreated, and figuratively mauled in his honest efforts. One must ask himself then

1. Is my enthusiasm and vigor viewed as youthful or temporary exuberance likely to wear away progressively, if not quickly, and to be tolerantly lived out by uncomplaining but relatively suffering colleagues?
2. Is my experiment and adaptation regarded as naïveté, a rather immature response to theoretical noise-making from college professors?
3. Is my possession and use of the jargon of the educationist considered both a revelation of smartness and a signal of potential irresponsibility in any community where public support is more closely congruent with the familiar than with the unfamiliar?
4. Is my espousal of the commonly recognized morale-building techniques, in-service improvement arrangements, and vigorous professional activity perceived as currying favor of the administration, as career and promotion bucking, as exploitation of others for reputation building?
5. Is my productive activity in developing classroom materials, in pushing course-of-study improvement, in taking courses at the nearby university felt as a threat to my colleagues' egos, by contrast embarrassing, discomfiting, devaluing in effect and creating hostility rather than warm admiration of creativity and imagination?
6. Is my attempt to teach better judged as a compulsive appetite to steal the affections of students, to build up a following based on compromises with the stiff and difficult realities of what is required to get a quality education with some honest standards of accomplishment?

7. Are my evaluating in groups and occasional "counseling" offers written off as improper and imprudent if not impudent excursions into the psychologist's domain?

When we are aware that such interpretations can be put on our behavior, we can see clearly the need for careful management of our own efforts. We may well look to ourselves to find ways of preventing such opinion from arising. We can help by diminishing our own stridency, by carefully avoiding a know-it-all approach, by moving ahead at a pace consistent with local conditions, while finding ways to move slowly with others to new levels of behavior.

KNOWLEDGE AND APPRECIATION OF OTHER COMMON INTERFERENCE FACTORS

In the preceding paragraphs we have pointed out that enthusiasm can flag rapidly if one finds it hard going with others or if personal efforts bring no breakthroughs or colleagues doubt the sense of our full effort. In this concluding section we wish to turn attention to some of these interferences that may depress morale and discourage effort and at the same time suggest some guides on how to deal with them.

Resistance to Theorists

Perhaps one of the commonest observations made by teachers about recent curriculum proposals is that "it sounds all right in theory but it will not work out in practice." Both the experienced and the preservice teacher, rather generally, join in expressing exasperation at college professors and supervisors who would promote a variety of adaptations. In fact a great deal of good curriculum development stalls because practitioners reject both the research and implications of research done by their leader colleagues.

Part of this, of course, derives from the suspicion widely expressed about those with new ideas. Further, changes proposed for the most part during the last twenty-five years have been suggested by a group held to be "progressive" and considered in part to be something less than completely realistic.

What teachers need to see is that there is a very important place for such theoreticians. They are not a threat. They too are not in possession of all the final answers. They are indeed in need of help in the corrective process related to their better thinking. Some are surely being driven to outlandish and bizarre proposals to maintain their "frontier-ship" badge, but these are exceedingly limited in number, fairly easily recognized, and appropriately ignored. Theorizing is rather the proposing of alternatives, as effectively supported as possible from the growing body of knowledge developed from the basic research which the usual classroom teacher does not see. In the mature college situations the best thoughts are presented as hypotheses and proposals, challenges, to be studied, examined, tried out—not as conclusions to be accepted without question.

Teachers often have difficulty in differentiating these theorists from the more dogmatic of their other mentors. They do not, particularly in the curriculum areas, see that much justifiable concern is with values and that with values there usually are no final and—correct—answers. One is left with his own choices to make, but at the same time invited to consider alternatives and deeper and varied aspects of choice.

The teacher therefore ought be constantly in search of outside challenges to his present line of thought and action. Only through a search for the better can he continue to grow. When he cuts off the theoretician, he severs his link to new perceptions and to ways of looking at things that might give him better methods and approaches. He denies himself the leverage the theoretical scholar offers in his familiarity with new knowledge.

As in other aspects of adjustment, rejection of the theorist can easily be a method of protection against the need for adaptation and for production that a new or different approach requires. In addition, attaching the "theorist" label to a supervisor serves as a means of resisting the efforts of the supervisor to improve the quality of instruction.

Frustration Unavoidable in Normal Progress

The more anxious we are to get rapidly on our way, it seems, the more extensive must be the evidence of progress. However, the lot of the curriculum worker is, as with nearly all reformers, still to be satisfied with small favors. Exasperation over one's own or a group's inability, or over some one else's lack of power to have multiple brilliant answers is thus bound to come. It may be quickly translated into criticism of the college professor, into disillusionment with one's childlike advocacy, into carping about colleagues, into a panicky and useless feeling, into the urge to withdraw to temporarily safer ground.

The defenses against this are not numerous and are all too often ineffective, yet there are some things we can do to help ourselves. If attempts to work on a wider scale and to affect remote decisions fail, there are still major improvements to be made in one's own classroom.

Spirit and hope can be maintained by the satisfaction to be derived from what is immediately better for children. Cutting our objectives down to size may well give us the comfortable evidence of success we need.

Advance recognition of the hardship to be endured has stood many before us in good stead. Change is slow and the way to it tortuous. To anticipate false starts and to expect many failures on the road to success, if they are part of every teacher's repertoire, will help make the small gain seem worthwhile. Getting Johnny willingly off to school is not always easy; but the example of the many devoted teachers who have already looked for an answer to this problem should give heart to the youthful and ambitious.

Complexity a Deterrent

Few undertakings are as simple as falling off a log; and simplicity is certainly not one of the characteristics of the school as an institution. Even in a single small school where there may be but a handful of teachers, practices and policies have historic rootage and both depth and entanglement compound the problems of getting at the source and of separating the significant from the insignificant.

Even in a small group almost everyone has an opinion about correct procedures, and very often his opinion is directly related to who has a new and different idea. Getting information on who believes what and who believes he is affected by change, although not easy, invariably is a necessary element in adaptation. Failure to do so leads very regularly to estrangement, subsequent behavior that seems to have no explanation, and counteraction in other situations.

Moves on curriculum changes can affect people at remote points, can precipitate attitudes that develop obstruction elsewhere, can produce effects that are never described and reported yet become hidden items on the agenda at subsequent meetings. It becomes obvious then that the proponent of change must extend himself in many quarters so as to feel and understand fully the impact of his choice-making. And repeatedly he must surmise wherein he can not or will not be informed.

More subtle even than effect of policy changes is the impact of adaptations by the individual teacher within the classroom. Although a teacher's classroom may be his personal domain, what one does there may make a difference in what other teachers may be expected to do. A novel way of dealing with pupils can easily disrupt another teacher's routine, increase his discipline problems, cast doubt in the pupils' minds about purpose and method, and threaten other teachers' self-confidence, particularly if supervisory interest and approval have been manifest.

Changes within classrooms that can cause a train of grievances are, among many, sharp reduction or increase in homework; extensive pupil-teacher planning; self-evaluation and self-marking by pupils; project work involving committees, field trips, and the use of out-of-school resources; introduction of new content and particularly independent decisions to de-emphasize or omit certain aspects; extensive use of student reports and presentation; dependence on a wide variety of audio-visual material; and intensive personal study of pupils.

It must be appreciated, then, that a school is a complex of relationships operating smoothly only when there are small tolerances in the fit of one part to another. When one teacher or group of teachers go beyond the limits they can easily put the whole apparatus out of kilter and in time may cause so uneven a function that simple tinkering will not restore unity.

Our constant thought then should be: how does this affect the other fellow, what does it mean to him, can he accept it in good grace, will it help him do a better job, will it create a positive feeling in him? At the same time we need to build up awareness as to why and to what extent we can help remove the causes of this problem.

The Many Duties of Participation

Like the farmer who already knew more about how to farm than he could do, the ordinary teacher usually has more ambition than he has either time or energy. Even the least interested of teachers has precious little time to devote to certain kinds of curriculum activity. The survey report on pages 88–91 illustrates this point clearly. For the most part teachers saw the tasks listed as proper roles for the teacher; however, in most cases many teachers indicated that they actually did not carry the role out. Reasons given are largely defensive rather than admissions of personal limitation.

The inclination then to be cautious if not resistant about being involved by the supervisor or by eager others is quite normal. There seldom are earth-shaking changes from the long and often tedious meetings of committees and we know our best efforts in devising new plans, in providing new materials, in trying new methods regularly do not bring about tremendous gratifications.

Fitting dreams and expectations to reality thus is imperative for the teacher. Helping the supervisor get a better picture of what can be done while health and a degree of personal life satisfaction are main-

Idea of Extent Done*

		Yes	No	1	2	3	4	5
1. Individual experimentation		150	0	16	30	51	32	5

133	a. Not enough time
46	b. Administration does not approve and makes difficult
22	c. Teachers do not think we ought to
31	d. Teachers do not get any credit anyway
10	e. Nobody else does is the attitude
75	f. No encouragement

		Yes	No	1	2	3	4	5
2. Individual production of materials, teaching resources (tests, contracts, worksheets, project and discussion guides, assignments)		150	0		4	10	47	51	36

57	a. Very good ones available commercially
70	b. No adequate typing, reproduction service
78	c. Not enough time
7	d. Do not believe in it

		Yes	No	1	2	3	4	5
3. Individual development, production of courses of study		103	47	15	26	60	37	11

37	a. Courses of study prepared by others and imposed
40	b. Textbook contains almost all that is needed
108	c. Not enough time
95	d. No motivation, pressure, expectation from superiors
43	e. Courses of study provided are excellent, more expert, more scientific and scholarly

		Yes	No	1	2	3	4	5
4. Active verbal deliberation on policies (load, teacher assignment, grouping)		138	10	30	31	36	27	20

15	a. Policies are set by administration
8	b. My job is to teach, administrators should run schools
80	c. Faculty meetings usually announcement periods
18	d. Too few faculty meetings to do anything
45	e. We talk endlessly about same things, seldom settle anything
21	f. People do not feel comfortable to talk in groups

* Rated on a scale of *very little* (1) to *much* (5).

[12] Survey conducted for Center for Curriculum Research, College of Education, State University, Albany, New York, 1957–9. Discrepancies in totals derive from incomplete replies to various questions or from selection of more than one reason for inaction.

5. Work with committee groups to   *Yes   No   1   2   3   4   5*
   plan new courses.   122   24   3 21 60 30 12

     5   a. New courses are determined administratively
    28 b. New courses are limited in number
     3   c. Install before we plan
    80 d. Courses come from the Department

6. Work with committee groups to   *Yes   No   1   2   3   4   5*
   revise old courses   133   13   3 19 70 46 10

    22 a. Too much time devoted to too little revision
    27 b. No help, blind lead the blind
    50 c. No leadership, no organization
    18 d. Can not change the textbooks

7. Work with committee groups to   *Yes   No   1   2   3   4   5*
   study, report on general policies   126   22   4 30 60 41   7
   (promotion, examinations, cur-
   riculum framework, special
   programs)

    83 a. Reports are usually filed
    30 b. Few appointments are made
    55 c. Too little respect for teachers' ideas
   100 d. Too seldom get significant changes

8. Work with committee groups to   *Yes   No   1   2   3   4   5*
   do research, evaluation, follow-   66   79   30 68 39   7   2
   up

   106 a. Teachers are afraid to do "research"
    42 b. Research usually is not interesting
    58 c. Technical skills are necessary
   110 d. Most school systems do not value these highly

9. Participation in promoting lay   *Yes   No   1   2   3   4   5*
   understanding   138   10   43 50 35 20   0

   130 a. Activities are too casual and too free
    88 b. Limited numbers of laymen are really interested
   116 c. A broadly organized, continuous program is lacking
    57 d. Teachers do not support the idea

10. Encouragement, seeking to stim-   *Yes   No   1   2   3   4   5*
    ulate colleagues   71   78   38 33 70   7   1

     12 a. Belief that this is *the* job of supervisors
     44 b. My business is my business; their business is theirs
     51 c. Belief that others are as professional or more pro-
            fessional
     30 d. Personal doubts and low morale

11. Continuing, extensive study of society and community needs

	Yes	No		1	2	3	4	5
	50	94		85	57	15	0	0

<u>106</u> a. This is the job of sociologists, economists, etc.

<u>108</u> b. Communities resist probing

<u>41</u> c. Schools can do little about major problems anyway

<u>49</u> d. Teachers are seldom really interested

12. Close and careful studies of pupils, their personal problems and needs

	Yes	No		1	2	3	4	5
	100	49		91	26	30	1	0

<u>131</u> a. Too many pupils, too little time

<u>71</u> b. Records and data are inadequate, incomplete

<u>69</u> c. Teachers are not, should not be psychologists

<u>32</u> d. Information seldom changes content or procedure

<u>85</u> e. The job is that of the guidance officer

13. Examination and review of the nature and effect of personal teaching, personally and with others

	Yes	No		1	2	3	4	5
	107	31		4	9	58	62	15

<u>16</u> a. Nobody requires that it be done

<u>6</u> b. No forms or procedures are provided

<u>56</u> c. Teachers are afraid of each other's opinions

<u>7</u> d. Evaluation of teaching is considered supervisor's job

14. Development and extension of professional interest, concern, scholarship

	Yes	No		1	2	3	4	5
	150	0		1	40	71	27	0

<u>121</u> a. Most teachers are not scholars

<u>134</u> b. Study is tied too often to salaries, merits

<u>101</u> c. College courses are very poor, kill interest

<u>41</u> d. Need of free time to earn money

15. Positive contribution to the esprit of the faculty and to the promotion of constant examination and revision of programs

	Yes	No		1	2	3	4	5
	135	14		26	39	60	20	1

<u>112</u> a. You seldom get credit for bringing work to others

<u>70</u> b. Most teachers are dead-tired to "programs of improvement"

<u>31</u> c. Contribution is looked upon as personal prestige making

<u>140</u> d. Schools are too busy

16. Extension of knowledge of curriculum; theoretical proposals,
examples, analyses of modern
practice

	Yes	No		1	2	3	4	5
	122	24		10	41	78	12	0

   59 a. Teachers think they do not make the curriculum

  105 b. Most curriculum writers are too progressive for teachers

   91 c. They all say the same thing

  138 d. Teachers need practical, down-to-earth details

17. Discussion of curriculum adaptation and changes informally, but
purposefully with colleagues

	Yes	No		1	2	3	4	5
	139	5		2	7	29	73	31

    9 a. Others are seldom interested

  37 b. Informal discussion is usually complaint, not constructive planning

  87 c. Salary, politics, rights, etc. usually come first

18. Active effort to improve the
quality and effect of small and
large group sessions

	Yes	No		1	2	3	4	5
	107	17		31	47	35	19	3

  85 a. Teachers think group analysis is "for the birds"

  72 b. There can be very little cooperation among prima donnas

  24 c. Few people want to be leaders

  92 d. Most people want to work for themselves, alone

19. Acceptance and assumption of
leadership responsibility willingly (e.g., committee chairman)

	Yes	No		1	2	3	4	5
	65	80		57	60	18	10	0

  131 a. Chairmanships are usually considered thankless tasks

  41 b. Most leaders, supervisors, do not want to share prestige

  140 c. Provisions are seldom made for relief of other duties

  71 d. Most people do not know how to get things done, no skills

20. Regular suggestion of plans,
proposal of solutions, encouragement of departures

	Yes	No		1	2	3	4	5
	118	30		35	51	37	12	0

  112 a. Eager beavers get the work

  68 b. Administrators get or take the credit

  41 c. Too often you are dismissed without thanks

  27 d. Colleagues suspect motives

tained is also a self-obligation. It lies then with each teacher to decide how much of himself he can give to trying to do better himself and to contributing to projects that will help both himself and others do better.

Instructional Leadership Often Absent

Although schools are getting larger and with their growth the ratio of teacher to supervisors is improving, probably more teachers lack adequate curriculum leadership than have it. A number of studies show principals and other administrators feel the need to put much more time on instructional improvement than they do. By their own admission these leaders neither provide the stimulus they would like to nor do they render the assistance as resource people they might expect of themselves.

The upshot of this is that the classroom teacher is left to his own devices and to his own self-motivation. The testimony of even first-year teachers[13] in one populous state is that they are seldom visited by superiors who, they sincerely believe, know very little of what they are doing.

Without a check point even the best, the most professional, of teachers may very well falter if not actually lose sight of his goal. If in addition there are no formally arranged groups or committees for study and production of resources, and there are schools where little effort seems purposefully devoted to curriculum improvement, the good teacher may find himself nearly in a vacuum. But nothing can come of defensively blaming "them" for their failure to exercise leadership properly.

One must either undertake to keep fermenting independently or actively undertake to promote in one's colleagues and leaders and lay supporters more helpful definitions of the roles of teachers and leaders. To ferment independently requires the self-concept examined in the beginning of this chapter, the constant utilization of media like those discussed in Chapter 5, and the regular reference to the theory and descriptions of practice presented in the good books on teaching method.

Despite the assertion sometimes or often made, depending on where you are, that teachers are a conforming lot, there are many of us who are vigorously independent and who are ambitious to exercise our professional prerogatives and to work out our destinies with our students alone. The idea of seeking help from others or of setting others

[13] Ruth Marschner, *Helping the First Year Teacher,* Capital Area School Development Association, 1950.

up to stand ready with or impose help does not come easily. In the same vein we know that colleagues and superiors more than occasionally feel criticized when we undertake to tell them what to do or help them see what their proper roles are.

In a preceding section we have stated that a teacher needs to examine carefully his own willingness to subordinate effectively. Part of good subordination is understanding of and insight into what a proper leader is like. We have remarked elsewhere that a good leader can not emerge without good followers who know what he is trying to be and to do and are willing to help. This point became vivid to Mackenzie and Corey when they studied instructional leadership. They emphasized in their conclusion that "the status leader who works with the group as a participant rather than as a director may face serious difficulties unless the other members of the group share his views about leadership."[14] Benne supports them in his observation that "the administrator can not function as a 'democratic leader' in the matter of policy formulation unless the teachers change with him by learning the role of democratic participants."[15]

So the classroom teacher again needs to know what democratic leaders are and can be like and he needs to know what he can do to help the leader who would be so skilled along the way. We shall not in any foreseeable time have less supervision and doubtless we shall have more cooperative efforts wherein each participant will have his leadership moments and roles. To be well informed about what can be and should be done seems imperative.[16]

Questions for Discussion

1. What are some "traditional" teacher urges that would have to be suppressed if a teacher is to work with cooperatively managed groups?
2. The traditional approach to teaching is generally considered by teachers to be safer. One could certainly not have any sure guarantees of safety with a quite different approach than the traditional. What kinds of helps and assurances would the ordinary teacher need?
3. A first-year teacher will seldom avoid hearing from some one or more of the experienced teachers that "all this curriculum work, committee meetings, are for the birds." Often the teacher will be invited to join groups who are disinclined to take much active part and quite likely scoff at the idea that

[14] Mackenzie and Corey, *op. cit.,* p. 138.
[15] K. Benne and Bozidar Muntyan, *Human Relations in Curriculum Change,* Dryden, 1951, p. 17.
[16] For discussion of what good instructional leadership involves see Mackenzie and Corey, *op. cit.;* Fred Ayer, *Fundamentals of Instructional Supervision,* Harper, 1954.

a classroom teacher can or should have much influence. How does the young teacher handle such attitudes and how does he keep his spirit up and his theory reasonably intact?

4. What channels or media should a good school have to help a teacher develop his self more fully? What is likely to be the behavior of individuals who would not see the value in or want to use such channels?

5. Several authors point out that in order to get change or altered ways of doing we have to develop dissatisfactions of sufficient magnitude to cause one to want to do something about them. What dissatisfactions ought to get teachers to want to change? Why don't the ones that cause you to want to become active affect the others?

6. One of the most persistent excuses of teachers who do not experiment or make contributions to groups or volunteer for production and writing jobs is that they never have any ideas, that they just can not generate bright and novel adaptations or have refreshingly new hunches. Very likely this is a proper description for many, but how can one increase his power to be creative and imaginative, to respond with good suggestions and insights?

7. Since World War II a great deal of attention has been given to the fact that in a group leadership really resides in each member of the group to a degree and that there is a distinct difference between status leadership and natural emergent leadership. How could this multiple leadership help one grow personally?

8. From your supplementary reading show how some of the common mental mechanisms are used by teachers to avoid or resist curriculum activity.

Suggested Bibliography

Bartky, John A., *Supervision As Human Relations,* Heath, 1953.

Benne, Kenneth, and Bozidar Muntyan, *Human Relations in Curriculum Change,* Dryden, 1951, Parts 1, 2.

Bills, Robert E., *About People and Teaching,* Bulletin of the Bureau of School Service, vol. 28, no. 2, College of Education, University of Kentucky, 1955.

Bruce, William F., and John A. Holden, *The Teacher's Personal Development,* Holt, 1956.

Kaplan, Louis, and Denis Baron, *Mental Hygiene and Life,* Harper, 1952.

Lecky, Prescott, *Self-Consistency,* Island Press, 1945.

Mackenzie, Gordon, and Stephen Corey, *Instructional Leadership,* Bureau of Publications, Teachers College, 1954.

Symonds, P. M., *The Dynamics of Human Adjustment,* Appleton-Century-Crofts, 1946.

Sharp, George, *Curriculum Development as Re-education of the Teacher,* Bureau of Publications, Teachers College, 1951.

CHAPTER 5

···

Building the Foundation for Choice

When the teacher accepts for himself the role of active participant, he will soon come to realize that no minor job has been elected.
The complex tasks outlined in Chapter 3 require extensive knowledge
and understanding. These attributes seldom exist to a satisfactory
degree in any one. In the main, preparatory programs in colleges are
not geared to give all the depth necessary, and it is the unusual person
or teacher who has sufficiently developed on his own the necessary insights and understandings. Most of us will have little difficulty in feeling equal to the task of deciding whether or not we should teach the
difference between a complete and incomplete sentence. Yet we may
wonder at our competence to decide whether or not calculus should
be taught to seniors, or what portions of mechanics should be replaced by specific portions of electronics. As we accept broad curriculum improvement roles proposed for us by the theorists, we are
virtually forced to extend the foundations on which our choices will
be built.

Much of what the teacher will need to know to make effective
choices will depend on the roles a particular situation requires and
how deeply engaged he may become. In some situations he may be
limited, by power he can not alter, to making assignment selections
from an arithmetic book, to deciding whether to take up spelling as an
independent unit or to integrate it fully with other types of work, or to
passing on the advisability of adding an easier course in chemistry. In
less rigid situations responsibility may include deciding with others
what objectives are appropriate for the school, whether to replace one
language with another, what to include as topics in general education
courses or as content in a course calculated to serve the clerical needs of
local business men. In an increasing number of places the teacher may
find himself within an extremely flexible framework, exploring with

youngsters their present level of maturity and need, and developing co-operatively out of that analysis activities to increase mastery of persisting life problems.

In such matters of choice the teacher can base his decision upon some knowledge and commitments. But he does not need to do so. In the first three illustrations given he can make his choices without much reference to broader considerations and without too much examination of deeper issues. He can use much of what has been provided by others without doing too much thinking or relating. The spelling list might have been prepared elsewhere—thus no problem exists in deciding what words to consider; the arithmetic examples may already exist in the book—thus there is no need to determine what number of skills need consideration; the alternative chemistry course may involve merely adopting a text—thus creating no burden in specifying the practical problems and in knowing the chemistry upon which their solution rests. In these decisions, then, the teacher may well act at quite an uninvolved level, and rely mainly upon others for direction, upon limited knowledge of a subject field, and upon minimal basic data on how children learn.

However, the more involved a man becomes, the more far-reaching the decisions in which he participates, the less possible it is to function on a superficial level. To do a proper job, the teacher will need comprehensive appreciation of the concerns and conflicts of our society and of the people in it. He will also require a great variety of skills to diagnose and deliberate upon needs. He will have to obtain guidance from a thorough grasp of the natures and attributes of those who learn, and he will depend for his wisdom upon increasing power over the areas of knowledge.

CURRICULUM AS SOCIAL POLICY

In the long run the program of the school exists to promote the total welfare of the people and to facilitate improvement of the quality of living in this society. Therefore, what happens in school should reflect the needs of the social group as a whole and should take into consideration the dislocations and changes which create for the individual and for his society new problems as well as different opportunities.

If the school program fails to provide enough young people skilled in mathematics and physics to pursue actively the secrets of interplanetary travel, the nation may suffer painfully at the hands of its competitors. If the program does not make provisions for developing in our young a strong but sensible loyalty to our basic creeds, we may ourselves soon be so confused about what we believe or stand for that we shall be easy targets for those who covet our wealth. If schools do not help many of our neglected youth attain respect and appreciation for such fundamental institutions as the family, in time great numbers of our young adults may make a mockery of monogamy and parental responsibility.

The school program is one instrument by which the society perpetuates ideals and beliefs, by which a people manage to develop skills and power to protect their interest, by which a nation at times even guarantees its continuance. Requirements for teaching American history, laws prescribing the celebration of Arbor Day, and regulations specifying the content to be taught in physics are consistent with this role. When a state education department or board rules that it is permissible to use funds for music education and to count instruction in music toward graduation and when the local school committee votes to support a band and to provide a music teacher, the justification usually lies in what we need and ought to do for individuals and for the group as a whole.

Those decisions that make the schools strong and responsible—that focus their effort on criticism and reconstruction or on perpetuation of the heritage, that permit special programs for special students, that delegate to the high school training for selected vocations—are all examples of social policy. Repeatedly they grow from the issues and the conditions of the moment.

National Curriculum Control Advocated

Had we a national educational agency or were our state agencies much more centralized, we could move quickly to meet our emerging curriculum problems. We could in one stroke change our objectives and promote intensive study of specific aspects. The classroom teacher would still be the key to quality, but he could very quickly be directed to apply effort to specific purposes. The priority of values on what to teach would rest with a limited authority. The limited authority would be accountable; and when unwise, tardy, or costly decisions were made, the blame for failure could be easily placed.

It seems quite improbable though that any time soon we shall have the responsibility for curriculum design transferred to some bureau of the national government. There may develop a far more influential United States Office of Education. However, the responsibility for determining how the school shall be organized—what particular objectives will be sought, how pupil time with a teacher shall be used and toward what ends—will doubtless remain a reserved function for a long time to come.

Depth Required in Continued Local Planning

It is important then that those who do have responsibility see the relationship between what they do, recommend, and propose, and the cumulative effect of the school. It is incumbent upon all those that determine the curriculum to know what the basic concerns and issues are so that, from policy at the state level to daily practices in the classroom, there can be a sensitive adaptation to personal and group needs.

With his usual modesty the classroom teacher may easily lead himself to believe, however, that his role is hopelessly limited. The assertion that he teaches a subject or the principal parts of weak verbs and that this kind of undertaking represents little in the way of social policy seems defensible.

On the other hand, it can be argued that it is a matter of some moment. Disgust and depression, in some cases aggravated frustration, have all too often accompanied attempts to teach grammar, for example. The consequence has been the withdrawal of youngsters and their further education in the school of hard knocks. Conflict over "correct" verb form and other English skills has driven learners from the school.

Aware of such outcomes from inflexibility or inappropriately chosen tasks, the teacher can make adaptations within courses and regularly help fashion other courses that will provide worthwhile tasks for the less able or the uninterested. When the teacher takes such initiative, he is casting a potent vote on educational policy.

The teacher then has some real freedom to espouse his cause, to fashion his own or additional objectives, and to relate systematically his work with his students to the solution of some social, community, or international problem. More than this, sensitivity to and understanding of the trend of events and of the "problems of our time" can lead to the expression of opinion and to the determination that action must be taken on them. From the casual conversation in the teachers' lounge to formal proposals for study by committees of the faculty the teacher has a range of channels through which to initiate action. The more informed the teacher is, the more alert and up-to-date his acquaintance with needs or with subtle and complex trends the more likely he will use these channels effectively.

OBTAINING INSIGHT FOR DECISION-MAKING

It is of course obvious that at any one point the curriculum is a product of a combination of reactions by many over a period of time. With some careful reflection, the reasons for changes in, and certain additions to, courses can usually be understood. For instance, many schools are now including a course in personal typing because increased production and wealth have made the typewriter a quite common possession. The addition of driver-training is a recent example of the response of the school to a social need.

Perception Blocked by Multiple Factors

However, sometimes changes that are most appropriate are a long time in coming whether they appear through election by a classroom teacher or by outside specification. Delay in such cases can simply be a matter of values on the part of those who can and should take the initiative. It can also be a failure to be sufficiently informed and alert. It may be a lack of clarity about who should start plans on their way. Or, as is the case in many places, there may be so much deliberation, red tape, and frustration connected with obtaining approval that those who have insight are simply disinclined to pay out all the energy required to put it into action.

Another complication is that some adaptations have been wrought by those with the power to do so in advance of the time when others who follow in their footsteps have responsibility for carrying them out. When those who inherit are uninformed of the reasons and can not fully benefit from the deliberations which have preceded, it is not uncommon for them to be disenchanted with the wisdom of their predecessors. Homeroom programs, supervised study periods, and club activities that outlive their sponsors or creators are examples.

Many Issues Already Thoroughly Studied

A great deal of our present argument over curriculum content and scope grows from similar gaps between those who studied and decided and those who did not and now have awakened to find things changed. Over the last quarter century, as shifts of major proportion have taken place in our economic, social, political, and ethical life, most public school leaders have seen the need of and have approved important curriculum variation. In this period a fairly well-defined group of "students of the schools as an institution" have grown in numbers, in influence, and some think, in wisdom and scholarship. Out of their numerous and intensive analyses and investigations has come the greatest portion of the proposals for changes in the school program.

The pained cries of the critics, lay and professional, who have recently discovered that adaptations have taken place in the schools reveal very nicely what has happened to those who have withdrawn from or neglected studies of cultural change and its implications for the school. Life adjustment education, driver-training, remedial reading, and functional courses of study have come as a surprise to those who do not know or do not admit that times are different. Exasperation has grown in them over the incompatibility of their concepts, formed under different conditions, and the newer roles of the school. For these critics and for those of recent and revived interest there is no alternative. They must catch up.

When that sobering review has been accomplished, there must certainly still remain differences of opinion as to what should be included in school programs and how teachers and pupils should employ their time. Eventually, in all American education, the final broad and general decisions will be and should be made by the public and their representatives on lay boards. But the school staff can not escape responsibility to advise, to counsel, and to recommend.

Teacher Growth Not Easy

Added to the already numerous duties of the classroom teacher, this may look like an impossible undertaking. Surely, it would be naïve to contend that it is not a very sizable assignment. Keeping up to date with, sensitive to, and informed about societal stresses and strains could be considered too much.

Yet the teacher must continue to extend his foundations for choice. Informed professional maturity demands continuing rigorous study of the state of affairs with continual examination by the teacher of his own views on what and how much the school should undertake.

In the next section of this chapter reference is made to several illustrative areas in which the teacher must keep up that constant vigilance. The readings in the footnotes contain more extensive analyses with which he should be familiar.

THE NATURE AND EXTENT OF CHANGES IN AMERICAN LIFE

It is commonplace now to observe that there have been vast changes in our way of living and that these changes, requiring increased knowledge, revised attitudes, and novel skills, have placed heavy demand upon the schools and thrust upon them new and different obligations. Dislocations have come about in every element of our culture and the interrelated effects are so complex as to defy an accurate tracing. Detecting the impacts, determining causal sequences, gauging the importance of shifts, judging their permanence and appraising their virtues and defects have thus become exceedingly difficult.

Doubtless some changes have more significance for the school than others, and they can perhaps be more quickly translated into proper curricular adaptations. But there obviously is no clear line of agreement on this.

Lessening of Home, Community, Church Influence

Perhaps the widely acknowledged loss of function by the historic institutions deserves to rank first among those developments of which the teacher should be keenly aware. For the reduced roles of home and family, church, and small community have in effect seriously altered and expanded the supplemental role of the schools.

Radical transformation in the American family[1] has had a widespread effect on the transmission and development of important attributes and skills, knowledge, and appreciations. Although much that is critical for modern living is still acquired from involvement in the processes which have replaced earlier home and family ways, a great deal has been lost. Among these are the character traits instilled and exemplified through long and intimate hours with parents. In the kitchen baking a pie or at one end of a crosscut saw the child had numerous opportunities to learn the meaning of a job well done, care and precision in the execution of a task, respect for loyalty and devotion. Constant association in work, play, and worship taught values by involvement that are now vainly sought after verbally. Semivocational skill and information were natural by-products of tillage, harvest, construction and repair. Responsibility, industry, a sense of obligation, respect for the rights of others came from daily identification in tasks and duties with those who possessed these traits.

Changes in the Face of Communities

In the same way that the home has, in changing, altered if not lost its influence on much of the growth of children, the community has, as

[1] For further reading on changes in the home and family and implications for schooling, see R. C. Angell, *Integration of American Society,* McGraw-Hill, 1941; E. W. Burgess, *The Family,* second ed., American Book, 1953; and R. W. Anshen, *The Family: Its Functions and Destiny,* Harper, 1949.

a positive educative influence, become increasingly ineffective. This has occurred mainly because of the complex social and physical organization of the modern urban center.[2] The warmth and friendliness, the responsibility of each for all, the vigilance of neighbors of the small village and hamlet have been replaced with impersonality; vigorous, often ruthless competition; and self-centeredness. The premium is in large part on how much an individual can "get by" with, be justified by what "they" are all doing, and take care of himself.

Struggle of the Church with New Conditions

The reduced level of the church's influence is equally apparent.[3] Although church membership has reached new levels in recent years and there is an apparent rededication of rather sweeping proportions, it is undeniable that the extent of the church's achievements in the way of maintaining and improving the moral status of the people is little more than depressing. In fact there seems to be nearly everywhere an increase in those evils the church stands against. Perhaps it can be argued that understanding and respect for those of different creed, color, and ethnic source have increased in America during this century and it might be reasonably held that more people have been baptized, that people are more generous with charities, that they support ideas and new laws that make a man his brother's keeper. On the other hand, it would be difficult to prove that there is anything like increased honesty in the marketplace, that God has not really departed from more lives than He has meaningfully entered, that the commandments are better kept today than they were before, and that families have not almost completely dropped Bible reading and study and even prayers.

The churches actually seem to have been fighting a losing battle in everything except membership. The now nearly desperate effort to force religious education into the public school reveals ineffectuality as much as anything.

Industrialization a Source of New Problems

What has happened to family, church, and community is probably more a result of invention, of mechanization, and of the wide-

---

[2] The significance of changes in community life is well treated in Jessie Bernard, *American Community Behavior,* Dryden, 1949; Edmund Brunner and W. C. Hallenbeck, *American Society: Urban and Rural Patterns,* Harper, 1955; and W. O. Stanley, *Social Foundations of Education,* Dryden, 1956.

[3] Difficulties of the church in maintaining its role are discussed in F. Ernest Johnson, ed., *American Education and Religion,* Harper, 1952, and W. O. Stanley, *Social Foundations of Education,* Dryden, 1956.

spread growth of industry than of any other factor. The shift from rural to urban living, the great increase in commerce and distribution, the radical reduction in self-employment and replacement of craft skill with machine-tending have followed upon the development and the use of machines of every description and type. Automation now heralds an even greater alteration with increased demand for technicians and specialists equipped to service and repair the involved apparatus being installed in all types of industries.

Preparing for and locating a job thus looms exceedingly large in the lives of youth. In fact, in recent years nearly every study of the aims of young people reveals their number one objective to be vocational education and education for work. The Educational Policies Commission acknowledges this in its report, *Imperative Needs of Youth,*[4] by citing as the *first* need that of developing "salable skills and those understandings that make the worker an intelligent and productive participant in economic life."

Whether the school should accept this need and seek its satisfaction as its primary goal doubtless has yet to be decided. There certainly are some who feel that the Educational Policies Commission has done education a disservice by emphasizing training so vigorously. In their estimation, despite the pressure from youth and the appetites created by industry, other objectives clearly deserve priority. Particularly is this so when there are still millions in jobs for which training may be effectively secured in a matter of a few weeks or months.

Individual Identity Lost

Another result of our industrial expansion is the gradual decline of individual choice and independence and with it increased insecurity, doubts of self-worth, and inclination to let someone else take the responsibility for making an innovation. Few people now avoid becoming a part of some pressure group or block, and many appear to lose their identity and become pawns in a game of economic class competition.

The great slum areas of our cities, the strident claims of advertisers, huge installment debts brought on by a need to distribute manufactured goods, and increasingly complex laws are incidental to the frenzied modern organization of people and machines to produce and to process more of everything. The citizen is surrounded, harassed, confused.

[4] Educational Policies Commission, "Imperative Needs of Youth of Secondary School Age," *Bulletin of the National Secondary School Principals Association,* March, 1947, whole issue.

It seems unlikely now that there will ever again be any remote Shangri-La to which modern American man may escape. The possibility of withdrawal to some isolated hermitage where the simple arts of lonesomely scratching an existence from the soil or contemplating a pond, Walden or any other, becomes yearly more remote.

Values in Flux

Related to the machine and affected by its dominance of American life is the matter of values. With nearly every development and addition to the tools used to transform our resources we have experienced some reflection in the expectancies and rules, formal and informal, by which behavior is guided. As our society has become more fractionated and face-to-face relationship reduced, many common ideas and beliefs have been diluted, discarded, or replaced.

Our value problem is thus acute. Available to us and reiterated by our institutions is a volume of maxims about proper and acceptable human behavior. Many are in the form of ideals not yet widely attained, verbalized but not acted upon. At the same time we are faced with rapidly changing conditions, with new evidence and information, with more insightful and critical interpretation. New guides are badly needed, but too often not forthcoming.

Currently, one of many debates and disagreements stands out as an illustration. At the same time that vigorous protest is being voiced over lack of discipline, there is a rising chorus of pain from a large group which is convinced that our society suffers grievously from a rampant conformity, a slowly ebbing vigor of independence, and a frightening lack of creativity and self-direction. The field of battle as usual seems to have been selected for its "either/or" advantages. The vigor of contesting positions defies rather than invites compromise.

Recently there have been repeated assertions that the public schools have neglected moral and spiritual values. There are some who claim that the schools actually deny them a place. Nothing could be further from the truth. In fact some of the pupils would argue that the schools really support one moralization after another. The work of Warner, Havighurst, Hollingshead, and others documents the fact that the public school purveys middle-class moral values.[5]

Nevertheless, there is much evidence that the school remains ineffectual in resolving the value crisis. There is no reason to anticipate

[5] Robert J. Havighurst and Hilda Taba, *Adolescent Character and Personality,* Wiley, 1959; August Hollingshead, *Elmtown's Youth,* Wiley, 1949; Otto Dahlke, *Values in Culture and Classroom,* Harper, 1958.

that the crisis will melt away or that the pressure for something to be done about the confusion will abate. And no agency or institution seems as adequate to the task as the schools!

Dependence on Education Increased

The faith of Americans in the school to protect them and get them ready for their struggles with the soil, the sea, and now the solar system has its roots in the convictions of our Puritan forebears, but it is only in this century and really since World War I that this faith has spread wide and deep and has been translated into numbers and buildings, laws and finance. It may be true that part of the growth has been forced by the technological revolution which required more skill and fewer young employees, but it can also be effectively argued that the momentum has derived from a belief of the masses, or at least their acceptance of their leaders' claim, that through education a man could not only be socially and economically mobile but also could raise his own personal experience beyond ignorance to enlightenment. The continual demand by industry and business for high levels of attainment in general—as well as in special—education has certainly provided impetus and encouragement, but it may be seriously doubted that anything but a vision of the people has created the ground swell which has brought over forty million children and youth into our schools.

The result is an increasingly literate society which now possesses concrete evidence of the power of education to make a difference. The requests for the school to expand its services, to attend to a greater variety of individual and special needs, and to adapt and shift its program thus multiply.

At the same time, the cultural transformations and immediate developments taking place in the world near and far are thrusting upon each society new concerns which apparently only the public schools can accommodate. Interracial and religious tensions, international issues, socioeconomic class aggravations, juvenile delinquency, vocational skill obsolescense, overpopulation threats, personality disturbances, health hazards, and a host of other ills and weaknesses or results of war, inflation, or political policy find their way to the school's doorstep. Although there is much uneasiness, particularly among the humanists and academically minded, about this tendency and periodic trend, there is little reason to believe that the pressure will decrease.

Even a temporary revival among the academicians and anxious moments of activity by life-adjustment advocates will not sterilize the school program for long. The swing to and emphasis on more mathematics and science merely testify again to the power of the school to serve emerging needs. And when the gap is closed, the faith that the school can and should help the nation and the individual will merely be more illustratively embedded.

GUIDES IN BASIC COMMITMENTS

Transfer students from liberal arts programs to teachers colleges have at times reported a pronounced discomfort with continual reference to democracy by their education professors. They are impatient with the instructor who would assume that any need exists for reviewing what we believe and what it means. Have they not all lived in America, been brought up in a social and political framework usually fiercely supported as the best example of the way man ought to live? Have they not all learned about our documents, our leaders, and our defenses on the average at least three times in precollege exposure and in almost every case at least once in college?

Repeatedly, however, when given an opportunity to express their convictions as to who should go to school, as to how standards should be determined, as to what should be taught, or as to the policies defensible for pupil management, they reveal not only inadequate understanding of such concepts as respect for personality, right to act on thinking, and dependence on intelligence, but also actual denial of these fundamental tenets.

This type of failure is not restricted to transfers. It is widely found among undergraduates in the teachers colleges. It is manifest everywhere in the actions of public school teachers. We all know, too, that many practices which are deeply etched in our culture not only violate the spirit and the vague, perhaps indefinable, quality of democracy but defy those agreements and specifications in the law which give substance to our beliefs.

The nature of democracy and its meaning for the schools, then, is something which the teacher and teacher trainee can not gloss over. Without careful and thorough examination and criticism, basic principles can be given lip service and curriculum choices made that are hopelessly inconsistent with the potent ideas and directives bound up in a series of statements. A great number of curriculum bulletins and courses of study actually carry nicely written forewords and first chapters or sections on elements of democratic thought, followed by provisions, conditions, and requirements so stated that the only charitable explanation seems to be that two different sets of people executed the inconsistent parts. The discrepancy is even more apparent when the contents of the handbook or syllabus are read, and actions in the class room then observed.

Some part of the trouble lies in the fact that even on basic tenets agreement is incomplete. The main fault very likely, though, is that decisions of the moment are not related constantly to general ideas[6] so as to furnish opportunity for increased insight, definition, and meaning.

GUIDES IN PSYCHOLOGICAL RESEARCH

As with the tenets of democracy, it is not difficult to locate summarizations[7] of the things "we know" about child growth and development or learning. Perhaps the assurance with which this knowledge is written is not justified, for there is certainly disagreement among the psychologists. Nevertheless, it is a fact that a quite similar set of ideas and conclusions has wide support in the literature and that a great many curriculum proposals and adaptations have been predicated on acceptance of certain generalizations. We know the study of these generalizations, of some of the original research which produced them, and of their implications is required of all teachers.

The outcomes of this study are in many ways similar to those which are derived from the passive acceptance of the statements about democracy. There are numbers of teachers who can reiterate what the professors say children are like, what they need, and how learning best takes place in them. Yet these teachers continue to carry on with children and to support in their schools practices which they know to be inconsistent.

This discrepancy, to be fair, very often lies in the actual difficulty of creating the conditions and situations which are consistent with the principles stated. Even when the desire exists, the obstacles are often too great to surmount. Overloaded with pupils, denied proper resource and supervisory aid the teacher can not get enough time, energy, know-how, and material to develop appropriate experiences.

[6] Note the agreement in statements by Johnson, Saylor and Alexander, and Hopkins: B. Lamar Johnson, ed., *General Education in the American High School*, Scott, Foresman, 1942, pp. 5–6; J. Galen Saylor and William Alexander, *Curriculum Planning*, Rinehart, 1954, pp. 122–127; L. Thomas Hopkins, *Interaction: The Democratic Process*, Heath, 1941, pp. 102–112.

[7] For an excellent summary see P. M. Symonds, *What Education Has to Learn From Psychology*, Bureau of Publications, Teachers College, 1958.

Rejection of Psychologists Pronounced

A still greater number of teachers, however, appear to have taken little heed of psychologists. Perhaps this is more true of the secondary teachers than of those who are in the elementary schools. Nevertheless, arguments continue over the method and subject, with a patent lack of conviction about maturational patterns, individual differences, the effect of punishment on interest and acquisition, socialization drives in children, the possibilities of transfer, the nature of retention, and uses of drill. Likewise, teachers regularly work long and diligently in selecting and producing content and in deciding what students will be asked to do without considering how their effort almost completely denies quality to learning activity.

Consistency with Principles Dependent on Careful Deliberation

There are several ways of approaching this problem of bringing choices—such as what to teach, where to place subjects, whether to have a subject organization, how to arrange for orderly build-up of skills, and how to schedule teaching of items of logically dependent relationship—into a defensible line with what is supportable in regard to behavior changes. The traditional approach is a comprehensive study of child development and educational psychology with the idea that the resultant deepened background will provide a map of such clear directions that turns into the byways of error will be impossible.

However, the most useful procedure for us teachers probably is the employment of some reverse English from practice to theory with emerging curriculum decisions being constantly studied firsthand against a set of generalizations we accept or develop ourselves. We can identify a great many such generalizations and have a whole volume of check points, or we can try to reduce them to a critical few and insist that our choices in each case be in accord with those basic points before we proceed. It might be that a few teachers have such a list and constantly use it in classroom planning or in work with colleagues, but a check with over a hundred teachers revealed no such guide sheet to be in use with anyone. Discussion revealed, too, an unusual mixture of beliefs about how behavior change is facilitated and little evidence of any careful effort even to think about the inconsistencies.

Many curriculum bulletins[8] do contain chapters on growth and development and on learning, but in selected interviews with teachers from systems where program guides apparently grew with stated positions in mind no widespread use was discovered.

[8] State Board of Education, *Alabama Course of Study*, Grades 1–12, The Board, 1954, Part II.

As more telling experiments are evolved by the psychologists and educational researchers, additions will doubtless be made to any set of generalizations we may propose. However, if at the present choices were viewed searchingly and fully by means of a chart something like the one on pages 110–121, we might move toward improved programs. In columns three and five some examples of violations and in two and four some examples of practices consistent with the generalizations are given.

GUIDES IN COMMON AND SPECIFIC OBJECTIVES

The work on objectives has been underway since formal education provisions were first made. The letters of New England Puritans contain ideas as to why schools should be set up in the colonies and what results might be expected. Among the statements of our political leaders, past and present, there are references to the value of education and to the competence one might derive therefrom. School critics and reformers from Horace Mann to John Dewey have written about how the schools have failed and have indicated possibly more worthy pursuits for them. During this century and particularly since World War II, considerable effort has been devoted to reviewing these earlier pronouncements on the aims and goals of schooling. The sentiments of the public at large about what the schools should do beyond education in fundamentals have not yet been systematically sought, but laws on the statute books in a few states imply what the aims of the school should be. Many citizen committees have indicated their convictions. A multitude of policy decisions by boards of education demonstrate that goals have had numerous evening examinations. As a result, we now have several rather impressive documents which propose purposes or objectives for our schools, and in numerous states and communities these statements have been accepted, added to, restated, revised, and constitute the approved purposes.

For the most part, these statements are well reasoned and defensible. They are broad in scope, and in the case of the *Purposes of Education in American Democracy*[9] document of the Educational Policies Commission fairly intensive treatment is given through the listing of some specifics represented by a general goal.

However, we should not be so naïve as to expect that any document could be without fault or should simply be accepted without ar-

[9] See Educational Policies Commission, "Objectives of Human Relationship and Objectives of Economic Efficiency," *The Purposes of Education in American Democracy*, National Education Association, 1938.

GENERALIZATIONS	VIOLATIONS IN TEACHER-PUPIL SITUATIONS	PRACTICE CONSISTENT IN TEACHER-PUPIL SITUATIONS	VIOLATIONS IN TEACHER-TEACHER PLANNING	CONSISTENCY IN TEACHER-TEACHER PLANNING
1. Quality learning requires genuine pupil purpose	1a. Pupils seek to please teacher b. Pupils seek marks only c. Pupil submits to assignment d. Why explanation is limited, not undertaken, or inadequate e. Goals are adult-valued f. Drill is based on teacher need for pupil mastery g. No time is available to relate purposes h. Extremely vague and abstract reasons are given	1a. Surveys of pupil concerns and interests are made b. Marks are reduced in favor of cooperative evaluation procedures c. Teacher plans are suggestions and invitations d. Choice of what to study is guaranteed e. Students plan possible tasks with teacher f. Teacher emphasis is on improving processes of inquiry and selection	1a. Required content is specified at grade level b. Minimum essentials of accomplishment are written in c. Selections grow only from subject logic d. Subject categories are made rigid. Skills, knowledge are not taught generally e. Activities suggested in courses are not adaptable to pupil concerns f. Exterior exam-	1a. Multiple suggestions are developed to increase concern for remote goals b. Persistent problems of living serve as the base for planning c. Immediate needs are considered to promote remote goals d. Teacher freedom is guaranteed e. Intensive studies are made of growth needs f. Instruments are developed to

i. Teachers use examinations and failure threats freely

2. Rapid acquisition takes place when tasks are set near ability level

   2a. All pupils are given same problems
   b. Need to get mark distribution imposes identical tests
   c. Frustration develops through too rapid increases in difficulty on a time schedule
   d. Pupils are berated for limitations, told that trying hard will produce results

   2a. Individual assignments are made
   b. Careful observation prevents frustration experience
   c. Varied levels of accomplishment are respected and acceptable
   d. Projects and activities permit ability level tasks
   e. Enrichment experience is provided the bright

inations are used to judge pupil and teacher
   g. Teacher is expected to dominate and direct

   2a. No diagnoses are made of differential ability
   b. Grade standards are fixed
   c. Re-assignment of pupils is not permitted
   d. Single texts are adopted and used exclusively

aid personal diagnosis

   2a. Resource units contain ideas for grouping
   b. Teachers provide time for planning
   c. Teachers agree to teach what is needed when pupils are ready

GENERALIZATIONS	VIOLATIONS IN TEACHER-PUPIL SITUATIONS	PRACTICE CONSISTENT IN TEACHER-PUPIL SITUATIONS	VIOLATIONS IN TEACHER-TEACHER PLANNING	CONSISTENCY IN TEACHER-TEACHER PLANNING
	e. Long and extended drill is substituted for insight f. Parents are threatened or goaded into tutoring g. Broader experiences are denied with excessive time demand put on limited objectives			
3. Learning process is most effective when sharp focus and enthusiasm are secured and maintained	3a. Explanations are short and off-hand b. Instruction is verbal c. Illustrations of application are not included	3a. Bulletin board, field trips, exploration are used to stimulate interest b. Method is varied to minimize fatigue and boredom	3a. Goals of instruction are stated too broadly b. Too many unrelated goals are set up for any one day	3a. Check devices are included in teaching suggestions b. Cooperative observation and supervision is arranged

4. Learning is an active process; qualitative learning involves thinking

4a. Teacher lectures, gives lists
b. Pupils recite mechanically
c. Tests are fact centered
d. Teacher identifies what is to be learned
e. Laboratory experience is reproductive and repetitive
f. Teacher monop-

d. Too much is attempted
e. Discipline via threat is misinterpreted as positive attention
f. Toc little provision is made for relaxation, change of pace

4a. The problem method is used
b. Pupils manage classroom program
c. Research and answer development are required
d. Questions are geared to cause, viewpoint, application

c. Objectives are stated in detail and reiterated
d. Teaching follows upon emergence of genuine work

4a. Restricted facts are identified for acquisition
b. Extensive knowledge is valued above broad know-how
c. Educational planning is future oriented, mainly steps for preparation

4a. Studies are made of appropriate community problems for student investigation
b. Sub-group study and reporting are encouraged
c. Extra-curricular activities are promoted
d. Classrooms are

GENERALIZATIONS	VIOLATIONS IN TEACHER-PUPIL SITUATIONS	PRACTICE CONSISTENT IN TEACHER-PUPIL SITUATIONS	VIOLATIONS IN TEACHER-TEACHER PLANNING	CONSISTENCY IN TEACHER-TEACHER PLANNING
	olizes the time			developed as laboratories for learning
5. Skill and knowledge are fixed and improved through continued use in normal and natural situations	5a. Massed drill is employed as the major technique	5a. Teachers constantly use content from other subject fields	5a. Subject content is included with little reference to its commoness of use	5a. Cooperative staff effort is devoted to skill development
		b. Papers inadequate in fundamental skills are rejected at appropriate levels	b. Outmoded subjects are continued in the program	b. High school content is vigorously appraised for its utility
		c. Re-teaching is done when need for skill arises	c. Subjects are improved only in behalf of antiquated requirements for the "educated man"	c. Activities are designed to call upon numerous skills; correct speech, graph making, idea organization, etc.
		d. Close relationships for evaluation are maintained with the home	d. Subject areas through which familiar attitudes and skills could be taught are	d. Extensive follow up studies are made of the employment of

			depreciated, e.g. driver training	graduates e. Analyses are made of student out-of-school activity
		6a. Student reactions and attitudes are seriously considered	6a. School responsibility for social and emotional growth is depreciated	6a. Home visitation is encouraged
	6a. Pupils are publicly criticized and evaluated	b. Student aptitudes are fully explored	b. Courses are put in prestige categories	b. Homerooms, core programs, counsellors provide for student relief
	b. Personal and deep psychological problems are ignored	c. Failure on tasks is positively treated as need for help	c. Scholarships, awards are restricted to certain academic pursuits	c. Remedial instruction is arranged
	c. Invidious comparison is practiced	d. Appropriate and well timed grouping is obtained		d. A long term program for developing sound self-concepts is planned
	d. Personal worth is related to passing. Passing is related to norms	e. Proper reading level materials are provided		
6. Continued excessive frustration interferes with and blocks effective learning	e. Simply too much work is required of growing children			
7. Transfer is obtained best when actively taught for, or sought	7a. Multiple isolated memorizations are not woven into a	7a. Learnings are constantly tested in novel, normal	7a. Subjects are defended on their formal discipline	

GENERALIZATIONS	VIOLATIONS IN TEACHER-PUPIL SITUATIONS	PRACTICE CONSISTENT IN TEACHER-PUPIL SITUATIONS	VIOLATIONS IN TEACHER-TEACHER PLANNING	CONSISTENCY IN TEACHER-TEACHER PLANNING
8. Higher levels of behavior, creative response, grow from integrations in the learner	meaningful relationship b. Excessive pursuit of marks puts emphasis on forgetting and learning for immediate use	situations b. Teachers demonstrate actual use of skills in other areas c. Careful discussion of where and when used accompanies all teaching d. Constant search is made for generalizations	contributions b. Utility and functional experience are rejected	a subject b. Claims are constantly exposed to research c. Lists of practical failure situations are made d. Extensive analyses are made by teachers of the application of facts and skills
8a. Tasks too often call on limited learning. They have no scope b. Separation of semesters sharply reveals failure to expect relating of material		8a. Constant attention is given to posing more complex questions b. Much writing, organizing, planning are done c. Time is provided for free explora-	8a. Much attention is given to forcing subjects down to lower levels b. Requirements far exceed electives c. Correlation and parallel teaching are neglected	8a. Much effort goes into locating exploration questions b. Science fairs, other plans for synthesizing information are sponsored

9. Learning is most qualitative when it involves acquisition to solve present, pressing problems

c. Pressure for acquisition is so great no time is granted for pupil planning and initiative
d. Everything has to be taught
e. Daily programs and hourly class meeting are routinized and stereotyped
f. Pupils are required to follow teacher forms and ways of doing

9a. No response is made to personal problems of adjustment
b. Value matters are avoided as too controversial

tion, independent pursuit
d. Multiple experiences are used to build understanding
e. Many media are provided for expression
f. Much opportunity exists for extended teacher-pupil discussion

9a. Person to person rapport is a major priority
b. Group warmth and unity is sought
c. Much time is spent

c. Teacher groups meet to find points of reinforcement

9a. Continuing census of youth concerns is made
b. Units are planned around youth needs
c. Adults, parents

GENERALIZATIONS	VIOLATIONS IN TEACHER-PUPIL SITUATIONS	PRACTICE CONSISTENT IN TEACHER-PUPIL SITUATIONS	VIOLATIONS IN TEACHER-TEACHER PLANNING	CONSISTENCY IN TEACHER-TEACHER PLANNING
	c. Knowledge of personal limitations and confusions is used punitively	in informal relationships	courses independently around subject content d. Treatment of adjustment problems is delegated and allocated to certain grade levels	are involved
10. Purpose levels rise in cooperative groups	10a. Teacher decides, assigns, demands independent work b. Competition for marks is major motivation c. Group projects are teacher directed	10a. Evaluation is a continuous integral part of program b. Teacher restrains urge to tell, to explain c. Veto power is seldom used d. Standardized tests are used in planning	10a. No time or room in specifications for cooperative planning	10a. Extensive alternative units are developed b. Longer periods for work are provided c. Awards, prizes are related to broader goals
11. Interest and focus fluctuate with growth	11a. No provision is made in the	11a. Expectancy and grades are re-	11a. Program is not flexible enough	11a. There is a plan to assess growth

patterns and rates

marking system for plateaus in learning

b. Each child is treated the same way at all times

c. Group re-assignments are used as threats

d. No re-teaching or post-teaching is offered

e. Periodic and varied positive motivation is neglected

lated to growth

b. Boy standards vary from girl standards during critical growth periods

c. Temporary introversion and withdrawal are overlooked. Regression in social and emotional behavior is acknowledged but not criticized

d. Activities are shifted to cater to strengths

e. Child is helped to a positive understanding of uneven growth

to permit intense pursuit during strong growth periods

b. No recognition is given to relief in special areas of weakness

c. Pre-requisites are maintained in course sequences

in a variety of dimensions

b. Records are developed to emphasize total performance rather than penalties for periodic arrests in growth

12. Learning depends on cumulative favorable impact of multiple

12a. Teachers are unconcerned about student life

12a. Teachers sponsor extra-curricular activity

12a. School is highly regulated, severe, and aus-

12a. The staff are personally productive,

GENERALIZATIONS	VIOLATIONS IN TEACHER-PUPIL SITUATIONS	PRACTICE CONSISTENT IN TEACHER-PUPIL SITUATIONS	VIOLATIONS IN TEACHER-TEACHER PLANNING	CONSISTENCY IN TEACHER-TEACHER PLANNING
stimuli, a good environment	b. Friendliness, interest in, respect for pupils is absent c. Criticism, sarcasm, personal abuse are practiced. Punishments are used in lieu of diagnoses, e.g. extra assignments, detention hall, zeros d. Certain subjects are ridiculed	b. There is familiarity with the student's past c. There is personal enthusiasm for knowledge, further study revealed to pupils d. Connection is made between school and community and national success and survival e. Teachers plan fun activities with pupils	tere by faculty restriction b. Program is narrow and academic. Areas for student relief and free expression are limited. Eligibility requirements are maintained for sports, etc. c. Little recognition is given to the limited abilities and needs of many students. There is thus resentment, a feeling of neglect, no loyalty	professionally creative b. Plans are employed to involve patrons in raising community level of respect toward education c. Vigorous staff action is devoted to securing appealing buildings, resources, equipment

13. Retention finally is product of personal value, what the learner selects and accepts for his own and uses

13a. Scores on end point tests are considered sufficient evidence of accomplishment
b. Teacher valued skills and knowledge are imposed arbitrarily on a captive group
c. Content taught has no meaning for the learner

13a. What to learn and why are the central focus. Learning how to value is the goal
b. There is cooperative determination of objectives
c. Teacher proposes, advises, recommends, encourages
d. Learning goals grow from much first-hand acquaintance with need to learn

13a. Discrete courses support learning for sake of learning and pleasing
b. What to learn is drawn from books written by scholars remote from immediate experiences of children

13a. Goals of education are set down as general behavior
b. Activities are proposed that contribute to increased personal adequacy in daily living
c. The value and importance of vocational orientation of subjects leads to graphic and vivid illustration of convictions

121

43855

gument or without analysis. There are many who object to such a specification as this, even as a suggestive one, by a group of educators; and
an appreciable number of the implied tasks for the schools in this volume is clearly without support from segments of the population. In
fact it is usually easy to locate teachers who doubt that the school
should actively undertake to obtain certain of the attributes and qualities indicated. The degree or extent of achievement is likewise an easy
subject for controversy.

This reveals the major limitation in the present use of the objectives lists. Generally, they are not carefully and extensively examined
and analyzed, and as a result they have all too little real effect on
specific aspects of curriculum planning. The common practice of adopting them as general guides and placing them in the first pages of
courses of study leads to little use of them thereafter. More attention to
objective clarification and more effort to follow general or ultimate
objectives down to specific purposes (with their logical counterparts in
teaching practice and outcomes) are therefore needed.

Such specification has been unpopular in curriculum writing for
some time now. The reason given is that the scientific method applied
to curriculum selection in the 1920's resulted in a mountain of labor
and the spawning of a mouse and so did the elaboration of general
statements into details. However, the abandonment of a concerted attempt to bring the general and specific levels of objective statement
closer together has only left a void that still has to be filled.

Replying to the criticism that itemization leads to an unwieldly
mass of specific objectives—so many that they swamp the school that
tries to take them seriously, instead of giving direction to its efforts—
Barton says "the specificity with which any school finally states its objectives for use is a matter of judgment by the school. The important
thing is to state them *specifically enough* so that everyone concerned
really knows what they mean. The writer once heard Charters advise,
'Stop one step above the obvious.' "[10]

This position is similar to that taken by Will French and his associates in their volume *Behavioral Goals of General Education in High
School*[11] when they say

Those responsible for this study believe that more specific illustrative
statements of the behaviors to be sought are essential if general education pro-

---

[10] George Barton, "Derivation and Clarification of Objectives," *Journal of
Educational Research,* April, 1948, p. 434.
[11] Will French *et al., Behavioral Goals for General Education in High School,*
Russell Sage Foundation, 1957, p. 35.

grams in high school are to be effective. Selection of content and other experiences will be improved if both students and teachers have a clearer idea of the principal specific behaviors which instruction is supposed to facilitate. Statements that go far enough beyond general objectives to provide examples of specific behaviors will give students and teachers the best proof available.

Two Levels Needing Teacher Attention

As the case stands now, most of us find ourselves somewhere on a distribution with a range including those with no systematic view of objectives and those with full experience in deliberating on school goals. Some have examined what specific experiences contribute to particular acquisitions or growth. Others have studied what cumulates into purposes like civic responsibility,[12] health, worthy use of leisure,[13] or an understanding of the significance of the family.[14] The majority appear to be on the "no systematic view" end. Even when those who are subject teachers are asked, they are generally unable to produce a comprehensive and well-organized outline of anticipated and suggested goals.

Nevertheless, there have been numerous publications by subject matter groups and professional organizations containing proposals and agreements as to the possible contribution of a subject or subject field. Few teachers have not at some time reviewed volumes of the national councils or associations or at least been made aware of their efforts through methods texts containing a chapter on objectives or the reasons for teaching a subject. But on the whole teachers usually seem to have forgotten these statements, and it is unusual to find one who has much of a personal and organized reference to give him both long time and immediate direction. His behavior more often seems to be intuitive. Tyler says of this, "Even broad and ultimate objectives then ought to be read with care and examined thoroughly with colleagues. At best of course they are but stated values. They should be consistent with our basic beliefs, our agreed upon needs, the known facts about physical, intellectual and emotional development and about the attainment potentials in humans. They further should be logically defensible and lead to consistent and defensible means."[15]

How shall the move up the scale be made then? There seems to

---

[12] Educational Policies Commission, *The Purposes of Education in American Democracy*, National Education Association, 1938.

[13] Commission on Reorganization of Secondary Education, *Cardinal Principles of Secondary Education*, Government Printing Office, 1918.

[14] Educational Policies Commission, *Education for All American Youth*, National Education Association, 1952.

[15] Ralph Tyler, *Basic Principles of Curriculum and Instruction*, University of Chicago Press, 1947, p. 1.

be no better starting point than to take one of the present ultimate or broad goal statements and determine to what extent it can be agreed the school should have a major role.

A specific example is included in the *Behavior Goals*.[16] Here there is extensive listing of behaviors that illustrate goal achievement followed by a chart presentation of a set of possible behavioral goals which a high school can stress. A rating scale is provided for indicating the extent to which one would accept these specifics. With this analysis the teacher has more than a single opportunity for expressing an opinion or for appraising how much effort his school is making. He has in addition a constant guide to the kinds of experiences he might develop with pupils that will lead to the behaviors sought.

Preparation of documents as comprehensive as the *Behavior Goals* volume or as detailed and integrated with respect to objectives in courses of study and units indeed does take time. If the result is a strait jacket, better the job be left alone. But if the framework's purpose is to turn broad and appealing goals into something more precise and more helpful in facilitating selection of immediate and limited experiences, it is clearly justified.

Cooperative Action a Help

Romine proposes in this connection that, where possible, objective formulation be a cooperative process to insure the closing of the gap between pleasant but largely indefinite statements and more limited and manageable purposes which lead to installing courses, blocking out units, setting up discrete learning situations. Feeling, as we do, that the analysis and range from ultimate to specific must be examined, he writes, "Once the objectives for the school are established, it is sometimes assumed that teachers will readily see a relationship to their respective fields (and to their teaching activities) and automatically pursue classroom and student-teacher objectives of a more specific nature which are consonant with those of the school. This is a fallacious assumption, and coupled with the typical approach, tends to promote a gap between stated philosophy and general objectives of the school and the outcomes actually sought by teachers."[17]

At this point we are not concerned with how this dual approach can and should be managed in detail. The point is that on a much

---

[16] Will French *et al.*, *op. cit.*

[17] Stephen Romine, *Building the High School Curriculum*, Ronald, 1953, p. 169.

broader scale there ought be developed more comprehensive and deliberately related specifications of objectives. Then using these for guidance the teacher curriculum maker could make his choices and later determine the extent to which they have led to outcomes valued and desired.

The probability that increased and wider attention will be given to restating and explaining more thoroughly what ultimate objectives mean and require in the way of intermediate and more discrete attainments is now greater than ever. Curriculum workers can expect more and more questions about what we are "trying to do with our schools anyway." The need repeatedly to check action against purpose and to insist on a true connection between learning exercise and valued and defensible outcome is thus upon us. It would be agreeable if all the work were done. But it is not.

GUIDES IN BROAD AND COMPREHENSIVE KNOWLEDGE

Inasmuch as decisions are made for pupils and must be acceptable to communities and are regularly dependent on what we know and value, we teachers can not escape the responsibility for adding to our data about those whom we teach and about the particular needs and concerns of patrons. Similarly, greatly increased knowledge in the disciplines growing out of man's study of himself and of his environment offers vast amounts of information which may serve as potential for solving problems. The teacher must constantly expand his control over these specifications too, if he is to serve responsibly in developing rich experiences for pupils.

Pupils' Needs a Constant Source of Data

Featherstone[18] says it would probably be taken as axiomatic "that a school should meet its pupils' needs." At least this seems to be so when one considers the persistent criticisms of the schools.

From many general inquiries of youth, we have gotten better ideas concerning probable common needs at certain age levels, among set groups, and under certain circumstances and conditions. In view of their range, order, and extent, we can make better decisions about courses, units, or patterns of teaching useful in dealing with those aspects of need appropriate for the school.

[18] William Featherstone, *A Functional Curriculum for Youth*, American Book, 1950, p. 67.

These general studies, however, will give at best only broad direction. They may serve quite adequately to suggest areas where more detailed and systematic studies locally will point up what can and should be done with particular pupils and groups of pupils.

Parent Values and National Needs as Bases

Inquiries will not tell the whole story about the needs of those who attend school. From the beginning of time, adults have apparently seen shortcomings in their offspring and have at the same time held convictions as to the attributes the uninformed and uneducated might well possess to tussle adequately with the present and better with the future. These predicated needs, to be sure, can not be dismissed. One may vigorously argue, as many have, that the pupil should never study or attempt to acquire knowledge and tools for dealing with a shortage he does not recognize, understand, or accept. In fact, they have argued so vigorously that the idea has grown up here and there that what they mean is complete dependence on unencouraged, unstimulated, and uncreated needs. Nothing could be more inane than such a conclusion.

The schools, we can be sure, exist because people want their children to obtain knowledge and skill to deal more adequately with life. Teachers are hired to help nurture and develop pupil desire to do just that and to point out whenever and wherever possible the degree and extent to which the pupil falls short of the ideal. This does not and should not mean crude imposition, but it certainly means for the teacher the obligation to be fully and extensively informed about what pupils could and should accomplish—not as adults—but as pupils.[19]

COMMUNITY ANALYSIS AND AREAS OF IMPROVEMENT

Review of local problems of living as a source of curriculum experience has been widely supported for years. For many the real evidence of the impact of the school is in what it accomplishes in improving the life of the community. Yet in few communities can any evidence be obtained of a planned and persisting effort to see if the school has raised the level of magazine buying and reading, affected the use of the public library, influenced the habits of voters, reduced traffic accidents, contributed significantly to health practice, diminished prejudice and stereotype, added appreciably to knowledge of the nation's history, increased loyalty or affected any number of other elements of community life.

[19] See Featherstone, *op. cit.,* pp. 85–86, for an excellent statement on needs.

Teachers' Scholarship a Critical Factor

Although we do subscribe heartily to the idea that a teacher must often be a companionate learner with pupils in pursuing solutions to problems, we do not believe this means that the teacher does not seek to accumulate more and more knowledge to provide a richer reservoir. Because a man knows, he does not need to tell. In fact when his telling will prevent the pupil from actively using basic tools and thought processes to discover the relationship of one thing to another and the extent of their affinity, he must restrain himself. But on the basis of a great deal of knowledge and insight, of full and rich experience, the teacher should be equipped to raise questions, to arouse interest, to stimulate thought, to give direction that will lead to increased knowledge, to the acquisition of skill, and to generalizations that will provide a basis for application in future remote and novel situations.

A teacher's job is to guide, and we can not guide without knowing in what direction and with what aim. The fuller our background, the more likely we will be able and want to propose, to tease, to test out, and to perceive relationship between potential interest, need, and gratification. Simply, the more informed we are the more we have to offer.

Teachers' Values Another Critical Factor

How much of what we will champion before our pupils or force upon them, of course, will depend on our point of view about the teaching process. In our view, as has been set out before, it is the responsibility of the teacher to balance what he knows against what pupils do not know and against what they say and feel they need. No teacher should be empowered to decide that his interests alone—what he possesses, what he likes, and what he uses—are subjects that everyone else should know. Our freedom as humans should assure us against having to value what some one other person values.

Nevertheless, each individual does have the prerogative to propose what he values to others. By agreement and consensus we, as teachers, are actually invested with the responsibility to pass on, to make available, what we know. It is clear that the laymen support education with the idea that the teacher they hire will give to their offspring or manage to inculcate in their offspring the knowledge, skills, values, and attitudes useful to a higher-quality living. When the teacher is without some of that knowledge himself or if he does not value it, for himself or his pupils, it does not take the laymen long to conclude that they want a different teacher.

Questions for Discussion

1. Argument often arises over the extent to which the school should pass on the cultural heritage, unexamined, and the extent to which it should be vigorously involved in reconstructing our beliefs and habits. What generalizations would you prefer to guide teacher curriculum makers?
2. The necessary breadth of the school's efforts is being more vigorously reexamined. What is the unique role of the school? In what areas is it supplemental? How shall we determine the extent?
3. Did your own education permit you to pursue goals and objectives meaningful to you? Were you exposed to learning activities of low quality? If so, what effect did this have on you?
4. What advantages and disadvantages do you see in having a national curriculum committee empowered to define goals, to set up courses of study, and to impose examinations?
5. Even if protected with a list of problem areas and with good resource units that contain many fine teaching suggestions and excellent materials, can a community take the risk of setting a teacher free with pupils to select their own learning activities and to decide what content they will acquire?
6. Should teachers study more complex, adult subject matter in their major field rather than methods and more general courses in varied fields?
7. In a group it is usually easy to find someone who will feel that taking Latin never helped him at all, having to write a précis was a waste of time, and learning a hundred chemistry formulas to pass the Regents—all to get into college to study journalism—were uncalled for and indefensible choices. How do you view the situation? What can be done about it, whatever position you take?
8. Suppose that in a democratic, teacher-pupil planning situation in the seventh grade the class completely rejected any effort to learn grammar. What position would a "modern" teacher take?

Selected Bibliography

Brameld, Theodore, *Patterns of Educational Philosophy,* World Book, 1950.

Counts, George S., *Education and American Civilization,* Bureau of Publications, Teachers College, 1952.

Educational Policies Commission, *The Purposes of Education in American Democracy,* National Education Association, 1938.

French, Will, *et al., Behavioral Goals of General Education in High School,* Russell Sage Foundation, 1957.

Gwynn, J. Minor, *Curriculum Principles and Social Trends,* third ed., Macmillan, 1956.

Havighurst, Robert J., *Human Development and Education,* Longmans, Green, 1953.

Henry, Nelson B., ed., *Learning and Instruction,* Forty-ninth Yearbook, National Society for the Study of Education, 1950, Part I.

Kearney, Nolan, *Elementary School Objectives,* Russell Sage Foundation, 1953.

Stanley, William O., *et al., Social Foundations of Education,* Dryden, 1956.

Stiles, Lindley, ed., *The Teacher's Role in American Society,* Harper, 1957.

Thorpe, Louis P., and Allen Schmuller, *Contemporary Theories of Learning,* Ronald, 1954.

CHAPTER 6

....

Working on the Broad Framework

There are a number of analogies one could use to emphasize the importance of a superstructure for the curriculum. The most familiar is from the construction industry where the framing of buildings is considered a most critical stage by architect, contractor, and public inspector alike. Each knows that unless there is a secure and sound skeleton upon which to fasten plates, strips, and pieces, there will be gaps, splits, and cracks. The final product will soon sag and settle. Fine workmanship, finesse with woodwork, plaster, and tile will be impaired, if not actually impossible. Craftsmen can do their best only when there is balance and stability, when there is protection against overload, and when their materials are not strained beyond their tolerance.

The frame of a house also affects more than the quality of the work of those who lay the floors, install the plumbing, and plaster the walls; more than the safety of the inhabitants. It actually determines in large part how the people in the house will live. If the living room and the picture window are in the front, proud owners will look out upon the traffic rather than upon the birds in the garden trees. If there is no entrance closet, they will have to put the visitor's wraps in the bedroom. The single upstairs bath may be good for the cuddle stage with the baby, but exasperating in the muddy boot stage of childhood. Full length windows may keep the beds in the same position for years. A too small kitchen may never give space for one of the lovely new refrigerators, and the dining-room ell forever may frustrate the desire for a real room for gracious entertainment. Compromises with desires may help and compensations may relieve discomforts. Still there will continue to be restrictions and limitations on what can be done in a house with rooms too small, no expansion space, or too shallow a cellar for fireplace and playroom.

Relief at times may be sought by additions and rebuilding, but this usually involves more than at first meets the eye. Walls have to be changed; wiring has to be extended and made adequate; flooring and clapboards have to be matched and so forth. Often the work required for remodeling costs far more than it is worth. The inconvenience is great and seldom is the general silhouette enhanced by additions. The remade structure is usually unbalanced and only partially successful in removing discomforts. In many cases the alterations wanted can not be managed at all. A bookcase will not go in where there is a steel post; a main bearing wall can not be removed to widen the hall. The roof must be removed to add a second story, and the joists on the first floor will not support extra weight. The heating plant is inadequate and larger ducts can not be installed.

Thus, the framework upon and around which a house is built can prescribe not only the quality of life in the house, but can create problems for the carpenter who would alter or add to its dimensions.

CURRICULUM DEPENDENT ON FRAMEWORK

Earlier it was pointed out that the curriculum is often defined as those experiences pupils have as a result of their attendance at school. This definition actually is inclusive but special. It seeks to emphasize that the pupil is the critical factor. It is he who puts value on what he seeks, hears, and feels; he decides in the end what to accept, to act upon, to approve, to respect, or to reject. In other words, what he possesses as a result of the impositions, suggestions, invitations which have been presented to him really is *his* curriculum. It is the pupil who finally gives his own exposure the quality of experience. Whatever the framework, he makes of it what he will.

We know that in most schools the pupil attends there will be some arrangement of his time and some focus of effort on the part of staff to encourage him to learn and to enlighten him about those items they value. The local staff or someone else will have decided whether to commit his time to health instruction, how much of it to give to calisthenics, and so forth. These same people will have decided what they want him to learn and at what time.

This collection of prescriptions and time allocations with titles and designations we know in common terminology as the program or the curriculum planned. We could say in keeping with the house analogy that here is the structure and the framework. In some communities it is but a list of subjects; in others it may be a lengthy document outlining purposes of schools and describing what provisions are or should be made during a six-hour day.

These fundamental prescriptions do not absolutely force what will go on in the pupil's mind, but it is a waste of time to argue that they do not have a powerful influence. When the high school credential may be earned only upon completing the study of certain facts of American history, the pupil usually attends to that requirement. Likewise the teacher has certain freedom almost everywhere to plan different activities, to proceed rapidly or slowly, to teach chronologically or around themes, but he is also limited by agreements or by pattern or by regulations set by remote agencies or by decisions in the local area.

Thus the quality of experience the pupil has in school, as well as the quality of living a person has in a house, depends in a very large part on the basic framework out of which the detailed impositions on and controls of living grow. If a pupil wants to change his curriculum, it is by this notion obviously possible that he may be restricted and hampered just as the imaginative homeowner is so often frustrated when he would remove his light switches or install a new window.

At present the pupil has precious little freedom. He asks constantly, "Why can we not study what we want to and why do we have to take so many required subjects?" Or he protests the need for material and tasks at his level of ability. He can not have his revisions because particular patterns can not be disrupted, because introduction of new approaches would put a strain on public relations, or because the graded system, like the arrangement of studs, requires a steady progression of intervals with no room for variance.

For the teacher there is regularly the same difficulty. He can not take his pupils on a trip because he can not infringe on the time allocated to another; he can not provide art experiences of a rich and systematic kind because the pupil schedule is filled with constants; he can not deal cooperatively and freely with pupils' problems because there are too many facts set out in advance for learning.

Both the pupil and the teacher of course can get along with a framework that is neither completely perfect nor completely flexible. There are as many examples of compromise and compensation in schools as there are in homes. An individual can live with what he must. Even so, we doubtless can agree that were it possible to set up a fully adaptable superstructure and to build around it appropriately nonrigid elements, we should have an ideal arrangement for accommodating emerging needs and changing conceptions about the kinds of specific experience we wish to have.

Remote Controls Reflected in Framework

For the most part, classroom teachers have been little involved in giving structure to the broad curriculum plan in this century. With the growth of the public school system, the increase in laws governing schools, and with the emergence of strong state agencies to administer the law and to direct schools, the classroom teacher has progressively lost the prerogative and great personal power he exercised a century ago. Commissioners and superintendents were delegated the responsibility to manage and supervise greater and greater numbers. They increased their regulations and set down more prescriptions and specifications to bring comparability if not uniformity into the schools. By the mid-1920's there was an almost furious effort to write down details of every kind and to establish a tight structure that would in effect be closely controlled and subject to scientific measurement.

When the teacher ran his own school he gave direct advice how the program should be set up and what his pupils should do. The nature of the one-room school made it possible for him to change as situations warranted and as it seemed he could best accomplish the ends desired. The master patterned his work after that of other schools he knew, but he had independence and a freedom seldom found now. The restrictions imposed on him by higher institutions of learning, by regulation, and by common agreement were few in number and limited in effect.

Now the teacher has to some extent been rediscovered as a participant in planning because of his really key role and because of the expanding theory of cooperative administration. By serving on local committees and on advisory groups, studying new organization and format for state programs, some teachers have lately contributed again to broad planning. However, the educational system has persistently become more complex, and in many places local action depends on what is set out or practiced at remote points where numbers of teachers are seldom continually involved.

Most of us as teachers are not much more than vaguely aware of what these remote conditions are and how they affect the broad framework within which daily classroom interaction takes place. We do know that certain state laws prescribe courses to be taught. Across the country state superintendents of instruction supplement the laws with regulations that determine how much time should be devoted to particular subjects or aspects of study. We are familiar with the bulletins prepared for departments of public instruction that recommend how the school day should be organized, what topics may be included, and how the basic areas are defined and should be approached. The influence of the colleges which rather generally list certain subjects as prerequisites for college entrance, we hear, is a powerful force in determining what will be done in the lower schools. Some teachers know a little about the accrediting agencies that from time to time study and evaluate schools; their influence in keeping uniformity against some standards of what a school should include in its program is, though, not much understood.

Several general curriculum books give some attention to these influences, but it may be fair to say the books give less attention than the influences deserve. The law and the college tradition are indeed extremely "well established," so much so in fact that when suggestions are made for curriculum revision without a very substantial bow in their direction, the likelihood of much adaptation is slim. In fact, until there is a change in the laws or regulations with the force of law in many states and until more colleges and state universities can be persuaded to alter and adapt their entrance requirements, we may expect there to be a rather effective hobbling of any noticeable new designing.

TEACHERS' CONTRIBUTION TO DESIGNS

All of this and more would seem to suggest that the classroom teacher actually has little to say and will for a long time to come have little to say about structural revision or adaptation. It might seem that strategic or over-all planning and plans are subtle combinations of many factors which the teacher is seemingly nearly powerless to do anything about himself.

However, there are many at work proposing and promoting presumably more adequate frameworks for the curriculum. In fact the attention devoted to a new design has been considerable since the late 1920's when Caswell and his associates sought to cast for the State of Virginia a model which would free the schools from their dependence upon the subjects for scope and sequence. But despite the effort there has been really very little change. Somewhat plaintively Caswell notes this in *The American High School.*

> Workers in high schools in some instances attach little importance to the general design of the program. They contend that really good teaching within the conventional plan will achieve whatever purposes may be desired.

According to this view, it is quite unnecessary and in fact undesirable to upset the general framework of the existing program; rather, attention should center on improving the teaching in the various subjects.

It is the opinion of this committee that this point of view is basically unsound. It is true that improved teaching always results in better education, but the conventional curriculum framework is the greatest single obstacle to the development of a program in the high school which provides the necessary assistance to youth in achieving in actual living the various developmental tasks which our society demands.[1]

In this admission Caswell frankly indicates that the curriculum theorists have not had much influence on the chief school administrators, policy-makers, and those who write and follow up regulations. In some respects, rather, the theorists have cried into the wind.

The consensus among the theorists now is that the classroom teacher should understand the influence of design on educational experience. He then can exert an enlightened pressure for the changes that in consistency should be made locally and that ought to be authorized by these more distant factors. The teacher should see that framework is pertinently related to the freedom to teach and to have ideas.

The way the teacher may or should go about speeding variations in design is treated in Part 4. The purpose here is to raise the point that the teacher ought to see how design is related to his effort in the classroom and how it figures in the combined effort of all teachers to obtain a more effective education. Now there is wide agreement among curriculum specialists on Caswell's opinion about the subject curriculum. However, it is more than likely, as events have shown, that curriculum specialists will not decide the framework. That which squares with the teacher's concept, sets well with him and works out for him will determine in the long run whether we shall have much of a different form for the curriculum. If the experiences teachers want to have with pupils are impossible or may be attained only at the cost of too much discomfort within one framework, we shall have in time a different one. Thus, what we obviously should want as teachers is a design that:

1. Makes it certain that the purposes for which the school exists are fully and properly provided for
2. Makes it possible for the teaching-learning process to be highly efficient, operationally respectable and defensible
3. Makes adaptations, additions, and subtractions simple and timely
4. Makes it easy and necessary to use pupil purpose and to engage in the direct development of meanings

[1] H. L. Caswell, *The American High School,* Harper, 1946, pp. 139–140.

5. Makes it indispensable for those who work within the design to do so in ways consistent with fundamental beliefs about education in American democracy
6. Makes it possible for us to feel competent and confident

THREE BROAD DESIGNS

Probably a good deal more has been written than deserves to be set down about the various types of curricula. Until a few years ago much effort was made to distinguish among them, largely because each writer was inclined to provide his own definitions. In addition there was considerable effort to be exact and discrete. We thus had rather detailed descriptions of the traditional, the subject matter, the subjects, the fused, the correlated, the integrated, the emerging, the broad fields, the pupil problems of living, the core, the unified studies, the experience, the child-centered, the activity, and other curriculums. At first, it might well be thought they should all be as distinctive as Dutch colonials, Cape Cods, and ranch types. But they are not. In fact they are in a number of cases names for about the same things with slight variations; and although it might be possible to arrange these names along a continuum from one nonexistent point to another that in reality doesn't exist, little can be gained from such an array.

Much confusion has arisen because it has not always been clear that most proposals for design have had to do with general education in elementary, in junior high, and in a limited part of the secondary school. In every case the organization of a good part of the senior high program by subjects, sequentially related to some vocation, has been tacitly admitted and provided for. Discussion of redesign for the three senior grades has been largely avoided. This neglect has left many readers and teachers thinking the authors meant that what has been proposed for general education ought be extended to special education. Some may actually have meant that, but they have not said so.

For all intents and purposes in thinking about curriculum design for this general education there have been proposed three fairly distinctive frameworks. In their book on *Fundamentals of Curriculum Development,* Smith, Stanley, and Shores[2] designate them *subject, activity,* and *core curriculums.* We have referred to the broad possibilities discussed here as subjects, controlled problem, and unrestricted frameworks, not to propose new terminology but to approximate in words

[2] B. O. Smith, W. O. Stanley, and J. Shores, *Fundamentals of Curriculum Development,* rev. ed., World, 1957, Part III.

the appearance in the administrator's office of the actual schedule of a teacher.

Before we proceed, we should like to illustrate this point. In the office of the administrator of a school program organized subjectwise, one would be likely to find this schedule for a single teacher:

GRADE IV—MR. JONES

8:45– 9:00	Opening exercises
9:00– 9:45	Number work (arithmetic)
9:45– 9:50	Diversion or recess
9:50–10:00	Lunch arrangements
10:00–10:40	Reading
10:40–11:40	Gym
11:40–12:45	Lunch and play
12:45– 1:30	Music or art
1:30– 2:15	Grammar or writing or spelling
2:15– 2:45	Science
2:45– 3:15	Seat work, library

In the office of the administrator of a school program organized around controlled problems one would be likely to find this schedule:

GRADE VIII—MR. SMITH

FIRST SEMESTER

8:00– 8:30	Review and planning
8:30–12:30	Group and individual projects
	Interdependence theme
	Unit 1—Farm and Factory in the 20th Century
	Unit 2—Inventors and Group Life
	Unit 3—Regional Planning for Resource Use
	Unit 4—East and West: Friends or Enemies
12:30– 1:45	Lunch
1:15– 2:00	Remedial English, quiet reading, number review
2:00– 2:45	Free
2:45– 3:15	Extracurricular

In the office of the administrator of a school program with an unrestricted framework one would be likely to find the schedule:

GRADE VII—MR. BROWN

8:00–12:00	Group A
12:00– 1:00	Lunch
1:00– 3:15	Special assignments
	Teaching of subjects *or*
	Remedial work *or*
	Planning, *etc.*

If one were to ask of Mr. Jones, "What number work?" he would very probably have a text available to show the observer. A glance at his plan book would specify pages and problems and one would not be long in discovering what probably would be happening in the fourth grade and what skills and manipulations were to be learned during the nine-o'clock hour.

Likewise a copy of any of the four units used by Mr. Smith might be obtained from the office. One would not after inspection know what necessary facts or ideas were being sought, but from study of the proposed and suggested activities he could easily speculate on what might be covered and what might be learned. With the help of a chart showing broad objectives and the aspects of living to be referred to in balancing activities an examiner could get some idea of coverage.

Mr. Brown, however, would present some difficulties. From the schedule no idea of what his group might be studying would be gained. Perhaps a broad statement of goals or an analysis of persisting problems of living would suggest what his age group might have found interesting or of pressing concern, but only direct participation with him would give any real intimation of the nature and purpose of his immediate cooperative work with his charges.

THE SUBJECT FRAMEWORK

Few who have completed school do not know what the subject framework for the curriculum is. Nearly all who read here have been exposed to some variety of it and remember the experience as not particularly bad. Some of the subjects in that framework stand out as having been perennials, and we all recall subjects listed in the high school handbook which we thought we would have liked but we did not have time to take. In some subjects we were good; some we liked; some we didn't; and we wondered why we had to take others. There are graduates among us here and there, of course, who are displeased that we did not have typing, or woodwork, more home economics, or some more help with matters like investment, house buying, and home decoration. Still, we know that one can't have everything and so we are not too petulant.

But when reference is made to course titles with common names and when memories of forty-to-fifty-minute class periods, presided over by a teacher who gave regular assignments and held recitations and discussions, are aroused, the total dimensions of the subject curriculum have not been touched. Neither has there been any proper recognition of the great variety of arrangements and approaches, teaching methods and procedures, adaptations, and creative adjustments made in the great many schools which have used the subjects to attain either vague or explicitly stated goals.

Thus experience in subject framework may be remembered by some as a fairly sterile, mechanical daily experience, pretty well detached from any personal problems or concerns, fortified with threats of poor marks and failure. For others, it was instrumental to many pleasant classroom experiences, the accumulation of knowledge with an accompanying sense of power, cooperative planning of pace and projects with an alert teacher, and a continuing opportunity for seeing the uses of knowledge and skill acquired.

However, the generalizers in curriculum development who have been struggling with the business of improving the outcomes of education do not view the framework, fostering either of the extremes in the above paragraph, with much enthusiasm. Their analyses have led them with Caswell to the conclusion that it is an impossible basis for sound curriculum planning.

That the subject framework should be distinguished from "the curriculum" or pupil experience derived through or from the teaching of subjects has already been implied. To agree on what that "curriculum" is would be well nigh impossible; but agreement on the nature of the subject framework is fairly easy to obtain. It is sketching the allocation of school time in terms of titles given to collections of facts, skills, generalizations and principles.

What then is the trouble with this framework and structure? Obviously poor quality experience, dreadful in some cases, can be promoted and created through it. But there are terrible teachers everywhere too; and in any business, is the tool any better than the artisan who employs it? Do we not have testimony that many have greatly enjoyed what has been done in the name of arithmetic, of American history, and of biology? Have not great American successes in political and scientific life, even in theoretical curriculum work, had their training through the subjects?

Faults in the Subject Framework

1. *Subjects compel too loyal adherents.* Each of the subjects is a title given to a collection of facts, skills, generalizations, principles, etc. This collection has been organized by scholars over the years. In every case a sizable group of people has come to know what is encompassed within that subject. They possess something—the existence, form, and relationships of which is pleasing. And they have rewarding tools for learning more about the phenomena included in the discipline. They

become engrossed in, if not enamored of, that which they possess. The urge to pass it along, to transmit it to keep it alive, to share it, to enlighten others is compelling. The scholar or the indoctrinated apprentice can even imagine that it is nearly a perfect model for training the mind. Thus the subject comes to have adherents, supporters, loyal and fervent advocates who are insistent to show why their knowledge is something which every man should know. But there is not room and time for every subject. Some subjects must be left out; some must be relegated to minor positions; some which are admitted must never be allowed to get respectable; some must remain with little rhyme or reason for their retention. There can not help but be jealousies, petty tyrannies, and vested interests.

2. *Broad newer objectives are neglected.* In recent years we have come to believe that the teacher is a counselor and advisor. It is now, we are told, a duty to know and study children. The intimacy of our knowledge will not only aid us in dealing with the broader aspects of personality, it will also give insight into appreciation, understanding of the conditions which attend the learning situation, the normal expectations we may have, how we may plan more wisely and effectively, and lead and teach more tellingly and tactfully. The subject demands excessive focus on its content, and the very nature of the multiple-period day makes impossible thorough careful study of youth.

3. *Abstraction and logic prevent adaptation.* By far the greatest claimed weakness is the logic of the subject itself. Arranged in the order of simple to complex, from easy to difficult matters, it compels the teacher to pose one task of learning after another, one dependent upon and growing out of the precedent ones, often without respect to what goes on either in the out-of-school life of the child or in other subject study. Occasionally the content, the facts and skills may be needed or usable or the child may even visualize and contemplate their future use in something he really wants to do, but usually such is not the case. What is learned is regularly learned because it is time, in terms of the inevitable march to more involved matters in the subject's domain, to learn it. The subject dominates, not the needs, concerns, and problems of the child.

4. *Nonfunctionalism is an inherent weakness.* Related to the logical unity of subjects is the problem of the isolation of their specific content items from the whole nature of the situations in which the items must come to function. This is the weakness so vigorously protested by those interested in transfer. The argument is that no experience in life is an arithmetic experience or a fraction experience, or a

common denominator experience alone. It is, rather, an exceedingly involved transaction in which many items of subject matter allocated to diverse disciplines are present and are being used by the learner in a coordinated, organized, and related way. Antecedent knowledge of, familiarity with, exposure to one item elsewhere and in relation only to other items of its own kind seem not to help the use and application of that item in the novel situation composed of items and conditions which are parts of other subjects and disciplines.

The very nature of a subject prevents each item from being total-problem oriented, for the subject is a distillation of units related to each other. Rather the item has to be approached as an entity itself in a long progression of specifics which have meaning in the perspective of the scholar. In time the interlocking of the parts and the logic of "next item" can make sense, but insight derives from the progression of elements in the subject, not from the fit of the element in the solution of some present natural problem. The item in a sense has been wrenched by the subject specialist from natural everyday problems and experiences and arranged in a kind of museum showcase to reveal all its properties.

5. *Time limits prevent effective learning.* Separated and isolated as the content is then, the approach to it may or may not be completely mechanical, but it inevitably must be by installments. The forty-to-fifty-minute period, seemingly inevitable with the subject curriculum, permits only a limited focus and emphasis. When the bell rings, the pupil must gather up both his books and thoughts, nearly literally tie them both off and put them out of sight and out of mind in order to collect his resources and level his attention upon a radically different objective and content. The requirement is an active and planned dismissal of his recent exposure; forgetting is actually at a premium.

6. *New content is not easily added.* Subjects, of course, like almost everything else are constantly growing and developing. The scholars add and subtract (very little apparently). The "school" subjects, with more flexible dimensions in recent years, have been expanded constantly to include new topics and content. Doubtless this has been more true of those subjects that are really less like subjects; such as, English (the language arts) and social studies (citizenship education) which are probably better called "broad fields" or areas since actually they encompass or include a number of subjects with more precise and descriptive titles like spelling, grammar, poetry, economics, anthropology, and government.

Yet is is argued that, despite their adaptability, the older "purer" subjects and the newer synthetic subjects are still restrictive and do not permit the rapid and easy addition of new content and experience, nor facilitate handling by the school of a wide range of issues and concerns properly within their scope. Concentrated on intellectual development and dependent on, if not restricted to, limited methods, it is said the subject design can not provide adequately the broad social development opportunity, nor encompass appropriately those experiences necessary to full personality development.

7. *Flexible and imaginative teaching is difficult if not impossible.* The final limitation is one which does not and obviously should not set well with teachers. This is the idea that the subject design itself spawns and nurtures, if not demands, a variety of teacher behaviors that are inconsistent with best teaching effort. Among these are meaningless drill, an uninspiring recitation, uniformity of instruction (telling), common group listening with consequent waste of time by the more able, limited and narrow minimum standards or attainment, persistent resort to marks and threats to secure application to material without meaning and of doubtful use.

As teachers and supporters of a subject and of a subject design, we may bristle at this budget of errors and insist that none of these practices need or must be and that poor teachers would resort to these techniques no matter what the design. It might be graciously admitted that this indeed may be so, but contrarily it can be argued that after fifty years of tinkering with the improvement of teaching the subjects, almost all abuses like these unfortunately are still very widely practiced.

Excellent Supports for the Subject Framework

The answer for many is that these faults indeed are not inherent and that already we have made very great progress in eliminating poor teaching of subjects. Teachers now often group students within the classroom; many of our texts contain suggested assignments and exercises of varying levels of difficulty; courses of study have been set up on unit bases, and drill and recitation have been all but eliminated; teachers study their students through the plentiful records of the guidance office; pupil-teacher cooperation determines pace, review, and coverage.

1. *The subjects are the most convenient and appropriate means to transmit the heritage.* Over the years the scholars have been able to implant in subjects the knowledge and skill which the race has acquired. In the most common subjects rests what a man needs to carry on his

daily existence. The school subjects encompass at least most of what is worth a child's knowing, and over the years they have been systematically organized from the simple to the complex, from the immediate to the remote, from the concrete to the abstract. In the hands of teachers they have been set up so as to move toward depth and complexity at a rate consistent with the growth of children.

The subjects therefore are efficient tools. They are set up sequentially; a child learns first what he needs in order to learn what comes next. Time is saved and pupil and teacher can be guided to attend carefully at points at which reiterated experience has shown learning will take place most easily.

2. *Subject framework is simple and visible.* Probably the most appealing attribute of the subjects' design is that it is neat. Specific items to be taught can be identified. Those responsible can easily manage the procedures required to determine the kind and degrees of attainment. The teacher is seldom at a loss to know what specifics to use in making up an examination.

This element of certainty frees the teacher to plan more effectively, and to study pupil problems of learning more carefully and extensively. Familiar with information and practiced in the application of particular skills, he is able to spend more time on diagnosis and enrichment.

When a student comes from another school or system, the exposures he has had can be fairly easily recognized, and some idea of what he has learned can be gained. Transfer is thus made easy; the student can adjust fairly quickly and easily; the teacher can locate a point and place of progress and development with some appreciable accuracy so as to promote and direct the next learning activities.

3. *Everybody knows and most people support this arrangement.* There are simply very many practical reasons for maintaining the subject design for the total program. The public at large are familiar with the basic subjects; they seem to feel they know what is being taught their children, and they are comfortable with the school in which specialists present knowledge to children.

The actual difficulty of managing any other design serves easily as a second reason for doubt. We teachers who are subject-matter specialists are reasonably confident of what we know. We have some assurance of what we can obtain in the way of behavioral change, and we have no urge to be cast adrift without a well-organized content to teach.

Materials and resources abound for the teaching of the subjects. Suggestions for projects, activities, and learning tasks have been refined and tediously worked through. They are easily accessible, and they have in many cases proved to be useful and adequate. The investment of communities in these resources is extensive, not to speak of the investment of each teacher (at least in the secondary schools) in years of specialized study.

4. *Subjects are responsive to alteration.* We have already mentioned the capacity of a school subject for expanding and developing. The metamorphosis of history into social studies and English into language arts and the emergence of general science clearly reveal the fluidity of school subject dimensions. The present redefinition of mathematics courses to relate geometry and algebra more closely in the traditional Grade 10 offering, the telescoping of mechanics in physics to permit the inclusion of electronics, the addition of sections on radiation and on the wonder drugs to biology widely illustrate maneuverability in the subject design. If that is not enough, we have examples of the radical unit organization of literature courses around human problems, and the recasting of history into spirited portrayals and studies of man's various struggles. We can start from the present problems or present heroes and work back to conditions of the dim past, or we can stay with present problems and accumulate the data significant to their solution. We can add content, activities, new objectives, and vivid experiences to the traditional subject.

5. *Subjects can emerge.* Even if completely convincing about the flexibility of purer subjects, few supporters of "subject-matter-in-advance" would argue for the retention of old labels. For the most part, "subject" people feel that elaboration and development of the traditional subjects into broader subjects or broad fields, or new categorization of information with modern labels is natural. In other words, to put a back dormer on a ranch house is sensible, and you can still call it a ranch house. What difference? The same idea is true with the broad fields. They are still a subject design: there is subject matter, content identified in advance, chosen through scholarly deliberation and judgment, considered significant both to the build-up of knowledge and to the cumulation of the wherewithal and skill to solve problems of living.

The broad fields do represent a nice compromise in design. Into a course like Science I there can be added a varied selection of content appropriate to topics like resources and conservation, energy and its application, and weather. In this way the year is not broken up into many parts for assignment to particular subjects.

Further, more content of pertinent use to children can be employed. The greater emphasis on practical problems also serves to relate knowledge more meaningfully.

6. *Pupils like to study subjects.* Often overlooked but significant in constructing programs are the wishes of those who must stand the exposure. For pupils the subject design does have many advantages, and in the interests of peace and harmony as well as good morale in the learning situation it would not be wise to ignore the reactions of students. Despite teacher modesty or denial, youth look to their teachers for answers. The thrill of going to junior high school in large part lies in the opportunity to listen to someone knowledgeable. Pupils at any level are not afraid or even reluctant to have a teacher turn their question back upon them or to be invited to investigate and search out an explanation alone or with others. At the same time, they come soon to appreciate the advantages of wise counsel and the potential value in the bank of human knowledge represented by the educated and experienced adult. The mature person who refuses to set up an arrangement for transmitting directly significant items of knowledge and skill he possesses can soon lose face.

Pupils like to shift gears, to change their focus from one subject or topic to another. They tire reasonably soon, in the junior high particularly, even after exposure to something they "love." When restlessness, disinterest, inattention, and unruliness set in, a new subject recaptures their application and energy.

CONTROLLED PROBLEM FRAMEWORK

For those who can not support the subject framework, the curriculum designers have sought to provide a structure that will be "subject-less" yet have scope, sequence, and content. Much has been written about this alternative, and a number of fairly detailed plans have been developed to provide direction. This is not the place to examine the relationship of change to the volume of writing nor to attempt to pass on the amount of actual departure. It is proper, though, in fact necessary, to say that teachers, who as curriculum makers are giving consideration to the framework for the curriculum, should be cautioned that the *general plans referred to here have as yet had but limited tryout in our public schools.* The arguments here and elsewhere are vigorous but change has been limited.

Nonsubject Structure Hard to Visualize

It is not easy for most of us to grasp what would replace the subjects. We are too familiar with the subjects, too close to our own past experience to "see" something new. Unfortunately we can not here devote many pages to the possibilities and variations for a nonsubject-divided, general education program. Adequate discussions and descriptive treatment have been provided by Smith, Stanley, and Shores,[3] by Saylor and Alexander,[4] and by Leonard.[5]

Mainly we know the idea is to devote the entire elementary day, the greatest portion of the junior high school day, and decreasing amounts of the senior high school day to the pursuit of a general education which includes (1) coverage of the traditional fundamental skills, (2) consideration of various aspects of emotional, social, and personal development, (3) acquisition of information about and insight into the pertinent concerns of society facing them as a group, and of the individual in that society as he faces them independently and as a group member, and (4) growth in the power to make choices and to promote values consistent with emerging ideas of what is democratic.

Probably the most widely known systematic analysis of the "problems" framework was made for the curriculum program in Virginia. The proposal was to set up experiences for children around issues, concerns, or problems that grow from the attempt of the American people to live a democratic existence more effectively. The over-all curriculum structure was tightly planned and organized. The tasks which society and learners in that society face were specified, in greater or lesser amount, and allocated to "levels" in terms of skills, knowledge, and appreciations useful and learnable at that time. Through such allocation, the sequence of things to be learned was controlled, and through distribution of problems or units adequate scope was guaranteed.

The original Caswell analysis takes up several lengthy volumes, as do the proposals of relatively similar kind prepared for several states and a number of cities. Widely referred to as an example is the format developed in Santa Barbara city and county schools (see pages 148–150).

Much confusion has arisen out of the variety of units suggested for developing the knowledge, skill, attitudes and values sought in these categories of personal social living. Units suggested in some local districts have been extremely personal and based on emergent and immediate, if not transient, interests, while elsewhere there has been pref-

---

[3] Smith, Stanley, and Shores, *op. cit.*

[4] J. Galen Saylor and William Alexander, *Curriculum Planning,* Rinehart, 1954.

[5] J. Paul Leonard, *Developing the Secondary School Curriculum,* Rinehart, 1956.

DEFINING THE SCOPE AND SEQUENCE OF THE CURRICULUM

The needs of the society that maintains a school determine the total range of experiences that children should have under the guidance of the school. The needs of growing children dictate the choice of the day-by-day experiences in this range.

To foster an adequate program of rich day-by-day living under the guidance of the school, the school must provide opportunities for three areas of educational experiences. These are: (1) opportunities for experiences that will develop social understanding and sensitivity to social needs; (2) opportunities for recreational, aesthetic, and creative expression; and (3) opportunities to develop special abilities and provide for individual needs. The scope of the curriculum must be defined differently within each area.

The following chart presents a possible organization of the day's program of schoolroom living when thought of as outlined here:

PROGRAM OF SCHOOLROOM LIVING

	GRADES 1-3
Integrated Program	An integrated program built around activities that children of this age are interested in doing. Problems of group living, needed skills of reading, writing, oral and written communication, number manipulations and concepts grow out of these activities and when acquired further the activities. Opportunities for recreational and aesthetic experiences also develop from the developing activities. These include opportunities for playing games and sports, making and enjoying art objects, singing and playing music, and reading and writing for fun.

Approximate Amount of Time	GRADES 4–6 7–9 10–14	
One-half of Day	Solving problems that arise in the community living of the school, as well as work on leads to the persistent environmental and social problems in the community. Leads are developed (1) to problems of health and science with their social implications, and (2) to problems of social science. A pupil group draws on all sources of information and suggestions from first and secondhand experiences that will help solve the problem or attain the purpose. In addition to science and social science problems, in grades 7–12 this core program includes the oral and written communication required of all pupils and much of the literature, and in grades 10–14 it may include all the skills in English required of all pupils.	
One-fourth of Day	Skill aspects of reading, writing, spelling, oral and written communication, number manipulations and concepts, that need special attention for mastery for effective use in units of work and in life outside the school.	Courses, clubs, and sports to provide for special interests and needs not required of all pupils, but some of these may be required in certain curricula set up for special needs such as college preparatory, vocational or general education.
One-fourth of Day	Opportunities for group and individual recreational, aesthetic, and creative experiences, including playing games and sports, making and enjoying art objects, singing and playing music, reading and writing for fun, in addition to opportunities for such experiences in the units of work in the core program.	

Kansas State Education Department, *The Kansas Program for the Improvement of Instruction,* Bulletin No. 6, 1939, p. 14.

erence for units and problem areas having student interest potential but clearly related to broad societal needs. Thus, some critics are inclined to observe that unit lists look like little more than a hodgepodge.

Actually, the scholarly casting of a problem framework, without seemingly innumerable elections and possibilities, without seemingly too much and too loose discussion of how teachers and pupils might or might not take up this or that aspect, without an exasperating "open-endedness," has yet to be made. A highly regarded Wisconsin bulletin, reproduced in Illinois, set the stage for the junior high school yet it covers only the problems a committee thought to identify. It does not represent the problems a highly qualified group of social analysts and psychologists would specify. This is not to say such a group would necessarily see any more situations than we confront as groups and individuals or see them any more clearly; it is merely to emphasize that a societally responsible problem framework is and ought to be difficult to make.

Now what are the claimed advantages of such a framework? Why should a teacher encourage the principal or the woman across the bridge table to believe the commonly used subject framework should be replaced with a nonsubject problem structure?

Numerous Advantages of the Controlled Problem Framework

1. *The teacher is granted freedom.* The major freedom in the problems approach is that no particular content is specified in advance. Surely much is implied, and securing control over many a problem clearly involves certain knowledge and skill. Yet the teacher is free to decide with pupils what is needed from a variety of sources and disciplines. From an extensive resource unit[6] the teacher can plan what to undertake, how long to spend, whom to engage, when to concentrate. The bell does not interfere with projects, and the relief and pacing desired can be easily adjusted to changing interests and fatigue.

The prerogative to make and to guide substantial choices permits the teacher to come into his own as a professional too. It relieves him of the compulsion to be a dispenser of someone else's knowledge and allows him to work directly with pupils as a counselor and a resource. He can relate himself thus more effectively to pupils and facilitate their growth into independent beings.

Further, the teacher is thrust upon his own resources and imagination to help locate information and to develop skills with which at times he is unfamiliar.

[6] See Chapter 8.

SCOPE

Developing and conserving personal resources
Developing and conserving other than personal resources
Producing, distributing, and consuming goods and services
Communicating
Transporting
Recreating and playing
Expressing and satisfying spiritual and aesthetic needs
Organizing and governing

SEQUENCE

First Year (Kindergarten)	Second Year (Grade I)	Third Year (Grade II)	Fourth Year (Grade III)
Growth in effective living through *self-adjustment within the immediate* environment.		Growth in effective living through *adjusting to the community.*	Growth in effective living by further adjusting to the community through the development of insights into the manner in which the *natural and controlled environment* is contributing to life *in our community.*

Fifth Year (Grade IV)	Sixth Year (Grade V)	Seventh Year (Grade VI)
Growth in effective living by further adjusting to the community through developing insights into the manner in which the *present culture-groups* are adjusting to life *in our community.*	Growth in effective living through developing insights into the manner in which *present as compared with former culture groups* carry on the basic functions of human living in *Santa Barbara* and *California.*	Growth in effective living through problem-centered experiences directed toward understanding how *modern technics* are being utilized in carrying out the basic functions of human living in the *United States.*

Eighth Year (Grade VII)	Ninth Year (Grade VIII)	Tenth Year (Grade IX)
Growth in effective living through problem-centered experiences directed toward understanding the interdependence of individuals in our school, our community, the regions of our nation, and in the countries of our American neighbors.	Growth in effective living through problem-centered experiences directed toward understanding how man's courage, knowledge, discoveries, and inventions have affected his way of living.	Growth in effective living through problem-centered experiences directed toward understanding and appreciating the individual's privileges and responsibilities as an American citizen.

Eleventh Year (Grade X)	Twelfth Year (Grade XI)	Thirteenth Year On (Grades XII and On)
Growth in effective living through problem-centered experiences directed toward happy, effective, personal, spiritual, social, recreational, and vocational living in the home, school, and community.	Growth in effective living through problem-centered experiences directed toward achieving the highest possible quality of experiences through striving for social, political, and economic democracy in local, state, and national setting and for peace and cooperation on the international scene.	

Santa Barbara City Schools, *Developmental Curriculum,* Board of Education, 1941, pp. 22–24.

SCOPE

Developing and conserving human resources
Developing, conserving, and intelligently utilizing nonhuman resources
Producing, distributing, and consuming goods and services
Communicating
Transporting
Recreating and playing
Expressing and satisfying spiritual and aesthetic needs
Organizing and governing
Providing for education

SEQUENCE

Kindergarten Grades 1, 2, 3	Grades 4, 5	Grades 6, 7, 8
Guiding the growth of children toward living more effectively in their immediate and expanding environment (home, school, neighborhood and community) through participation in activities involved in carrying out the basic functions of human living.	Guiding the growth of children toward living more effectively in a changing world and understanding it through investigating man's relationship to his physical environment, comparing and contrasting our increasing control of the environment with the simpler adjustment techniques utilized by people of simpler cultures.	Guiding the growth of children toward gaining increasing effectiveness in carrying out the basic functions of human living through developing the ability and desire to react to the total environment according to a pattern which is based upon (1) an adequate understanding and appreciation of scientific principles and methods involved; (2) an understanding of the resulting increased possibilities of control, and (3) an understanding of resulting rapidity of change.
Integrating Theme for Grades 9, 10	Integrating Theme for Grades 11, 12	Integrating Theme for Grades 13, 14
Planning with respect to educational, vocational, personal, and social goals and gaining in understanding of the relationship between the problems of the individual and those of the school, community, state, and nation.	Developing in understanding of the ways man has met and is meeting his major problems with emphasis upon the solutions now proposed and upon the historical foundations of present problems.	Developing in understanding of democratic ideals and their implications for social organizations.

Santa Barbara County, *Curriculum Guide for Teachers in Secondary Schools,* Board of Education, 1941, pp. 38–39.

SUGGESTED PROBLEMS OR UNITS FOR
SANTA BARBARA PROGRAM

Ninth Grade	Preventing Accidents, Planning for My Education, Making Our Water Supply Serve Human Needs, Planning My Vocation, Becoming Acquainted with Our School, Securing Mental and Physical Health
Tenth Grade	Using Leisure Time Wisely, How Can We Better House the Nation, Influencing Public Opinion, Improving Relations with Latin America, Promoting International Understanding, Spending Your Money Wisely, Conserving Our National Resources, Proving for National Defense, Appreciating the Contributions of Other Cultures
Eleventh Grade	Agencies of Mass Communication, Building a Happy Home Life, Regional Planning for the Use of Our Resources, Securing Justice, Making Machines Serve Mankind, Protecting Civil Liberties, Keeping the Government Responsible to the People
Twelfth Grade	Improving Our Relations with Latin America, Preventing Crime, Building a Happy Home Life, Providing Public Education, Protecting Civil Liberties, Improving Relationships Between Racial and Cultural Groups, Keeping the Government Responsible to the People, Finding the Right Job.

Santa Barbara County, *Curriculum Guide for Teachers in Secondary Schools,*
Board of Education, 1941, pp. 41–42.

2. *Guidance is really possible.* In a problems-organized general education the responsibility to know the pupil well, to diagnose in him a variety of needs, and to guide and finally lead him to maturity is one of the keystones. The teacher has time enough to see the pupil in many situations and to help him relate one part of experience to another. Reduction in numbers allows intensive examination of personnel records; the flexibility of the time arrangement facilitates individual conferences; reports can be more extensive and searching, and planned redirection and therapy can be applied with regularity and consistency. The teacher is not at his wit's end to locate pupils, and he is not over-

SUGGESTED LEADS TO UNITS OF WORK FOR THE CORE
PROGRAM IN GRADES 7 TO 9 IN KANSAS

What shall I do in traffic accidents?

What do your gardens and fields wash?

How is coal mined?

Why shouldn't I drink beer and smoke cigarettes?

Can dust storms be prevented?

What personal hygiene shall I practice?

How can I prevent accidents in the home?

How can I help keep my school and town clean?

Why can't I thumb a ride?

How shall I spend my money?

How do machines serve me and my family?

How does money help us to trade?

Why does industry depend upon land?

How is water power developed?

How can I learn to dress neatly and attractively?

How can we entertain our guests?

How are my town and country governed?

How do state and national laws affect my living?

Where shall I play?

How does my community provide opportunities for music, art, literature, drama, and museums at public expense?

Who pays for my education?

How do trains, trucks, airplanes, and ships affect the clothes I wear,
the food I eat, etc.?

Kansas State Education Department, *The Kansas Program for the Improvement of
Instruction*, Bulletin No. 6, 1939, pp. 19–20.

loaded with papers and the details needed for the management of many
people.

3. *Extraneous subject matter can be dropped easily.*   Perhaps
more optimistic than justified is the assertion that if a group of pupils
attends to acquiring knowledge and skill appropriate to helpful action
in solving social problems, the pupils will learn only what is useful,
practical, and functional. Yet the protagonists of problems are enthusiastic in their belief that through appropriate activities, selected
cooperatively, there will be less learning for the sake of learning alone.

4. *Broader and more fundamental goals are pursued.*   Pursuit of
facts and information clearly stands out as the purpose of subjects
study. Although teachers often list other objectives for their courses, it

is seldom that an intensive evaluation reveals them working very hard on anything but names, dates, classifications, formulas, explanation of phenomena, and the like. On the other hand, dependence upon the unit approach, it is asserted, encourages if not guarantees the development of socially interactive habits and skills. It increases decision-making opportunity and promotes deliberative selection. It builds resourcefulness and leads to competence in research and investigation. Out of cooperativeness and reliance upon group planning come ability and enthusiasm to use the method of intelligence. There is a premium on independence and creativity.

5. *Pupils are more actively engaged.* "You do it well, but we do it better" might be appropriately used in regard to this point. An inherent part of the problems approach is the involvement of pupils in determining goals, deciding on activities, managing the use of resources, and going through the process of reflecting on and evaluating progress toward anticipated outcomes. Inasmuch as the emphasis is on dealing with problems of immediate concern to society's groups, pupils are constantly motivated to seek help, novel information, and methods of problem resolution from many places.

Not all working on the same tasks, they are regularly considering some means of presentation and transmission of their information, plans, and conclusions. They are more likely to write, to paint, to draw and sketch, to perform and dramatize, or to make recordings. They seldom need wait for the teacher to be told what to do, how much time to spend, or when to terminate.

6. *Learning is natural and unforced.* It is further argued that when pupils are planning together with teachers, when they are diagnosing their own needs, when they are seeking answers to personal questions, they are driven by highly estimable purposes. They are assumed to be genuinely seeking information to clarify a view, to build a case, or to reveal a position. They are improving speech and writing to communicate something they want to say more effectively. Poems are read to stimulate sensitivity to or knowledge about their purpose—seldom just to be covered as an example of authorship.

7. *More modern teaching procedures are usable.* When longer periods of time are available, a group can plan projects, trips, investigations, surveys, and research that may take them out of the classroom and even away from the school for substantial periods of time. Arrangements are more easily made for visitors and resource personnel who may be called on to help. Student demonstrations and exhibits are easier to manage. Groups are freer to deliberate and plan, to expand

ideas and report. The library and the community become much more extensively used for information.

Arguments Opposed to the Controlled Problems Framework

Both the more conservative and the more radical have objected to the controlled problems structure. For the confirmed subject advocate, the problems proposal is on the one hand much ado about nothing—an attempt to make molehills into mountains—and on the other quite an irresponsible invitation in the face of present conditions and of any forseeable future. The present most widely expressed objections are stated in the five points which follow.

1. *Teachers are inadequate to do this properly.* Although there are now a number of universities training teachers for a problems framework, it is true that teachers who consider themselves qualified are extremely few. A very large number eschew any interest. Over 90 percent of undergraduates and graduates in selected secondary training institutions[7] where general curriculum courses are offered respond, "This is for the birds. How could anybody possess so replete a collection of resources to presume to be really competent and useful?" they ask.

Teaching this way presents difficulties that appear to be overwhelming. Students will have less and less common knowledge. Despite vigilance in diagnosis and occasional direct group teaching of specific skills, immense amounts of teacher time will be devoted to instrumental teaching when errors and misunderstandings appear. The need for individualized teaching, regardless of longer hours, will grow greater than the teacher can manage.

However, more important than this is that few teachers want to be party to the transmission of inaccurate information, partial insight, and confused notions. To many, even this modification of the subjects framework, supported by well-organized and rich resource units, puts the teacher in the impossible situation of having to know everything.

2. *It does unnecessary violence to good servants.* Language arts and social studies teachers can look at the problem lists and come away dismayed. First, most of the suggested units closely parallel liberal social studies program offerings. Second, the neglect of topics or problems associated with the language arts is pronounced. It is clear also that arithmetic is slighted and science is bootlegged in as some kind of a

---

[7] Survey conducted by the authors in four training institutions.

distant cousin of problems of social evaluation. Many of the problems are actually old subject-matter units turned around into unconnected participial phrases, like "becoming aware of the current scene," "understanding and appreciating the American heritage," and "exploring the problems of living in a family"; or turned into questions such as, "How can we learn about us?" "Why is education important?" "How shall we get along best in school?"

Many of the units suggested for consideration, problems presently included in published material for "experimental" schools, look just like the titles of chapters from up-to-date texts. In fact, many resource units differ only in that they include more activities and less general presentation and discussive material.

3. *The cart is before the horse.* Involvement of adolescents and even of children in the examination of major social issues long before they can actually do anything about these and before their opinion and judgment makes any difference seems nearly foolhardy to many. All that eventuates, they feel, is more a youthful exuberance than a sense of reality about what is possible. A few flash-in-the-pan changes in communities have been reported, but in the main we can not expect school groups to run communities and states and the idea that students should get involved in action stages before they know what to do appears unnecessary if not unwise.

4. *Problems can be contrivances too.* Although it is possible for there to be flexible units with great teacher freedom allowed, it goes without saying that instructional procedures may be rigid too. The content considered necessary to problem understanding and solution can be ordained in advance; and the projects assigned and undertaken can as well be done for the purpose of obtaining marks and teacher approvals. When one looks over the subquestions listed under a problem area like "How to Live More Effectively as a Family," it is obvious that an activity entitled "Investigation of Present Conflicts Between Home Standards and Community Standards" may prove to be quite a deadhead for a large percentage of pupils.

Despite lengthy and careful study of adolescents—their needs and their interests—and despite brilliant analyses of persistent problems of living, it must be admitted that few children are sensitive to the same problem or concerned about it at the same time. Keeping healthy, which may be rationalized into some project like "knowing what communicable diseases children often contract," actually can be as abstract as learning that the circumference of a circle can be obtained by using a formula involving a constant and the diameter.

5. *Responsible authorities have no adequate way of checking progress.* When the matrix of problems has been determined, the freedom which the teacher is afforded in selecting projects, activities, and content will make it extremely difficult and probably inconsistent to develop examinations to provide any evidence of comparable accomplishment. The breadth of items considered and learned will be so great that no examination will be able to provide fair coverage. Those in charge of the schools will not know what crucial and critical information is being acquired.

UNRESTRICTED FRAMEWORK

The idea that a teacher should freely take a group of pupils and move with them from one interest to another, from one concern to a subsequent one, from limited to complex activities, from one level of maturity to the next has actually had few sponsors. What it has lacked in number, it has, however, made up for in vigor and enthusiasm. The consequence is that many educators and a number of citizens are aware that there has been proposed an "experience" curriculum which pupils and teachers with all those who affect them and whom they affect, immediately and indirectly, should plan together, in advance when necessary, and in process as befits the situation.

Contentious to put it mildly, this approach to curriculum framework (nearly no framework at all, except teacher, time, and pupils) has precipitated violent argument as well as bewildered shaking of heads. Much of the argument doubtless arises out of misunderstanding and misinterpretation, but even many of those who understand have grave misgivings and serious reservations.

We can not hope to present a detailed or even a reasonably complete "recap" of this frontier position. It is obvious the combined version offered here can not help but leave tremendous gaps. Thus to be recommended is a complete reading of two books by L. Thomas Hopkins[8] which present this concept of curriculum designing. Smith, Stanley, and Shores[9] have a shorter analysis covering much of the general picture of the idea. In the revised edition of a volume by Stratemeyer *et al.*[10] two sections deal with how a teacher can work with such a free arrangement.

[8] L. Thomas Hopkins, *Interaction: The Democratic Process,* Heath, 1941; and Hopkins, *The Emerging Self,* Harper, 1954.

[9] Smith, Stanley, and Shores, *op. cit.,* chaps. 12, 13.

[10] Florence Stratemeyer *et al., Developing a Curriculum for Modern Living,* Bureau of Publications, Teachers College, 1957.

Essentially the no-design curriculum delegates to the teacher and his group the responsibility for studying themselves, locating their deficiencies, determining the goals on which to work, and cooperatively deciding how to use available resources in books, teachers, and other adults to acquire knowledge and skill. Free to select from many proposals, the group can and should consider the proposals of others, the criticisms of elders, the problems of the larger social group as well as the incipient needs of members. It has to check progress against the goals of others, elders, as well as against its own. As the individuals see their own needs and those of the group emerging from their examination of purpose and progress, they will identify new areas for study, new outcomes to pursue and new activities to which to devote time.

No formal written scheme is contemplated for such an emerging developing experience. The group members live daily within a culture, conducting themselves independently and together in all ways common to human behavior. They acquire, and operate on, a pattern of values; they use the cultural heritage in search of aesthetic satisfaction; they call upon language to tell and to ask. Their constant orientation is "Is this the best level of living possible and attainable for us? How can we develop greater control over our environment immediate and remote? How can we enhance ourselves as humans?"

The group uses as method an ever improving cooperative, democratic, and interactive effort. Needs which can be identified as personal constitute the focal points for study, examination, and instruction. If all can and want to work on the same thing, so much the better. If an individual cannot share or support group concerns yet himself has legitimate goals, he can easily be cared for. The persisting isolate, however, would be subject to diagnosis and reasonable therapy to help him become the group member he must become in our society.

Thus, there is no prescribed coverage except living itself, and no predetermined sequence of what to be concerned about and what to learn. Movement from one experience to another more complex or difficult is a product rather of maturation itself. Increased alertness, greater sensitivity, wider exposure, additional power to observe, to wonder, and to ask, advancing capacity to notice, to respond, and to act will expose new skills, generalizations, facts of a useful kind which will then be sought and taught.

The prototype for the "experience" curriculum or framework is the life of a preschool child. Here we have nearly a perfect example of living which daily brings new exposures and opportunity, new demands and needs. Getting up the stairs involves skills and knowledge.

Successful management leads to know-how and to skill. It also leads to conscious and unconscious generalizations about other problems in climbing. Dressing, toileting, resolving play issues with neighbors' children, pushing a cart, eating, tieing up shoes, obtaining a lollipop, and so on, represent emergent impasses to be negotiated through reference to imagination and intelligence and through resort to resources possessed by others.

Similarly would the teacher relate himself to the *group* in the subject-less situations. With a group he would work through the total dimensions of their continuing experience together, exercising the prerogatives and the privileges of parent-advisor, suggesting, stimulating, encouraging, and supporting. In other words, he would not abdicate nor absent himself. Obviously as the most mature and the officially delegated societal agent in the situation he would neither encourage nor permit his younger colleagues in the search for maturity and self-enhancement to indulge in useless whims, irresponsible transient diversions, or persisting negative actions. Rather, as the maturer participant, he would seek constantly to open new doors, to stir up higher level interests, to develop more legitimate purposes.

This would mean for the teacher immense responsibility to guide toward even more responsible choosing and toward even more exacting criteria; but it would also mean avoidance of domination, compulsion, compromise and subterfuge. It would entail operation at a risk level where violation of freedom of choice is permissible only in the face of the destruction of the process of positive growth itself. For example, with children one can, and doubtless should, permit experimentation in climbing the stairs but hardly encourage practice in climbing high-tension wire poles.

There is thus no way of telling exactly what pupils would cover or what they would know as a result of their planning with a teacher at any one grade level. They would know what they needed to possess to *do* what they had found useful to enhance and develop themselves. They would work on "how" to acquire knowledge and skill, and they would build in their information and skills as a part of their own pursuit.

Vigorous Objections to the Unrestricted Framework

Needless to say, there are violent opponents. There are also some sympathetic critics. The most common reaction is consternation and amazement. How could rational people even contemplate the possibility of turning the fate of the public school's general education effort over to the uncertain, ill-equipped, fumbling teacher next door! Isn't it bad enough that our elementary teachers have so little knowledge about the mysteries of simple science that they avoid it, that we have had to hire art, music, physical education, and recently, even reading specialists to support them, and that in desperation we are on the threshold of introducing the platoon system again in the lower school? How could one then be fantastic enough to think that in the junior high school and in the senior high school an ordinary human would be competent to advise on a myriad of problems calling for knowledge from almost all the great disciplines? Where the critics are disturbed by the kind of teacher competence required for the controlled problems plan, they are nearly speechless in their response to an "experience" curriculum proposal. There are other reasons for objection.

1. *Much that is important will be neglected.* People who possess highly valued facts and skills are ever apprehensive that what they know will not be transmitted to others. As has been pointed out, what a man can do with what he knows often means little to the possessor. On the other hand, we do have a cultural heritage. Common knowledge holds us together, makes us comfortable in each other's presence. Responsible adults in a culture ought to know what they believe in and what they want their offspring to be familiar and equipped with. The only practical way to insure this is through delegation of responsibility to authorized people who can make decisions in manageable situations. Expectation should be that such delegates will identify what is to be covered.

2. *Management of the schools will be impossible.* Custody of the public school enterprise must in the end be vested in some one. The taxpayer entrusts his children to the schools confident that highly qualified leaders will be in charge. He spends his money in the belief that he is hiring personnel who are responsible and who will have command of the situation; and, rightly, he is entitled to expect that there will be wise and efficient management and that at any time, as stockholder, he should be able to get a full and accurate accounting.

With the experience curriculum neither of these expectancies can be approximated, far less guaranteed. Except in very broad and happy terms, what a class or group or a school or school system is up to will not be known. Remote patrons and leaders will have no idea what a teacher may be doing. Further, to assess his products in any accurate and comparable way will be impossible.

The school program will be a veritable uncoordinated jumble. A child who must move from one community to another will have virtually no chance of having had common exposure. With textbooks used throughout the country and fairly uniform in their grade coverage, the transfer problem even now presents innumerable difficulties. Imagine the panic in a child and the consternation in a teacher when it is discovered that the new registrant either has covered a unit about to be undertaken or has experienced nothing of what his new class has successfully accomplished.

3. *Thoroughness and perfection in the basic skills will be neglected.* Despite the persisting attack upon traditional teachers for resort to organized drill (very little of which is now meaningless), it is still true that accuracy and precision with a skill is gained from its use and evaluation of its performance. Granted that the way to true realization of the use and value of a skill or an item of knowledge is in the discovery of its appropriateness for the accomplishment of a legitimate goal of larger dimension, it still remains that realization and appreciation and single and limited exposure do not fix. Dependence upon a sometime or occasional future use or upon fairly periodic demand for building up sufficiency is not enough.

Systematization is necessary. Errors in any group are so numerous, so common, and so well known that common sense dictates we plan direct instruction, prepare exercises involving normal areas, and secure accuracy through concentrated study followed by subsequent correction and reteaching in novel situations. We can not afford to leave a teacher free to omit, to neglect, or to fail to pursue a proper level of efficiency at selected growth stages. A teacher should know what spelling skill, arithmetic knowledge, punctuation accuracy can and should be attained and should teach directly for those well-known goals. Otherwise left to instrumental and individual diagnosing, pupil and teacher will be able to establish no efficient order for special study.

4. *Resources, learning materials can never be adequate.* Perhaps the greatest difficulty now encountered by teachers is the differential reading ability of pupils who can not properly use the texts available. Some adaptations have been made and several texts covering much the same material but with different reading difficulty are now sometimes used. However, the restrictions are still painful and there seems no likelihood they will be appreciably eased. How could it then be anything less than inane to contemplate casting away the few bits of cork now available and to propose striking out on an ocean of problems with next to no resources at all. The supplementary materials in pamphlet, brochure, and leaflet form now available, in appropriate slang, amount to "peanuts." But beyond that, practically none of it is

carefully graded with respect to reading difficulty. If it is a sin to send a child to a textbook with too high a reading level, it is conscience-less to perpetrate on him material of literally unknown difficulty.

Whether we like it or not, schools are places where pupils learn from printed material. Some information can be derived from visits, observations, films, and lectures, but the storehouse of civilization now is in the written word. Very little has been prepared at appropriate reading level about many, many personal, local, or even remote prob-lems pupils identify as concerns. To anticipate pupils will find informa-tion, obtain data without frustration and discouragement, is to delude oneself with the fancy of a wild goose chase.

Another objection in connection with sources is that the school teacher is hired to teach. Expectation that everyone from the local milk-man to the president of the bank turn over his place of business and his time to being interviewed and to helping school pupils is patent ad-mission of inability to do the job assigned. The place for pupils is in school, not decorating store windows, peddling handbills on "why to vote," and interfering with adult responsibility to administer the laws in the community.

Further, the supposition that parents want or ought to engage with teachers and pupils in long hours of planning what they should study is hardly short of daydreaming. Children are sent to school to learn what teachers know; parents work long hours to secure the where-withal to support the teachers in their work. They can and they ob-viously will not be bothered with hours upon hours of curriculum planning.

5. *The burden upon the teacher will be excessive.* Allied with the reality that parents will not and can not exercise continuing judg-ment about what ought to be studied and learned, is the fact that the teacher would have no substantial guide outside his own prejudices and possessions. Thrusting the teacher into the role of mature guide, and legal arbiter, of what to attend to is both too great a social risk and too inhuman an assignment. We can depend on parents to nurse and nurture through five years, but we can not afford to expose ourselves to the mercies of a million or more selectors and planners in the highly complex and intricate business of getting our citizens ready to deal individually and as a group with the threatening world about them. We value some things more than we do others; we treasure certain parts of our heritage; we believe certain facts should be known. These can not be entrusted to decisions made by a teacher.

More than that, we can not expect the garden variety teacher, and there are many of them, to be a sufficient scholar, a sufficiently informed person, a brilliant enough analyst, a wise enough judge to provide or to secure the reflective surfaces through which students will identify the critical learnings for our time.

Support for the Unrestricted Framework Possible

1. *Pupils will acquire the most basic fundamentals for which our education exists.* Above all, we have our schools to free the minds of our children and our people. We want our graduates to be skilled in the making of critical decisions for themselves individually, for others, and for themselves as part of groups. Presently they are educated by a means completely opposed to the outcomes in behavior which are sought. The experience curriculum insures that the pupils will study themselves and their needs as well as those of the social group of which they are a part. Opportunity will be ever present for selecting among alternatives, for reflecting on and judging the worthwhileness, the moral justification, and the meaning of these choices. The highest level of cooperative interaction will be obtained. The participants will learn how to share, to contribute, to affect and improve, to criticize and appraise, to manage and direct, to review and revise. They will learn how to use and respect the resources of others.

Along with these, they will at the same time learn through meaningful use the facts and skills they need to carry on as citizens. Pupils will be equipped to think through their problems when they emerge, locate quickly and efficiently what they need, and function properly with what they have previously learned in genuine situations.

2. *Education will be self-explanatory and worthy of time and energy.* When a man has problems and wants solutions, he seldom denies himself the accompanying satisfaction of attainment of or control over what accomplishment requires. On the contrary, forced action to acquire unwanted or unvalued outcomes, as we have emphasized before, leaves bad taste and few traces. The power of the "experience" curriculum lies in its focus on felt needs.

The natural outcomes of purposeful study are higher retention, vivid revelation of the relationship of knowledge and skill to outcome, legitimate practice effect, and, more important, personal reward and satisfaction in the learning process. This is what builds up respect for guidance, confidence in teacher leadership, faith in promises, and in the long run respect for knowledge, retention of the student in school, and reduction in discipline problems. The teacher is not forced to lengthy, contrived explanations, nor is he impelled to rely upon cajolery and threats of failure. Rather his task becomes one of helping to define better, to reduce a large purpose to manageable proportions, and to diagnose a variety of shortcomings that could be remedied.

3. *It will extend and unify education effort.* Making present living in all its dimensions better is the goal of this unfettered design. What emerges as important in the lives of the group will serve as the starting point. The whole range of living effectively will become substance for appraisal and study.

Thus, having fun, enjoying oneself, finding relaxation do not need to be escapes from drudgery and self-denial. Neither does school have to be a place for one type of behavior, and home and community an excuse for another. Likewise, the future hardly needs to be divorced from the present and exist as some "out there" possibility.

The unstructured, unrestricted framework guarantees freedom to look at all of one's existence. Every dimension of the formal and informal resources can be used to provide facts, to mature sentiment, to extend appreciation, and to monitor the development of skills.

4. *It will recognize the personal dimension in education.* Long neglected in American education has been the very core of growth and behavioral change, the basic and evolving sentiments and perceptions of the child himself. The whole paraphernalia of education has been geared to what those in legal command desire.

Properly managed, the unrestricted framework reorients the program to its proper place and allows the struggling, pushing, probing efforts of youth to find acceptable expression. It accents exploration and initiative and respects the integrity of the organism to find its own direction and to build into itself the attributes to deal more successfully with subsequent experience. This is a creative education. The process of growth itself becomes the focus for the learner, and through his attempts, analyses, and evaluation he can break through the wall of dependent relationships and protective skills that keep development arrested.[11]

5. *It is consistent with what happens anyway.* The amazing thing about schooling is that those schooled always decide what they will learn. Many teachers are deluded by pupils who pass their tests and promptly forget all they have acquired to negotiate the examinations successfully. The world is full of the "educated" who proudly recall that they took some subject but do not remember a blessed thing about it and do not remember ever having used any of it. This then is

[11] A brilliant analysis of the way schools produce "arrested selves" is available in *The Emerging Self,* by L. Thomas Hopkins.

the great sham pupils for generations have perpetrated. From their studies they have always taken what they have needed to solve present problems, and well-defined and clearly envisioned future problems. A good number of dutiful trucklers have led themselves to believe they had future need only to discover they did not. Some have bemoaned their inevitable losses, but most of the dutiful have learned, forgotten, and let it go at that.

People, pupils, are constantly at work on their own problems. What they see as valuable and worthwhile to them they learn "for keeps." What they use constantly and normally they retain; what is excess baggage they shed as rapidly as self-protection permits or the ravages of time prescribe. Instead of hours of waste motion then, we should content ourselves wisely with the differences that will make a difference.

Selection of Alternatives

It is unlikely that the unrestricted framework will soon be widely accepted. With the re-emphasis on subjects, standards, and academic performance, the trend is actually the other way. It is clear that most teachers as well as most administrators, patrons, and pupils prefer organization around the traditional subjects. Therefore, for some time to come, the major work of teachers will remain that of improving the subject-organized curriculum. Yet each teacher should appreciate not only the reasons for but the possibilities of re-design. Development of the broad background and study of the techniques needed in the unrestricted framework will certainly not handicap a teacher, and thorough general preparation together with tryout of the skills and approaches in modified form will provide both for increased insight and for inclination to make adaptations in the subject organization.

Questions for Discussion

1. To some, it seems like turning back the clock to return to a general education program guided by a single teacher, with no subjects identified. In this day and age, with books and with many people with special knowledge, we would not be going ahead but back to days even before the one-room school. Is this not so?
2. Why do we need a specialist to teach the English, the useful scientific facts, the arithmetic we all as liberally educated humans ought to know and use properly anyway? Hasn't the subject curriculum vividly demonstrated its inherent fallacy by failing to produce in us just what it presumes to secure for our children and youth?

3. Some critics of the controlled problems framework see it as just a "gim-mick" to slide in the wanted content in a new guise. In other words, the problems selection group know what information, what skills they desire children to possess, what they want them to think and conjure up solutions about. Does it seem that way to you?
4. Could college professors ever really come to agree that subject study—for general education—in high school is not necessary, maybe even not ap-propriate? Why would they resist the idea?
5. It looks as if the unrestricted framework would make quite unnecessary special methods of teaching, except for those courses in the upper secondary school that would represent the first steps in a disciplinary approach? What do you think?
6. On what basis would it be possible to select pupils for college with an experience curriculum?

Selected Bibliography

Faunce, Roland, and Nelson Bossing, *Developing the Core Curriculum,* second ed., Prentice-Hall, 1958.

Featherstone, William, *A Functional Curriculum for Youth,* American Book, 1950.

Hopkins, L. Thomas, *Interaction: The Democratic Process,* Heath, 1941.

Hopkins, L. Thomas, *The Emerging Self,* Harper, 1954.

Lurry, Lucille, and Elsie Alberty, *Developing a High School Core Program,* Macmillan, 1957.

Smith, B. O., William Stanley, and J. Harlan Shores, *Fundamentals of Curriculum Development,* rev. ed., 1957.

Stratemeyer, Florence, *et al., Developing a Curriculum for Modern Living,* Bureau of Publications, Teachers College, 1957.

Wilson, Howard, *The Fusion of Social Studies in Junior High Schools,* Harvard University Press, 1933.

Wright, Grace, *Core Curriculum Development: Problems and Practices,* Bulletin 1952, no. 5, Government Printing Office, 1952.

INDIVIDUAL ACTION FOR BETTER EXPERIENCE

PART III.

INDIVIDUAL ACTION FOR
UNITED EMERGENCY

CHAPTER 7

....

Planning for Learning Experiences

We have said the real curriculum is not what is projected but what is experienced by students. Thus what is often called methodology for purposes of discussion is the most critical nexus in making the curriculum. This means that the teacher needs to be a tactician of the first order. In the preceding chapter we have drawn attention to the more general role of the teacher in concerning himself with the way in which the curriculum is designed and set up. We have argued that the teacher must be vigilant to lend his counsel in planning the broad and basic structure for the curriculum and that he must be critical of the arrangements made and permitted to secure the objectives agreed upon. But still the sharpest focus for the teacher must be on the more personal aspects of planning which are necessary for good tactical behavior in the classroom. From that planning more than anything else will come high-quality behavior in the classroom.

There are some who would avoid this responsibility and some who would hope that good and useful plans could always be devised elsewhere by others. But neither is possible. Each teacher must plan and he must plan for himself and for and with his group. No one else can really plan adequately for him. Others may aid but they can not substitute. This every seasoned teacher has come to know.

Even when a teacher plans carefully, however, he has to acknowledge that good plans remain theoretical until the moment of implementation. Many situations arise unexpectedly in the classroom and dealing with them calls for judgment and skill. No amount of planning can anticipate everything. Everyone recognizes that opportunities arise occasionally so rich with learning potential and so sufficiently manageable that teachers can move forward without much that is preplanned. But without plans most of the time, the entire process of directing learning usually becomes one of uncertainty and emergency and it leads to inefficiency. On the other hand, good planning reduces this uncertainty. It helps diminish teacher anxiety. It reduces confusion. It guarantees that needed materials will be on hand, and it gives greater assurance of efficient learner action.

We do not then deny the importance of instrumental tactics in teaching, of intuitive skill in the actual direction of learning activity, or of the capacity to seize upon golden learning opportunity. We know there are people who know what to do but are unable to do it and so make ineffective teachers. And we know that there are those who rely on luck with hardly a bow to forethought. But good teachers must be strategists as well as tacticians. They must not only be able to carry on brilliantly in face-to-face relationships and under the pressure of classroom action, they must also be able to formulate plans in such a way that educational policy is furthered and the purposes of education are realized.

DIMENSIONS OF PLANNING

We might call the more personal and immediate planning the teacher does with or for a class or group "tactical planning." The kind of decision-making on a whole program and organizational patterns for that program discussed in the last two chapters might so be thought of as policy and general strategic planning.

More personal planning or tactical planning, as we see it, has largely to do with courses of study, instructional units, and daily agenda-making. Often the first two involve group or committee activity and could possibly be called *local strategic* planning because they are advanced planning of rather lengthy periods of time with a variety of alternatives proposed. But not much is to be gained by splitting hairs at this point. The teacher's real "field of battle," so to speak, is the classroom or the class group requiring month-by-month and day-by-day decision-making and choice.

Whether the teacher is planning with others or "going it alone" in setting up his course of study or daily activities there are some basic tasks to which he needs to attend. Good experience can seldom be provided for pupils until some consideration has been given the following.

Goals and Objectives

Whenever we make arrangements to go somewhere we obviously need to know where we are going. There are those who from time to time start out without a destination and are content just to wander, hoping that what happens may be stimulating and satisfying. Happily we do not find too many of them; but more often than should be the case there are pupils in school who are hard at work on tasks the purposes of which are extremely vague to them. Some of this occurs because they have never been informed. Some occurs because pupils rather regularly slough off or give little heed to what they are told about the reason for doing something. Some occurs because teachers are not particularly clear themselves as to why certain studies have been undertaken.

OBJECTIVES OFTEN NOT CAREFULLY IDENTIFIED

In many situations we inherit the goals we are obligated to pursue from previous decisions made by departmental groups and by more remote agents. Often the broader objectives have been determined by a curriculum committee or are contained in general statements approved for a system as a whole. More generally, the broad goals are implied in the decision by a board of education to sponsor a course on glove-making, or dramatics, or cooking for boys.

Specifics are usually left to the teacher. Most often, however, the decision to teach a particular item is taken because someone else has actually identified what to teach.

OBJECTIVES EASY TO SET

The process of identifying and selecting related and detailed objectives[1] is really not so difficult. For the most part, our limits are set by what we are employed to teach and by the broader goals determined before our time. The time allotment provided further restricts the field of choice. The grade level involved and the nature and needs of pupils at that point give us further direction. We know or can find out easily what others seek to teach or have been successful at teaching within similar prescriptions. Long lists of objectives have been made by students of the subject fields. They can be examined for hunches about what ought to be included. Course objectives can be drawn from more general statements of expectancies; unit objectives grow naturally out of the purpose set for the longer study of which they are a part. Lesson aims come from systemically breaking down bigger goals and from appraising the extent of progress against them.

[1] Edgar Wesley, *Teaching the Social Studies in High School,* third ed., Heath, 1950, p. 117.

Diagnosis of Needs

Diagnosis of needs is of course not separate from determination of objectives and much of the time must precede any really logical approach to them. We can state what our goals of instruction are without reference to what pupils lack or what society near at hand or far away requires in them. We should be fairly foolish however to try it for long.

On the other hand, we have pointed out above that sharp statements of goals does make evaluation possible. If we know what attributes a person should have, or we would like him to have, or he himself would like to have, we have a ready-made measure to see how far short he is. Which is to come first then, the chicken or the egg, is hard to say. At the outset someone must have seen some alternatives, i.e., knowledge of correct verbs or no knowledge, and decided which was more important. Need thus may have preceded the objective, but it did not precede the value, and the value may be easily thought of as a goal.

NEED OR VALUES SERVICEABLE

Arguing then over whether we should consider diagnosis the first dimension or the second would not gain us much. We must be alert to deficiencies before we set goals. At the same time we can not be aware of shortages until we have decided something is worth having. The point is that we can not hope to plan well for pupils unless we are well prepared to determine what they are lacking. Intermediate and more immediate objectives serve this purpose well because they are really hunches, proposals, and hypotheses. They are ideas about what ought to be and could be learned, whether they are put down in advance by a teacher or after rather thorough exploration and discussion by pupils. In certain of the more highly organized and preparatory subjects, objectives may be considered more as imperatives because they are logical relatives of a more general commitment. Even so, the instructor will have to ascertain constantly how much his pupils have secured of what was determined as required knowledge. Some might wish to call this evaluation or measurement rather than diagnosis. However, we prefer to think here of it, when planning is discussed, as a step in the planning process.

REMOTE AND IMMEDIATE ASPECTS OF DIAGNOSIS

In Chapter 4 there were identified a number of approaches upon which the teacher should rely in developing broad sensitivity to pupil needs. Some of those should be useful in sketching out courses of study and in conceiving units. However, the burden of more implicit planning and particularly that for limited periods of time requires that the teacher extend himself to develop procedures for obtaining data in much more specific and detailed form.

This is the aspect which is so often overlooked in the planning process, particularly where plans are drawn well in advance. Courses are set up, units are written against a cross-sectional picture of conditions, against common needs sometimes referred to, but suggestions made, content identified, and materials listed are without reference to individuals who compose a group. Naturally, preplanning can seldom get closer because teachers do not usually know in advance the names of the pupils they are to have. Thus, diagnosis can not take place sufficiently in advance to provide all the alternative specific plans needed. Tentative plans must be altered and discarded, and new ones developed as more detailed gaps in expected or desired growth are identified.

Selection of Content or Subject Matter

Probably the most difficult problem for the teacher is the question of what content should be used or called upon to accomplish the purposes and objectives set out. This is more so the case where objectives are very generally stated; so broadly stated as, for instance, "to learn to distinguish between good and cheap literature." Thus, one may have many alternatives for groups that differ in ability.

In practice, we are all aware that the most common procedure in "selecting" has been simply to adopt[2] the content, usually a textbook, and to frame objectives to fit that content or to justify it. In many places the course of study identifies the textbook to be used or claims to be based upon it. This means simply that a committee of teachers have carefully read the text and chopped it up into "units" to fit the yearly calendar; so much before Columbus Day, so much before Thanksgiving, and so on. Lesson plans, if there are any, are merely further reductions of chapters to pages per day with the monotonous repetition of ultimate objectives and a quite inaccurate listing of other more precise sounding goals. Where the slowness of the group does not permit

---

[2] Interesting examples of this were secured by simply asking several teachers to explain how they went about selecting a text. Each teacher explained he secured texts from hopeful salesmen, looked them over, and decided what he liked. Each admitted that he did not consult the state syllabus or handbook in his field. Two said they could not get the syllabus.

full coverage, pieces are left out. "We have not got time to take that up. We will skip that. I never liked to teach that anyway."

The concern here, when it exists, is whether what is included in the text is what ought to be taught or all that should be taught. Despite the fact that many a good high school text contains more factual information about a subject than some teachers have at any time truly known, we must presume and admit that well-trained teachers possess and have access to information well beyond that contained in the text. Each teacher has considerable latitude within which to decide then what part or what more to teach even if the goal is facts. Sources useful to a teacher are the opinions and advice of others, consensus studies, and the reactions and attitudes of pupils, the abilities and interests of students, and analyses of life activities. But seldom are these avenues thoroughly employed by the individual teacher.

PROBLEMS COURSES AND MORE ACTIVE SEARCH FOR
APPROPRIATE CONTENT

The course which is more focused on process, on teacher-pupil planning, on general social and personal problems, and on adaptation and adjustment requires the teacher to have a different view of subject matter. Faced with a problem, the student must locate information that will give him a solution. Thus, what he needs to know is not set out ahead of him by someone but is instrumental to and dependent upon his action to gain an insight. Content is data and awaits ferreting out when it will be useful.

Now does this mean the teacher does not locate or identify subject matter? Hardly. For the most part, the "problems" students will be working on will be ones with which the teacher has some familiarity. Also the teacher will be participating in the process of judging what information has been obtained, *i.e.:* Is there enough? Have all the angles been examined? Would this or that make a difference? So even the subject-less "core" teacher will have to be involved in discovering content.

GOOD GUIDES TO SELECTION

Over the years various criteria[3] have been identified for the teacher to use in selecting subject matter. The chart on page 174, pre-

---

[3] Hollis Caswell and Doak Campbell, *Curriculum Development*, American Book, 1935, p. 255; J. Paul Leonard, *Developing the Secondary School Curriculum*, Rinehart, 1946, chap. 4; Vernon Anderson, *Principles and Procedures of Curriculum*, Ronald, 1956, pp. 415 ff.

pared by Romine, is a synthesis from several sources. Smith, Stanley, and Shores[4] in their volume have analyzed five that they find as common references:

1. Is the subject matter significant to an organized field of knowledge?
2. Does the subject matter stand the test of survival?
3. Is the subject matter useful?
4. Is the subject matter interesting to the learner?
5. Does the subject matter contribute to the growth and development of democratic society?

These can be compared to an earlier list prepared by Hopkins:[5]

1. Have a high frequency of occurrence in the common activities of present social life. For this reason it ought to be taught in the schools.
2. Have high frequency of occurrence in the common activities of present social life, but not be taught by any outside social agency.
3. Have a high frequency of occurrence in social life as it ought to be in the next generation.
4. Be of interest to pupils.
5. Serve as the basis for acquiring more learning.
6. Be within the capacity of individual pupils.
7. Be within the training and experience of individual pupils.
8. Be of value in meeting the basic needs of a possible future career.
9. Include those topics of the greatest relative value out of the total possible range of topics.
10. Include an intensive treatment of a small number of topics rather than an extensive treatment of a larger number of topics.
11. Include the same topics or activities in the same subject in succeeding grades, only when there is new material, a new objective, a new approach, or a new outcome.
12. Be selected in such a way as to contain the maximum amount of the most desirable indirect content.
13. Make possible the maximum correlation with other subjects.
14. Be selected for its value in reaching the objective as determined by scientific experimental studies.

In any case criteria like these are not all usable at once. Some may apply more to subject-centered teaching where the purpose is vocational or the filling in of a sequential array of facts or skills. Some may apply only where the goal is process or the attainment of quite undetailed behaviors related to personal and societal improvement. More

---

[4] B. Othanel Smith *et al., Fundamentals of Curriculum Development,* rev. ed., World Book, 1957, p. 132.

[5] L. Thomas Hopkins, *Curriculum Principles and Practices,* Sanborn, 1929, p. 133.

EVALUATION OF EDUCATIONAL CONTENT FOR INCLUSION IN THE CURRICULUM

CRITERIA   RATING

1. Is the proposed content significant, valid, and useful in interpreting, understanding, and appreciating contemporary life?   _____

2. Does the proposed content relate definitely to one or more of the pertinent areas of life problems with which the curriculum should deal?   _____

3. Will the proper use of the proposed content promote the well-balanced growth and development of boys and girls in terms of stated educational objectives (abilities, attitudes, habits, sensitivities, etc.)?   _____

4. Is the proposed content important in terms of its contribution to the over-all roles of the curriculum-conservative, critical or evaluative, and creative; has it real significance in human experience?   _____

5. Does the proposed content have use in satisfying the immediate challenges, interests, needs, and problems of boys and girls?   _____

6. Is the proposed content consonant with the maturity level and the experiential background of the learner?   _____

7. Is the proposed content readily capable of adaptation to meet individual differences?   _____

8. Does the proposed content contribute to a continuous and interactive learning situation which promotes the progressive growth and development of the learner?   _____

9. Does the proposed content permit effective associations and has it useful application in present-day situations pertinent to the learner?   _____

10. Does the proposed content have sufficient intrinsic motivational power to encourage satisfying learning activity?   _____

11. Will the inclusion of the proposed content promote a well balanced curriculum free of unnecessary repetition and does it take into consideration other educative agencies and forces?   _____

For rating use the following scale:
- 2   Meets the criterion to a high degree
- 1   Meets the criterion to some degree
- 0   Does not meet the criterion sufficiently

Stephen Romine, *Building the High School Curriculum*, Ronald, 1954, p. 200.

for-the-moment criteria might be used when one is selecting a poem, let us say to illustrate social conscience in the poet. These would include:

1. Can this poem really be meaningful to the group?
2. Does it contain good examples of poetic tools for concomitant learning?
3. Is it easy to use, accessible, reproducible, etc?
4. Will it increase pleasure in a respect for poetry generally?
5. Is it valid, will it have impact, be remembered?

At any rate the teacher has no small task on his hands where he is free to select his own content or obligated by the absence of higher-level specifications to make the choices or to participate in making them. Still he ought to take greater advantage of his freedom than he does.

Choice of Activities

In an earlier chapter it was emphasized that activity which does not produce high-quality learning has characterized the schools too much. Over and over pupils have gone through the paces: written compositions and not learned how to express ideas; solved problems and not increased power over decimals; committed to memory and not developed any feeling at all. The result has been distressing not alone to the pupils. Many of us have turned to each other and asked what will produce better results. What can we have pupils do that will assure the accomplishment of the objectives set out?

There are many kinds of activity that will result in learning. There are those which are mental as well as those which are physical. There are direct and indirect ones. There are enjoyable and tedious ones. There are those that require great concentration and those that are all but casual. There are individual ones and those that require groups to be present.

CLARIFICATION ON THE MEANING OF LEARNING ACTIVITIES NEEDED

In the years since Lois Mossman wrote her book on the activity movement there has been an unusual amount of confusion about what activities are appropriate for the schools. Unfortunately, in many minds activity has come to mean only rather gross and obvious physical expression, best exemplified in the use of hammers, paint brushes, and tape-recording machines.

It is doubtful that more than a handful ever had only this in mind. Rather it is all too clear that those people who earlier insisted that learners be more active agreed that increasing learner participation meant increasing it in the mental areas as well as in the physical.

What they were after was a situation wherein the pupil might have a clear purpose in mind. Through active effort of the pupil to obtain that purpose, it was felt there would come legitimate and valid learning. The basic idea was that the learner himself had to be on the move. He had to be involved; he had to interact and partake, to want to do what he did for purposes which were his and which coincided with what a teacher was hoping to accomplish.

Activities ought always to support perceived objectives. If the goal is composition skill, appreciation of *Oliver Twist,* or facility at figuring percentage, the pupil ought to write, he ought to read, and he ought to figure, but only as he sees the activity related to his achieving his goals.

A ninth grader may decide independently that he wants to know how certain people lived in Dickens' day. If so, reading *Oliver Twist* is something he ought to do. At the same time, a ninth grader may agree with the teacher that he just ought to read and so get on with the story just as happily and purposefully. Whether the original impetus to read comes solely from himself or from the encouragement of the teacher makes little difference. If reading is satisfying and produces knowledge, increases social perception, builds attitudes, and so on, it is a good activity. But if the activity—reading *Oliver Twist* or painting a mural—is forced on the child, we have lost much of its value to legitimate learning. This is where we so often fail. We can find good activities, but they are not what pupils want to do.

Some would say this is so inevitable, in the face of objectives and content prescriptions, that we just have to live with it. Most teachers, nevertheless, know better and feel differently. The alternatives open to us even in a fairly rigid subject matter course are numerous.[6]

Developing Organization and Approach

In addition to selection of what to learn and how to learn, the teacher must consider the order in which learning may take place most quickly and easily to make possible further and higher-level learning. A lesson, a unit, a course are all links in an enterprise to change behavior and to help the pupil move from one condition of competence to another.

Probably more instructional activity fails because it is not very well organized than for any other reason. We often hear from pupils that Miss Jones is swell, but she just can not "put it across." Others re-

---

[6] For a master list of usable types, see Paul B. Diederich, "A Master List of Pupil Activities," *Educational Research Bulletin,* December, 1936, pp. 166–169.

port that if they only knew what the teacher was getting at, they might follow. Many are the pupils who complain that they were never really *taught* the fundamentals. Observation in many classes reveals pupils wasting their time or so busy learning details that they never see what they all mean. Review and reteaching are widespread because pupils have not been prepared or too little time has been provided for full exploration to take place. Pupils get lost because too rapid shifts are made from one topic to another or they are too uncertain about what precedes to use it well in what follows. Goals are presumably being pursued which the teaching procedure is not at all likely to produce.

Thus, problems of where to start, toward what, how much to cover with any learning enterprise, and how to manage it are sizable. The subject teacher again has fewer difficulties. By now the content of subjects taught year after year is pretty well pegged.

With a number of the more flexible subjects, such as social studies and English, there has always been a less consistent logical order. As a result, at any level what may come first and what may follow is not so clear, although practice is fairly standard. Social studies courses have regularly been organized into units bearing little relationship to each other, with little need for any one preceding another. Commonly, though, the over-all organization in the grades has been consideration first of immediate and local social and historical information and later expansion as well as extension to further times and places.

The teacher in a subject-less setting has even more open a situation and doubtless a more difficult job. His obligation at the outset is to work along with pupils in deciding what problems are and can be of concern to them and what goals they see value in pursuing. Inasmuch as there is no preordained content, the problem of getting items in at any one specific point does not exist. The teacher nevertheless helps pupils see what they need to accomplish their purposes and in general forestalls their undertaking tasks beyond their level of competence. The burden of choice lies with the group, but it is still not irresponsible choice. What they discover to be the first leg on their progress forward sets the order of events. Sequence grows naturally out of the occurrence of need. But direct teaching and telling, systematic approaches to accepted goals are consistent with the theory and follow upon the request for illustration and explanation. To make his decisions on such direct teaching, the teacher draws upon his knowledge of what pupils can learn with reasonable ease and upon his funded knowledge and analysis of the order of topics in the normal course of learning.

Actually both the subject teachers and the less restricted "core" teachers may, except in a few cases, use similar guides although the subject teacher may make his actual choices in advance and largely without any pupil participation. The "core" teacher must contribute his weight while the class is deliberating. Obviously both have to function within the broad lines of organization set down by state and system planning groups. The following guides seem to us appropriate for both.

1. *Organization should consider if there is anything so fundamental that it must precede, come at the outset, be included early.* This is the claimed pronounced advantage and fault of the subject approach. Someone has thought the whole thing through in advance. Main topics and subtopics have been identified. Declensions and conjugations have been numbered, living things have been classified, and distinctions have been made between the concept of function as related to equation-solving and the concept of demonstrative proof as related to shapes and sizes, and so on. What is simple, what is definitional, what is initial has been determined. The teacher knows what is coming next or at least later on so he can lay the ground work. $2 \times 2 = 4 = 2^2$ then gets into the picture before $a \times a$ and $(a + b)(a + b) = a^2 + 2ab + b^2$.

Still we must accept that there is nothing necessarily and absolutely rigid about a school subject. Much flexibility has been obtained through organizing courses around themes, around issues, and around problems. Thus an outline may suggest "magnets" as a topic, or more specifically "electromagnets," or even "factors affecting the strength of an electromagnetic field," but the topics may be taken up first or last.

2. *A syllabus seldom sets a rigid outline.* Teachers working in circumstances in which state syllabuses or course of study outlines are available are undoubtedly ethically obliged to "follow" them when this is expected, but no syllabus was ever intended as an excuse for poor teaching. The only legitimate meaning of "following" a syllabus is that the planning done by teachers *follows* that done by those who prepared the printed guide. The syllabus is a map which provides a general orientation to the area to be traversed and a reference for occasionally checking progress; it is not a series of trail markers to be followed one to the next. Once teachers have prepared their own courses of study, using the syllabus as one of many reference materials, mislaying the syllabus probably results in little harm.

3. *Suggested sequences have been proposed for the "core."* Some attempt has been made at the overall program level with this kind of allocation even for the subjectless "core." The identification of per-

sistent problems of living[7] by age groups with subpoints about likely concerns and questions is an effort to prevent the teacher from getting "in over his head" and to alert him that certain facts and skills may need to be taught before others. These guides are, to be sure, extremely flexible. Even so, we must recognize that analysis of persistent problems shows the teacher that counting, adding and subtracting numbers, and so on precedes calculating averages and figuring discounts. Learning basic punctuation precedes "using knowledge of grammar and rules of usage to proofread."[8]

This means that the teacher is encouraged to use his personal, rationalized and logicalized experience to promote student awareness and pursuit of problems in order to obtain quick learning at the best time. We know pretty well what can be learned and emerges to be learned because of what children can do and try to do. Children do not learn how to repair gasoline motors before they can distinguish one motor from another. Responsible guidance requires that we help them see what ought to be undertaken first.

Sequence has always bothered teachers. The discomfiture has been even greater since a fair portion of the literature seems to suggest that expectations for age or grade attainments should get minor consideration. Actually few teachers, when pushed to it, will stand on absolute essentials even in the subjects. However, when a faculty group plans a program, for health or social development, they can and ought to come to agree that in terms of pupil growth and natural experience, emphasis should be given to the pursuit of certain skills, understandings, and concepts. In order to *diminish* the utter confusion which can easily arise in any normal teaching situation, there can be general agreement on what will be striven for and when.

4. *Organization should consider what provides the most inclusive and manageable overview.* A great volume of criticism has been heaped on teachers because they have seen what the details and parts lead up to, when their pupils have not. Moving piecemeal toward larger goals, teachers have confused and "lost" their learners.

In organizing any learning experience then, we ought to seek the best map with broad outlines that we can find. This will make possible the constant relating of subtasks to a more general purpose, provide a binding force, give a sense of direction, and help keep motivation at a higher level. Whether the learning enterprise is of long or short

---

[7] Florence Stratemeyer *et al.*, *Developing a Curriculum for Modern Living*, rev. ed., Bureau of Publications, Teachers College, 1957, pp. 196–7.

[8] *Ibid.*, pp. 206–207.

duration, a course or a single lesson, this principle of orientation and unity is appropriate. The unifying element might be a meaningful question, an idea, a problem, or a theme. If it is sharp and clear, students will know where they are going and how fast.

5. *Organization should consider what coverage should or might be anticipated and at what rate.* Experienced teachers know well that whether they plan for or with groups, it is not at all difficult for there to be bitten off more than can be chewed. Few ever finish a year having touched thoroughly upon all that was contemplated or possible. A common joke about teachers is that they just get to their pearls of wisdom and to the next day's assignment as the bell rings.

Some of this is simply the problem of management: setting limits on reports and insisting on them, politely shelving opportunities for digression, arranging other times for special explanation and remedial teaching. At the same time, it also involves discovering and determining what is necessary to solve a problem, to produce a generalization, or fully to expose a topic. What should a group postpone, what is it unnecessary to examine, how deeply should the matter be investigated? When we set up a learning experience, particularly where purpose is common (and that is possible and regularly to be sought in the subjectless program), we can expect that there will be various levels of attainment, more effort and attention needed by some than by others to grasp an idea, to fix some valued facts, or to master some skills. Our organization is faulty if it does not provide for those differences.

6. *Organization should consider what steps seem most logical and likely to move us forward toward our goals.* What is logical to one person is not at all necessarily logical to another. Teachers ought not need to be reminded of this, but it is amazing how nearly all of us continue to be dismayed that our students do not see why they should take up this or that even after we explain it to them. Yet students can and do see the logic of many, many approaches and on the whole are anxious to be guided into logical approaches. A student who really is aware of why it would be better to deal with one aspect before another and can see how he has progressed because of a systematic relationship of the parts gets a real satisfaction out of learning.

7. *Organization should contribute to focus and impact.* The limitations of the highly isolated daily lesson are numerous, to be sure. Initiative is denied the child; planning and self-direction are prevented; over-all grasp is impossible, and so on. But one thing the lesson has done for very many of us is to provide us with something we could encompass, we could begin upon in ignorance and could complete

with confidence and a sense of accomplishment. It seems useless to argue the point. You and I have had a lesson on the piano, on homonyms, on the constituent function of legislatures, on sharpening knives, on any number of things. In many cases we needed only one. We did not need to string out our insight-getting over a long period of time; and we needed nothing in the way of drill to understand, and little in the way of drill to fix our knowledge or our skill.

In much of our recent writing all too little emphasis has been given to the lesson and its proper place in a subject or a subjectless "core." Teachers can teach and they should. We should not be led to think that exposition is inconsistent with guiding learning.

Obtaining clear-cut dimensions is, it must be agreed, a sadly neglected part of planning and organizing for learning. A few visits to classes where pupils are reporting on what they investigated will soon render testimony to the fact that someone might be getting practice at telling but a greater number are getting good practice at being politely inattentive and uninterested. In this book we have made the point that one of the sins of subject teaching has been exactly this difference on lack of purpose by the teacher while teaching. But having long units and student reports does not close the gap. We need more thorough consideration of how and when to pinpoint a learning task and to relate it to wholesome pupil purpose.

8. *Organization should contribute to retention and transfer.* These two items take up much space in books on educational psychology and figure prominently in all discussions on the curriculum. They require not the least imagination. If what pupils acquire flies away or makes no difference in the multiple experiences to be encountered in life, we waste our time.

We have said that much of the content to which secondary pupils are exposed is lost since it is so seldom used or not learned sufficiently. Some would reply, "That is good. If it is unused it is unworthy of much attention until it is used." Although we can agree with that in part, we can not do so completely. We are the better for anything we know, no matter how incidental, as long as more significant items are not neglected while we pursue once-to-be or never-to-be recalled facts.

The proponents of the persistent problems approach comfort themselves that most effective drill will be provided by the regular recurring demand for skills and facts, and correction or reteaching each time will gradually and eventually build up accuracy. The teacher should take advantage of the natural error and opportunity to explain or require explanation!

This does not look systematic enough to old hands at grammar or even sane to some arithmeticians, but we do not propose to quarrel with either side here. Actually where a fairly tight subject structure exists, the teacher is constantly correcting and reteaching, after long periods of drill have regularly proved ineffective. So the major argument with the subjectless proponents may be over how much forced immediate drill is defensible after the initial teaching of principal parts or of decimal placement.

A more difficult matter is how to get retention of the common "one-shot" teaching, let us say about the Congress of Vienna, *Ozymandias,* the qualifications for voting, and the layman's lexicon of proper words to identify body parts for the doctor. No sensible educator wants to make a quiz maniac out of an ordinary Joe, but we are faced with the fact that man can profit from remembering. Some thought is necessary then on making arrangements for review, recall, and reiteration.

The other matter of getting skills and information to function in novel situations which call for them to be fitted in as subparts or which call for them in slightly adapted form is no more easily managed. Research emphasizes that transfer comes best when we reach the generalization level and discover a common principle which has such force and obvious applicability that we can hardly avoid using it. It also emphasizes that we get transfer when we teach for it, when we reach out to show in how many places and ways the specific element or the generalization fits. We can discover all by our own wits that grease, soap, and oil make things slippery, but if we can see the principle only with respect to frozen bolts on a license plate and not with respect to a hot drill on a piece of strap iron, we have not got much. Instruction that fails to build up applications of some number and consequence by arrangement, even if it does pursue generalizations, will always fall short.

We can have faith that the natural course of events is so rich as to insure a demand upon the generalization or we can push things a little in the way we organize a course. The very existence of the public school calls for us to push a little more than casually for both retention and transfer.

Measurement of Progress

In several places which follow, consideration is given to the place of evaluation in the improvement of activities to secure better learning. In the discussion above of objectives and diagnosis of needs it has been shown that direction is obtained from finding out what deficiencies and shortages there are. The other values of measurement and evaluation are common knowledge or easy to figure out.

The unfortunate matter, however, is that to date measurement has been very much restricted to a check-up on facts and a number of relatively limited intellectual and mental skills. Evaluation as a participating enterprise by the pupil to set the stage for his more adequate personal selection and management of experiences has been almost completely neglected.

COURSES OF STUDY

It is conventional to divide the school's program of studies into sets of related experience known as courses. Common parlance has it that teachers teach courses; geometry, eighth-grade general science, and biology. Bright critics remark regularly that here is the major fault; nobody remembers that he always teaches pupils. But there is not much point in belaboring that matter. What teachers do with pupils in an assigned period of time is a course. Whatever their plans, written down in detail or broadly sketched, they are known to all of us as the courses of study.

The earlier view of the course of study was that it should provide a rather rigid set of dimensions and prescribe what content had to be covered. In the main, courses written in the 1920's and 1930's bore heavily on outlining content areas to be covered and occasionally included a discussion of approaches which might be used in teaching a subject. They were more often properly called syllabuses, and they were usually prepared for teachers by state officers or by a local committee and installed to become the standardized reference for all those teaching in specific subjects.

The most recent view of a course of study is that it is a general examination of what is involved in accomplishing a series of objectives having a relatively close relationship. It is held out to the teacher as analysis and as a set of suggestions about what might be included and about how the teacher could approach his work with pupils most effectively. It may include a presentation of general philosophy, a statement about learning, a discussion of what good planning and teaching are, a review of children's growth characteristics, ideas about the social and personal needs of pupils, and techniques for discovering and diagnosing pupil deficiencies. Modification and adaptation are written in and the teacher is invited to expand as well as to fit dimensions to the local situation. More generally, and more properly perhaps, such resources are referred to now as guides.

The teacher's *own* course of study more properly includes less philosophy and fewer methodological considerations and much more of the sticky details of content, order of subparts, tests, and so on.

Most commonly the teacher's course of study deals with a recognized subject, e.g., "Plane Geometry" or a unique organization of a recognized body of subject matter, e.g., "Science for the Consumer." However, in some instances it is organized around (1) an area of living, e.g., "Family Living," (2) social problems, e.g., "Problems of American Democracy," or (3) an area of student needs and interests, e.g., "Health." Older established courses are easier to plan because there are numerous sources of suggestions—state outlines, textbooks, materials from many other schools. In planning newer ones, especially those not encompassed within a subject, a great deal of imagination and careful thinking is necessary.

Clarification of General Goals

Unfortunately many courses just grow, and even years after a teacher has begun teaching he may have really little grasp of what his course is about or how it is organized to obtain the ends he, together with his pupils, seeks. This may be because he has never set down his objectives or clearly specified to which of a conglomerate of objectives he is actually devoted. It may be because he has borrowed, lock, stock, and barrel someone else's logic and has never stopped to think whether the arrangement contributes to what he ought to be doing. For instance, few teachers who pursue love of country have carefully thought through what steps should follow one on another to nourish the seeds of patriotism from simple beginnings in flag salutes to intricate and subtle defenses in the heart and mind.

This failure arises because too many think of course-making as a synthetic process. Naturally it can be and as we have said it all too commonly is. Rather, good planning is analytical. It is the art of getting a good scope, a clear objective, an identifiable whole and then of discovering what the parts and elements are, what is consistent and what is not, what guides and augments, and what carries one aside and perhaps even interferes.

This means that units should be decided upon and out of the concept of a course. We should perhaps have a unit on "Fighters for Freedom" if we wish to develop a deep emotional commitment to our way of life. On the other hand, if our objective is just to be able to name the representatives of the Virginia dynasty and to know the names of the big men of an historical period, we may want only a unit on "Early Presidents."

A course of study intended to make students more effective consumers of the products of modern science will obviously differ from one which aims primarily to commence the preparation of future scientists. If both these aims are sought by the same course of study, still another design is necessary. A course supposed to impart detailed knowledge of the chronological history of the United States should be planned differently from one concerned with developing understanding of the historical roots of current social problems or the evolution of American institutions and ideals. If the purpose of a course in English is to make students knowledgeable about the authors, plots and characters of the "best in English literature," a quite different plan is required than for a course which purports to provide insight into persistent human problems and values through a literary approach. Consideration of the outcomes sought is clearly one of the first steps in planning a course of study.

The desired outcomes also determine the specificity of a course of study. As was indicated earlier, there are times when the nature of the activities engaged in is of more concern than the content with which they deal. Hence, in a course in which the major outcomes desired are skill in scientific method or democratic processes, the plan may be prescriptive with respect to activities, but only suggestive regarding content. In other courses aiming at certain definite understandings the content may be quite specific and the activities only suggested.

Nothing in this means that units have to be fixed, nor even that they need be completely developed in advance. In the unrestricted framework we should expect units to be built actually in progress and only be describable at their completion. On the other hand, if we are committed to rather precise preplanning and our goals are more devoted to products than certain democratic processes, then our units ought to be derived from a logical analysis of objectives rather than a happenstance teaching of what we know or of what is arranged in a text in which the author may have had in mind only a few of the objectives we claim to pursue.

Consideration of Content

In the discussion of dimensions, reference has been made to the selection of content. We need not review the general ideas advanced there about all planning. If the curriculum design requires specific content, we can do little else but identify it in the course of study. If no particular facts are to be required, we may want to give focus to the course by clarifying what concepts, generalizations, or broad gauges for behavior we are seeking, or what problems are appropriate. These in effect are content, but they should be at a general enough level to free the teacher to determine what specific information to use in providing the richest and most valid background for attitudes, appreciations, and ways of looking at and approaching matters.

Out of good analysis of broad goals there should come the ideas for units and manageable, highly meaningful, shorter duration efforts. These titles or subquestions can be listed with some fairly simple discussion of what scope and depth could be expected.

Until the teacher has located these subpoints, he actually has little line on what his activities may be calculated to produce and he actually has little idea of what materials, resources, and references to use. For example, if the subgoal of the theme that man has had a long struggle to emerge, develop, and get his house in order is to get an insight into how the search for religion and the struggles to practice it have affected man's behavior across the ages, the teacher may want to show how religion has been related to wars, how it has influenced politics, when and where it has figured in poetry, and what contribution it has made to art. When these or other questions or areas for investigation and study are identified, he can think about motivation techniques, debating questions, bulletin board displays, suggested readings, independent research papers, community expert resources, *ad infinitum.*

Decisions on Style and Approach Required

We can not anticipate that we will want ever to teach the same thing the same way twice. It seems that good teachers pride themselves on the fact that they are wedded to no particular set of steps or procedures even though they may have the same facts or generalizations in mind year after year. Occasionally a major event offers an excellent star to which to hitch the learning wagon. It may be a centennial celebration; it may be the martyrdom of an author; it may be the awful impingement of a war or the draft that provides a continuing reference point. More regularly, variation is simply the teacher's desire to start differently, to play another angle, to try out some theory.

Outwardly, the typical teacher just seems to get rolling when the school year opens, but most of those who have a few tenure stripes cogitate and reflect over the summer, or more often in the midst of this year's effort they consider how to proceed next fall. On the whole, old-hand teachers do not write out at length their schemes for carrying on throughout a semester or a year. However, if a committee or group of teachers is developing a course or guide to be widely used, we ought to expect a number of suggestions about the general methods for handling the subject. At the same time, individual teachers certainly ought to do more of this credo and "intention" kind of writing for themselves.

Chapter I of the Pennsylvania course of study for social studies[9] in the secondary schools attempts to do some of this. There, attention is given to what is involved in teaching for social learning and certain of the teaching techniques now highly recommended are identified and encouraged. The Denver home economics[10] guide includes sections on philosophy, governing commitments in the program, and suggestions about teacher-pupil planning.

Planning Units Still Important

State subject bulletins and local system guides now commonly contain modified resource units. These are, so to speak, teaching fodder and include limited objectives, activities, suggestions for evaluation, and so on.

Probably more productive teacher and course-of-study activity has gone into accumulating these resources for teaching than into anything else. No one would want to quarrel with that effort, for teachers do need a great deal of ready help. Yet there are some critics who would claim that once units get written down and developed for a course, they are difficult to dislodge and replace. They get used over and over in exactly the same way.

This of course does not at all have to be the case. Loose leaf notebooks and manila folder files are used in many systems and by many teachers to facilitate addition and discard, and systematic reporting on materials discovered and used and projects tried out is always possible in the bigger system. A teacher, if he has the time and inclination, can weed out the extraneous material and those at-the-moment, brilliant idea flashes he has previously recorded for posterity in his notes.

The Individual Teacher and the Final Course of Study

Units do take time to develop and the production of a dozen or so homemade ones for each of three or four courses is not common practice. Although no one should expect a teacher to turn out his

---

[9] Pennsylvania Department of Public Instruction, *Course of Study in the Social Studies for Secondary Schools,* The Department, 1951.

[10] Denver Board of Education, *Home Economics in the Senior High School,* The Board, 1948.

personal and novel set of units all at once, a good course of study is not likely to exist until the teacher has got his own produced.

This means that we should anticipate that courses of study will grow as the teacher grows. We can start with guides provided, and pick and choose. We can, without guides, do our best to look the field over and draw ourselves a map at the outset. But with experience we ought to discover that neither those who have filled books with suggestions nor our own initial hunches are all we want and feel comfortable with. In time, there ought to emerge for us our own form and outline that release both the pupil's and our own best efforts and make the relationship something unique.

OUTLINE FOR COURSES OF STUDY

TITLE

This seems obvious but is noted because title may do much to restrict or to increase the scope of a course. *Elementary Algebra* is more limited than *Ninth Year Mathematics. The Geography of the United States* restricts more than does *Basic Geography. Problems of Democracy* permits an extremely flexible arrangement.

FRAME OF REFERENCE

First, attention should be given to the reason the area or subject is included in the program of studies. An overview should include something of the history of the course, its place in the offerings, and any general point of view about the area for study, factors which have affected it, and conditions which do or should influence. If the course is part of a sequence, the general pattern should be summarized and a chart included to show both scope and sequence. Either here or in the section on method and approach, particularly with general elementary courses, continuing high school subjects, and "core" guides, some meaningful statement should be made about continuity and sequential learning.

GOALS AND OBJECTIVES

Courses are usually considered to serve rather ultimate and broad goals of education. The extent of service to these should be clarified. More limited objectives and those likely to be attainable in very large part should be identified as understandings, abilities, attitudes, skills, and generalizations. Sometimes anticipated and proposed pupil objectives are included in the unit outlines. They should more often be developed as the teacher works out the teaching unit. Statements on goals and objectives may be introduced with a review of the general concept underlying the teaching of the subject or the field.

STATEMENT OF PURPOSES AND POTENTIAL USES

A general committee-prepared course outline should be a resource for the teacher and provide him with a mine of information. The possible appropriate teacher uses of the guide should be clear. The material in the guide and why and how teachers may use particular parts should be explained.

METHOD AND APPROACH

In this section the accepted fundamental principles of educational psychology applicable to learning may be restated. The basic ideas as to how good teaching is given should be set forth. How the units proposed are conceived and how the teacher should utilize them ought to be considered. Attention may be drawn here to any agreements or impositions about essentials, time allotments, and prescribed tests. Ideas about appropriate teacher-pupil planning should be expounded.

UNIT SUGGESTIONS AND OUTLINES

Illustrative planning units should include a statement of unit purpose and relationship to course purpose and other units, objectives, general content anticipated to be covered or used, activities and references. Evaluation suggestions may be included separately from activities.

TEACHER REFERENCES AND RESOURCES FOR EXTENSION

No course of study is complete. New units need to be added and developed. Teachers ought to extend their understandings and ideas about the course as a whole. Good bibliography should be provided.

EVALUATION

There should be means for teacher criticism and evaluation of the whole course and for teacher influence on changes to be made by committees near at hand and by more remote groups.

THE INSTRUCTIONAL UNIT

As an organizational subdivision the instructional unit falls between the course of study and the lesson. Earlier practice omitted this level and learners progressed through a course on a lesson-to-lesson basis. This procedure was like traversing a maze in that the student did not know which direction the next turn (or lesson) would take him nor could he look back very far to see where he had been.

More recent concepts associated with Gestalt psychology have stressed the importance of a total configuration in giving meaning to its component details. It is argued that daily experiences become more meaningful when perceived in terms of the larger unit of a study and when the units are related as parts of an entire course. Learning is not a process of the accretion of experiences, but rather of their incorporation into a pattern. The unit makes possible this integration.

A second strength of the unit approach appears in the maintenance of purpose on the part of the students. Unless activity is to be aimless groping, it must receive direction from purpose. In the isolated lesson arrangement purpose may exist for each lesson; but when the lesson is completed, the purpose ceases and must be re-established again for the next. The unit provides for a persistence of purpose over a longer span of time and the learners' purposes for each lesson become, for the most part, the furtherance of the broader purposes of the unit.

Accompanying the more sustained purpose is a third value of the unit organization. The learning products most likely to be both retained and transferred are the broader ones—concepts, generalizations, and attitudes. For these to be developed well some amount of induction is necessary. A single lesson is seldom enough for this process. Several, and often many, lessons are required to attain these products. The unit organization shifts the emphasis from the necessary, but less significant, details to the broader, more significant outcomes to which the details all contribute. Learning becomes more permanent and more functional.

Lessons of course remain but their meaning has changed. Instead of self-contained recitations, they have become stages in the fulfillment of a larger plan. The same may be said with respect to units which to a lesser degree are stages in the development of a course. Externally, however, units need only be appropriate as foci for organization of a course, whereas internally they must be organically organized. Therefore, lessons must differ according to their functional position in the unit, rather than all be constructed along a standard pattern.

Several Types of Units

The unit approach is employed by teachers under various educational philosophies and curriculum plans. It is used where all classroom learning experiences are organized by subjects, where some are organized around projects or "activities" and where a "core" curriculum is present. Consequently, units vary somewhat and a confusing terminology has sprung up to indicate these variations. Actually, *all* instructional units are sequences of learning experiences designed to achieve certain educational objectives. Since each consists of experiences, units are similar in that all possess content, involve activity, mental as well as other kinds, and culminate in some degree of satisfaction and evaluable results. Hence, the differences among units lie in the *kinds* of objective, in the relative *emphasis* placed on the content and the activity aspects, and in the *type* of culmination and evaluation.

What are commonly called "units" in educational books on method are actually *plans* or aids to planning. Thus a distinction is made between teaching units and resource units. The *teaching unit* (or *unit plan*) is an outline for a specific learning unit to be engaged in by a particular group of learners. It may be modified, extended or condensed as it is applied but, subject to such flexibility, it specifies the learning experiences to be provided, the instructional materials to be used, and the evaluation procedures to be employed. The *resource* unit, mentioned previously, is an organized collection of suggestions for a possible teaching unit—in other words, a planning aid.

In classifying learning units the first consideration is the relative emphasis placed on the content and the activity aspects of the experience. When content is the major consideration and is specified in advance, it may be called a *content* (or *subject matter*) unit. When, on the other hand, the content is not the major concern, but rather the activities engaged in, the term *activity unit* is descriptive. Such units are sometimes labelled *experience* or *process* units.

Variations within these two categories result from differing objectives. Thus content units may aim for (1) acquisition of specific information and skills, (2) general understanding of an area, or (3) some change in the pupil's total behavior. But the assumption is that there is something about the particular *content* dealt with which will achieve these objectives. The activities which are employed are secondary, though certain kinds are perhaps favored.

Activity units, on the other hand, may aim for growth in ability to (1) solve social, personal, and intellectual problems, (2) make decisions and form opinions, or (3) make evaluative judgments. The assumption here is that the experiences must provide for such activities and the particular content dealt with is secondary. If the topic meets certain criteria and the activities are properly carried out, much worthwhile content will be encountered but it will serve as means rather than as an end.

The opposition of these two basic approaches has been at the root of much of the educational unrest, attempted reform, and alarmed resistance of the twentieth century. In discussions, proponents of each seemingly exclude all possibility of merit in the other. Yet there is probably no school so traditional nor one so very "modern" that within its curriculum some use is not made of both the content and activity approaches. Considering the multiple objectives of the modern school, it is quite probable that all varieties of both categories would under some circumstances be found to be the most appropriate.

There are certainly a considerable number of specific skills and items of information which students need to learn and concepts which they need to develop systematically. But because these products are often as readily lost as acquired, carefully chosen experiences, properly organized, are necessary to improve *retention*. Then there are areas where it is not the details but the broader understandings and insights they lead to which are of greatest significance, and a somewhat different unit organization is called for. Generalization rather than retention is the main concern. Doubtless there are also occasions when it is desirable and not unreasonable to seek to bring about a definite adaptation of pupil behavior through an appropriately designed learning unit. Behavioral change requires *application* of learning.

Neither One nor the Other Necessary

Further, it is unquestionably desirable that pupils learn the techniques of problem-solving and the methods of inquiry which yield necessary facts and lead to the discovery of principles. Therefore, while activities of this nature undoubtedly can be provided in units mainly designed to achieve subject matter outcomes, their importance suggests the desirability of *also* providing occasions where the use of these problem-solving activities will be the *dominant* concern. However, it does not follow that this discovery approach is either the most effective or efficient one for *all* learnings, nor that the techniques and attitudes associated with it are so difficult of attainment that it must be used in *all* situations. Similarly, it is no doubt justifiable to organize some experiences primarily to provide practice in group deliberation, clarification of values, democratic process, and critical thinking, but, again, not exclusively and not without regard for the subject matter of the issues, problems, and propositions to be considered. The matter of most importance is that objectives be clearly defined and defensible. Then the learning experiences must be given *whatever* unitary organization best leads pupils to accept or set purposes consistent with the objective, and pursue these purposes through that sequence of consequential learning experiences which offers greatest promise of their attainment.

THE UNIT PLANNING PROCESS

There are no rules for planning instructional units. They depend for their quality upon a highly creative process. The purpose of much of the discussion in this chapter has been to develop an understanding of the position of the unit in the over-all planning scheme, the importance of unitary organization, and the variations in units. It having been suggested that all of the various types have some place in the curriculum, it is now appropriate not to select one type nor to attempt to describe the process of designing each of half a dozen types, but rather to emphasize those aspects of construction generally common to all.

To construct anything satisfactorily one must know what characteristics the finished product should possess. It is suggested that the following attributes should be sought in evaluating a unit plan and hence in developing it.

1. *Unity Is Paramount.* This is self-evident, yet it must be emphasized that any random collection of learning experiences, say a month's work or that of a "marking period," does not make a unit. There must be an appropriate focus or center of organization. Some authorities suggest that the only suitable center is a problem. Some problems do make excellent foci for units, particularly when problem-solving technique is a primary objective. But, as Bellack[11] has suggested, while problem-solving is of course the method by which new knowledge is discovered, it is not necessarily the best approach for transmitting what is known.

Furthermore, as stated earlier, many problems as formulated for learning are nothing more than topics in interrogatory form. It is true that pupils always have the problem *of* learning, but they need not always have a problem *for* learning. The unifying theme should be determined by the main objective of the unit and may be a topic, a problem, a technique, a concept, a principle, a generalization, a period of time, a structure, a process, a geographic area, an area of human activity, a phenomenon, an aesthetic form or medium, or a project.

2. *There Should Be Careful Organization.* The structure of units resembles that of a play. The action is ascending and then de-

[11] Arno Bellack, *What Shall The High School Teach,* Association for Supervision and Curriculum Development, chap. IV.

scending. Like all noncyclical sequences there are three phases—beginning, middle and ending, although the demarcations are not necessarily clear cut. The well-known Morrison unit plan provided five stages: exploration, presentation, assimilation, organization, and recitation. Less formal methodology today recognizes initiatory, developmental, and culminating aspects. The conventional five steps in problem-solving—defining the problem, gathering relevant facts, proposing hypotheses, testing hypotheses, and drawing conclusions—might also provide an organizational structure.

Many other arrangements have been advocated and used, stemming back to Herbart's original five formal steps of instruction which, it may be recalled, were preparation, presentation, comparison, generalization, and application. Robinson's helpful "SQ3R" formula for study also illustrates the same general scheme in recommending that students approach an assignment by surveying, questioning, reading, reciting, and reviewing. Thus it appears that the diverse organizational designs for units are variations on a single theme differing in the emphasis placed on each part and the kinds of experiences provided. Introductory, evolving, and consummatory stages are always discernible.

3. *Appropriate Learning Experiences Should be Selected.*   In both content and activity the experiences which constitute the unit should (1) promote learning and (2) be appropriate from the standpoint of the learners, society, and the learning products sought. Experiences promote learning according to their *novelty* and *impact*. If all novelty is lacking, *i.e.,* if something entirely known is dealt with, the possibilities for learning are neglible; if there is too much novelty, the experience assumes the quality of a puzzle and learning occurs only by chance or after tedious, often discouraging effort, seemingly too great for the reward finally attained.

The impact of an experience derives either from its vividness or from recurrence. Extreme vividness may be traumatic and, while powerful in producing learning, often dangerous. Even at that, for many types of learnings a recurrence of experiences is necessary. This should not be construed as strictly repetitive, but rather as progressive variation of performance. Increased insight is gained by a combination of differentiation and integration, or analysis and synthesis, leading to a re-interpretation of earlier experiences in the light of each successive one.

4. *Experiences should fit the learners.*   Many terms refer to the appropriateness of experiences. In relation to the learner it is often said that they must be meaningful. In ordinary parlance this means they

must "make sense." Meaningfulness is a product of relationship to previous learning and to either the logic of a subject or the perceived application of what is learned. These factors obviously vary to some extent among individuals within even the conventionally graded group
and, hence, a further criterion of appropriateness involves *individualization.* Numerous efforts have been made to make experiences individually appropriate. Compromises have been sought by providing for
several levels of difficulty. Sometimes the *number* of experiences has
been varied on the basis of quickness to learn. Often *preliminary experiences* are provided for individuals lacking the necessary background. Another approach is to *vary the goals* sought commensurate
with the learner's potential. An approach increasingly employed is to
provide broad common experiences, the *components of which are assigned* on the basis of the differential ability of individuals to contribute
to the group's undertaking.

From the standpoint of the learners, then, the appropriateness of
experiences is essentially a question of the likelihood that each individual will derive meaning from them. The term purposeful is also
frequently used in this connection. Experiences do not have purposes;
only people do. Meaningful experiences will either have had their conception in the prosecution of student-originated purpose or, by virtue of
being meaningful, will, though adult-inspired, be conducive to the en-
listment of such student purpose. Hence, purpose on the part of learners is a necessary condition of the learning situation but is not a characteristic inherent in the experience. Learners establish such purpose
with respect to an experience either (1) because the value of the anticipated learnings is recognized; (2) because it is integral to a larger
endeavor being pursued for some broader purpose; or (3) because,
despite its apparent lack of value, it is perceived as a necessary means
to some unrelated or remote goal, such as admission to college or staying on an honor roll.

Similar statements may be made regarding the claim that experiences should be *interesting.* It is the learner who is or is not interested.
It is questionable whether either the content or activity associated with
any meaningful experience can be said to be inherently interesting or
uninteresting. Learners develop interest in an experience either (1) because the activity is pleasurable, which in turn is dependent upon the
stage of development they are in, the strength of their desire for new
experiences and their previous degree of success with similar activities;
(2) because the content promises to satisfy a curiosity which has been
permitted or encouraged to flourish; or (3) because the learning prod-

uct itself is seen to be consistent with their welfare, *i.e.,* in their best "interest."

5. *Experiences should have social impact.* Beyond being meaningful to individual learners, experiences must also be socially significant. A scale of significance might range from that of indifferent significance to that which is absolutely vital. Any choice should of course avoid the detrimental and among the remainder give priority on the basis of nearness to the vital end of the scale. Unfortunately, no such convenient scale actually exists and hence judgment as to significance is necessary. These judgments will not be unanimous but if made by people well schooled in the requirements of a free society, they will not likely be grossly in error. At least, it is better that this characteristic be given consideration than ignored entirely, for time is short and society can indulge pursuit of fancies only after its own needs have been served.

This is not to argue for *utilitarianism* as it is widely conceived. Learnings may be socially significant without being immediately useful or readily convertible into cash. But some may make little or no difference to society either immediately or ultimately and therefore should be given time grudgingly. In most cases the significance of experiences should be evident or readily demonstrable to students.

6. *Experiences should guarantee valid learnings.* The third sense in which an experience is or is not appropriate relates to the likelihood of its leading to the outcomes desired from it. Some content may not be appropriate for the development of a generalization or attitude, even though increasing the student's factual knowledge. A particular kind of activity may be suitable for developing broad understandings, but not skills. Decisions in this regard naturally depend upon an understanding of the psychology of learning which the teacher is presumed to have. A brief summary here of kinds of experience appropriate for various types of learning outcomes may serve as a helpful reminder.

Skill
1. Witnessing illustration of use of the skill and its place in some total process through direct observation, motion picture, reading, or oral explanation.
2. Observing demonstrations of the skill in its entirety at normal speed and then slowly.
3. Telling the steps while performed by instructor.
4. Telling the steps while performing them himself.
5. Performing the entire skill.
6. Practicing component steps analyzed as giving most difficulty.
7. Alternately practicing components and performing entity for rhythm, form, accuracy and speed.
8. Using drill.

Memorization
1. Reading and discussing entire selection for its total significance and for meaning of all words, phrases, or symbols.
2. Indicating recognition of the desirability of memorizing based on teacher's persuasion or own conclusion regarding convenience, e.g., a formula; enjoyment, e.g., a poem; etc.
3. Reading and reciting the largest manageable, meaningful unit while seeking cues from inherent or contrived associations.
4. Alternating practice of the whole and of difficult parts.
5. Continuing practice with increased spacing of periods for overlearning and later occasionally for maintenance.
6. Making contrasts with similar material to reduce retroactive inhibition.

Concept Formation
1. Directly or vicariously observing specimens or representations of the referent or, when more abstract, considering various manifestations of it.
2. Formulating a definition of the concept in own words and ascertaining the name conventionally applied.
3. Refining the definition through further contact with referent to determine cases included and excluded.
4. Memorizing a formal definition if desirable.
5. Applying the concept in thinking.

Generalizations
1. Encountering a series of selected phenomena illustrating the principle, law, rule, etc.
2. Noting similarities and differences to formulate a generalization.
3. Applying the generalization to specific cases through prediction or explanation with attention to apparent exceptions and related but nonidentical generalizations.

Attitudes
1. Extending the generalization procedure to commitment for or against attitudinal object.
2. Encountering the attitudinal object in pleasant or unpleasant affectively charged situations.
3. Participating in group decision regarding opinion toward object.
4. Subjecting own present attitudes to logical and empirical scrutiny.

Problem-Solving Ability
1. Stating a problem and analyzing it for subordinate problems.
2. Defining terms, identifying concepts, making assumptions explicit.
2. Recalling facts known about the problem and the situation in which it arises.
4. Speculating as to possible solutions, and where applicable estimating quantitative answer.
5. Identifying further information and opinion required.
6. Deducing probable consequences of various proposed solutions in terms of additional data obtained.
7. Testing favored solution when possible, or in group situations seeking consensus as to which is preferred.

Systematic Approach for Planning Units

Teachers who understand the value of unitary organization and who keep in mind the characteristics of a good unit can with a little practice develop a suitable procedure for planning teaching units. Probably all approaches will involve, in one way or another, the steps described below.

Almost invariably the first step must be to determine the objectives of the unit. At this level they can no longer be expressed in the generalities used for the course of study or the total curriculum. It is most useful to state them as learning products or outcomes; as an aid in doing this many teachers find it helpful to classify them as generalizations and concepts, factual information, skills and attitudes. It is probably best to express them in terms of what pupils should do or be able to do as a result of this set of experiences. When this is done, as we have said before, valid evaluation is more readily made because then the kind of evidence for which to look is clearer. It also provides a check on the worthwhileness of the objectives for if the changed behavior anticipated from certain experiences is seen to be inconsequential, the experiences may then be questioned. Further, it prevents the inclusion of grandiose objectives incapable of achievement, or reiteration without any real attempt at accomplishment.

Objectives should be specific but the list for a given unit should be kept as short as possible by limiting it to outcomes which it is reasonable to anticipate. Caution is needed particularly in the areas of personality, character, and certain broad attitudes and complex habits. When these are included, it is well to use the verb "to improve," rather than "to develop."

When what is to be accomplished has been determined, the next step is to determine how to accomplish it. Here the three phases of the unit enter the picture. The first is the *introduction.* Its function is to assure readiness and establish purpose. To *ascertain* readiness it may be desirable to discuss out-of-school experiences students may have had relating to the forthcoming unit, to review background material they may have learned earlier in school or even to give a pretest which will reveal individual weaknesses as well as areas which may be omitted. To *increase* readiness it may be desirable to provide a common experience through a film, a discussion, a trip, or even a lecture.

To establish purpose it may be desirable to raise an issue or pose a problem, to give an overview of the unit indicating its significance to the students and society, to provide for broad orientation reading, or to propose a concluding activity toward which to work. Here, of course, teachers who are inclined to encourage student participation in planning will guide the class or committees in reaching agreement as to what shall be undertaken and the approach to be used. The important task in that event is to assure that the purposes set by the group are consistent with the objectives sought through the unit. To this end, and also to have suggestions ready, the preliminary planning discussed here is just as essential as if the teacher were to impose a specific set of experiences.

The second phase—the "body" of the unit—must include experiences likely to lead to the desired outcomes—whether skills, understanding, or attitudes. In addition they must be varied, not only because of interest, but also to allow for differences in rate and method of learning of the students. By variety of experiences three aspects are to be understood.

One is the complexity and abstraction of the content and hence the reading difficulty of printed materials used. It should be recognized that the development of a concept or generalization can proceed to different levels or degrees of understanding, and therefore the content dealt with by the various students in a group must differ to permit each to achieve the appropriate depth for him. For example, the study of a dry cell may involve for some only a can, a rod, paste and posts, but for others ions, electrons, inhibiting agents, and internal resistance.

Another aspect of variety concerns the sensory avenues to learning. The experiences should be selected so that they include nonverbal as well as verbal approaches, visual as well as auditory, manipulation and direct observation as well as vicarious contact. The third aspect is closely related but differs sufficiently to be noted. Variety is also desirable in regard to the kinds of opportunity to deal with the content. Provision should be made in the unit plan for experiences involving written and oral reporting of independent reference reading; creative expression of ideas through dramatization, art work and the fashioning of objects of various materials; and all these variously as individual, small group, and total class arrangements. To assure that each student has appropriate experiences methodological skills are required, but the basis for such individualization is established by the inclusion of varied experiences in planning the unit.

In his planning the teacher should also consider interrelationships between the unit at hand and other units of the course, learnings from other courses, and students' lives in and out of school. Call it correlation, integration, articulation or application, the selection of experiences should provide for reinforcement of both present and previous learnings. Few units fail to offer opportunities for strengthening basic skills of language and computation. Literature, music, and art relate to many social and scientific concepts. Most learnings in some way bear upon the affairs of the family and the immediate and more remote community. Most are associated with some concern of students at any level of development, whether they belong to the velocipede set, the bicycle gang, or the jalopy crowd. Making these connections may well capitalize existing interests, which is all to the good, but the chief justification is the increased meaning with which both current and former experiences are invested.

Phase three of the unit is the conclusion. There are three aspects of this phase. One is the use of summary and review to fix learnings and improve transfer. The second is evaluation. Although evaluation should take place throughout the entire unit, the concluding phase should provide for appraisal of both individual achievement and the success of the class in carrying out the work planned.

A third kind of experience which is appropriate in terminating the unit is a class activity toward which the work of the unit may have been directed. This "culminating activity" frequently involves public performance or display, such as an assembly program, a presentation before another class, or a corridor exhibit. However it may also consist of a trip, a community service, or a publication. Its major value is not the learning it yields but the continuing purpose it provides for the entire unit.

The unit plan's structure is implied in the foregoing discussions of the characteristics of a good unit and the process of planning one. It may be helpful, nevertheless, to summarize the many considerations mentioned in such a way as to furnish a basic skeleton for a unit plan. Since there are, as pointed out earlier, a number of different kinds of units and since differences also exist in the most effective approach for various subject areas, this outline can only be suggestive with modification, and departures not only permissible but desirable. It is not suggested that a stereotyped pattern for planning be adopted, but some rigidity is considered preferable to a situation in which unit planning is omitted or is so haphazard that the quality of learning experiences is open to serious question.

I. Title:
   What unifying theme, problem or process provides a center around which
      to organize this unit?
   Is it appropriate logically in terms of the subject area, psychologically in

terms of the students for whom intended, or philosophically in terms of significance to society?

II. Objectives:

What is the major contribution of this unit to the course of study and in turn to the development of students and the furtherance of the society?

What specific outcomes in terms of skills, understandings and attitudes are sought?

III. Introductions:

How will the readiness of students for this unit be ascertained and increased?

Is it likely that some lack the necessary background?

Is the topic entirely new to them or have they dealt with it before?

How will student purpose be established?

How can students get an overview of the area to be considered?

To what extent can students participate in the specific planning of the unit?

IV. Body:

What kinds of experience are dictated by the nature of the outcomes sought?

How can sufficient variety of experience be introduced?

What variation in difficulty can be provided?

What variation in source of information is possible?

What variation in ways of organizing content can be offered?

How will the relationship of this unit to previous and concurrent experiences be brought out?

What other subject areas and school activities can be brought to bear upon the present experiences?

What connection can be made with the local community, with contemporary society, and with the daily lives of students?

V. Conclusion:

How will the unit be summarized and reviewed?

What culminating activity was planned for inclusion here?

What evaluation can be undertaken to determine the extent to which the proposed outcomes were achieved?

Resource Units as Source of Background Help

It is evident that the task of planning good instructional units places a considerable burden upon teachers' imaginations in devising a variety of appropriate experiences and upon their memories in recalling the many materials which might be used. To make it easier to design good units for specific groups, resource units have come into use.

A resource unit is a compendium of ideas regarding suitable experiences and materials for a unit, available for consultation when the teaching unit is planned.

For many subject areas such as foreign languages, advanced science, and mathematics, resource units have not been extensively developed. However, there have been many produced for English and social studies and for "core" programs. Recently an excellent series for consumer science has been published by the New York State Education Department.

(The next chapter is devoted to a discussion of resource units and contains suggestions for their development and effective use in providing a basis for teaching units.)

CLASSROOM MODIFICATION AND REFINEMENT OF PLANS

Just as the *process* of planning is more important than the resultant *plan* so it is more important to *have* a plan for each meeting of a class than to *follow* one. It is impossible to specify precisely in advance what should or will occur in the classroom. The unit plan cannot even state with precision how many days will be required for each phase. Therefore, unit plans provide broad guide lines for daily planning but do not eliminate the need for it.

The daily plan will differ according to its position in the total unit. It is not necessary for the daily plan to have the systematic organization of a unit. It need not come to a conclusion; often the activity is left for continuation the following day. Many changes in specifics are to be expected, particularly if students are given a share in determining them.

When based upon a well-constructed unit plan, the daily plan serves the functions of providing tentative agenda for the class and a set of notes or reminders for the teacher. It aids in preventing the results of an extensive process of careful curriculum planning from getting lost at the critical moment when they are to be transformed into experience.

Anticipation of Planning with Student Groups

In preceding chapters we have indicated our conviction that pupils should have a part in the curriculum making process. In the daily adjustments which are inevitable with any unit, the most direct and appropriate situation exists for the teacher to act on his democratic commitment and to take advantage of pupil maturity and interest in determining what may best be covered and how.

The extent to which the teacher can permit participation here or embark on experimentation will of course depend upon experience, the nature of the framework, local point of view, and so on. We know some teachers can allow students to choose among alternative approaches deemed equally suitable by the teacher. Some are inclined to create among students the impression of choosing freely when in reality they are skillfully being led to a decision predetermined by the teacher. Some will permit students to help decide over-all course objectives and select topics they would like to study, leaving to the teacher the specific planning of units for dealing with topics and for achieving the objectives. Others will favor the reverse by specifying for students the objectives and scope of the course and then permitting them to share in planning the experiences through which the learnings will result. Very few can risk the extreme position of allowing experiences to evolve, unplanned in advance, entirely through the process of pupil-teacher planning.

The point of view expressed in this chapter clearly makes the teacher the key person in planning learning experiences. It stresses the importance of very careful and deliberate "laying out" of courses of study and instructional units within a framework of the curriculum broadly drawn against the prevalent mandates. By no means, however, does it preclude student participation with each other and with the teacher in the process of establishing purposes and devising means for carrying them out. But if the professional teacher is to be circumscribed by rather precise frameworks, it is obvious that the students must also operate within the same ones and further be guided by the mature insights of the teacher.

Hence, in those situations where a problem-solving process is called for, students must of course have the opportunity to project solutions and to decide upon sources of data. In this undertaking the resource unit is valuable in reminding the teacher of possibilities to suggest to students. In this sense preplanning has taken place. But, further, teachers must constantly be aware of objectives which require other kinds of experiences than those planned by students, and they must be alert to the differing requirements of individuals within the class. Never can all the necessary experiences be planned cooperatively with students and, indeed, in many of the courses now offered in the secondary school the opportunities for such student participation may be very slight. Pupil-teacher planning should be used, then, where it is appropriate and eschewed where it is not.

Careful Introduction of Pupil-Teacher Planning

Most teachers lack training in the technique of planning with students in the classroom. Therefore, even when they perceive that a particular situation is one in which this approach would be advantageous, they frequently hesitate attempting it. Clearly, however, if the benefits of such experiences are to be realized, teachers will have to experiment with them until proficiency comparable to that with more conventional methods is achieved. In order that this may be done without an intolerable loss of security, it is important that they introduce the newer procedures very gradually and follow certain suggestions offered by teachers experienced in them.

The first thing which must be borne in mind is that usually the students also are unfamiliar with this mode of classroom operation and therefore must be helped to learn the new ways without their feeling too insecure. At first, the choices offered them must be relatively minor ones[12] until they become accustomed to being permitted to participate in planning and somewhat proficient in the process. For example, a starting point might well be the planning of some culminating group activity to summarize and apply the learnings of a unit. This provides practice in several skills, such as, (1) encouraging all members of the group to participate in the discussion without domination by a few, (2) anticipating the results of various proposals and some of the difficulties which may be encountered, (3) reaching consensus on a plan of action, (4) accepting individual responsibility for contributing to the enterprise, and (5) judging the results of the project when it is completed to identify effective procedures and those in which the group needs to improve.

When most of the members of the class demonstrate that they are able to exercise these group skills, a next phase might consist of having students also decide what sources might provide information answering the questions posed by the teacher for the unit and how the information can best be presented for everyone's benefit. In doing this such further skills as the following should begin to develop: (1) determining how to locate needed data, (2) using the library, particularly its reference materials, (3) working as small committees, and (4) developing and presenting individual and group reports.

Next the planning of entire units can be undertaken by the class with the teacher's guidance. To the skills already developed must be added those of (1) analyzing a problem or topic, and (2) deciding upon the learnings which should result from the study of the unit. Finally, a particular course may be such as to permit students to share in *identifying the problems to be considered*. This then will be the final phase of the gradual introduction of pupil-teacher planning. Here the

---

[12] Alice Miel *et al.*, *Cooperative Procedures in Learning*, Bureau of Publications, Teachers College, 1952.

skills to be developed will include (1) taking a problem census, (2) setting criteria for the acceptability of a problem for study, and (3) selecting and establishing a priority for problems on the basis of the criteria.

The design suggested above for inducting students into the curriculum planning process is by no means infallible and is only one of many possible approaches. The important point is that both teacher and students must gain confidence in their ability to work together in planning, executing and evaluating learning experiences. If the progress of either party is slow, undertakings should remain limited until a more extensive involvement can be attempted. Even so, a number of cautions should be observed. They are discussed at some length in Chapter 11.

Questions for Discussion

1. Identify some kinds of personal or immediate problems youth is likely to have. Show how they could *lead* to more important and significant issues or concerns.
2. Contrast how such issues and concerns were identified or focused upon in the traditional subject approach. Which in your estimation is better?
3. Do we have any likelihood of finding teachers whose wisdom is so sufficient that we may leave the major part of tactical planning to the classroom teacher?
4. Interview some teachers. Ask them to differentiate between courses of study and textbook. Ask them to show you their courses of study.
5. In your estimation could a course of study seek both content about American democracy and full development of the creative, problem-solving process?
6. Illustrate how a course of study you know provides for a series of lessons supporting and crystallizing broad generalizations or concepts.
7. How shall we balance out, decide upon the number of content units, activity units?

Selected Bibliography

Douglass, Harl, ed., *The High School Curriculum,* Ronald, 1956.
Krug, Edward, *Curriculum Planning,* rev. ed., Harper, 1957.
Leonard, J. Paul, *Developing the Secondary School Curriculum,* Rinehart, 1953.
Risk, Thomas, *Principles and Practices of Teaching,* American Book, 1957.
Saylor, J. Galen, and William Alexander, *Curriculum Planning,* Rinehart, 1954.
Stratemeyer, Florence, *et al., Developing A Curriculum for Modern Living,* rev. ed., Bureau of Publications, Teachers College, 1957.

....

CHAPTER 8

Production and Use of Resource Units

In the overview of the planning process presented in Chapter 7 brief mention was made of the resource unit. Because the preparation of resource units seems to be a promising approach to the improvement of instructional units and is almost essential to effective pupil participation in planning, some elaboration of this topic is desirable.

It should be understood that a resource unit is not a plan. A general plan for a year's or semester's work in some area of instruction is a course of study. This is often divided into a number of instructional units. The specific plan for teaching a unit to a specific group of students is generally known as a *teaching unit.* A *resource unit,* on the other hand, forms the basis for planning teaching units tailored to the nature of various groups. Or, if the plans are to be developed with the students, the resource unit offers the teacher a source of security by making available suggestions which will aid students in formulating and carrying out their plans. The resource unit is rather a file of ideas.

Just as the development of the instructional unit helped teachers break away from the discrete daily lesson approach, the resource unit first came into being to help teachers organize work on topics not found in the textbook. These were topics of current significance and also topics which were not limited to a single subject and therefore could not adequately be considered by any subject textbook.

THE VALUE OF RESOURCE UNITS

The advantages of resource units when students engage in planning of learning experiences are generally accepted. However, many teachers do not employ cooperative planning and often, therefore, fail to see the value of resource units in their work. Yet not only would their use improve teacher-directed instruction, but it would also serve as a first step toward greater involvement of students in the planning process. Of all the values which might be claimed only two will be suggested here: better individualization of instruction and greater efficiency in planning.

Individualization of Instruction

The thought of providing differential learning experiences in a diverse class of thirty students is for many of us so formidable a task that although we accept the desirability of doing so, we conclude that it is quite impossible. This is because we think in terms of fixed unit plans and daily lesson plans which must be adapted extemporaneously in the classroom to meet individual requirements. This is indeed difficult, if not impossible.

The only feasible way of differentiating instruction is to accumulate in advance a variety of materials and ideas for activities suitable for various student characteristics and needs. A resource unit should provide teachers with materials of all types and all levels of difficulty and activities appropriate for different groups and individuals as well as for the class as a whole. Furthermore, it should suggest experiences consistent with differing interests likely to be found in the classroom. Motivation is therefore aided. Enrichment for the more able students can be accomplished by selecting more challenging experiences, while provision may be made for the slower progress of other students by choosing from proposed activities and materials at a lower level of difficulty. To make such adaptations on the spur of the moment while teaching is almost impossible; equipped with a resource unit, the teacher should be able to approach this ideal much more closely.

Efficiency in Planning

In terms of efficiency of planning, the resource unit saves far more time than its production takes. Extensive daily lesson planning is extremely time-consuming. The use of teaching units makes the process of deciding upon a given day's work an easy and natural one. But to develop a different teaching unit for each class is also burdensome if it must be done *de novo* each time. Resource units permit this to be done expeditiously, however.

The fact that resource units are best developed cooperatively also increases efficiency. The burden can be shared and thus made lighter. Needless duplication of effort is avoided. Good ideas are made more widely available instead of being kept personal secrets. All of this makes for improvement.

CHARACTERISTICS OF RESOURCE UNITS

A resource unit is essentially a file and indeed may be located in a folder, but it is an organized file. If it is published or duplicated, the necessity for it to be organized may be more obvious, but organization is no less important to a folder. Unless the folder is organized, it cannot be used efficiently. Furthermore, since it is meant to be expanded, the process of adding items is facilitated by a clear-cut organization. Finally, its completeness and adequacy can be more easily assessed if it has an orderly arrangement.

However, the resource unit is a working tool not an academic exercise, and therefore the exact nature of its content and the specific manner of organization are not matters of great importance. Each group of teachers should find a format convenient for that group. The suggestions presented here may clarify the idea of resource units, demonstrate their value, and provide a basis for beginning to develop them.

Introduction

Assuming that such identifying information as title, course, and level has been set down, the first part recommended is an introduction. This may appear superfluous and, perhaps, ostentatious, but it serves three purposes. A statement of orientation for the unit serves (1) as a reminder to the teacher, (2) as a source of information to another professional person who may examine the unit, and (3) as a basis for introducing the unit to a class.

It is a worthwhile exercise for a teacher to state for a particular topic its significance in the contemporary world, its place in the logical development of a subject, its relationship to other topics and subject fields, and its bearing upon the lives of students. But even more important, *students* often need understanding as they embark upon a unit of work. The introductory statement provides a basis for teacher remarks. The teacher's presentation may be oral. More often, however, a teaching unit is duplicated and put in the hands of pupils as a guide. When this is done, an initial statement is very important in establishing the tone of the teaching unit and "letting pupils in on" what they are expected to get from it. Good guidance from the resource unit can be very helpful.

Outcomes

The second part of the resource unit ought to consist of a list of possible outcomes which might be sought through this unit. It is helpful to classify these as understandings, skills, and attitudes. Understandings include facts, concepts, principles, rules, and generalizations; skills include both specific actions and broader habits to be initiated or strengthened; attitudes include interests, appreciations, and values to be fostered.

The list of outcomes should be much longer than would be anticipated for any given class because the unit should lend itself to use with several age and grade groups. However, the list should be limited to important and realistic goals lest it become so long it cannot readily be comprehended. It can then serve as a check as to the adequacy of provisions for activities and materials. In this manner improbable or unrealistic objectives which there is no intention to seek or for which no materials or activities are available can be eliminated.

Content Outline

In most cases the resource unit relates to a subject course, and it is desirable for the teacher to have a logical outline of the major topics to be dealt with. The outline may not need to be detailed because any other teacher of that subject will be aware of the components of the main topics and, furthermore, the details will not be emphasized to the same degree in every class for which it is used. The outline is useful for checking against a syllabus or course of study which may be required or desired to be followed.

In certain "core" programs the content cannot be specified in advance and may be drawn from various subject areas. The unit then centers around a broad *problem* and the content outline becomes an analysis of that problem into relevant subproblems. In developing a plan for attacking the problem, students may suggest other component problems, but it is unlikely that these will differ greatly from those anticipated by the teacher. The teacher's analysis is important not only as a source of suggestions for the class, but as a basis for knowing what kinds of activities and materials are likely to be needed. With such pre-planning it is easier for students to participate extensively in planning how they will approach a problem.

Learning Experiences

Perhaps the most crucial, and certainly one of the most extensive, portion of the resource unit is the compilation of possible learning experiences. In developing this list, it is necessary to consider all of the outcomes, several ability levels of students, and various kinds of interests. Each experience must involve some activity with respect to some content.

What are learning activities? They are what students *do* to learn.

The following list may serve as a reminder of the types of activities which might be applicable in a particular unit. It by no means exhausts all of the possibilities. Teachers must consider with what content each activity is to be concerned in order that a learning experience may result.

ILLUSTRATIVE LEARNING EXPERIENCES

ACTIVITY	CONTENT
1. Reading—Text	Parts:
—Reference	Topics:
2. Reading—Oral	Selections:
3. Writing	Topics:
4. Observing—Demonstrations	On:
—Projections	Topics:
—Charts, models, etc.	Topics:
5. Listening—Teacher Lectures	On:
—Guest speakers	Topics:
—Recordings, programs	Topics:
6. Visiting	Places:
7. Constructing—Models	Of:
—Charts, maps, graphs	On:
8. Reporting—(Oral)	Topics:
9. Discussing	Questions:
10. Collecting	Items:
11. Displaying—Bulletin board	Themes:
—Table, diarama, etc.	Themes:
12. Problem-solving—Group research	Problems:
—Individual solution	Problems:
13. Practicing	Exercises:
14. Dramatizing	Topics:
15. Experimenting	With:

Even a random list of experiences of this sort is a helpful source of suggestions in making a unit plan. However, classification increases its usefulness. Two categories are possible and both can be used simultaneously.

One relates to the position in the unit at which the experience is most appropriate. Thus a three-way division into initiatory, developmental, and culminating experiences results. The developmental section is ordinarily the longest.

The second category is in terms of the participants. Here four main subparts are possible: entire class, interest groups, ability groups, and individuals. The experiences listed for the entire class are those which all pupils should have. Those under "interest groups" should be of the type that are suitable for committee work. The suggestions for the last two parts, ability groups and individuals, must, to be most useful, be further classified in terms of difficulty. For this, three divisions are satisfactory: high, average, and low. A symbol may be placed in front of each experience to indicate its level or, better, the suggestions may be sorted into three different lists.

When both of these schemes for classification are used, a grid results with twenty-four spaces.

Participant	1. Initiatory	2. Developmental	3. Culminating
A. Entire Class	A1	A2	A3
B. Interest groups	B1	B2	B3
C. Ability groups			
(a) High	C1(a)	C2(a)	C3(a)
(b) Average	C1(b)	C2(b)	C3(b)
(c) Low	C1(c)	C2(c)	C3(c)
D. Individuals			
(a) High	D1(a)	D2(a)	D3(a)
(b) Average	D1(b)	D2(b)	D3(b)
(c) Low	D1(c)	D2(c)	D3(c)

The chart is illustrative only and is not suitable for actually listing suggested experiences. The simplest way to begin this phase of construction is to take twenty-four sheets of paper and label them with the symbols in the chart along with their meaning. Ideas can then be entered on the appropriate page and additions can be made at any time, using additional pages when necessary. As the process advances, occasional reference to the list of illustrative learning experiences will suggest ideas which have been overlooked.

Learning Materials

Because it is impossible to keep in mind the variety and number of possible materials and other resources, an orderly way of listing them is essential. Perhaps the best way is to classify them according to the units for which they are most applicable. One section of each resource unit, then, should consist of such a list. It is helpful to arrange it according to the type of resource and to include needed information regarding how each item may be obtained or where it is located.

The most extensive part of the materials section ordinarily consists of reading materials. Included here we should find reference books and related literature, such as fiction, biography and other nonfiction, and fugitive materials of the pamphlet type. When the number of books is relatively extensive, teachers ought to classify them roughly on the basis of reading difficulty. Three levels—easy, average and difficult —may be used; but if the unit is to be used at several grade levels, more careful estimation of placement may be necessary. Needless to say, because this is time consuming, it is far too often neglected.

In addition to reading materials, such other resources as motion pictures, film strips, slides, models, charts and maps of possible relevance to the unit should be listed together with their sources and any data needed for planning their use. Speakers, places to visit, and other community resources may also be indicated, although more complete information should be available on them in the school's community resource file mentioned in the chapter on instructional materials.

Evaluation Procedures

It is often advocated that a complete resource unit contain a section devoted to possible procedures for evaluating outcomes and particularly to sample test items. If methods other than conventional testing are applicable, it is undoubtedly desirable that they be listed for future reference. These might include records to be kept by either students or teacher, a guide for observation by the teacher, checklists for student performance in various situations, or an inventory of students' attitudes. The resource unit should include samples of these instruments.

Good questions of the essay type also might well be recorded as part of each resource unit. But, except for a few model objective type items, this type is better handled in a separate card file.

Since the construction and validation of test items is a separate and continuous process, it is suggested that the evaluation section of the resource unit incorporate a discussion of that process rather than the items themselves. This discussion might well be standard for all units and should be prepared by someone on the staff who is well versed in item analysis procedures and the philosophy of testing. Improved evaluation is essential to improvement of curriculum and including this statement in each resource unit may help emphasize good testing procedures.

CONSTRUCTION OF RESOURCE UNITS

Since resource units are never used as plans but merely as a basis for planning, they may be developed at the state or system level, published commercially, or prepared by the teachers who will use them.

Whatever their origin or permanence of binding, they should never be construed as finished products. They should always be subject to continual revision and augmentation. Those obtained from external sources should be evaluated in terms of appropriateness of level and completeness, with respect to the structure suggested in the previous section and with respect to their adequacy for fit against local controls.

Most production of resource units must and probably should be done by teachers at the local school level. This task is one which can be done by a teacher individually or in cooperation with others. In fact, it is perhaps the most fruitful activity in which teachers can engage together in improving the curriculum.

As a joint undertaking, it usually involves the members of a department or a group of teachers teaching the same course. Two basic approaches are possible. It may be decided to assign specified units to the various individuals for independent development or it may be preferred that all contribute to each unit. The latter permits more pooling of ideas but requires more time for meeting together and for incorporating various suggestions into a single list. The gains outweigh these difficulties, however, and it is probably preferable to use the cooperative approach even though fewer units are developed in a given time. Not only does the team approach strengthen the program and help participating teachers improve, but the experience also forms a basis for wider group effort on curriculum problems throughout the school.

Initial Decisions

The first step in constructing resource units is to agree upon the topics or areas to be encompassed by each. If a teacher considers it an invasion of his professional prerogatives to consent to a group determination of this matter, it will of course not be possible for him to participate. It should be remembered, however, that resource units do not prescribe the manner in which instruction is to be carried out, but leave complete freedom of choice to teachers in formulating their own *teaching* units. Their order of use is also left to the teacher. Therefore, it should be possible for most teachers to sit down with colleagues and come to some agreement on the themes or problem statements which should constitute the major divisions of the course in question. Ideas can be derived from state syllabuses and course-of-study outlines from other states and systems, but these should remain suggestive. If a local system course of study exists, the extent of possible deviation from it should be determined. Indeed, if the course of study was developed cooperatively, several steps in the resource unit development process will already have been accomplished.

However, it should be pointed out that there are two types of resource units. The type that has been implied above is an intermediate kind which, since it falls within the framework of an established course of study, is narrow in scope and permits only slight variations in teaching units in accordance with the characteristics of the classes with which they are used. This is the type that an individual teacher can readily construct for his own use.

The other type, a "full-fledged" resource unit as it were, is much more extensive and can form the basis for work in various subjects or core courses. The topics for these are likely to be broad, lasting problems of society such as conservation, communication, democracy, peace, health, and the like. From a resource unit on freedom, for example, teaching units at various levels and in various courses might have such topics as "Men Who Fought for Freedom," "Great Documents of Freedom," "Dark Days for Freedom," "Civil Rights in America," and "The Freedom Theme in Literature," to name but a few. The content of such units is traditional subject matter, but it is reorganized in a form different from the conventional.

Joint Deliberation

When the type and topic has been decided, the next step is the determination of feasible outcomes applicable to the resource unit. If they are not already stated in a course-of-study guide, this is a proper matter for the group to decide upon. The outcomes should stem from the stated objectives of the course as a whole in accord with the nature and scope of coverage of the particular unit. As noted earlier, the unit outcomes probably are best classified as understandings, skills, and attitudes.

The content for each unit may then be outlined. If the organization of units is somewhat novel, it may be necessary to check off each item of subject matter in a syllabus or course-of-study guide to assure that all of the required or recommended content has been incorporated. It must be remembered that teachers operate within a total framework of curriculum determination and do not possess such complete freedom that they can proceed independently of mandates imposed at higher levels of responsibility. Nevertheless, the same body of cultural or curricular content can be organized for instruction or emerge in a vast number of ways. Therefore, teachers should enjoy great freedom to be creative with respect to the organization of courses and units as long as they responsibly demonstrate that the schemes they evolve comply with expectations or at least do not vary so radically as to be confusing.

The outline of content for a unit need not be detailed and usually does not need to be extensive or cover many pages. Great detail is unnecessary because it is to be used by specialists or well-qualified generalizers who are quite aware of what is encompassed by a particular topic. Furthermore, general phraseology preserves freedom for the teacher and to some extent preserves for students the freedom to select the specific subject matter needed to effect understanding.

Pooling Ideas

On the remaining parts of the resource unit collaboration can be of a somewhat different nature. The joint deliberation and decision which are necessary with respect to the unit themes, outcomes, and content outline are not required with respect to learning experiences, resources, and evaluative items. Suggestions for these portions can be accumulated simply by pooling the independent ideas of the participating teachers. Ideas for learning experiences derive from previous successful teaching, from the reading of books and periodicals, from attendance at conferences, from visiting other schools, and from sheer professional creativity. (Sources of information about materials are discussed in Chapter 9.)

As for activities, a convenient method of cooperation consists of having individual teachers write suggestions on file cards which can later be examined together and classified. Particularly in general education areas, it is useful to ask various specialists to contribute suggestions for activities relevant to the unit theme involving their special fields. Some even advocate categorizing certain activities under such headings as music, art, manual, and the like so they may easily be selected later for pupils with special interests.

In deciding which of the contributed activity ideas to include in the resource unit, it is important to keep in mind that at this point it is not possible to consider appropriateness for specific pupils nor suitability in terms of available time. This must be done when the teaching unit is developed, but in constructing the resource unit the object is to provide as many suggestions as possible. The criteria for inclusion, therefore, are whether the activity is relevant to the theme and outcomes of the unit and whether it is definitely of educational value and not likely to be wasteful of pupil time. The major task is one of classifying for ease of use and noting the categories in which more ideas are needed.

Two kinds of cooperative activities are worthwhile with regard to developing test suggestions and guidance. Test items constructed by each teacher can be shared by the others if a file of the type mentioned earlier is maintained. Each individual can still prepare his own tests even though items are selected from a common pool. Whenever an item is used, an entry regarding difficulty and discrimination should be entered on the card by the teacher using it. In this way, information accumulates as to the worth of the items. Thus cooperation aids both in the construction and in the validation of test items.

In the production of resource units there is no conflict between individual initiative and cooperative action. When conditions are not suitable for cooperation, nothing prevents the individual teacher from proceeding on his own. A superior individual may indeed produce something better than can a group of less capable people. But when joint action will save time and create a better product, it would seem highly desirable to facilitate such action. In either case, resource unit production is one of the most effective approaches teachers have toward improving the curriculum and their own instruction. They should understand clearly, therefore, what a resource unit is and how to create one.

ILLUSTRATION OF A RESOURCE UNIT

Without question, it is desirable to examine a number of resource units before attempting to develop one. A clearer idea of what they are can be gained in this way than simply through reading about them. The difficulty of including a sample resource unit in a book is that, if a really thorough one is used, it will occupy too much space, and if it is not thorough, it may give the wrong impression as to its usefulness. Furthermore, of course, it can only deal with one subject field or problem area and hence the reader must try to imagine one for his own field. In addition, a published illustration gives the appearance of being complete whereas working units are continually expanding. A sample will seem quite neat and concise whereas the ones teachers make for their own use will ordinarily be dispersed over many sheets of paper in a file folder. Finally, in considering an illustration as a model, a reader may conclude there is only one form for a resource unit and that the one presented is it.

The example presented on pages 219–227 was produced by a student preparing to be a secondary school teacher as an assignment in a college course and was not intended by him to be complete or to be a model. He has graciously consented to its being included here and to its being subjected to critical comments by the authors. Actually, as a student exercise it is excellent and indeed with further expansion would do credit to any teacher. The authors' remarks about it are intended to aid the reader in critically appraising published units and in preparing better ones himself.

1. Introduction

In terms of the discussion in this chapter the introduction is much too brief even for an "intermediate" type unit. However, what there is gives an idea of what should be found in an introduction. It emphasizes the social justification for the unit and would provide some basis for "setting the stage" with a class. It does not suggest how the unit relates to previous or subsequent work in the course or in social studies in general, and it does not relate the topic to the lives of eighth graders. In its brevity, it does not reveal to the teacher the full possibilities of the unit nor refer him to readings to enlarge his background.

2. Objectives

These are what the authors have preferred to call "outcomes" and they are classified in the manner which has been recommended. They are reasonably few in number and for the most part realistically attainable or at least likely to be reflected in the teaching. Under "skills," it might be more accurate to substitute "improve" or "strengthen" for "develop," where it appears, since this single unit would not be relied upon for the complete development. Some of the skills might be made more specific, such as the ones referring to critical thinking and to study habits by indicating what aspect of these complexes will receive emphasis through this unit.

3. Content Outline

This is a logical outline of the subject matter which will come into use in the development of the unit. It is not as detailed and lengthy as many which appear, but it could probably have been confined to two levels of subordination after the main headings and still be meaningful to another social studies teacher. However, the detail does no harm as long as it can be kept in mind and it may serve as a helpful reminder and check.

The content in this illustration is conventional and derives from a single course of study. As such, it does not differ greatly from a textbook outline. Again, it should be understood that a broader unit would encompass far more content than would be associated with just one course.

4. Learning Activities

These are organized, as suggested, in terms of the phase of the unit to which they pertain and in addition the developmental activities are classified as appropriate for whole class, small group, and individual. Some of the individual activities are marked as especially appropriate for the better students. A further distinction of "average" and "slow" might have been made here, and the group activities might have been classified as those for "interest group or committee" type and for "ability groups." The list of activities could be expanded easily to include many other types by referring to the checklist presented earlier. However, each of the objectives sought is reflected in one or more of the activities listed. All in all they suggest a variety of interesting and worthwhile things for eighth graders to do in studying this important phase of national history.

5. Materials and Resources

These are classified into two main types. Other types might have been included: pamphlets, charts and maps, field trips, film strips, etc. All of the books appear to be nonfiction; another list of fiction related to this historical period would be useful. Both lists might well include notations revealing the approximate level of reading difficulty of each item. The list of films would be more useful if it provided information on source and length, at least.

6. Evaluation

Here a complete sample test has been included. As suggested earlier, it is probably more helpful merely to accumulate as large a number of good items as possible from which various tests might be constructed and keep these in a separate card file.

As in all cases of evaluation, it is difficult to find ways of checking progress toward many of the objectives. Understandings, particularly facts, are easily tested but some provision for evaluation in the area of attitudes and skills is also needed. Thus various checklists, performance tests, opinion inventories, and the like would be useful. These, as well as occasional brief quizzes, also help make evaluation a continuous process rather than something concentrated at the conclusion of the unit. In addition, evaluation of oral presentations, of group discussions, and of other aspects of the process, as contrasted with the content, should be appraised and students should participate in that. Lists of criteria for these purposes can be used for any unit.

The actual test items in the illustration need not be analyzed in detail here but it may be noted that while the multiple-choice items are in the main soundly constructed, some of the completion items are weak. Number 1, for example, is not an appropriate completion item and some of the others relating to men's names might better be combined, with a few additions, into a matching question. The essay questions are appropriate in their aims but might be more explicit to help the student grasp what is expected of him.

TITLE: ESTABLISHING OUR NATION[1]
FOR: Social Studies, Grade 8

INTRODUCTION

In view of the omnipresent threat of the Communist ideology and totalitarian government in today's troubled world, it is of increasing import to strengthen our democratic ideals and cultivate a love of human freedom in the hearts and minds of our young citizens. We are now engaged in a global contest, the stakes being the preservation of our values and indeed our very existence as a nation. In this continuing struggle we must produce worthy citizens and promote democratic ideals which will ensure our ultimate victory and the perpetuation of our free society. The knowledge of the founding of this nation, which includes the winning of independence and the framing of the Constitution, is essential for good citizenship. This is an integral part of our heritage—from this period come most of our basic rights and freedoms as Americans. The War for Independence expressed the conviction in the fundamental rights of man, rights that were written into our Constitution. This early struggle for liberty exemplifies our determination to be a free people. We can learn much from a study of this period that will strengthen our values and help to unite us in a common effort to sustain these values and defeat the forces working against them.

OBJECTIVES

Understandings:
1. A belief in the natural rights of man led the colonists to revolution and the establishment of an independent nation.
2. The Constitution provides the framework of our government and is the supreme law of the land.
3. The Constitution, the Declaration of Independence, and the Bill of Rights promote freedom and the democratic way of life.

[1] Prepared in 1958 by James A. Linderman as a class assignment at College of Education, State University, Albany. Used as an example with his permission.

4. An acquaintance with the major incidents and heroes of the struggle for liberty in America.

Attitudes:
1. Appreciation of the struggle and sacrifice of the colonists to establish this nation.
2. Appreciation of the ideals and contributions of our early leaders.
3. Respect for our Constitution and its principles.
4. Respect for our democratic form of government.
5. Realization of the continuous nature of the fight for democracy.

Skills:
1. To develop oral skills through class discussion.
2. To develop self-expression through oral and written reports.
3. To learn how to interpret documents.
4. To learn how to make use of the library.
5. To develop critical thinking.
6. To acquire a tolerance for the views of others.
7. To cultivate good study habits.
8. To develop the ability to make valid generalizations.
9. To learn how to use maps and charts.

CONTENT OUTLINE

I. Colonial Resistance to British Rule
   A. Unpopular British policies and effects
      1. Stamp Act
         a. Taxation without representation
         b. Stamp Act Congress
         c. Sons of Liberty
         d. Boycott of British goods
         e. Colonial resoultions in legislatures
         f. Repeal
      2. Proclamation of 1763 and Quebec Act
      3. Townshend duties
         a. Boston massacre
         b. Boston Tea Party
      4. Intolerable Acts
         a. Boston closed to commerce
         b. Revocation of colonial charter
         c. First Continental Congress
         d. Commerce boycott
         e. Militia
   B. The Outbreak of War
      1. Lexington and Concord
         a. Paul Revere
         b. Minutemen
      2. Second Continental Congress
II. Fighting for Independence
   A. Tom Paine's *Common Sense*

B. Declaration of Independence
   1. Franklin, Adams, Jefferson, Hancock, Washington
   2. July 4th, a historic occasion
C. Campaigns
   1. Saratoga
   2. Valley Forge
   3. Yorktown
D. Advantages for Americans
   1. Geography
   2. Foreign aid
   3. Great leaders
E. Disadvantages for Americans
   1. Financial difficulties
   2. Small population
   3. No standing army
   4. People divided in support
F. Advantages for British
   1. Greater wealth and population
   2. Trained armies and officers
   3. Aid of Hessian troops
G. Disadvantages for British
   1. Divided support for war
   2. No great leaders
   3. Fighting on foreign soil
H. Great American patriots
   1. Patrick Henry—great orator
   2. Sam Adams—organizer of resistance
   3. George Washington—"father of our country"
   4. Nathan Hale
   5. George Rogers Clark
   6. Ben Franklin
   7. Thomas Jefferson
   8. Robert Morris—financier of the war
I. Treaty of Peace (1783)
III. The Need for Stronger Government
   A. Structure of the Confederation
   B. Accomplishments of the Colonies under the Articles
      1. Conduct of the War
      2. Cession of western lands
      3. 1783 Peace Treaty
      4. Northwest Ordinance
   C. Weaknesses Under the Articles
      1. No tax power
      2. No power to regulate commerce
      3. No chief executive
      4. No federal court system
      5. No power to settle disputes between states
      6. No respect from foreign governments
      7. No support for an army and navy

IV. The Constitution
    A. Constitutional Convention
    B. Founding Fathers
       1. Washington—presiding officer
       2. Ben Franklin—wisdom and experience
       3. James Madison—"Father of the Constitution"
       4. Alexander Hamilton—strong central government
       5. James Wilson—strong and popular government
       6. Roger Sherman—Connecticut Compromise
    C. Main Compromises
       1. Connecticut Compromise
       2. North-South Compromise
    D. Democratic Features of the Constitution
       1. Separation of power
          a. Executive
             (1) approves or vetoes laws
             (2) makes treaties
             (3) appoints justices to supreme court
             (4) spends money
          b. Legislative
             (1) passes laws
             (2) approves treaties
             (3) controls money
             (4) approves judicial appointments
          c. Judicial
             (1) review laws
             (2) judge law cases involving federal government
       2. Federal Principle
          a. U.S. Government (delegated power) controls:
             (1) Foreign relations
             (2) Foreign and interstate commerce
             (3) Defense
             (4) Money system
          b. State governments (residual power) controls:
             (1) Education
             (2) Public works
             (3) Police power
             (4) Health and safety
             (5) Local governments
       3. Limited Power
       4. Amendment process

Word List

actual representation	minutemen	declaration
virtual representation	repeal	patriot
resolution	massacre	Hessian
intolerable act	Continental Congress	campaign
boycott	delegate	treaty
militia	document	standing army

financier

provision

delegated power

residual power

veto

amendment

federalist

antifederalist

Bill of Rights

dictator

tyranny

common interest

common danger

oppressor

national unity

monarchy

parliament

checks and balances

executive

legislative

judicial

convention

loyalist

turning point

Articles of Confederation

ratify

ordinance

interstate commerce

central government

Founding Fathers

presiding officer

compromise

House of Congress

popular government

equal representation

separation of power

federal principle

LEARNING ACTIVITIES

A. Initiatory:
1. Stimulate interest through a class discussion of rights and freedoms that the students have as American citizens. Compile this list on the blackboard.
2. Prepare a bulletin board exhibit of things pertaining to American freedoms. Have class participate in this.
3. Read a patriotic poem and discuss its points that have bearing on the unit. Several poems may be found in Joy E. Morgan's *The American Citizen's Handbook.*
4. Show pictures of early U.S. History. Emerson M. Brooks' *The Growth of a Nation* contains some excellent pictures, posters, and maps.
5. Raise questions on the origins of our rights and freedoms and leave them unanswered temporarily; solve them during the unit's study.
6. Talk about the 4th of July as a holiday and get a discussion going on what is behind this occasion.

B. Developmental:
Whole-class activities
1. Map study illustrating isolation of colonists from England. Discuss how distance and slow communication fostered a spirit of independence in the colonies.
2. Discuss how geographical factors helped develop self-reliance and spirit of freedom for colonists.
3. Have class members make a list of words pertinent to the unit that they should know.
4. Show movie "American Colonies." (Tells story of daily life in the colonies and what happened to make colonies to band together to meet a common oppressor.)
5. Show movie "Colonial Freedoms are Threatened." (Shows ways British threatened colonial freedom and how the colonists resisted oppressive laws.)
6. Have class members make a summary of the various acts passed by parliament and give colonial objections and reaction.
7. Make a list of respective advantages and disadvantages of both Britain and Americans in Revolution.

8. Play phonograph record "Stamp Tax Proposal." (Gives English view and colonial objections.) Discuss.
9. Show movie "Fourth of July." (Shows importance of this holiday and provides background for the momentous act of 1776.)
10. Read aloud Longfellow's poem about Paul Revere—also "The Concord Hymn" by Emerson. Discuss.
11. Have class do outside readings, selecting books from the school library which pertain to the unit. Brief reports on these readings may be given.
12. Map study to show how Cornwallis was trapped by French and Americans at Yorktown.
13. Show movie "Beginnings of the American Nation." (Discuss weaknesses of colonies under the Articles of Confederation.)
14. Make a graph or chart on the Articles of Confederation giving provisions and specific weaknesses.
15. Choral reading of the Preamble to the Constitution and discussion of the ideas involved.
16. Dramatize the Constitutional Convention by having class members act as delegates.
17. Class discussion of rights, duties, and responsibilities in the Constitution.
18. Show movie "Amendments to the Constitution." (Explains why amendments are needed and how they protect our rights as citizens.)
19. Class discussion to summarize unit material.

Small-group activities

20. Divide class into groups. Let each group alternate in asking and answering questions pertinent to this unit.
21. Divide class into several groups. Have each group prepare a bulletin-board display on different aspects of the unit.
22. Have a committee prepare and put on a play in which a few patriots try to convince a few Tories that they should join the side of the patriots.
23. Divide class into groups and have each group prepare a brief newspaper on some aspect of the unit.
24. Panel discussion on whether or not we should have separated from England.
25. Panel discussion or debate on small state vs. large state controversy in framing Constitution. Emphasize issues that were compromised.

Individual activities

26. Have each student do a biography on one of America's early great leaders.
27. Have each student write a letter to a friend in England encouraging him to come to America. Try to convince him of the freedom and opportunities to be enjoyed in the colonies.
28. Draw cartoons on various topics such as the Boston Tea Party, etc.
29. Oral reports on famous early leaders: Washington, Jefferson, Hamilton, etc.
30. Have each student assume he is a citizen of Boston. Write a letter to a friend in Virginia or some other state telling him of events which happened in Boston.

31. Report on Tom Paine showing how he influenced the move toward a complete break with England. (For gifted students).
32. Write an account of discussions for and against declaring independence in a meeting of the Second Continental Congress. (For gifted students).
33. Write newspaper editorials from both patriot and Tory viewpoints concerning the conflict over independence. (For gifted students).
34. Write an entry which might have appeared in James Madison's diary. (For gifted students).

C. Culminating Activity:
1. Take a field trip to a nearby historic site which is relevant to the unit, such as the Saratoga battlefield.
2. Visit a session of the state legislature to illustrate "democracy in action."
3. Organize class as a self-governing body and draw up a constitution for it.
4. Class discussion of the unit and its importance.

MATERIALS AND RESOURCES

A. Books
1. Albjerg, Marguerite Hall, and Knight, Frederic B., *We, the Guardians of Our Liberty,* Atlantic, Chicago, Dallas, Beckley-Cardy Company, 1940.
2. Brooks, Emerson M., *The Growth of a Nation,* New York, E. P. Dutton and Company, Inc., 1956.
3. Brown, Marion Marsh, *Young Nathan,* New York, Junior Literary Guild, Philadelphia, The Westminster Press, 1949.
4. Carmer, Carl, *Cavalcade of America,* New York, Crown Publishers, Inc., 1956.
5. Coy, Harold, *The First Book of Congress,* New York, Franklin Watts, Inc., 1956.
6. Findlay, Bruce, and Findlay, Esther, *Your Rugged Constitution,* Stanford, University Press, 1950.
7. Fisher, Dorothy Canfield, *Our Independence and the Constitution,* Eau Claire, E. M. Hall and Company, 1950.
8. Kelty, M. G., *The Beginnings of the American People and Nation,* Boston, Ginn and Company, 1930.
9. Kottmeyer, William, *Our Constitution and What it Means,* St. Louis, Dallas, Pasadena, Webster Publishing Company, 1949.
10. Mason, F. Van Wyck, *The Winter at Valley Forge,* New York, Random House, 1953. (Fiction)
11. McGee, Dorothy Horton, *Famous Signers of the Declaration,* New York, Dodd-Mead and Company, 1956.
12. Moon, Glenn W., and MacGowan, John H., *Story of Our Land and People,* New York, Henry Holt and Company, 1957.
13. Morgan, Joy Elmer, *The American Citizen's Handbook,* Washington, D.C., NEA, 1941.
14. Norton, Thomas J., *The Constitution of the United States,* New York, World Publishing Co., 1943.

15. Rodell, Fred, *Fifty-Five Men,* New York and Harrisburg, The Telegraph Press, 1936.
16. Schachner, Nathan, *Alexander Hamilton,* New York, Toronto, and London, The McGraw-Hill Book Company, Inc., 1952.
17. Swift, Lucius B., *How We Got Our Liberties,* Indianapolis, Bobbs-Merrill Company, 1928.
18. Tappan, Eva March, *American Hero Stories,* Boston and New York, Houghton Mifflin Company, 1906.
19. Tappan, Eva March, *The Story of Our Constitution,* Boston, Lothrop, Lee and Shepard Company, 1922.
20. *The Living Democracy Series: No. 13, Men to Remember,* Civic Education Center, Medford, Tufts University, 1956.

B. Audio-visual Materials

    Films: "Amendments to the Constitution"
           "American Colonies"
           "Beginnings of the American Nation"
           "Colonial Freedoms are Threatened"
           "Fourth of July"

    Recording: "Stamp Tax Proposal"

EVALUATION

Sample Test Covering this Unit:

I. Fill in the blanks with the correct answers.
1. The Colonists objected to the Stamp Act because _____.
2. A famous incident in Boston in which several colonists dressed like Indians was _____.
3. The opening battles of the Revolutionary War were fought at

_____.
4. "Common Sense" was written by _____.
5. _____ was signed on July 4, 1776.
6. The great patriot who regretted that he had but one life to give for his country was _____.
7. Our country's first constitution was called _____.
8. The man who is often called the "father of the Constitution" was

_____.
9. The great compromise that provided for two houses of Congress was _____ compromise.
10. The Constitution provides for three departments of governments. They are: _____, _____, and _____.
11. The first ten amendments are called _____.
12. The branch of government that makes laws is _____.
13. _____ secured French aid in the Revolutionary War.
14. _____ wrote the Declaration of Independence.
15. _____ presided over the Constitutional Convention.

II. Multiple choice. Underline the correct answer in each item.
1. The battle which ended the Revolutionary War was fought at (a) Valley Forge (b) Yorktown (c) New York (d) Saratoga.

2. The country which aided the United States during the Revolution was: (a) Germany (b) Canada (c) Russia (d) France.
3. The main reason we needed a new constitution was that: (a) we were at war (b) we were poor (c) there were many rebellions (d) our government had little power.
4. A power of the executive branch is: (a) making laws (b) reviewing laws (c) approving or vetoing laws (d) judging law cases.
5. The division of the government into three branches is called: (a) limited power (b) separation of power (c) delegated power (d) residual power.
6. The supporters of the Constitution were called: (a) Federalists (b) antifederalists (c) patriots (d) minutemen.

III. Answer *two* of the following:
1. Discuss briefly colonial resistance to British rule.
2. Discuss briefly the advantages and disadvantages of the Americans during the Revolutionary War.
3. Discuss some of the democratic features of the Constitution.
4. Discuss some of the weaknesses of the Articles of Confederation and tell how these weaknesses were corrected after the adoption of the Constitution.

EFFECTIVE USE OF RESOURCE UNITS

Although the place of resource units in the total process of planning appropriate learning experiences has been considered in Chapter 7, some further comments may be appropriate because obviously no matter how faithfully and well resource units are constructed, they are of little value if not used properly. The most important point about them is that they are only aids to instructional planning and do not in themselves constitute plans for teaching. Specific plans for teaching must indicate definitely the activities which will be included, the materials to be used, the timing sequence and duration of the various experiences, the assignment of tasks, and the diagnostic procedures to be employed. After careful study of a good resource unit, a teacher with some familiarity with a class should be able to lay out several weeks of work rather quickly.

If it is preferred that students participate in the final decisions as to what is to be done, the teacher's study of the resource unit, decision as to the extent and nature of student participation to be permitted, and notation of suggestions he may make, represent necessary preplanning. Besides preparing to aid individual students and groups to make selections of projects on which to work, the teacher must give thought in advance as to how the groups are to be formed and managed and also to the practice opportunities which must be provided. Resource units often do not specify the latter since it is assumed that the teacher will make appropriate provisions for strengthening skills and promoting retention.

Furthermore, since resource units are more or less independent of position in a course, attention must be given to the way a particular unit can be introduced which will relate it to previous learnings. The initiation should also be planned with due regard for the interests of the specific class. Often a decision on how the unit is to culminate will determine how it should be initiated, and at times making this decision is actually part of the initiatory phase during which students should participate.

While the resource unit is intended to improve instruction, the actual teaching of a unit also serves to improve the resource unit. When pupils participate in planning and proposing ideas, many of their suggestions are worth recording for possible use another time. On the other hand, some of the ideas in the resource unit do not always work out as well as it seemed they might, and this information should be noted. Rather than delete items, it is probably more useful to insert cautions or suggestions for their improvement.

There is another reason for keeping logs or records of the units studied by a group of pupils—namely, to prevent gaps and repetitions in future years. This is particularly true of course when specific courses of study are not rigidly followed. For example, the teacher alone or with students might select from a wide number of possible topics in seventh-grade science. If the same procedure is used in the eighth grade, it is necessary to know what was done the previous year. These records should be quite detailed so that the exact nature and extent of the work will be clear. In this way the same resource unit may be drawn upon in two successive years without duplication.

It should not be construed that in developing teaching units from resource units the teacher merely lists certain experiences and materials and routinely presents them to students. The teacher must assure that concepts are developed systematically and thoroughly and that skills are practiced sufficiently. This requires presentations by the teacher, teacher-led discussions, various diagnostic procedures, and intensive practice opportunities for selected students. In planning the unit and each day's work, the teacher must make provision for these activities in addition to those suggested in the resource unit. Otherwise, the desired learnings will not take place and the resource unit, intended to improve the instructional situation, will have adverse effects instead of those anticipated.

Questions for Discussion

1. This chapter has been exhortative with respect to the use of resource units. What objections, if any, might be raised regarding their use? What obstacles to their preparation might be encountered? How might these obstacles be overcome?
2. If it were necessary for some reason to eliminate one of the recommended sections of a resources unit, which would you do without? Why?
3. Is there a way of expressing desired learning outcomes or unit objectives which you consider superior to the classification into understandings, skills, and attitudes? Can you think of any outcomes which do not fit into these categories?
4. What criteria should determine the selection of experiences and materials from a resource unit for use with a particular class?
5. How could a school principal stimulate resource unit production among his faculty?

Selected Bibliography

Biddick, Mildred L., *The Preparation and Use of Source Units,* Progressive Education Association, *circa* 1940 (mimeo.).

Bristow, William, and Dorothy Furman, *The Unit in Curriculum Development and Instruction,* New York City Board of Education, 1959.

Bureau of Secondary Curriculum Development, *Tall Tales and Tunes: A Resource Unit for Junior High School English,* New York State Education Department, 1959.

Garrett County High School Workshop, *Technology of Living,* Garrett County (Maryland) Board of Education, 1950 (mimeo.).

Hand, Harold, ed., *Living in the Atomic Age: A Resource Unit for Teachers in Secondary Schools,* College of Education, University of Illinois Press, 1946.

Hanna, Lavone, Gladys Potter, and Neva Hagaman, *Unit Teaching in the Elementary School,* Rinehart, 1955.

Krug, Edward, *Curriculum Planning,* rev. ed., Harper, 1957.

Leese, Joseph, *Education for Better Use of Our Resources,* CASDA, College of Education, State University of New York, 1952.

Lurry, Lucille, and Elsie Alberty, *Developing a High School Core Program,* Macmillan, 1957.

Quillen, I. James, *Using a Resource Unit,* National Council for the Social Studies, no date.

CHAPTER 9

....

Development, Selection, and Use
of Instructional Materials

That aspect of curriculum work in which teachers devise learning experiences and select suitable activities and appropriate content for specific groups of students inevitably leads us to instructional materials. Most activities designed to produce learning involve materials of some sort, either because they are implied by action, as in the case of throwing or reading, or because they serve as a source of the content. Much cultural content either is represented by or recorded in material objects.

The schools of an earlier day were characterized by both a physical barrenness and a paucity of materials for use in instruction. Books were dominant but even those were scarce. Even today many teachers limit the activities of their students to listening and to reading a single textbook.

In the nineteenth century a movement known as object teaching flourished. It was based upon the pedagogical ideas of Pestalozzi but reached the height of its popularity under Edward Sheldon at what is now the College of Education at Oswego, New York. In this approach some sort of object was made the center of a lesson in which pupils sought to observe as many characteristics and to form as many relationships as possible. The method soon became very formalistic and probably assumed somewhat the same character as the meaningless drill and rote memorization which was prevalent. But the idea of learning from direct as well as from vicarious experience was later to be extensively promoted.

The so-called "new education" had, of course, as its central thesis the value of personal experience as a basis of learning. This idea stemmed from the growing tendency to favor scientific experiment over reliance upon authority as a source of truth. Therefore, in addition to observation and manipulation, the use of many literary sources instead of a single textbook "authority" also came to be favored.

However, learning, or the acquisition of knowledge, is not the same as investigation, or the extension of knowledge. It does not therefore necessarily follow that the methods of the latter are the best for the former purpose. But if one of the goals of formal instruction is to develop the ability to continue learning independently, the use of such methods is justified since most such informal learning takes place in the face of some problem which requires solution. If students have been limited entirely to a type of instruction in which their learning activities are specified in detail and their source of content is circumscribed, it is unlikely that the ability to engage in individual study or problem-solving will develop. However, even for the conventional goals of instruction, there are psychological reasons for favoring the use of a wide variety of materials.

The Obvious Need for Instructional Materials

Several arguments for varied learning activities were presented in Chapter 7. Variety of activity implies variety of material, and the same arguments are valid in each case. Interest is enhanced, differences among pupils in mode of learning are recognized, and reinforcement is effected when learning is not limited to a single type of material.

However, two further points should be noted. There has been a tendency to rely heavily upon a textbook as almost the sole source of instructional content. Aside from giving the impression that the particular book used is infallible or singularly valid, this practice ignores the striking differences in reading ability within most secondary school classes. If learning is to be dependent upon the ability to comprehend what is read, it is incumbent upon those who teach to give the pupils books within their level of comprehension. The desirability of a multiplicity of reading materials is thus indicated.

Yet even this provision overlooks a shortcoming inherent in verbal materials of any sort. This is exemplified in the Chinese proverb about a picture being worth a thousand words. Except for people of unusual ability in abstraction, verbal symbols have severe limitations in conveying concepts faithfully. Not many secondary school students are sufficiently sophisticated in this respect nor have they an extensive enough background of actual experience to provide the framework for purely verbal elaboration of ideas. The "boners" frequently attributed to them testify to the inaccuracy of the constructs they form in the absence of adequate direct or nonverbal vicarious experience. Even pictures cannot do justice to Niagara.

While such excellent devices as motion pictures and television are now available for teaching, it should be emphasized that none of these supplants books and other printed materials. In fact, the latter are needed in greater abundance than ever when modern methods of teaching are used, not merely because of the range of difficulty to be provided for but equally because these methods stress research from literary sources, frequently involving contemporary topics not yet included in textbooks. Although poor readers may profit especially from nonverbal materials, even for them the use of such materials must only be supplementary. To spare them from reading is to do them a disservice; more than anything they need assistance in improving this skill and this requires verbal materials at their level of comprehension.

LOCATING AND EVALUATING MATERIALS

The production of instructional materials has become "big business" in the United States. The commercial interests involved put before the teacher a bewilderingly wide assortment of their wares, necessitating his choosing from among them the materials which best fit the learning experiences planned. At the same time, there are many kinds of material which are not profitable to produce commercially or which by their very nature cannot be so produced. They exist, but their existence is not as widely proclaimed as that of products which benefit from extensive advertising and promotion. The teacher is faced with the task of locating them. Finally, the kind of material needed for some learning experiences simply does not exist, commercially or otherwise. If the desired learning experience is to be provided, the teacher must make these items himself or have them made.

Selection Essential in Procurement and Use

The goal of selection is, of course, to have the right material at the right time for the right students. There are therefore three aspects to the problem. The broadest aspect is that of having *potentially* valuable materials on hand. The other two relate to timing and differentiation at the actual point of use.

1. *Practical considerations must guide choice.* That there is an economic consideration with respect to choosing materials is self-evident. Some highly desirable items may be financially out of the question in some school situations. In other cases, the relative importance of

one expensive item must be weighed against the educational value to be had from the many less expensive materials which could be obtained for an equivalent sum. There are many instances in which the budgetary allotment for materials is niggardly and much desired items can not be obtained. Teachers should recognize, however, that increase in budget provisions will be brought about only through steady and forceful insistence by teachers. Certainly it is unrealistic to expect boards of education to implore teachers to use more instructional materials. Yet it is not uncommon for administrators to wish teachers would ask for more. The old adage about the squeaking wheel getting the grease applies.

A further practical consideration in the selection of materials is durability. For equipment or books which are to be used by many people and are expected to last many years it is false economy to choose shoddy goods. On the other hand, the opposite may be true with expendable supplies; when foolscap is satisfactory, it is prodigal to use bond paper.

2. *Educational value is paramount consideration.* Important as cost and quality are, they are overshadowed by the educational factors to be considered. First among these must be *validity.* This concept, so pre-eminent in the area of testing, has two aspects when applied to instructional materials. One is the accuracy or truthfulness of the material—its objectivity or correspondence with reality. Qualified teachers should be competent to judge whether materials are consistent with current scholarship in their fields. But unless teachers keep abreast of developments in their subject areas, as was emphasized in Chapter 4, they cannot effectively evaluate the instructional materials they use. Only constant scholarship will guarantee identification of out-of-date and false information.

In this regard the matter of sponsored materials arises. A vast quantity of films, magazines, pamphlets, samples of products or raw materials, and other items useful in the classroom is made available each year by industrial firms, political groups, and other special interest groups. Most of it is free and of high technical quality, often surpassing similar material prepared specifically for instructional use and expensive to obtain. The temptation to use sponsored materials is therefore very strong.

Yet there must be awareness of possible ulterior motives underlying these materials and the accompanying fear of subverting education and of indoctrinating children. It would be naïve to think that sponsors made such materials available solely out of a desire to contribute to the educational system, but the very recognition that this is not the case and the awareness of possible undesirable effects of their use are themselves the best safeguards against the inherent danger. With such realization, the teacher will understand what precautions are necessary.

Both to aid and protect the teacher it is desirable that the board of education establish a policy regarding sponsored materials. This policy should be implemented by a statement of regulations in the preparation of which teachers, librarians, the director of audio-visual aids, and perhaps laymen participate along with the administration. Such rules should be clearly stated and made known to all who must apply them. Within such policy and rules, however, the teacher must be free to make the final decisions whether or not to use any particular item.

It is obvious that the first necessity is that materials of this nature be carefully examined by the teacher before being used.[1] This applies to all instructional materials, but time does not always permit teachers to carry out the rule. With sponsored matter the time must be found. In examining the material two points should be checked. One is the validity of the content, as mentioned above. The extent to which there is distortion through omission or misstatement must be noted. The second point is the offensiveness of advertising. In some instances, the sponsor's name is only used unobtrusively to identify the source and as such is no more objectionable than the nameplate on a film projector or the imprint of the publisher on any book. In others, the nature of the content necessitates frequent reference to the sponsor, particularly when a product or process unique to that sponsor is being described. In contrast to these types are those in which the content is obviously incidental to the commercial message, or the impression is falsely created that only the firm in question is to be credited with a particular accomplishment, or there are subjective claims of superiority or entreaties to purchase or support.

The second precaution can be exercised through the manner in which sponsored materials are used. For certain purposes some of the objections cited actually become assets. For example, if the purpose is to learn to analyze advertising or propaganda, flagrantly biased illustrations are desirable. Or if it is desired to learn what the views of various parties to a controversy are, then highly partisan presentations are

---

[1] American Association of School Administrators, *Choosing Free Materials for Use in the Schools,* The Association, 1955; Association for Supervision and Curriculum Development, *Using Free Materials in the Classroom,* The Association, 1953.

legitimate sources. Of course, in each case it is essential that students clearly understand these purposes and, particularly in the latter example, that all positions regarding an issue be as equally represented and effectively presented as available materials permit. When distinct one-sidedness is unavoidable, this fact should be noted so that students may recognize this as they form their own judgments. Similarly, when the purpose requires strict objectivity, the teacher can compensate for sponsor bias, if not excessive, by calling attention to it.

To sum up, then, the primary concern with regard to instructional materials, sponsored or not, is the validity of the content. But validity is dependent upon the purpose for which the material is to be used. Moreover, materials selected despite shortcomings in terms of validity can be made satisfactory by drawing attention to their inadequacies when they are used.

3. *Materials must contribute to outcomes sought.* The idea that materials may be perfectly valid in the sense of truthfulness but still not be valid for the particular purpose for which they are intended suggests the importance of deciding upon outcomes before selecting materials and of keeping the outcomes in mind when examining the materials. That materials are but tools which should serve, not determine, the objectives of instruction seems obvious, yet textbooks have for years been permitted to determine courses of study instead of vice versa, and with the growth of audio-visual aids many of these have been employed for little reason other than to use them. No real harm comes to students from such random use of materials anymore than from browsing in the library. But browsing is not effective scholarly activity, and the use of instructional materials without careful regard for objectives is not good teaching.

Materials may be valid and even consistent with instructional purposes and still not be appropriate for a given individual or group. It is important for a teacher to be aware of the conceptual or vocabulary level involved or the degree of manipulatory skill required. A film on the frog designed for primary pupils may be a waste of time for biology students, and of course many films are too advanced for junior high school students. In the case of printed materials, the matter of difficulty and interest level is even more significant since materials at too great a level of difficulty will yield little or no meaning to the reader. Proper use of materials will take this factor into account but this can not be done if the correct selection has not been made in the first place.

The Teacher and Active Search for Materials

It is not an easy task to keep informed on the ever-increasing number of materials available for use in instruction. If a school or system has a curriculum library or materials center with one or more people staffing it, the teachers can be greatly assisted in the task. In most instances, however, each teacher must take the responsibility upon himself.

Just as there are many sources of materials, there are also many sources of information about the materials. Commercial enterprises mail their catalogs and brochures to schools, departments, and individual teachers. These should be filed for ready reference. The United States Government Printing Office furnishes a free semimonthly listing of its publications. Professional journals usually feature book reviews and lists of free and inexpensive instructional materials. By scanning those to which he subscribes and others in the school's professional library, a teacher can be assured of keeping up with a large proportion of the current output.

Teachers who attend state or national professional meetings learn of many items from the displays and literature at the customary manufacturers' and distributors' exhibits. See the example on page 237. Bibliographies may be had from many sources—books, libraries, state education departments, and the United States Office of Education, to name but a few. Five helpful listings which should be in every school are:

1. *Free and Inexpensive Learning Materials,* eighth ed., Nashville, Division of Surveys and Field Services, George Peabody College for Teachers, 1957.
2. *Educator's Guide to . . .* (Volumes no. 1. Free Films, 2. Free Slide Films, 3. Free Tapes, Scripts, and Transcriptions), Randolph, Wisconsin, Educators Progress Service.
3. *Educational Film Guide* (and *Filmstrip Guide*), New York, H. W. Wilson Co.
4. *Catalog of Government Publications,* Washington, D.C., United States Government Printing Office.
5. *Selected Bibliography for Curriculum Workers* (Yearly), Washington, Association for Supervision and Curriculum Development.

One could not specify all the means by which teachers may learn of materials. Knowledge may result from conversation with another teacher, from a study council workshop, from reading a newspaper, or from written inquiry to a firm, embassy, or the headquarters of some organization. Certainly a teacher who is on the alert for such things is more likely to find out about them than one who is not. A teacher who is professionally active has more opportunity to come across such

YOURS . . . FOR THE ASKING

Now is the time to check over the items listed in this column. Indicate on the coupon which you can use and your requests will be forwarded to the advertisers promptly. Please be sure to fill in your address completely and without abbreviations.

105. *Arts and Crafts of New Mexico Indians.* A three-fold 17" x 22" sheet in full color shows examples of Indian water colors and various other Indian crafts. (New Mexico State Tourist Bureau)

107. *Alaska.* A new teaching unit on our 49th state for intermediate grades; includes 34 activities which take into account children's varying interests and abilities; an outline of major topics. (Compton's Pictured Encyclopedia)

110. *Information* about part-time or summer sales opportunities representing Dr. Zim's "Our Wonderful World." (Spencer Press, Inc.)

111. *Summer Session Bulletin* outlines the various courses and special programs planned for the summer of 1959. (University of Vermont)

118. *The Re-Living History* booklet tells of historic New England Shaker Village recreated and restored by high school students, for use as summer project for enriching leisure activity. (Shaker Village Work Group)

6. *What Every Writer Should Know* is a 24-page manual of helpful hints, do's and don'ts for writers. (Exposition Press)

19. *List* of free teaching aids on coal, coal mining and the use of coal. (National Coal Association)

27. *Posture Posters* set of 5—designed for use in the classroom to illustrate the principles of healthful posture. (American Seating Company)

32. *List* of hard-to-find teaching material aids the farm, forest, mines, inexpensive science materials and arithmetic devices. (Practical Aids Company)

33. *Brochure* outlines the assistance available to persons who wish to know how to go about having a manuscript published. (Greenwich Book Publishers)

43. *An Application Form* shows teachers how to professionalize their applications and put their best foot forward when applying for a new position. (The Advancement and Placement Institute—Crusade Journal)

49. *This Brochure* lists a different kind of tour through Europe and a corner of Africa. Describes itinerary and gives costs for 20 countries in 70 days, summer 1959. (Europe Summer Tours)

57. *The Library Catalog* lists children's books in picture-in-buckram library bindings, with recommendations and curriculum areas noted. (Follett Publishing Company)

67. *Aviation Teaching Aids Folder* lists free materials available for aviation education teaching. (United Air Lines)

68. *Florida Future*, a folder showing Florida real estate opportunities designed for middle income families of America. (Florida Realty Bureau, Inc.)

81. *Brochure* on the Disney technicolor science and entertainment films includes the 1959 Feature Film supplement listing 16 mm. films for schools, churches and clubs. (Ideal Pictures)

82. *Samples* of cut-out letters for use on bulletin boards, signs, posters and other uses. (Mutual Aids)

91. *France,* a 24-page booklet in color, contains much helpful information on what to see and look for in various regions of France. (French National Railroads)

108. *1959 Summer Session Bulletin* gives the details of all courses offered. (University of Minnesota)

115. *Western Summer Tours* is a 72-page booklet describing all-expense escorted vacation tours of the West. (Union Pacific Railroad)

120. *Information* on unique group tour service to Hawaii and the Orient. Explains how a group member who organizes and conducts a group of 15 or more persons can receive free air transportation on the tour. (Transocean Air Lines)

122. *The Facts about School Furniture Today.* A 16-page booklet of enlightening illustrated discussion of the importance of classroom seating as it relates to teaching, learning and other activities. (American Seating Company)

-------------------------- USE THIS COUPON --------------------------

State Teachers Magazines, Inc.
Dept. D, 307 N. Michigan Avenue
Chicago 1, Illinois

Available in
school year of
1958–59 only.

Send me the items covered by the numbers circled. I indicate quantity desired where more than one copy is available. 4¢ is enclosed for each number circled.

105.   107.   110.   111.   118.   6.   19.   27.   32.   33.   43.   44.
49.   57.   67.   68.   81.   82.   91.   108.   115.   120.   122.

Name..
Subject...Grade.......................................
School Name...
School Street Address...
City...New York
Enrollment: Boys.......................................Girls...

New York State Teachers Association, *New York State Education,* The Association, March, 1959, p. 471.

237

information. Then finally some information, but by no means all, will come to the teacher with little or no effort on his part.

THE SCHOOL LIBRARIAN AS SOURCE

The school librarian usually has acquired many resources for enrichment of classroom teaching. As the job of librarian has developed during the present century, he has become a sleuth in search of multisensory aids as well as books, pamphlets, and other written materials. As instructional procedure and technique have changed, he has been called upon to locate materials of all kinds and to serve students or teachers in search of varied information and experience. Student reports, student forums, panel discussion, presentations, and debates usually require a wide array of resources.

In order to discharge instructional obligations wisely and to improve teaching, the teacher must increase his acquaintance with the library and must develop a suitable working relationship with the librarian. This may be done by meeting informally with the librarian, by visiting the library and looking for materials with him, and by enlisting his help in selection of texts and other resources.

The major function of the librarian consists of finding, selecting, and ordering the resource materials that strengthen the school curriculum. While students, teachers, and administrators are normally consulted as to purchases, the librarian usually makes his own ultimate decisions. By training and experience he is well prepared in the techniques of selection. He has access to guides and aids of various kinds. He also is familiar with well-established standards by which style and slant or bias can be judged. Still he can not and usually does not wish to exercise his prerogatives alone. Few librarians overlook the advantages of cooperation with the staff in locating items to be purchased. Most are extremely anxious to have suggestions from their colleagues on what to order. Both periodically and whenever the need arises in most schools teachers are urged to make up lists for library addition.

In most cases, librarians are ever ready to reciprocate and make suggestions and give advice about possible requisitions by departments. Many distribute monthly lists of accessions and constantly bring to the attention of specialists new and revised publications in various fields.

In the area of curriculum planning and revision the librarian is a particularly important contributor. Even minor changes in content or class procedure are almost immediately reflected in the library. Librarians often know whether materials are available for new ventures or can be made available for proposed course modifications. Success after course changes have been made will depend on how well the librarian is informed of what is needed and how his role has been affected. If the emphasis is to be shifted to research, independent study and exploration, and the preparation of reports, the burden on the library will increase significantly. Preparation for what may come through participation and through opportunity to sketch guidelines should not only make for better rapport but should also identify the librarian with the desire for full accomplishment of the ends sought.

AUDIO-VISUAL AIDS DIRECTORS AS SOURCE

There is one school of thought which holds that the library should be a complete instructional materials center. This would mean that it would be responsible for securing, storing, and distributing all kinds of audio-visual materials as well as those in printed form. Specialists in audio-visual materials disagree with this point of view. They maintain that theirs is an area requiring special training which most librarians lack, and that for adequate service to teachers someone should be specifically charged with the management of audio-visual aids. The majority of librarians probably agree, since they recognize that their major interest is in printed materials, and that they do not have the time, help, or space even to do the kind of job they would like to with these.

Therefore, some school systems have developed centers for audio-visual materials and individual schools have designated a staff member to be responsible for these aids to teaching. These centers should of course work closely with the library. The librarian often learns first about new materials; some items, such as records and film strips, may best be stored and circulated in the library. But for advice on motion-picture films and help in their procurement the teacher should turn to the director of audio-visual materials. Often he is also in a position to assist the teacher in developing new materials through photography or tape recording.

CURRICULUM SERVICE BUREAUS AS SOURCE

Larger school systems have recently developed instructional resources centers[2] or curriculum centers, often in connection with the offices of curriculum assistants and supervisors. Somewhat similar

[2] Amo DeBernadis, "An Instructional Materials Center, "*Education,* January, 1957, pp. 306–309; J. W. Rendell, "Leadership Role of the Educational Materials Specialist," *Educational Leadership,* April, 1955, pp. 423–429; P. W. Witt, "Your School Needs a Materials Specialist," *Teachers College Record,* May, 1957, pp. 425–430.

facilities are also to be found now in many colleges. Several state education departments maintain curriculum libraries or laboratories at which they have accumulated a great variety of materials including courses of study, textbooks, models and *realia*, film strips, files of current and fugitive material, and so on.

The simple existence of a rich collection of this type can do a great deal for the teacher. Browsing alone often turns up references which can be useful and lead to additional materials. When the library or laboratory is properly staffed and there is someone charged with "digging out" appropriate supplements and they are made available from curriculum programs elsewhere as well as from the established publishing houses, the teacher's coverage is greatly increased.

Curriculum laboratories also serve in many cases as the basic resource for teacher committees engaged in the writing of courses of study and in the preparation of resource units. Meeting regularly with supervisors and specialists, teachers can bring group judgment to bear on grade level placement for books, on pamphlets and free materials to recommend, on what ideas to include in locally written leaflets and brochures, on newsletters and teacher notebook circulars.[3]

TEACHER-DEVELOPED MATERIALS AS SOURCE

Regardless how much material for instructional use becomes available on the market there will always be a need for teachers to develop some of their own. Some clever and ambitious teachers spend a considerable amount of time improvising items which could be purchased. If students participate in such activity, a very valuable learning experience may ensue, which, of course, is highly desirable. If the activity is solely on the part of the teacher, however, even though it may be greatly enjoyed, it is likely to be a poor use of the teacher's time. There are times, it is true, when the item would not otherwise be obtained and there are times when superior results can be attained by the "do-it-yourself" method. But as a general rule commercial materials are likely to be of superior quality, and the teacher should insist on their being purchased whenever possible rather than making this unnecessary at the expense of his own gratuitous efforts. There are enough materials which cannot be obtained elsewhere to occupy the teacher's energies in developing without his also working on things which can readily be purchased.

Teacher-developed materials can be classified in many ways, but

[3] See excellent series of single page bulletins prepared for elementary teachers in the Schenectady, New York, schools: A. Hulstrunk, *Elementary Science Topics,* Science Research Office, Board of Education, Schenectady.

perhaps it is most helpful to consider them in terms of their purposes. Materials may be needed to (1) heighten motivation, (2) indicate standards, (3) provide summarization, (4) furnish information, (5) give directions, (6) make assignments, (7) facilitate practice, and (8) supply illustrations.

To heighten motivation, the teacher may develop a display for a bulletin board or for a table which will pique the interest, arouse the curiosity or encourage the comments and questions of students. It may have the characteristics of a puzzle, game, riddle, or unexplained phenomenon depending upon the particular subject matter.

To indicate standards, such things as a chart listing criteria for performance or an actual sample of an excellent finished product may be used. Some may be the teacher's own work but often students' productions will serve. Students may also be guided in formulating rules for written assignments, oral presentations, laboratory reports and the like, and in preparing charts for displaying them.

To provide summarizations of class discussions or of a unit of work, it may be desirable to list main points on a chart, or prepare a time-line on a long strip of paper, or even duplicate an outline for the students' notebooks. Summaries can be put on film strips or recorded on tape for later play back as a review.

To furnish information, it is often necessary for the teacher to prepare two-to-three-page typewritten essays on a given topic to supplement what is available to students in printed sources. This is frequently a more efficient and effectual way of providing information than to do so orally as a lecture. Ideas for such essays emerge as teachers become aware of topics which are not treated at all in textbooks, discussed too sketchily, or presented in a manner which is confusing to students. The preparation of such information sheets is an excellent activity for cooperation among teachers in the same field and often particular specialties of individuals can be capitalized upon for the benefit of all. Certain topics, such as the history of the local area or the occupations of the community, call for a more extensive project which may result in lengthy pamphlets instead of a few pages.

To give directions for certain procedures to be followed by students it is often desirable to prepare "job sheets" so that students may proceed independently. These are particularly important in science, industrial arts, homemaking and, occasionally, art. However, they may also be useful in other subject areas to indicate how to proceed in doing a "research paper," increasing reading speed, making an outline, and so forth. The following contract illustrates one approach used to promote individual reading and study.

STUDY CONTRACT FOR THE NOVEL *Northwest Passage* BY
KENNETH ROBERTS

(Example of Locally Produced Plan for Individualization
of Instruction)

INTRODUCTION

Northwest Passage is built around the life of Major Robert
Rogers whose dreams of fame and fortune are shattered by the
schemes of petty but more practical minds. Although history has
proven Rogers wrong, his indomitable will, his magnificent spirit
have made him a hero to all those who search in vain for a Northwest Passage of their own.

The story is told by Langdon Towne, a young New England
artist, who, having served under Rogers, appreciates the weakness
of his character but admires him for his true strength.

ASSIGNMENTS

Daily: Each day hand in a written report (about a half page
in length) summarizing the reading done for that day. Note any
dialogue, descriptive passages, or other evidences of good writing
which you like.

Assignment for Thursday, April 7

Read chapters 1–23 (inclusive) and be prepared to discuss the
following with your group.

1. What are your impressions of Langdon Towne?

2. Contrast or compare the social situation existing in the colonial
New England village with that in a modern city or village.

3. What characteristics made Rogers successful as leader of the
Rangers?

4. Why were the Rangers more successful in their campaigns than
were the British regulars or the Provincials?

Assignment for Friday, April 8

Read chapters 24–43. Discuss.

1. What enabled the Rangers to endure the hardships attending
their march in St. Francis?

2. It has been maintained that history is merely the story of the lives
of great men. Interpret this statement in connection with the
Rangers' attack on St. Francis.

Courtesy of Department of English, Milne School, Albany, New York.

3. Do you note any similarities between the Stephen's incident and Braddock's defeat?

Assignment for Monday, April 11
   Read chapters 44–55. Discuss.

1. What similarities, if any, do you find between the Brawnes and London society?
2. It has been said that the only consistency some know is inconsistency. Does this apply to Elizabeth Browne? How? Why?
3. What part does the Northwest Passage play in Rogers' life? Is it real to him?
4. In your reading experience have you met another person whose environment was similar to that of Anne Potter? Illustrate.
5. Special topic (optional)
   1. Albany of this period
      a. Social life
      b. Description
      c. Activities

Assignment for Tuesday, April 12
   Read chapters 56–67. Discuss.
1. Contrast Rogers and Johnson.
2. Contrast Anne and Elizabeth. What differences in their environments might have resulted in differences in character?
3. Characterize Natty Potter. (Note his treatment of Anne.)
4. What evidences have we of Rogers' ability as an author?
5. How does the opinion of Langdon Towne's father change regarding his son's profession? What factors might be responsible for this change?
6. How does Langdon's feeling toward Elizabeth change? Why?

Assignment for Wednesday, April 13
   Read chapters 68–end. Discuss.
1. Why do you think Towne returned to America?
2. Give some reasons for Langdon Towne's rise to success.
   a. Character traits
   b. Coincidence
   c. Relations with other people
3. What are some of the factors contributing to Rogers' failure?
   a. Character traits

b. Coincidence

c. Relations with other people

4. How do Towne and Rogers' other associates feel toward him at the end of the book? Why? Do you agree or disagree with them? Support your opinions.

5. Throughout your reading of *Northwest Passage* you have been noting passages which you liked—or disliked. Using these to support your arguments, discuss Kenneth Roberts as a literary artist.

a. style

b. story teller

c. thinker (discuss theme; possible symbolism of title)

SPECIAL TOPICS (OPTIONAL)

1. Perhaps you have read another novel by Kenneth Roberts. If so, how does it compare with *Northwest Passage?*

In style

In setting

In plot

Do similar characters appear?

2. Have you read a historical novel, the setting of which is in the same period, by a different author. Compare this author with Roberts, noting

a. style

b. background

c. accuracy (historical)

To make assignments, an assignment sheet is frequently helpful. This consists primarily of questions to be answered or general directions for carrying out some learning activity outside of class. It may easily provide for differentiation by having required and optional items or by being divided into several sections on the basis of difficulty. In certain cases provision may be made for doing the work on the sheet itself in the manner of workbooks, but more frequently the sheet is only a guide. It offers the advantage of enabling the teacher to use items from many sources, including his own imagination, rather than being restricted to questions at the end of the chapter in a single book.

To facilitate practice another kind of material is needed. A practice sheet should contain only items requiring a specific type of response or operation. Such sheets can be purchased and workbooks often include them. When available and satisfactory they should by all means be purchased, since they are time-consuming to prepare. Often there is no choice and the teacher must produce them. They are needed in every subject in which drill is essential, and they should be in a form which permits their being used individually with those students who give evidence of needing the additional practice, either in class while other students do other things or as an outside assignment. Commonly such practice sets are duplicated, but, particularly in mathematics and languages, they may be placed on cards with separate answer cards to permit students to check their own work.

To supply illustrations teachers create all kinds of devices. This is, in fact, one of the most creative facets of teaching. Most teachers realize they are not going to be able to make scholarly contributions toward advancing knowledge in their subject field, but too few realize they can make original contributions toward better ways of teaching their fields. A better way of illustrating a scientific principle, a geometric theorem, a grammatical rule, or an historical event is worthwhile seeking. It may involve a model, a diorama, a set of transparent overlays, photographic slides—the possibilities are limitless. Some teachers have marketed their inventions, and indeed one of the regrettable facts about the profession is the lack of sufficiently effective means[4] for making some of these excellent ideas more widely available to other teachers. But at least the development of such instructional materials offers each teacher a source of considerable satisfaction.

TYPES OF MATERIALS

To this point, the discussion has contained reference to various kinds of instructional materials. To some extent they have characteristics in common which permit their being considered as a whole. However, each also merits some special consideration.

Textbooks Still the Major Resource

One of the incongruities of some professional textbooks is their disparagement of the use of textbooks in teaching. It is true, as mentioned earlier, that an inordinate emphasis has been placed on the textbook in American schools, although this practice probably made a great contribution formerly by compensating for the inadequate

---

[4] The Study Council Movement has provided one means of sharing. See *CASDAIDS*, Capital Area School Development Association, College of Education, Albany, New York.

preparation of teachers and by providing some uniformity among school programs. Now that most teachers are professionally competent and school systems are well organized and administered these justifications no longer exist.

But this does not mean that textbooks do not have an important place in modern education. In fact, textbooks are better than ever, not only technically but educationally. The question is not whether, but how they should be used.

The manner of using a textbook varies to some degree with the subject. Its place in mathematics illustrates the extreme of one role, as a major source of learning activities and, to a great extent, a guide for the course. Where large numbers of exercises and problems are needed, as in mathematics and foreign languages, it is too time-consuming for the teacher to prepare them. Therefore, in the selection of a textbook the number and range of difficulty of these items is a matter of primary concern. Their realism and appeal to pupils at the age for which they are intended are important factors. Since much of the work the teacher will assign pupils will be selected from the textbook, it should contain as closely as possible the kind of experiences the teacher would design for the type of pupils concerned. The textbook will be used much as a resource unit would, not as a list of identical assignments for all, but as a source of varied experiences from which appropriate assignments may be developed.

Other experiences of a more direct nature involving demonstrations and application will supplement those centering around the textbook. The teacher maintains control over the planning and execution of the course, although in some cases the sequence employed by the textbook may be followed strictly. Even in mathematics there are instances in which the order of topics is of little significance and the teacher arranges them without regard to the textbook. However, when it is significant, the teacher conforms to the desired order. The arrangement of the content, then, is sometimes an important consideration in choosing a textbook.

In most other subject areas the textbook need not occupy such a central position. Two functions are appropriate. One is to furnish an overview for a unit of work. Even the lengthiest of textbooks is necessarily lacking in the detail necessary for adequate development of most concepts and generalizations; but, because of its conciseness and careful organization, it serves as an excellent starting point for the more extensive reading which is usually necessary. A rather rapid reading of the appropriate portion of the textbook serves to orient the student to the scope of the topic, familiarize him with terminology, and raise questions for further reading and discussion. The second function is to provide a summary at the conclusion of a unit. After the problems associated with the topic have been explored and data from numerous sources examined, the material in the textbook should be familiar and its organization should be helpful in consolidating what has been learned.

No textbook, however excellent, is of much value to a student if he cannot read it. It is not unusual to find a range of eight grades with respect to reading ability in an unselected secondary school class. This means that in a ninth-grade class some students may read as well as the average college freshman and others no better than the average fifth grader. Few would expect an average fifth-grade pupil to have to study from a ninth-grade textbook, yet that is essentially the situation some students face when a single textbook is used. Few would advocate college students learning from ninth-grade textbooks but when a single textbook is used some will be doing the equivalent of that. The opinion is sometimes expressed that this range should not exist, that it is the result of poor reading instruction in the elementary school. It may well be that all pupils could be brought to higher levels of reading ability through some sort of different approach in the elementary grades, but the *range* would still exist because this is the natural result of all instruction. Indeed, if the instruction were improved, it would be expected that the range would become even greater.

Neither deploring nor accusing eliminates or solves the problem. The range exists, and in many situations the only feasible course seems to be that of using more than one textbook. Sometimes easier and more difficult books purportedly intended for the same course and level are available and some copies of each can be used. In other instances no book designed for a particular course is at a sufficiently easy reading level for some members of a class, and it is necessary to use a book designed for a lower grade but dealing with many of the same topics. Some argue that such a book would not be satisfactory because it would not include all the material to be dealt with in the course. True, but a student who cannot comprehend the normal book gets the benefit of only a small portion of its content; with a simpler, though less complete, book he at least comprehends all that he reads. With such a basis, class discussions become less bewildering and from them he can gain much he otherwise would have got from reading. Some students, too, having read a simpler book for the overview may be able to deal with the "regular" textbook as a summary after the concepts are familiar. This the teacher must determine and decide upon. But the basic rule must be to attempt whenever possible to provide each student with a book appropriate to his reading ability— one he is likely to be able to comprehend. Instances are known when a textbook has had a vocabulary level two grades higher than the grade for which it was intended, with the result that over half the class was unable to read it. Therefore, another point which should be checked in selecting textbooks is that of reading difficulty. There are several formulas for doing this.[5]

There are, of course, a multitude of qualities which might be considered in choosing a textbook, but many are either such that they may almost be taken for granted if the book is to be considered at all, or else of minor importance and decisive only if two books are in more significant respects essentially equal in merit. These include factors such as durability of binding, size of type, quality of paper, number of pictures, use of color, and even price. These matters are not un-important, but in terms of the curriculum making process and the teacher's role in it other questions are far more central. Some of these have been mentioned and the teacher, or preferably a group of teachers, faced with the opportunity of selecting textbooks should give them first consideration.

1. The question of use. Has design of the course preceded the selection of a textbook? Will the text be the main source of information and exercises and determiner of sequence, or will it serve only as one of many sources?
2. The question of validity. Is the book under consideration authoritative, up to date, free of undesirable bias, and lacking serious errors?
3. The question of difficulty. Is the level of difficulty suitable for the group for which it is to be used? Are several textbooks going to be necessary?
4. The question of psychological soundness. Is the factor of student interest recognized? Are concepts developed adequately? Are descriptions clear? Are applications realistic and significant? Are there sufficient practice materials of suitable range and interest?

In making a selection it may be desired to locate a detailed checklist. These can be found in most subject-area methods books and in some of the ones listed at the end of this chapter. They may be helpful, but no rating instrument is likely to be completely satis-factory in a given situation and no sum of weighted scores can

[5] See Edgar Dale and Jeanne S. Chall, "A Formula for Predicting Read-ability," *Educational Research Bulletin,* 27:11–20, January 21, 1948, and 27:28, February 18, 1948; Rudolph Flesch, *How to Test for Readability,* Harper, 1951; Gerald A. Yoakum, *Basal Reading Instruction,* McGraw-Hill, 1955, Appendix I.

SYNOPSIS OF A STATEMENT ON TEXTBOOK SELECTION
BY THE
AMERICAN TEXTBOOK PUBLISHERS INSTITUTE

School authorities and publishers have a common purpose in studying the problem of textbook selection; to determine those procedures which best assure a fair and objective evaluation of every textbook under consideration. This means an understanding not only of what each book contributes to good teaching, but also of how well it meets the school's objectives for the grade and subject. Obviously such an understanding benefits both children and schools; it also works for better textbooks by making the publisher an active partner in the teaching profession.

The details of any desirable procedure for textbook adoptions must vary with the subject, the grade level, and the peculiarities of each school system. Large cities will follow different procedures from towns and villages. Elementary school arithmetic poses problems quite different from high school science; adoptions from a state-approved multiple list require procedures different from those of independent school systems. Yet, underlying these many variations, there are several basic principles for the sound and successful selection of textbooks.

First and foremost, the selection should be largely influenced by classroom teachers. After all, they are the ones who meet the children each day and should be best able to judge the kinds of materials that are most effective. Guidance and counsel by supervisory authority is frequently necessary to make certain that selections meet the objectives of the contemplated program; but teachers will be responsible for the use of new materials in the classroom and they should have a strong voice in the decision. A committee on elementary textbooks might well consist of four to six teachers, along with an administrative or supervisory official. On the other hand, textbook selection for a small independent high school might be informally assigned to the two or three who teach the subject. But whether the committee is large or small, formal or informal, elementary or high school, classroom teachers should have the primary responsibility for making textbook decisions.

No committee is stronger than its members. The wise superintendent will, therefore, evaluate candidates not only for their expe-

Sales and Distribution Committee, *Desirable Procedures for Selecting Textbooks*, American Textbook Publishers Institute, no date.

rience and proved teaching competence, but also for their individual judgment and resourcefulness. They should be able to recognize imaginative teaching when they see it in well presented and well organized materials; above all, they should be teachers who appreciate what good textbooks, properly used, can contribute to the learning process. Poise is essential. The teacher who feels she is already overworked, who can find no time for interviews or study or who develops a prima donna complex over the competition for her time, has no place on a textbook committee.

But the best committee, be it informally or formally organized, can be hamstrung by arbitrary rules and restrictions. Granted that some regulation is essential, such policies as the following, if wisely adapted to the peculiarities of the special situation, will do much to assure a wise textbook selection.

1. The committee should not be secret
2. The committee should be small
3. The committee's task should be kept within reasonable bounds
4. The committee should be given adequate free time
5. A time schedule should be part of every procedure
6. Publishers should be notified of pending adoptions
7. Provision should be made for interviews
8. Hearings may be desirable
9. Outside consultation should be prudent
10. Committees should be encouraged to study all aspects of the publisher's program
11. Development of a course of study and the selection of textbooks should go hand in hand
12. Individual judgment should be emphasized

The foregoing suggestions assume a committee procedure. But there are obviously many situations where such a procedure is not practical, for example in most of the independent junior and senior high schools. However, the same principles apply in these instances, even though the selection procedure may be informal. Teachers should actively participate in choosing textbooks, and the publishers should be encouraged to seek interviews with these teachers at hours which do not interfere with classroom programs. In many instances the teacher may be relatively inexperienced and her judgments must be carefully checked by the principal or department head. But study of various textbooks, along with interviews, will help to mature that teacher—to make her more aware of different approaches and techniques and of the special skills required to evaluate any textbook intelligently.

The procedures assume informed publishers' representatives, an assumption that is generally true. Textbook salesmen, with few exceptions, are college graduates with previous experience in teaching or school administration. It is a type of work that appeals to educated men and women vitally interested in ideas, in teaching and teachers, and in education as an institution. Publishers aim to employ representatives with those interests. Many of the editors and administrative executives of the educational publishing houses have had the benefit of long experience in the field with close contacts with schools. The textbooks they develop reflect this experience and enable them to interpret correctly the recommendations they get constantly from schools and from their sales representatives. Textbooks and textbook selection can be improved if the school people will encourage and stimulate the development of alert, intelligent, and helpful textbook representatives.

---

adequately depict the suitability of a book. The people making the selection must know what they need and then seek the book closest to their specifications. None will be entirely satisfactory, but this is all the more reason why the choice should be made with care and deliberation and why planning should precede rather than follow the selection.

Supplementary Book Selection a Problem

The textbook provides for intensive reading; in order to allow for extensive reading also, many supplementary books are needed. These are usually purchased and controlled by the librarians although some may be housed permanently or temporarily in the classroom. Teachers should select these books or aid the librarian in selecting them. They cannot nor need not be chosen with the care that the textbook requires. But most of the same considerations are applicable.

Books should be selected for their contribution to the actual courses and units included in the program of studies. Their validity should be assured, except if they are deliberately used to illustrate a bias. A wide range is desirable so that the better students can get advanced material and the slower ones can find something manageable.

The matters of adequacy of exercises or development of concepts need not be of concern but clarity of style should be. More well-written books are available than most schools can acquire, so there is no justification for buying poorly compiled ones. Interest, too, is worth con-

CHECK TEST FOR EVALUATING A HIGH SCHOOL
ENGLISH PROGRAM (Book)

Rate each question by the scale: 2 for excellent; 1 for fair; 0 for poor. Possible total—100 points

FORMAT   POINTS

1. Are the covers of the books attractive? _____
2. Are the pages uncrowded and well designed for ease of teaching? _____
3. Is the print easy to read? _____
4. Are the books easy to carry, handle, and shelve? _____
5. Are the illustrations well done and suitable to the grade placement? _____
6. Are the illustrations an integral part of the teaching program? _____
7. How much is color used for illustration and for teaching helps? _____
8. Are the quality and texture of the paper good? _____
9. Is the binding strong? _____
10. Will the books lie open? _____
11. Are introductory materials, instruction, and learning exercises easily distinguishable from one another? _____

Organization and Authorship

12. How well is the material arranged for continuity and progression in teaching the book? _____
13. How useful is the table of contents to show the complete organization of the book? _____
14. Is there a full, easy-to-use index? _____
15. How well organized is each individual lesson? _____
16. Are there numerous study helps such as italics and boldface type, footnotes, cross references, parenthetical explanation, color? _____
17. Is there provision for individual differences? _____
18. How easily can the material be adapted for teaching in the unit, the core, the traditional-type lesson? _____
19. How well qualified are the authors? _____
20. Is there a statement of their philosophy in a preface? _____

By permission of Row, Peterson & Company, Evanston, Illinois.

CONTENT   POINTS

21. How well do the books deal with the four areas of communication; speaking, listening, reading, writing? _____

22. Will the material be easy to teach? Are the activities practicable? _____

23. Will the material appeal strongly to students? _____

24. Are the lessons strongly motivated? _____

25. Is the material suitable for the grade? _____

26. How well are vocabulary and style suited to the grade? _____

27. How clearly is the explanatory material presented? _____

28. Are the directions for carrying out lesson assignments clear, concise, and complete? _____

29. Do the books stress the fundamentals? _____

30. Is there a strong drill program? Is there consistent provision for oral drill and original drill? _____

31. Can the diagramming be omitted without damage to the sequence of instruction? _____

32. How much provision is made for creative work? _____

33. How strong is the program in vocabulary? _____

34. What emphasis is there on dictionary work? _____

35. How extensive is the spelling program? _____

36. Will the books contribute to character development and social growth? _____

37. Are brief quotations and other selections having literary worth used for illustration or practice whenever possible to stimulate appreciation for literary style? _____

38. Is the subject matter accurate? _____

39. Do the books include numerous examples of student writing? _____

40. Is there (at the junior and senior level) complete, step-by-step teaching in writing the research paper? _____

41. Do the books teach levels of usage? _____

42. Do the books teach literary types? _____

Aids to Instruction

43. How strong is the maintenance and review program? _____

44. Do specific and practical cross-references provide for maintenance of skills? _____

CONTENT POINTS

45. Is there provision for measuring progress in oral and written work? _____

46. Is there a well-developed testing program to diagnose weaknesses and to check mastery? _____

47. Are the tests published separately? _____

48. Are there *manuals* and *keys* having complete answers for all exercises, tests, and diagramming? _____

49. Do the *manuals* have helps and suggestions for teachers? _____

50. Are there *workbooks* available? _____

---

sideration both in terms of the age-level of the students and with respect to variety. Appeal to boys should perhaps be particularly stressed because of their frequent reluctance to read and because books of interest to boys are usually also liked by girls, while the reverse is seldom the case.

Many of these qualities are difficult, if not impossible, to judge for supplementary books for the simple reason that it is usually not practicable to obtain examination copies as is always done with textbooks. However, teachers do have opportunities to look at some in other libraries and at book exhibits. To a large extent it is necessary to rely upon descriptions and reviews. The librarian aids greatly by accumulating such information and passing it on to the teacher or department most concerned. In turn, the teacher should maintain a priority list of the titles most wanted for his courses so that his preferences will be taken into account when the librarian orders.

Reliance on Fugitive Materials in Modern Instruction

It is well, perhaps, at this point to recall the purpose of having all these additional books and other printed materials. When instruction centers largely around the textbook, students are often encouraged to do further reading to deepen and widen their understanding of a topic. Although Jefferson may be mentioned frequently in the textbook, a biography of the man will provide a deeper insight into his qualities and contributions; although the essential features of frontier life in the nineteenth century are presented in the text, a book dealing exclusively with this theme will widen the student's knowledge to include many more aspects. Thus, these additional materials as conventionally used are literally supplementary to the textbook.

In another instructional approach they occupy a position more nearly coordinate with the textbook. Students are confronted with problems for which many sources must be consulted to obtain the necessary information. The textbook serves only as a starting point; indeed, the questions left unanswered by the text suggest the problems to be investigated. Often these problems involve contemporary matters on which new information is continually becoming available. This is especially true with respect to science, business, and current affairs. Such information often has not found its way into books. Much of it is available in the form of pamphlets, charts, and other miscellaneous items. Because these are available from a great variety of sources, difficult to discover, they are commonly referred to as *fugitive materials*. The materials are valuable in enriching instruction, in providing for ability and interest differences, and in making recent information available. Pamphlets, being briefer than books, are more flexible. Some materials such as the "Roadmaps of Industry"[6] graphs are useful in many subject areas—in business, social studies, and science—on the basis of their content, and in mathematics by reason of their form. Teachers improve curriculum very concretely by using a large variety of such materials in a discriminating way.

Much of the same could be said for pictures, specimens, charts, maps, and models. The four-color printing process and the widespread use of photography in news-gathering have made magazines a rich source of material for a picture file. Every good library has one, but every good teacher also has his own. Specimens of rocks, flowers, insects, and the like have always been essential to a good science program, but every subject area suggests objects which are readily obtainable. Certainly for such items as road maps, timetables, insurance policies, banking forms, weather maps, and a host of other things there is no justification for using anything but the "real McCoy." Many companies make available samples of products or raw materials which teachers find it profitable to secure although they present the same problems with regard to location and storage that the fugitive reading materials do.

The value of maps in teaching social studies, science, literature, and languages requires no discussion, although it is probably a fact that not a great enough variety is found in most schools and too few experiences with them are provided. Charts are perhaps best when prepared by teachers or students to illustrate or summarize various aspects

[6] Published weekly by the National Industrial Conference Board, Park Avenue, New York 22, New York.

NEW YORK STATE

The following leaflets and pamphlets are available from the New York State Department of Commerce, Albany 1, N.Y. Single copy free to teachers on request.

Business Fact Book—New York State Houses of History in New York State Map and Guide to New York State—The Vacation Empire

New York, The Empire State. A 12-page leaflet describing the history, government, industry, etc.

This is New York State. A 65-page illustrated booklet describing the state's history, geography, government, industries, etc.

The following materials are issued by the New York State Education Department.

Historic Sites of New York State. A guide to the historic shrines of the state.

Hudson-Champlain Reading List (Bureau of Secondary Curriculum Development, 1958). A 21-page bibliography describing the state and city historical fiction; reference books; etc.

Additional Sources

Loan Exhibits from the New York State Historical Associa-

SCIENCE

Science Materials Center offers a catalogue of tested, age-graded science materials for pre-school through high school age. Catalogue is free to teachers. Science Materials Center, 59 Fourth Ave., N.Y. 3, N.Y.

The Moon and Beyond is a booklet which will help teachers answer questions about Operation Moon Shoot. Provides background information on the moon and the solar system. National School and Library Division, Grolier Society, 575 Lexington Ave., N.Y. 22, N.Y. Single copy free to teachers.

U.S. Office of Education Publications. Single copies of leaflets, reprints, and bibliographies on a variety of educational subjects are available free to teachers. Some recent publications are: *Using Pictures in Schools; Bibliography of Recent Books About Jets, Rockets and Space Explorations; Bibliography of Professional Literature for Elementary Science Teachers* (Revised Feb. 1958). Write to U.S. Office of Education, Washington 25, D.C.

Studying Space Beyond the Earth is a teaching guide con-

NEW YORK STATE

tion and the Farmers Museum, Cooperstown, N.Y. Teachers may write for a leaflet describing the twelve loan exhibits which may be rented. Some of the titles are: This was New York; The Old-Time School; Folk Art; Lighting; The Kitchen.

Historic Societies of New York State. A list of names, addresses and officers. Write to State Education Department, Division of Archives and History, Albany 1.

SCIENCE

taining suggested activities for elementary grades. Write to Compton & Co., 2 East 44th St., N.Y. 17, N.Y. Single copies free to teachers.

The Best in Children's Science Books. Growing Up With Science Books is a 36-page booklet for teachers and parents. Lists 250 informational science books for children of all ages. Prepared with the help of Julius Schwartz by age and subject and fully annotated. R. R. Bowker Co., 62 West 45 St., N.Y. 36, N.Y. Single copy 10¢; $3.35 per hundred.

Science and Foreign Policy. A pamphlet discussing science education in the U.S.S.R. and the U.S. Foreign Policy Association, 345 E. 46th St., N.Y. 17, N.Y. 35¢.

---

of a unit. However, the available commercially prepared charts should be carefully explored by teachers in planning because some are excelled by no other material for certain purposes. Nothing, for example, can take the place of the periodic table, chart of the electromagnetic spectrum, or a series of anatomical charts.

The construction of models is a valuable learning activity for students even if only following directions carefully is involved, but especially if the process is one of translating mental constructs into concrete form.

Many teachers, too, have developed ingenious models, often with removable or movable parts. In determining whether to purchase a model, the chief consideration would seem to be whether the size, cost, or inner complexity of the object itself makes a model actually superior for instructional purposes. A model of a large steam turbine makes sense; one of a wall-type fire extinguisher does not.

The selection of these materials is not a problem of great consequence. Most are free or inexpensive and the greatest difficulties lie in locating, ordering and storing them. Suggestions as to how alert teachers become aware of the availability of materials were provided earlier. Ordering free materials is as simple as sending a post card or letter, although the process can be simplified even further if the school prepares a standard form for this purpose. The procedure for ordering those with a small cost varies from school to school, sometimes requiring elaborate vouchers and often having to be ordered by the librarian. In the case of federal government publications, the most convenient method is to use the special stamps which can be purchased in large quantities for this purpose. For other sources a system whereby the teacher has access to a petty cash fund is the most convenient.

The best way of storing fugitive materials also varies with the situation. Some which are of general value should be in the library; others are probably best kept by the teacher if he has any storage facilities. In a filing cabinet these materials can conveniently be arranged according to the instructional units for which they are most applicable. When the collection becomes too large for this kind of storage, library bulletin cases prove satisfactory. Where resource units have been developed, these will indicate the titles which are potentially useful for each unit and hence the materials themselves can be arranged alphabetically for use on various occasions.

The selectivity suggested earlier regarding sponsored matter is particularly applicable. Each newly acquired item should be examined carefully to determine how it may best be used as well as if it should be used. Its level of difficulty should be noted, and in the case of particularly good items, the possibility of obtaining adequate quantities for classes investigated.

Careful Consideration of Audio-Visual Materials Needed

The newest additions to the arsenal of instructional materials are those involving the projection of images and the amplification of sound. Properly used, they afford the teacher some highly effective tools. In fact some enthusiasts forget they are tools and predict that they will supplant the teacher. The authors recall after the armed services' extensive use of motion pictures in their training programs during World War II hearing speakers at educational conferences herald the approach of the teaching film on which master teachers would present entire lessons and courses. The same predictions are currently heard with regard to television. In the face of growing automation in industry, it is difficult to combat the arguments and make it understood that teaching is not a manufacturing process.

Yet even if it is kept in mind that these materials are only tools, the fact of their newness prompts some teachers to use them almost indiscriminately simply to achieve the status of being modern. At the same time, the two processes of image production and sound reproduction are basic to a large portion of current commercial entertainment, and so their use has for students an identification with entertainment which is not present with other forms of instructional material. This in no way diminishes their educational value, but it does create an ever-present danger which only emphasizes the importance of basing the use of all learning materials upon sound curriculum planning. When instruction regularly involves a variety of activities and materials, audio-visual devices fit in naturally; it is only when the learning situation centers almost exclusively around a textbook that their use creates a holiday atmosphere.

Each type of audio-visual material has its unique advantage which should be recognized in determining which to use in a particular situation. All share in varying degrees the disadvantage of being relatively expensive and somewhat bothersome to use. Many improvements have been made through such means as brighter projection and better screens, reducing the darkness requirements for rooms, and reduction of weight in machines, by slides made of film instead of glass, and by records of light plastic, long-playing and unbreakable. The development of color photography and high fidelity sound reproduction have increased the value of some materials for certain teaching purposes.

In planning learning experiences, two kinds of selections must be made with regard to audio-visual materials. One concerns which medium is best and the other relates to the particular material. For certain purposes the medium needed is obvious. If students are to experience Schubert's "Unfinished Symphony" or Robert Frost reciting his poetry, a recording is indicated. When motion in normal, accelerated, or slowed form is an important factor, the motion picture is needed. When motion is not important or when the cessation of motion is desirable, slides or a film strip may be superior. When continuity is necessary, the film strip is convenient, but slides, although somewhat more costly, can readily be arranged to provide continuity and also have the virtue of flexibility. When it is desired to project pictures or diagrams which are not transparent, the opaque projector is clearly the only means. When an emotional impact is sought, the musical background on sound motion pictures makes a worthwhile contribution, but for strictly rational study it may be an undesirable distraction. Indeed, even the narration may be inappropriate for the purpose at hand in which case it can be turned off and either omitted or replaced by one by the teacher. It seems probable that for many purposes less expensive silent films would be satisfactory and possibly superior, but few are made today. The captions and explanatory frames might well contribute to students' reading ability.

In determining the appropriate medium, then, either one is uniquely suited for the purpose, or, if two or more will serve, the simplest (and usually least expensive) is preferred. In selecting the particular material the factors proposed previously apply, but their application often entails somewhat more time and effort. One can scan a book but not a motion picture. It simply must be sat through in a previewing. This is admittedly difficult when film arrives barely in time for its scheduled use but it is in most cases imperative. Unless a complete description of a film made expressly for classroom use is available as assurance of the nature of the content, the teacher has an obligation to view the film before showing it to a class. The story, now a legend, of the teacher after World War II who unpacked a film on hygiene developed for the Army and began showing it to a junior high school class before learning that it contained material which could not be exhibited to a mixed group should serve to convince and remind teachers of the importance of checking in advance. Lists like the excerpt on pages 261–263 help, but they have faults too. The four questions on page 263 suggest some.

One of the difficulties with rented and borrowed films is that of se-curing them at the time plans call for them. Often they must be ordered months, and sometimes a year, in advance. The situation is better in the case of teacher-planned courses than of those in which pupils help decide the sequence, but even when the teacher can be reasonably certain when a film will be needed, it may not be available. It is prob-ably preferable that a film be used late than early. At least then it may be used for review, but the review should be carefully planned.

This need to introduce and follow up a showing is of course not limited to review situations. One of the weakest aspects of teachers' use of films is the lack of related planned experience. Too often it is a case of "Now we're going to see a film" and then "Now let's get back to our book." Pupils should know why they are viewing and what they should note. Afterward they should explain what they saw and benefit from further elaboration by the teacher. The introduction and

1198 *Portrait in Plastics*—23 min. color. From photography to plastics, here's the story of George Eastman, the beginnings of modern photography and the movies, and the development of plastics for industrial and consumer end uses.
—Eastman Chemical Products, Inc.
—Subsidiary of Eastman Kodak Co.

1196 *The Eighth Wonder*—19 min. color. Available ONLY in: Ala., Ark., Fla., Ga., Ill., Ind., Ky., La., Miss., eastern Mo., N.C., Ohio, S.C. and Tenn. A fascinating tour of the natural wonders of beautiful Rock City on Lookout Mt., Tennessee.
Rock City Gardens

1193 *The Missile Man*—28 min. color. Operational crews working on the development of American guided missiles.
The Martin Company

1187 *The Land Is Yours*—22 min. color. Available ONLY in: Conn., Del., D.C., Me., Md., Mass., N.H., N.J., N.Y., Pa., R.I., Vt., Va. and W.Va. What you should know about land titles, including defects arising from fraud, unpaid taxes, etc., and about owners title insurance.

—American Title Association
—Atlantic Seaboard Conference

1185 *The Making of Fine China*—27 min. color. The designing, molding, firing, decorating and burnishing of beautiful American chinaware, with a number of lovely pieces shown.   Lenox, Inc.

1182 *Cows, Milk and America*—14 min. color. Delightful cartoon on the history of milk in America, from the early settlers landing at Jamestown to the present.
American Dairy Association

1180 *This Is Bermuda*—29 min. color. Beautiful travelogue of the sun-drenched Bermuda vacation land. The color is superb!
Bermuda Trade Development Board

1179 *A Message to Sir Walter* 27 min. color. Lavish costume production with a Hollywood star cast, tracing the origin of the potato and its fascinating role in history. Produced by Metro-Goldwyn-Mayer Studios.
California Long White Potato Advisory Board

1178 *A Fortune in Two Old Trunks*—29 min. color. A *completely new version* of this popular historical film about

Modern Talking Picture Service, *Pocket Guide to Free Films*, The Service, New York, 1959.

the development of fruit growing in California's beautiful Santa Clara Valley.

Sunsweet

1176 *More Than Just Steel*— 20 min. color. Behind the scenes of one of America's most spectacular industries, where amazing new kinds of steel are custom made.

Armco Steel Corporation

1174 *The Cardinal Tradition*— 27 min. Thrilling moments in baseball, including highlights of world series games, close-ups and slow motion, and great stars like Grover Cleveland Alexander, Dizzy Dean and Stan Musial.

Anheuser-Busch, Inc.

1172 *Color & Texture in Alcoa Aluminum Finishes*—19 min. color. Aluminum's design possibilities. "Probably the most striking imaginative industrial short subject ever filmed in the United States," says The New York Times.

Aluminum Company of America

1171 *You Decide*—28 min. color. *Quiz show* on American business with a unique opportunity: *you* make important business decisions and judge their wisdom for yourself. Here's an insight into what it takes to make American business grow and prosper. The Ohio Oil Company

1166 *The Chocolate Tree*—27 min. color. With charming sets, beautiful-soft color photography, special music—this is the story of cocoa and chocolate products, their importance in world trade and in history.

The Nestle Company, Inc.

1165 *For God and My Country* —13 min. color. Photographic coverage of the 1957 Boy Scout Jamboree at Valley Forge.

★ —Pure-Pak Division —Ex-Cell-O Corporation

1163 *A Highway Hearing*—28 min. color. Road improvements coming your way? Here's how you can support your highway officials in the public hearings required for roads to be built under the new Federal Highway Act.

The Dow Chemical Company

1160 *Homes for a Growing America*—15 min. color. NOT available in: Ariz., Cal., Ida., Mont., Nev., N.M., Ore., Utah or Wash. Beautiful, exciting new homes for contemporary living—and the streamlined methods of the modern home building industry.

National Homes, Inc.

1157 *You and Your Ears*—9 min. color. Sprightly Walt Disney cartoon, starring Jiminy Cricket, about the complex operation of the human ear and the importance of proper ear care.

Zenith Radio Corporation

1153 *Adventure in Dairyland*—

28 min. color. Walt Disney introduces this delightful story of two young "Mouseketeers" who spend two weeks on a Wisconsin dairy farm and learn the ABC's of dairy farming.

American Dairy Association

1147 *Moving Mountains*—27 min. color. The fascinating story of "materials handling," from the methods of antiquity to the fabulous mountain-moving machines of the 20th Century.

Clark Equipment Company

1. At what grade level are these appropriate?
2. What teaching objectives would they serve best?
3. When should they be shown? As preview? As explanation? As summary?
4. For what purpose were they originally made? Entertainment? Instruction? Motivation?

---

the discussion should be planned by the teacher during the preview, and they should be filed in the resource unit for use another time.

Audio-visual materials offer pupils experiences which they could have in no other way. These materials can amplify, widen, and deepen meanings based on reading. But they can also be a shameful waste of time. Through careful planning, discriminating selection, and enlightened use, the teacher must see that they are not wasteful.

An evaluation record of each film used should be kept by the teacher. This record should include a discussion of how the film was worked into the unit being studied and suggestions for possible future use of the film. These records should be available for all interested

TEACHER FILM EVALUATION SHEET

Title_____ Producer_____
Source of film_____ Address_____
Length in minutes_____Sound___Silent___Color_____Black and white_____
Grade used_____Subject_____Unit_____
Date of use_____ The film may be used to: Introduce a unit_____
Present material_____ Summarize main points_____
Grade levels for which the film is appropriate_____
1. What educational purposes can the film serve?_____
2. What major questions are raised in the film?_____
3. What major questions are answered in the picture?_____
4. What preparation should be given students before using the film?_____
5. What suggestions or cautions do you have for the use of the film?_____
6. Summarize the major points in the film briefly._____
7. Photography   Excellent___Good___Fair___Poor___
8. Sound   Excellent___Good___Fair___Poor___

teachers in the building. In this way it is possible to build a valuable resource of teacher judgments that is not available from film company literature. The records also serve as a basis for the purchase of new materials and thereby reduce waste in purchasing. While check forms are especially helpful to directors of audio-visual aids, pupils and teachers in the classroom do not really need appraisal forms in order to evaluate a particular film.

COMMUNITY RESOURCES

Margaret Mead has characterized the American high school as having withdrawn behind a fence atop a hill, aloof from the on-going life around it. The highly verbal approach of the academic high school has in part been modified through the increased use of the materials described in the preceding section. These are designed to bring reality or faithful representations of it into the classroom. It is only one more step to take down the fence and establish two-way communications between the learning situations of the school and the life of the community.

There is considerable disagreement regarding how extensive this intercommunication should be. This issue is discussed at some length in Chapter 15. Here the only matter considered concerns the use of community resources in learning experiences.

Oddly, teachers may be less aware of the resources available in the area immediately surrounding the school than of those which may be ordered from distant points. Often the reason is the lack of a "catalog." Unless a teacher has lived in the community for some time and has made it a practice to use its resources in teaching, he cannot be expected to know what is available. It appears essential, therefore, that every school maintain a community resource file.

Such a file can best be developed by the faculty cooperatively. A good start can be made by pooling the information already in the possession of various members, but further research is necessary and the information must be classified for convenience in use. The major classificatory breakdown should probably be between human and material resources.

Many people in every community have unique contributions they can and are willing to make to pupils' learning. It may be because of their (1) vocation, (2) hobby, (3) country, state or city of origin, (4) travel experience, (5) college attended, (6) war exploits, (7) possessions, (8) political office, (9) organizational affiliation, and the like. Their contributions can be made by speaking or showing films directly in the classroom, by being interviewed by designated pupils, by loaning materials, or by providing teachers with information or assistance.

The material resources consist of both cultural and natural types. Cultural resources include: (1) industrial plants, (2) stores, (3) offices, (4) civic buildings, (5) museums, (6) libraries, (7) communications studios, (8) architectural illustrations, (9) water filtration and sewage disposal plants, (10) transportation terminals, (11) dams, (12) canal locks, and the like. Natural resources include (1) geological formations, (2) swamps, (3) ponds, (4) waterways, (5) woods, (6) parks, (7) zoos, (8) gardens, (9) farms, (10) mines, and other habitats of plants and animals and sources of minerals. Some of these are sources of materials which may be brought into the classroom but for the most part they represent places to which class groups may be taken.

The information which ought to be on the cards of the resource file varies with the type of item. When applicable, the card should reveal (1) the nature of the contribution, (2) names, addresses, and telephone numbers of those who are involved, (3) methods of contact, (4) costs involved, if any, (5) restrictions as to hours, days, or size of group and (6) comments regarding special attractions, dangers, or preparations needed. Upon using a resource, the teacher doing so should indicate on the card the date, class, and evaluating comments for the guidance of others who may wish to avoid duplication, forego an unsatisfactory experience, or otherwise profit from the remarks.

Several aspects of planning are evident with respect to community resources. The preparation of the file represents long-range cooperative planning. Before taking a class on a field trip the teacher must first visit himself or consult the remarks on the file card. This teacher-planning can be supplemented by specific planning and preparation by students. Indeed, planning for such a trip or for receiving a visitor to the classroom is perhaps one of the best starting points for student participation in planning. Field trips make good culminating experiences for a unit because they provide an opportunity to observe applications and vivid illustrations of concepts and skills which were learned. However, as in the case of audio-visual materials, they sometimes serve better as inciters to interests and curiosity in initiating a unit, and when they constitute an important source of data they belong in the developmental part of the unit. Thus, when a community resource should be employed and whether its employment will be a worthwhile expenditure of time depend equally upon the teacher's being very clear as to its purpose.

The use of community resources in the school probably requires a greater degree of cooperation than using any other materials. Of course, teachers must occasionally make mutual adaptations over a conflict in scheduling a motion picture projector or in desiring a set of library books on the same topic for classroom use. But a field trip often requires more than a single classroom period, and in order that one may be carried out perhaps half a dozen teachers may have to excuse all or part of their classes. Only when a staff is in general agreement on over-all objectives and when the purposes of a trip are clearly in line with these, can such concessions be expected. Indeed, they may not otherwise be justified. No teacher should unilaterally make arrangements which will interfere with colleagues' schedules. However, with proper planning, communication, and understanding it should be possible to secure endorsement of such excursions and very often to convert them into joint endeavors whereby the purposes of a number of subject area teachers may be served simultaneously.

Questions for Discussion

1. Discuss the proposition that the brief development of a concept in a text-book is less adequate for students who learn more slowly than for the brighter ones and therefore outside reading is more of a necessity for the former than the latter.
2. What kind of help should a teacher be able to expect from the librarian? From a director of audio-visual aids?
3. What abuses have you experienced as a student with regard to instructional films? How might this be avoided?
4. How could a single field trip serve the purposes of teachers in several subject areas? Consider a specific example.
5. What advice should industrial firms receive on the preparation of materials for school use?

Selected Bibliography

American Association of School Administrators, *Choosing Free Materials for Use in the Schools,* The Association, 1955.

Cronbach, Lee J., ed., *Text Materials in Modern Education,* Scott, Foresman, 1947.

Department of Elementary School Principals, *Instructional Materials for Elementary School,* The Department, 1956.

Henry, Nelson B., ed., *Audio-Visual Materials of Instruction,* National Society for the Study of Education, 1949.

Kinney, Lucien, and Katherine Dresden, *Better Learning Through Current Materials,* second ed., Stanford University Press, 1952.

National Citizens Commission for the Public Schools, *How Good Are Our Teaching Materials?* The Commission, 1955.

"The Textbook in America: A Symposium," *Saturday Review of Literature,* 35:13–70, April 19, 1952.

CHAPTER 10

....

Toward Improved Experience in the Subjects

Biologists have identified a number of conditions needed by all living things for survival; or, in other terms, a number of functions are common to all organisms. They have also found that, in what they consider the higher forms of life, there is an increasing specialization of function on the part of various structures in the organism. While it is dangerous to draw analogies between organisms and society, it may be noted that certain common needs and functions are shared by all members of a society, but that as the society develops an increasingly complex culture, a specialization of function or division of labor is essential. In education, then, provision must be made both for the general needs of all members of the society and for the differing specific needs of diverse individuals. Thus, the distinction arises between general and specialized education.

Specialization is reflected in another way. All of the content or subject matter available for educative experiences must come from the culture or, as it is sometimes called to indicate its transmission, the cultural heritage. The culture includes everything man knows, believes, and can do. Some of this is, or needs to be, shared widely among most, if not all, of the members of the society; the remainder is possessed by relatively few specialists who either need it to perform their functions or who are engaged in adding to some segment of it through scholarly inquiry. Some cultural content may be in the possession of only one or two people and, indeed, certain skills and knowledges have been held as closely guarded secrets, passed on only to selected people.

There are, then, two bases upon which cultural content is specialized—namely, by lines of endeavor and by scholarly disciplines. The latter are grouped into three broad areas—the humanities, the natural sciences, and the social sciences—but the extensiveness and complexity of these has made it essential that scholars concentrate their inquiries along very much narrower lines.

Without such specialization neither our present stage of cultural attainment nor further progress would be possible. However, it is not without disadvantages, chief among which, perhaps, are the increasing difficulty of interdisciplinary communication and the correlative inability to integrate the various insights necessary for dealing with complex problems. Since specialization is indispensable, ways of eliminating these undesirable concomitants are urgently to be sought.

One issue of considerable consequence is how early in life specialization should begin. Two opposing demands create the issue. On the one hand, the increasing length of time required to acquire a specialty argues for an earlier beginning, whereas, on the other, the increasing complexity of the culture to which specialization gives rise calls for a more extensive and, hence, prolonged general education. For the secondary school the result is a disturbing uncertainty of purpose and inconsistency of practice. There is for the most part a feeling that this level should concern itself predominantly, if not exclusively, with general education. Certainly the idea that the secondary school should prepare youth for specific vocations is far from universally accepted. Yet it is almost universally expected that teachers in the secondary school will to some degree at least be specialists either in an academic field or in some functional area.

One of the factors complicating the situation is the difficulty of distinguishing at that level whether a particular study is general or special education. It is clear, of course, that if a student devotes several years to some industrial field such as the machinists' trade or some technical subject such as aerodynamics, he is engaged in special education. In a field such as business, however, shorthand may well be considered special education, but introduction to business or typewriting might easily be deemed to be general education and the call for business law would be quite indeterminate.

Even less clear is the status of such academic fields as mathematics, science, and foreign languages. For some students they may indeed represent the beginning of a long period of specialization, but for more of those who elect them this is not the case and these courses serve actually as a part of their general education.

From the standpoint of the student, therefore, the question of specialization is not always clear-out. From the standpoint of the teacher, however, the matter is usually quite definite. Secondary school teachers by and large are expected to be, and regard themselves as, specialists in one or two areas.

Several advantages of such restriction of concern are apparent.

The teacher himself feels more secure in knowing his fields well and is enabled to deal with matters which interest him most. To the extent that special techniques of teaching are needed for different kinds of subject matter, it is helpful to be able to perfect those techniques rather than have to master many others. The same is true with respect to knowing what materials are available as sources in those subjects.

Disadvantages have also been cited, however. A narrowness of outlook is often attributed to secondary school teachers. They are charged with being so immersed in their own subjects that they are unable either to deal with problems which transcend these subjects or to understand pupils and their needs. Being quasi-specialists, they are accused of failing to recognize that their students do not also intend to acquire such specialization. As a result, it is maintained, they tend to stress relatively unimportant details to the neglect of more broadly significant and enduring outcomes.

It is not the purpose here to debate this issue again. It is recognized that almost all secondary school teachers are, and most will continue to be in the foreseeable future, subject specialists. The purpose of this discussion, then, is to inquire into ways in which such specialists can be most effective in realizing the objectives of the secondary school. In particular, consideration will be given to what a teacher should know about his own field and why he should have a fuller understanding of other fields than is often the case.

THE TEACHER AND HIS OWN SPECIAL FIELD

High on every checklist of the characteristics of a good teacher is the phrase "thorough knowledge of his subject." Seldom, however, is there any indication of what this phrase means precisely. Within any field of study other specialists who are not teachers also need a thorough knowledge of their subject. In what ways is the requirement for a teacher any different from that demanded of these other specialists?

For those who adhere to the view that anyone who knows a subject can teach it, the answer presumably would be that the two requirements do not differ at all. The position advanced here, however, is that there is a distinction between a student's knowledge of a subject and a teacher's knowledge of it.

The student's knowledge consists of a comprehensive acquaintance with the major concepts encompassed by the field including the finer distinctions among them; an understanding of the principal generalizations or theories, including the evidence supporting them; a moderate degree of skill in the more essential operations or manipulations; familiarity with the methods by which knowledge in the field is extended, and a thorough grasp of the scheme by which it is organized and classified. The practitioner extends this primarily in the direction of a high level of proficiency in certain of the skills, developing them into an art. The scholar augments it primarily with respect to the skills of acquiring new knowledge on the basis of more extensive knowledge of the entire field and more intensive knowledge of some narrow aspect to it. In what respect does the teacher's knowledge of the field go beyond the student's?

Six important ways may be considered. The teacher is concerned with (1) how his field is learned most readily, (2) what aspects of it are most significant to the nonspecialist, (3) its relationship to other fields of study, (4) its bearing upon the present lives of young people, (5) the kinds and sources of materials useful in teaching it, and (6) avenues for keeping "abreast" of developments in the subject.

The Teacher and the Requirements for Transmission

Knowledge of how immature learners most readily acquire the understandings and skills of a particular field gives rise to modifications of general teaching techniques which are often known as special methods. Acquisition of the rudiments of such special methods is a part of most programs of teacher preparation, but continued extension and perfection of them is a major activity of teachers in improving curriculum. On this more than anything else the teacher is expected to be an expert.

One of the essential characteristics of the special methods of teaching a subject is a scheme of organization for the purposes of learning as contrasted with the organization of the subject itself. As was indicated in Chapter 6 these two schemes are seldom the same; the second is the result, not the basis, of the first. Scholars frequently fail to recognize the distinction, and indeed this same failure on the part of teachers represents an area in which perhaps the greatest improvement of teaching in the subject fields can be accomplished.

Perhaps the best way of clarifying this point is by suggesting an absurdity. If the field of biology were introduced to learners on the basis of its logical organization, the kind of animal life studied in Grade 1 would be protozoa. Mammals would not be reached until the high school years. While this is an extreme and hypothetical illustration, similarly ridiculous instances could be found in the manner in which subjects often are actually organized for instruction.

A corollary of this misconception is the notion that one element of a complex learning must be thoroughly mastered before proceeding to the next. If it were true, a student would have to know all the words in a language before attempting to put them into sentences and be able to write sentences without error before forming paragraphs. This is somewhat like insisting that a golfer perfect his driving before attempting other shots or playing a game.

Each teacher should carefully examine his subject field and various methods of teaching it in relation to these and other facts about how learning takes place. Traditional practices which conform to this knowledge should be retained, but those which do not should be revised, unless other compelling reasons argue against it.

Need to Identify General Values

Most teachers are very much aware of what an expert in their field ought to know, but often they labor under the misapprehension that everyone needs that knowledge. High school English teachers, for example, frequently seem to proceed as if their goal were to make English teachers of all their students.

The difficulty, of course, is that it is not possible to tell whether certain students in high school will or will not become specialists in a given area. If time were unlimited, it might be desirable to treat every student as a potential specialist. Since it is not, the best approach would seem to be to assume they will *not* be specialists, concentrating on what is of most general value and then supplementing this with those students for whom time permits. With priorities well established, students might be spared from bothering about matters of lesser consequence to them and concentrate on more thorough learning of the more vital portions which might then be better retained to serve them well later. This would in no way prevent the more able ones from filling out their learning in as great depth as they find possible.

Suppose, for example, during the study of the period after the American Revolution a student, after attention to a great many details, manages to learn and retain four weaknesses of the Articles of Confederation, four provisions of the Northwest Ordinance, and two articles of the Bill of Rights. If, with different emphasis, he knew none of the weaknesses or provisions mentioned, but did know all ten amendments of the Bill of Rights would this be more or less desirable? Or, in the study of nitrogen, if a student spends considerable time trying to learn the characteristics of the various oxides and the valence changes exhibited by nitrogen, would this be worthwhile if partial success in the endeavor were at the expense of a thorough understanding of the relationship of nitrogen to plant life? In both of these illustrations teachers may answer differently, but the point is that teachers of a subject should set priorities and not leave the matter to chance by trying to expose students to everything in their field.

Setting these priorities is a matter of judgment and no single basis will suffice for all situations. The teacher's own knowledge of his subject suggests certain things as more basic than others for further study. His knowledge of contemporary life indicates that some learnings will find more frequent use or be more vital than others. It should also be recognized that in our society there are certain things which all people are expected to know and others for which there is not such an expectation. All these factors enter into the decision, along with an awareness of what kinds of learnings are most readily retained and transferred.

The Teacher and Ways to Reinforce Learning

The teaching of a subject can be improved by attention to its relation to other fields of study. This is not to say that all subjects are in every respect closely related nor to advocate that awkward efforts should be made to exploit a remote connection. But there are many instances where the relationship is apparent and natural, and these should be capitalized. Too often teachers proceed as if such instances do not exist.

A worthwhile undertaking for a teacher, elementary or secondary, is to make a chart listing the various units of a course at the left and forming columns at the right of it for each other subject field. In the boxes thus formed notations may be made indicating relationships that are apparent. Several kinds will stand out.

First, there is the use of skills from another subject in learning the one at hand. The various language and numerical skills are most obvious, but also included are those of art, industrial arts, homemaking, business, and even music. An effort to apply as many of these skills as possible can not only improve the learning experiences of the subject at hand but also strengthen the skills through the practice provided.

In addition to the activity relationship, there are a number of bases with respect to content. There is, for example, a time basis. Some pe-

CHART FOR RELATING SUBJECT CONTENT TO UNITS

	ENGLISH	SOCIAL STUDIES	MATH	ART	HOME ECO.	INDUSTRIAL ARTS
PLANT AND ANIMAL HABITATS	Composition on field trip. Habitat descriptions in animal stories. Relate to "setting" in literature.	Habitat maps. Effect of white man on original habitats on this continent. Economic significance of habitats.	Estimation of animals per acre. Mesh screens and area. Volumes of ponds, aquaria.	Dioramas of habitats. Sketches of plants and animals. Colors in living things.	Plants and pets in the home. Lawns and gardens.	Construction of cages, traps, nets.
FOODS AND HOW WE USE THEM	Advertising claims for foods on TV, in magazines.	Food habits of various nations. Food problems of explorers, settlers. Salt and spices in history. World Health Organization.	Graph of food components. Caloric calculations. Proportions in menu enlargement.	Diagrams of digestive systems. Charts of food types.	Menu planning. Effects of cooking, freezing. Lunch selection.	
MAGNETS AT WORK	Meanings of: magnetic personality, polarized views.	Magnets and navigation. Maps with variations shown.	Degrees and compass rose.	Field diagrams.	Doorbell circuit.	Magnets in motors. Magnetized tools. Construction of electromagnets, telegraphs.

riod of historical time is represented by the life span of every author, composer or other artist, by the setting of most literary works, and by each scientific discovery. Each of these therefore can be related to well-known historical events contemporary with it. Space, too, is a basis. Every person studied was a native of some country or resided in some section of this country and every event took place in some geographic locus. These locations can be identified on a map or globe and related to some other fact regarding the place. Then there is a literary basis for a relationship. Biographies, poems, novels, nonfiction, as well as musical selections and art works have dealt with virtually every topic encountered in any subject. Further, there is frequently an application basis whenever a concept from one subject is basic or analogous to one in another. An illustration might be the concept of dependence which may be developed in mathematical equations, in clauses in English, in a political sense, and in scientific explanations. Finally, vocabulary provides a basis for relating subjects, particularly through the use of word origins and technical uses of common terms. It seems inconceivable, for example, that either the term iconoscope in physics or osteoclast in biology could be studied without reference to the word, iconoclast.

It is not necessary, actually, to combine subjects in order to help pupils establish intelligible interrelationships among their various studies. Some teachers enrich their instruction in the manner suggested almost as matter of course; to others the idea apparently does not even occur. Deliberate planning through some device such as the chart mentioned above will assist any teacher to initiate the practice and with time to make it automatic.

A Subject's Significance

Learning should be functional. No one can teach effectively without being able to put himself in the position of his students. The teacher of any subject must consider its significance for the lives of young people.

The older the student, the closer he is to adult life and the better able to perceive adult implications in what he learns. But throughout most of high school, students' interests and concerns do not coincide with those of adults. All subjects affect those of youth in various ways, however, and these instances should be capitalized as fully as possible. Nevertheless, in no sense should it be thought that everything studied must bear a close and vital relationship to students' immediate lives.

Any interest or problem may, for example, serve as a theme for composition writing. Since human relationship problems are prominent for teen-agers, both classical and contemporary literature dealing with such problems can be employed to good advantage. Romeo and Juliet can be viewed as a tale of love involving two people of junior high school age. Interest by pupils in their bodies, appearances, and performances can be recognized in biology, home economics, and physical education. At an age when adventure appeals history can satisfy their desire. Geometric forms of every kind can be found as well on the automobile as in any other context. Teachers who know what pupils are thinking about and what they need to move successfully to the next phase of development can search their subjects and find contributions of many kinds. When they do, subjects begin to "make sense" to students.

What is taught should be up to date. The last two aspects of a teacher's knowledge of his field relate to knowing what materials are available and where they may be obtained, and keeping abreast of new developments in the subject. The first of these was treated in the preceding chapter. The second is, of course, the main characteristic which the teaching specialist and the scholar specialist share. Science and social studies teachers have, perhaps, the greatest inherent need of continued study, but certainly none is entirely exempt. New machines and processes annually add to such areas as home economics, industrial arts, and business; new creative productions add to literature, music, and art. At mid-century, mathematics teachers suddenly found the assumption that their field was more or less static to be quite erroneous and many found themselves quite outdated in their own subject.

THE TEACHER AND OTHER SUBJECT FIELDS

The teacher needs a somewhat different view of his own field from that of the scholar or practitioner in the same field, but further, he needs a knowledge of other fields in the program of studies. One reason why he must be familiar with other subject areas has already been suggested: in order to teach his own subject more effectively by taking advantage of its relationship with others. A second reason, however, is based on the idea that the curriculum of a school is the business of the entire staff. Instead of taking the attitude that what takes place in other subject areas is no concern of his, each teacher should feel responsible for every aspect of the program. Similarly, he should welcome the suggestions and concern of other members of the staff with respect to his own subject field.

It should be recognized that some subject specialists disagree with this point of view. They resent what they consider to be interference on the part of people uninformed about their fields and, consistently enough, they refrain from concerning themselves about the subject areas of others. When teachers in general are uninformed about other fields, there is of course some justification for the "isolationist" viewpoint. But the trouble is that this is circular. Concern for other areas is rejected because of the lack of knowledge, and the need for acquiring the knowledge is denied because of the lack of concern. Obviously, if teachers were to become well versed on all phases of the program of studies, the objection noted above would disappear. But still there would have to be some reason for being informed, and it is this: subjects are not taught for their own sakes! They are taught because they contribute to one or more accepted objectives of education. No single subject can alone achieve a major educational objective; therefore in order to assure that the functions of the school are being carried out properly, the staff must view the entire program in terms of the accomplishment of the school's purposes.

Knowledge of Current Practices Needed

The most obvious kind of knowledge a teacher should have about other subjects pertains to the nature of present offerings in the particular school as well as nationally. This means knowing rather specifically what is taught in each course. There are many courses which a given teacher did not take while in school; some new ones have been added and probably most of those studied have changed in the interim. Often a teacher disparages a certain course, sometimes even in public, simply because he does not know what it actually entails. If upon careful scrutiny he feels it could be improved, he is in a position and has the responsibility to urge modifications.

Knowledge of what is being done in other subject areas elsewhere offers a basis for appraising the local offerings. While at first thought this may appear to be only a method of keeping other teachers "on their toes" with respect to their own subjects, further reflection will suggest that it is likely to result in a teacher being able to find support from the others for practices he would like to institute, because they will understand the desirability of the innovations.

In schools where it is the practice to develop course-of-study outlines and summaries of the program of studies, it is relatively easy for the entire staff to become familiar with every subject area and course. Where these materials are not available, local or state syllabuses may be studied, and if these do not exist, professional books may have to be consulted. All of these types of sources should be available to students preparing to be teachers, thus permitting them to have a thorough understanding of the total curriculum before entering the profession. Nevertheless, some means should be established in every school to permit all staff members to become conversant with the local curriculum. This is very neatly done in the New York State Bulletins, *Charting the Curriculum* and *Elementary Curriculum: An Overview.*[1]

Knowledge of Aims and Goals of other Subjects Necessary

In addition to the content of courses offered by the school, each teacher should be aware of the objectives espoused by other departments. Specialists in each subject develop a more or less unique orientation as to what they are trying to do and it is well that others learn what this is. What is the orientation of the science teacher? What is the art teacher trying to accomplish? Toward what goals is the physical education instructor working? There is no better way for each of these to clarify his own set of purposes than to have them subjected to the critical appraisal by colleagues in other areas.

Often a teacher hears of certain activities being carried out in other fields which he is unable to explain or defend. By knowing the point of view of those working in these fields, he can understand the reasons for their practices and hence interpret them intelligently to laymen. Furthermore, when a whole staff is thus thoroughly conversant with each other's aims and goals it can more readily deliberate together on questions relating to the objectives of the total school program.

Understanding of Trends in the Subject Curriculum Necessary

What a trend is in education it is difficult to say. How many years or what proportion of incidence is necessary for a practice to be considered a trend cannot be specified. Nevertheless, certain tendencies can be illustrated sufficiently, perhaps, to give some insight into significant characteristics of the subject-organized curriculum as it has developed. Not all of these tendencies may be found in the future to be desirable; indeed some are currently the target of considerable criticism. However, they evolved as the result of continuous experimentation and deliberation by countless educators over a period of many decades, and therefore should be known by all teachers.

[1] Both publications are obtainable from New York State Education Department, Albany.

Expansion and Increase of Subject Areas

An inescapable observation regarding changes in the programs of studies of high schools since their inception is that the number of subject fields offered has increased. The so-called academic fields of language, history, science, and mathematics have been augmented by fine and practical arts, technical and commercial fields, and physical education in response to broadened purposes and to a widened range of clientele.

In some schools additions and substitutions have been made more quickly and on a wider scale, but few schools have escaped the impact of burgeoning knowledge and specialization. As with most growth, there has been considerable strain. The advent of new courses has not always been met with enthusiasm, and numerous proposals for additions have had active opposition with considerable effort expended to maintain the *status quo*. Some of the more recent subjects have been assailed for their excessive vocational flavor, for their lack of difficulty, and for their inappropriateness for high school study. Proponents of additions more than occasionally have discovered that they are less "respected" than those who teach the traditional subjects. It is not uncommon now to find staff members who are resentful over the reluctance of some of their colleagues to place much value on some of the newer subjects.

Doubtless, "jockeying for position" is natural. We may very well have to accept that for a long time to come new school subjects and new content emerging in old subjects will not be favorably viewed by those who place high value on established content. However, it apparently is inevitable that changes do and will take place. Certain subjects and parts of subjects do outlive their usefulness and in time they do succumb to replacements.

The teacher then should have some idea of the emergence of the various subjects and subject fields common to the high school program. With the perspective even a limited history of a subject provides, we should better understand why subjects have emerged, what contribution they originally were expected to make, and how they have come to have their particular brand of respectability.

English was not taught in the Latin Grammar School, for example. It was presumed that the scholars had learned to read and write from a tutor at home, at a public reading and writing school, or at a "dame" school. English was introduced into the academies and early high schools in the nineteenth century with an emphasis upon selected English literary classics and upon formal grammar. Mental discipline was a major consideration. By the twentieth century contemporary American literature was included, wide reading was encouraged, and composition and elocution had been added. The subject of English, which a century before had not been considered worthy of study at the secondary level, had become the one most required. During the present century it came to be viewed as consisting of the four language arts with literature of all types as its source of content. Facility in use became the goal, and numerous situations in which speaking and writing are required were employed in the classroom. Grammar and spelling were taught in connection with their use rather than in isolation. Reading instruction, formerly considered finished at the elementary level, was extended to the high school in both remedial and developmental form. Centers of interest were used to relate literature and the skill learnings to each other and to the lives of students.

Social studies as a combination of various subjects based on the social sciences did not come into being until the 1920's. History was studied incidentally in the Latin Grammar School in the literature of Greece and Rome. Modern European history and particularly British history were introduced into the academies and high schools of the early nineteenth century, American coming somewhat later as it became more substantial. During the latter half of that century, the pedagogical ideas of Herbart, who stressed history and literature, brought about their introduction into the common schools and strengthened their position in the high school. Similarly, Pestalozzi's influence encouraged the teaching of geography at the elementary level, and undoubtedly the tremendous amount of immigration stimulated the inclusion of civics. When the reorganization movement put the seventh and eighth grades into the secondary school, these two subjects, along with history, became important components of the high school curriculum. Economics has never been widely taught and sociology has been almost nonexistent. Of course, concepts from both of these disciplines as well as from the three mentioned previously are incorporated into the social studies fusion, but history still dominates. American history has increased in emphasis, and current problems have been given greater attention. To some extent there has been a shift away from a strictly military and political history to one which also deals with the development of social and economic institutions. The earlier preoccupation with name, date, and place facts has given way to a concern for important generalizations, significant movements, and an analysis of cause-and-effect relationships.

Some mathematics, chiefly arithmetic, was incorporated in the Latin Grammar School curriculum in its later period. It was the academy with its emphasis upon applied mathematics that gave the subject its boost. Algebra and demonstrative geometry found favor during the nineteenth century because of their presumed disciplinary value. It was not until 1842, however, that Harvard required algebra for admission and geometry was not required until 1866, indicating that these were college level subjects previously. By the twentieth century, mathematics through advanced algebra was well established in the high school, although as the enrollments climbed and the character of the student body broadened, the proportion taking mathematics declined, many students going no further than eighth-grade arithmetic. With the development of the junior high school, emphasis at that level was placed upon the application of arithmetic and the introduction of geometric and algebraic concepts. A second track in the form of a general mathematics course was instituted in the ninth grade to parallel elementary algebra. Many schools began to require a year of mathematics beyond the eighth grade. By 1955 it became apparent that the well-established sequential program of the high school had failed to keep pace with mathematical advances, and the need for modernizing the content was realized simultaneously as the pressure for encouraging the greater numbers of students to study the subject mounted.

The humanistic Latin Grammar School, like the universities of its day, refused to admit science into the curriculum. The early academies, with their practical orientation, first included astronomy and physics, and with the great rise of science during the nineteenth century both they and the high school added biology, chemistry, and other sciences. At first some were grouped under the heading of natural philosophy, but by the turn of the century the individual subjects were well established only to be recombined again at the junior high school level as general science around 1915. With the shift from nature study to elementary science in the lower grades, science became a dominant subject, though not yet is it as extensively taught as are English, mathematics, and the social studies. With the further development of consumer-oriented courses for the senior high school, it may become more widely studied than it now is where only academic courses are available.

While the offerings in science have grown steadily since World War I, foreign language provisions have continued to follow their somewhat uncertain course during this century. With the shift in emphasis from grammar and translation to speaking ability and with the introduction of language instruction at the elementary level, an increased emphasis upon foreign language consistent with wider international contacts may take place. The first languages taught and for a long time the only respectable ones were, as has been mentioned, the classical languages of Greek and Latin. Greek nearly disappeared entirely in the early part of the present century, and while Latin survived it yielded its dominant position to French which grew in popularity but more recently has been surpassed by Spanish which became popular during the 1930's and 1940's. German thrived after the turn of the century along with science and mathematics but virtually disappeared in the changed climate of World War I. Scandinavian languages, Italian, and Hebrew have been taught primarily in bilingual regions, but have never achieved general acceptance. Russian now appears to be a candidate for rapid growth in the last half of this century.

The American culture has never been overly hospitable to the aesthetic areas of art and music, and with the exception of singing and drawing in the elementary schools and performing music groups in the high school, the curriculum in both of these fields has been limited. General music classes in junior high schools have varied greatly in their success, although art has in recent years developed considerably at this level with increased emphasis on creativity and the use of a wide variety of media. The vast improvements in recording and music reproduction and their correspondingly increased popularity may result in more emphasis on appreciation of fine music.

The practical arts, contrarily, have grown much during this century. Industrial arts originated in a manual training setting derived from a highly refined Swedish system called *sloyd* which was introduced here late in the nineteenth century. Industrial arts, a general education program aimed at increased familiarity with the industrial world based on direct experience, should not be confused with industrial education which aims at specific vocational training. The latter was introduced both in trade schools and comprehensive high schools in response to industrial expansion and the decline of the apprentice system. Homemaking and agriculture were first promoted with the establishment of land-grant colleges and the extension service toward the end of the last century. Further federal encouragement specifically for high schools came with the Smith-Hughes Act of 1917 subsidizing these departments and requiring double periods of instruction and home projects. Additional vocational education development occurred with the inception of technical subjects, often provided in separate technical high schools, accompanied by a considerable amount of related instruction in science and mathematics.

Perhaps the most extensive vocational area in comprehensive high schools is business. The academies offered bookkeeping, but the later emphasis on secretarial work awaited the invention of the typewriter, the development of a system of shorthand, and the rapid expansion of the business world toward the end of the nineteenth century. More recently, retailing or distributive education has entered the picture along with related work experience. Business subjects have also received some acceptance in recent years as part of general education, particularly introduction to business, personal typing, and business law.

It was World War I and its revelation of the physical condition of the nation's manhood which gave the initial impetus to organized physical education in the high schools. Many states enacted laws requiring such instruction. Its development was accompanied by a growth in intramural and interscholastic athletics and a recreational emphasis became dominant over the traditional calisthenics and body-building. The number of gymnasiums, swimming pools, and playing fields increased greatly, and although World War II revealed little improvement in the fitness of youth, faith in the program persisted. A study in the 1950's showing American youth to be inferior to their European counterparts in strength and stamina caused some increase in careful physical testing and some shift away from games toward more exercises. But the athletic emphasis remains strong, although a tendency toward sports which can be continued in adulthood is noticeable.

Health instruction has been closely associated with physical education. The great advances in medicine in the past century, particularly those relating to immunization and other preventive measures, undoubtedly spurred the introduction of health teaching in the schools. Legislation pressed by various groups interested in the alcohol problem also had an effect in the early 1900's. The listing of health in first position in the so-called "cardinal objectives of secondary education" issued in 1918 undoubtedly had some bearing upon the extension of health teaching to the high school level. At present it perhaps receives greatest emphasis in the junior high school, particularly as part of science.

Problems Presented by Proliferation

The introduction of new subject areas would itself have increased the number of courses, but in addition so many more courses did develop in older fields that by 1955 over five hundred were offered at the secondary level. Some schools, of course, still offer very few, while others may provide as many as two hundred. It is difficult to determine how many different courses exist because different titles are used for substantially the same course and in some cases the same title may refer to two quite different courses. Strictly speaking, every course of study differs somewhat from every other so it is a matter of judgment whether two are to be considered the same.

While the number of courses has been growing, the number specifically required of students has been decreasing. This indicates that the elective system has become widespread and students are permitted to plan their own unique programs with the assistance of parents and counselors. Many applaud this progress toward individualization, but some feel that students are not mature enough to select a balanced program and they deplore the fact that students can complete high school without having had certain courses.

Many states and school systems have adopted a position avoiding both extremes, whereby about half of the credits are required and half open to choice. Even of the latter, it is common to require a sequence in one field, further avoiding too much scattering of courses.

REQUIREMENTS FOR GENERAL STATE HIGH SCHOOL DIPLOMA
IN NEW YORK

Group I	English	4 units
	Citizenship Education	3 units
	General Science	1 unit
	Mathematics	1 unit
	Health	$\frac{1}{2}$ unit
	Physical Education	0 unit (90 min/wk directed activity)
	Total constants	$9\frac{1}{2}$ units

Group II	Sequence—3 units in:	
	Agriculture	Industrial arts
	Art	Mathematics
	Business subjects	Mechanical drawing
	Foreign languages	Music
	Homemaking	Science

Group III   Electives—to make total of 18 units

Presently, there is extensive pressure for reducing even more the elective opportunities in both high school and college. Perhaps the "constants-with-variables" arrangement will prevail, but it obviously will be continuously reviewed in the years ahead. We can not stop the increase in knowledge nor, it seems, successfully avoid vocational and special training in the high school. The emphasis upon fitting the curriculum to the needs of the student will also continue, and we can expect development of many new courses.

Apparently, school staffs will increasingly be called upon to appraise new courses and variations on old courses. We find now a pronounced trend to truncation and to the telescoping of programs in the secondary school. Subjects have been, since World War II, placed at lower grade levels to permit some college subject teaching at the high school level. New subjects will continue to challenge the established ones.

Choice may not be easy. Every proposal is likely to have an enthusiastic proponent. Our colleagues are likely to be quite anxious to obtain approval of their special courses and pet schemes. We can anticipate that it will get increasingly more difficult to choose among many appropriate, useful offerings for high school pupils. If we stick to very precise subject areas, it is obvious that the problem will even be greater, perhaps impossible. The alternative in many cases seems to be some synthesis of subjects or more comprehensive organization.

Emergence of More General, Broader Courses

Under the pressure of fitting more and more content into a limited period, many schools have experimented with several administrative devices to keep the staff happy. They have found ways of combining content and of selecting it more effectively within a large scope well enough to please the proponents of new areas as well as to satisfy those who desire to retain established content. Sharp breaks and complex schedules have thus been avoided. Although new and more inclusive titles have been used to name courses, teachers have been able to identify within the courses the content which could, if necessary, be ordered again into a specific subject. Departure from familiar terminology has been troublesome in some cases,[2] e.g., social studies; but in other areas, e.g., English, there has been limited protest from either teachers or parents.

Development of broader school subject offerings came of course for other reasons than competition among subjects alone. Some of these causes or bases for more inclusive organizations of content are included in the discussion which follows.

[2] Note how general science in Grades 7–9 was particularly misleading to a number of critics who tried to compare American and Russian education. The critics claimed that American schools teach no "physics" in Grades 7–9. Actually general science does include many elements of elementary physics.

Development of Survey Courses

During the decade following 1910 a new type of introductory survey course was developed in a number of fields. Usually offered in Grade 9, these courses served both as an introduction to a subject area for those who would do further work in it and as an over-all survey as part of the general education of students who would not be studying the subject further. Thus general science,[3] mathematics, business, shop, music, and art are widely offered today.

These new subjects or courses have permitted the instructor to include units from a number of specialities and to provide the student with a general acquaintance, if not a comprehensive treatment. Appeal has been greater because students have had opportunity to explore numerous areas of interest. The teacher has been able to select the more stimulating highlights and leave to later courses those aspects particularly needed for specialism. Also from time to time the teacher has been able to relate better the content from heretofore rather discrete areas.

The design for these general courses has never attained much standardization because it has never been clear exactly what purpose they were to serve. In some cases, they have represented little more than a series of relatively unrelated samplings of more advanced, specialized courses in the field. In others, they have centered around the major generalizations or principles which in later courses are developed in greater detail. In still other instances, they have stressed those aspects of a subject area which find greatest application in everyday affairs. Thus, in many cases they have not been as useful everywhere as they might have been both in relieving competition for more time for special subjects and in making possible a much more effective teaching of the subjects and parts of subjects included. Yet it does appear subject teaching can be appreciably improved through greater attention to the purpose and the design of these general courses.

Several pitfalls in these courses have been revealed in experimentation with them. The danger of superficiality is especially great, particularly if too much is crowded into them. So many concepts may be included that few can be really well developed. Or the concepts se-

---

[3] General science is often also referred to as a broad fields course. The distinction between a survey and a broad fields course, as we see it, is that as between function and structure. The general science survey course is one consisting of units drawn from or based on a series of science subjects, e.g., weather from meteorology; electricity from physics. A broad fields course in general science is one consisting of units which have no particular subject origin or base, e.g., air or the environment.

lected for consideration may be kept so elementary that they represent little more than common knowledge which the students may already possess before beginning the course. A related danger is that the material will be so disjointed that few broad understandings can emerge. Thus careful selection as well as organization, using a "scheme with a theme" as suggested in Chapter 8, are essential to the improvement of these courses.

Merger of Subjects

Somewhat similar to the general course is the merger of subjects in the same or related areas. English as taught in most schools, for example, is not a single subject but a broad field course encompassing literature, composition, spelling, grammar, declamation, and other subjects. A fusion of history, geography, political science, and economics led to the arrangement known as social studies. Biology is a fusion of botany and zoology. English and social studies have usually been the bases of courses known as unified studies. All of these schemes represent attempts to overcome one of the chief criticisms of the subject-organized curriculum, namely, its compartmentalization.

Thus when two or more subjects deal with similar phenomena and it is desired that students recognize the interrelationships, it is possible to rely solely upon methodological means of bringing out these connections or they can be facilitated by organizational means. The various kinds of mergers mentioned above represent organizational approaches to the problem designed to diminish the effect of subject divisions on the establishment of organic relationships among learning products.

There is, however, another purpose of subject mergers. Particularly when skills are of primary concern, it is often desired to spread out certain types of experience over a period of years rather than concentrate them all in one course. Hence, in English as now usually constituted, the language skills are part of each year's work, thus providing for continuous practice, whereas if they were taught in a single year they would tend to deteriorate from disuse. In New York State a revision of the sequential secondary mathematics program during the 1950's introduced a merger of intermediate algebra and plane trigonometry as an eleventh-year course in order to emphasize relationships, but it also revised other courses by including attention to arithmetic skills in all of them and to algebra skills in geometry. These latter mergers were primarily for skill maintenance.

Attempts to Functionalize Subjects

The teaching of subjects has also been improved in recent years by deliberate attention to their functional features. This does not mean that immediate practicality or social utility becomes the exclusive criterion for selection of content and activities, but that whatever is selected is dealt with in a way that emphasizes function rather than obscures it. A former attitude seemed to be that the more pedantic and remote from ordinary affairs subjects were, the more valuable they were. The view that has prevailed in recent curriculum changes is the contrary one that if intelligent behavior is to result from learning, the ways in which learning may be used must also be learned. Furthermore, while advanced scholars may well be driven to learn for the love of learning and acquire knowledge for its own sake, few students in the lower schools are so motivated. The latter are characteristically less interested in a subject, and hence inclined to learn it more readily, when that subject is seen either to affect them personally or at least to be relevant to the affairs which they observe going on around them.

There are three main ways in which functionality is achieved. One is by the acquisition and practice of skills in a setting involving their actual use. A second is by learning facts not in isolation but in connection with a problem or for the purpose of arriving at generalizations. The third way consists of examining the applications which may be made or by considering principles.

1. *The development of skills through projects in industrial arts and agriculture and through family situations in home economics is a rather obvious illustration of the first-mentioned approach of functional teaching of skills.* However, much has also been done in the more academic fields. In English, for example, where language skills are involved, situations have been planned wherein writing, speaking, or reading is done not just as an exercise but for a purpose. This does not mean that spelling may not be given separate deliberate attention nor that time may not be devoted to specific drill on troublesome grammatical matters, but that in addition and so far as possible opportunities for the actual *use* of these skills will be provided. Similarly, while mathematical operations may be brought to a functional level through practice exercises, problems in which they may function are also made an important part of mathematics and the less contrived these problems the more clearly the functional value is established. In social studies such skills as the reading of statistical charts

and graphs, of maps and of reference materials are employed in connection with any and all topics or problems. In business education and science instruction the use of office or laboratory settings for the practice of skills is by no means new, but even in the foreign language program such practices are found as listening to authentic foreign conversation on records, preparing newspapers in the language, using current periodicals and papers for reading, and stressing conversation in the classroom. These illustrations show how good curriculum planning in the subject areas—old and new—provides for skill development in functional settings.

2. *The second functional approach cited earlier related to the use of facts.* There are, perhaps, in every subject certain "important facts" which people in general, or at least those who have studied the subject, are expected to know. They are probably less numerous than it is commonly thought, but whatever their number they should be learned by whatever means is effective. For the most part, however, the facts encompassed by a subject ought not to be treated as ends in themselves as they so frequently are (though no one would admit it), but rather they should be discovered as needed for some purpose. The purpose of facts is, as discussed in Chapter 7, to serve as data in the solution of problems. As such they should lead to generalizations. Generalizations which are not based on an abundance of facts make for glib superficiality. Therefore, good subject teaching makes use of even more facts than is conventional. What is more, students learn how, when, and where to seek them.

In English courses students, far from all having to read identical selections, derive from a variety of literary works insights which when discussed with others or contemplated alone lead to conclusions both with respect to recurring human problems and to the essential characteristics of literary genre or particular authors' styles. With help, students can formulate rules of usage from examples of good usage. In writing, they can develop habits of basing what they write upon facts obtained through increasingly perceptive personal observation or from available printed sources.

Instead of memorizing lists of dates or little known facts of the television quiz-show variety, social studies students now make use of primary and secondary sources, ranging from field trips to government documents to historical novels, to collect the information needed to examine important problems of mankind. From historical accounts they learn that these problems usually are difficult to solve and recur in altered form to confront generation after generation. From other social science sources they are confronted, however, with new data, the fruits of scientific inquiry, which as yet have not been applied to the age-old problems and in this direction many learn to place their hopes. Similarly, in science courses, the facts obtained from experimentation, their own or that of others more skilled, serve as raw materials to draw conclusions about the universe in which they live. Even in mathematics, where the deductive art of drawing necessary inferences is a matter of major emphasis, opportunity can still be provided for students to experiment and measure and study numerical examples as a basis for formulating general rules. Further, by gathering some of their own data to solve problems involving measurement, they appreciate better the source of the data they manipulate in solving textbook problems.

In foreign language courses the appreciation of an exotic culture can not be gained by memorizing a list of authors and composers or by learning the location of places of interest. Just as a feeling for a period of history is best gained from the vivid and detailed delineations in movies, historical novels and contemporary materials pertaining to the period, so too a feeling for another culture comes from wide contact with its content. The information thus gained, from books or at firsthand from people or recordings, in restaurants or museums, serves as a basis for drawing conclusions and forming ineffable impressions.

The value of the practical arts is also much enhanced by frequent appeal to the reflective process to formulate principles empirically derived from manipulative experiences. From the specific materials, processes, and operations dealt with in industrial arts should come broad understandings of the ways of industry; from dealing with specific problems in home economics should come an understanding of the principles underlying wholesome family life. In the fine arts the statements made in regard to literature apply also, and in art, particularly, the experimental approach to artistic principles is a fruitful one.

3. *The third functional trend in subject teaching concerns the application of principles, which is in a sense the converse of what has just been discussed.* Indeed, good curriculum planning provides for continual alternation between experiences from which principles can be derived and experiences in which they can be applied. What is learned in English should be applied in written and oral work in other subjects, in activities such as school newspapers, debating and club meetings as well as in the communication problems of everyday life. The applications of science to health, to gardening, to the operations of the technological products in home, farm, and industry should receive

attention. Mathematics programs today give considerable emphasis to enabling students to apply the subject to personal and business finances, to problems of the shop and home, and to the field of science. Art principles are put to use in connection with matters of dress, interior decoration, community beautification, stage design and poster work, as well as creative leisure. The learnings of social studies are viewed in terms of their implications for the local community, the school's student government, and the small group of the classroom, homeroom, or club. Thus the several subject areas of the curriculum, however academic, become functional as a result of experiences whereby skills are practiced for a purpose, facts are used as data, and evidence and principles are applied in varied situations.

SUBJECTS AND THE OBJECTIVES OF THE SCHOOL

The various subject fields together make up a single organism: the school program of studies. They are not independent entities but parts of a whole. It has been shown how the number of areas and courses within areas have increased in response to the requirements of an enlarged and altered clientele, how general courses have arisen to serve commonly shared needs, how mergers of courses have helped bring out relationships and distribute the learning of skills, and how the functional aspects of subjects have been emphasized. Each of these trends is exemplified by most, if not all, areas.

In spite of these similarities and common tendencies, each of the fields has to a great extent progressed independently with its own specialists acting like private corporations. Each has developed its own sets of objectives reflecting the orientation of many specialists. To some extent this is good, for it avoids the restriction of adhering to an over-all "party line" and encourages initiative. But it also invites duplication, omissions, and inconsistency in the total school program.

Individuals and special interest groups within the educational pro-fession derive authority to make curriculum decisions only as it is delegated by the profession as a whole. Within a school it is the staff as a whole, not individuals or subgroups, which carries the responsibility and authority for developing a curriculum. The controlling element is the set of purposes which that curriculum is designed to achieve. These, therefore, are the purposes of the school, not of any one subject, and *it is only as the various subjects contribute to the broad objectives of education that their continuance is warranted.*

The broad objectives, both national and local, promote understanding and commitment; the broader pronouncements furnish guidance and serve as a check. Subject specialists should ponder the contribution not only of their own fields but of all others to these general objectives. Staffs, jointly, and students preparing to teach, individually, can profit greatly from examining each subject area in the light of the "Seven Cardinal Objectives" or some other preferred list. To illustrate this process a brief analysis is presented here using the four purposes of education in American democracy promulgated by the Educational Policies Commission.

1. *Self-realization.* "To realize" means both to be aware of and to accomplish, and both connotations are relevant to an individual's gains from his educational experiences. One of the purposes that experiences in all subject areas should serve is to promote an awareness of the potentialities which lie within each self and to provide means by which they may be fulfilled; to clarify the priority of conditions needed by the self and to develop ability to achieve them.

Fundamental to self-realization is the need to know, and the ability to find out about that which is outside the self. To the extent that the learning experiences in any field involve the activity of inquiring, discovering, exploring or experimenting, self-realization is promoted. To the extent that the individual learns to invest these experiences with reflective thought, his awareness of his own mind grows and so do his benefits from its use. Symbols are essential to thought and, hence, growth in ability to use language and number is central to self-realization. Prescott[4] made the same point when he identified the integrative needs of personality: *contact* and *harmony with reality* gained through as many direct experiences as possible but accompanied by *progressive symbolization,* that is, growth in ability to represent reality symbolically.

It is not necessary to call attention to the obvious contributions of English, mathematics, and foreign language to this purpose, although often the teaching of these subjects degenerates into a formalistic manipulation of symbols as if an end in itself, instead of offering experiences in using them for inquiry, thinking, and genuine communication of ideas. Less obvious is the fact that good curriculum planning in other subject areas can provide not only for the application of language and computational skills but also for their improvement. In every subject, vocabulary is increased by the addition of technical terms. The best ways of reading and studying in the particular field

[4] Daniel Prescott, *Emotion and the Educative Process,* American Council on Education, 1938.

may be given explicit attention, assuming the use of the library and the availability of a variety of books encompassing the level of reading ability of each student. Nearly every subject also permits writing, discussion, and oral reporting.

Well-planned experiences in social studies provide frequent occasion for the use of mathematical concepts in statistical charts, graphs, and maps. Science of course involves great amounts of quantitative thinking, but in addition introduces other symbolic systems such as the chemical formulas, the electronic diagrams, meteorological maps, and astrononical symbols. Problems in business nearly always call for computation; measurement is essential in both industrial arts and home economics; rhythm in music and scale in art both involve numerical relations.

While all subjects can contribute to self-realization through the improvement of ability to express ideas symbolically, and through both the satisfaction and encouragement of intellectual curiosity, there are other aspects which some subjects are particularly well suited to foster. Self-realization is largely contingent upon good health and certainly depends utterly upon survival. Therefore, any subject which increases understanding of and inclination toward safer and more healthful behavior contributes to this over-all purpose. The content of science has many applications to health and the laboratory presents many considerations of safety. Learning safe practices is also a major concern in the industrial arts shop and during physical education in the gymnasium and on the playground. Safety in the home and principles of nutrition, sanitation, disease prevention, and other aspects of health maintenance are inherent in the content of home economics. It is often argued that these matters should be the concern of the home rather than the school, but statistics relating to the health and safety record of the populace cast considerable doubt on the suitability of many homes as a source of such instruction.

Recreation is another aspect of self-realization for which skills are developed in physical education quite apart from the contributions to physical health. However, while sports are a major diversion of many individuals, hobby-type skills of the sort learned in art, music, home economics, and industrial arts also serve as a lifelong source of personal satisfaction for many others. The literature phase of English can scarcely be said to have high utilitarian value for the business of everyday living or for many vocational pursuits. If it is to be studied, it must, except as an ideational source, be primarily as a foundation for enjoyment in leisure hours. This being the case, experiences with literature must be such as to nurture interest and enjoyment rather than to create revulsion. It is essential for teachers to respect honest differences in taste, not only those due to immaturity but those inevitable among adults. Self-realization is genuine only when it involves the release of unique potentialities, not when it assumes the snobbish affectation of devotion to alleged refinement. This is not to imply that the school should espouse Philistinism or that it should not seek to develop accepted good taste. But it ought not to extol literary appreciation and disparage woodcraftmanship; it ought not count that person who can create beauty in a home, in clothing, or in a flower arrangement inferior to the one who can roam the art museum knowingly; it ought to recognize that being a dilettante performer on a musical instrument can be as much a source of fulfillment as being a connoiseur of classical music.

The American standard of living makes everybody a member of the leisure class. It also, however, places many people in positions wherein they derive little satisfaction from their vocations. For these persons leisure pursuits are their only real opportunity for self-realization. Every subject in the curriculum offers possibilities for finding outlets for talents and avenues of interest in which leisure skills and appreciations may be developed. Sports and the several fine and practical arts mentioned above have wide appeal, but for some a similar attraction may be found in mathematical puzzles, in dramatics or creative writing encountered in English, or in collecting butterflies or rocks based on experiences in science. In view of the diversity of people's interests, a broad school program is indicated, and it is incumbent upon each subject teacher so to view his subject and plan learning experiences that individuals may find opportunities for self-fulfillment. To do so is not to subvert learning to frivolity, but actually to promote a liberal extension of the humanistic ideal. Not to do so restricts the curriculum to exclusionist pedantry or illiberal vocationalism.

Finally, self-realization demands ability to think. Thinking always involves problems and requires proficiency in perceiving, defining, and analyzing them, as well as in the process of deduction and induction. Representing the highest level of intellectual activity, thinking is a difficult ability to acquire and therefore must be a concern at every level and in every subject. It cannot be learned in a single course such as geometry, nor in a unit on the rules of logic, nor through a classic illustration of the scientific method. There is as much need to think in the industrial arts shop as in the science laboratory, as many genuine problems to be solved in home economics as in the mathematics course. In every subject area there is a commendable tendency to organize learning experiences in such a way as to stress the *process* of finding solutions to problems rather than to place the emphasis upon the *product* of others' thinking, that is, upon the answers. Today's answers will not all serve for tomorrow; the problems of tomorrow are unknown. Our only reliance is upon the process for solving those problems and this process in one form or another is applicable to every subject area. In most cases, perhaps, the process is highly individual and calls for initiative and self-reliance; in some instances, however, it becomes a group process, particularly as a democracy solves its problems, and as such calls for cooperativeness. Opportunities for both kinds abound in the various subject areas, but only if the experiences are organized around questions or problems to stimulate thinking activity.

To summarize, then, each subject contributes to self-realization to the extent that it

1. Encourages inquiry into the nature of reality through direct and vicarious experiences
2. Develops the abilities involved in effective expression and accurate communication
3. Strengthens the basis for safe and healthful living
4. Arouses and sustains unique, constructive interests
5. Provides tools for individual thinking and group problem-solving

2. Human relationships. A second area toward which the subjects of the modern curriculum have been directed involves those learnings which make for greater effectiveness in dealing with others in the more intimate relationships of family and other primary groups. Every subject *can* be taught in such a manner as to make possible many occasions for actually practicing mutual respect and accomodation among students. Small study groups in social studies, the teamwork-sportsmanship setting of physical education, the working relationships in laboratory science, industrial arts and home economics, the strict demands imposed by conjoint action in performing music groups —each emphasizes somewhat different aspects of human relations. Yet the same subjects taught through other learning activities might yield very little along this line.

The content of many subjects also bears upon these relations, if it is but recognized and brought out. Literature—English or foreign— deals with all kinds of human relationships. History and the sociological aspects of social studies provide opportunities for analyses in terms of human values. Home economics in its most intellectual aspects is a psycho-sociological study of home and family. Business subjects can stress the relationships involved in employment, in dealing with customers, and in working with colleagues. English, again, furnishes basic skills for conversation and correspondence which are essential avenues of human relationships.

In short, teachers make their subjects instruments for improving human relationships when they plan learning experiences which (1) permit interaction of students with each other in which respect for opinions, rights, and sensibilities is stressed, and (2) entail investigation of the play of human values in all matters under study.

3. *Economic Efficiency.* Mundane as economic matters are, they form the basis for all other aspects of living and the school has both the opportunity and the obligation to develop students' effectiveness in this realm. There are two aspects here—vocation and consumership.

Some subjects are frankly and primarily vocational in purpose. This is true of industrial and technical subjects, many business subjects, agriculture, and, if "homemaker" be considered an occupation, then home economics also. Industrial arts, as distinguished from industrial education, is not primarily vocational, but by dealing with the materials products and processes of industry is aimed instead at increased understanding of our industrial society as part of general education.

However, every subject has some vocational implications and applications, and each teacher should be aware of these so that he may both contribute to students' vocational guidance and take advantage of the motivational value which practicality has for some students. The development of language skills in English is related to vocations in many respects. In addition to identifying the occupations which are obviously primarily concerned with writing, reading, or speaking, the English teacher strengthens such broadly applicable skills as reading and listening to directions, writing letters of application and business letters in general, being interviewed, making sales conversation, and using the telephone. Furthermore, reading ability can as well be improved using materials pertaining to occupations as with anything else, and even the study of literature, particularly biography, furnishes opportunities to consider vocations which are described.

Mathematics enters vocational pursuits at all levels from simple computation to the highest forms of abstraction, often through the process of measurement. Science, too, involves both theoretical and technological fields of work. Art and music teachers seek to identify talent with professional potentialities, and particularly in art the commercial possibilities have expanded greatly as a result of developments in packaging and product design, television, and printing. Even in foreign languages the opportunities for interpreters and translators have increased in both government and business.

Mathematics, especially at the junior high school level, focuses upon computations involving money and measurement, both of which are clearly involved in the consumption of goods and services. In science the principles underlying the operation and maintenance of the products of technology form the basis for more intelligent use of them.

Business departments have assumed major responsibility for consumership learning, but again the other subjects have their own unique contributions to make. Both industrial arts and home economics provide an understanding of the qualities of various materials and the evidences of good workmanship, as well as the necessary skills in many instances for making articles oneself. Art instruction properly improves students' abilities to select and arrange items of various uses on the basis of aesthetic principles. Also good taste in the areas of music and literature, developed in these respective subjects, should have its effect on the types of records, books, and magazines selected, and the ways in which time and money are spent for entertainment, whether at the concert, theater, or cinema.

Even the social studies, which at first glance may be thought to have little bearing upon economic efficiency, have perhaps the most far-reaching implications of all. Through the study of economic systems the scope and importance of the "world of work," as well as the place of specific occupations, are stressed. Often a unit of study relating to occupational choice and progress is included. In addition to the social significance of work, this field also stresses the importance of conservation in consumption. Wise consumership entails such understandings as the legal safeguards of personal interests, the bases of standards of living, society's obligation for the welfare of the underprivileged citizens, and the economics of the greatest of all consumers —government.

Subjects contribute to economic efficiency, then, by

1. direct vocational training
2. emphasis on vocational guidance and applications
3. providing skills and understandings relating to the personal management of time and money
4. stressing the social aspects of production and consumption

4. *Civic responsibility.* All subjects contribute to citizenship education and although social studies are concerned with this primarily,

changing the name of social studies to citizenship education, as was the case in New York State, does not diminish the role of other subjects in this regard, even if it does unnecessarily obscure it. Even social studies may do little to make better citizens unless deliberately pointed in that direction. Knowledge about American history or government does not alone assure better democratic citizenship; if it did, teaching *about* Communism and Russia might be dangerous. But social studies may be concerned not only with knowledge but with the skills involved in critically examining social institutions in the light of fundamental democratic values. Thus knowledge of history and content from the social sciences becomes important for the insights it permits into modern social problems.

In the teaching of all subjects, including social studies, there is of course an effort to teach responsible citizenship through actual practice in classroom behavior. However, other subjects also promote this objective through their content. English can include experience in analyzing propaganda, in improving newspaper reading, and in using parliamentary procedure and effective discussion techniques. Some English teachers see value in giving some attention to the fourth of the language processes—listening, inasmuch as its importance has been greatly increased by the development of electronic media of mass communication.

Almost every social problem has quantitative aspects, and mathematics can therefore play an important part in developing civic responsibility. Although these problems are usually ultimately of a value-judgment type, the judgment often hinges on questions of scientific fact. The citizen today must be literate with respect to basic scientific principles, if for no other reason than to understand the recommendations of technical specialists and preserve his own basic right to participate in deciding matters of policy. Science courses have a further effect insofar as they stress the social significance of scientific discoveries.

Foreign language indirectly influences citizenship by enabling somewhat better understanding of other nations, but its study is made even more valuable when it includes deliberate emphasis upon understanding and respecting cultural differences. Art and music, being universal languages of a sort, may contribute in the same fashion if they are taught with such emphasis. Business subjects supplement the social studies in developing economic literacy through consideration of specific business practices and in strengthening respect for law through the study of business law. Health education can provide opportunities for considering public, as well as personal, health problems.

In summation, subjects further the development of civic responsibility when they are taught in a way which

1. requires increasingly mature acceptance of responsibility for classroom conduct
2. permits discussion of contemporary social problems in an atmosphere of respect for the opinions of others
3. provides an understanding of the development and functioning of social institutions
4. increases facility in understanding other cultures

THE IMPROVEMENT OF SUBJECT TEACHING

The foregoing section indicates that all subject areas in the curriculum, if properly directed, can contribute to the broad, accepted purposes of schooling. Intellectual purposes can be served simultaneously with the meeting of individual and societal needs. The two are not in conflict.

Much improvement in subject teaching has resulted from teachers paying increased attention to the purposes of the school and to specifying the objectives of their subjects and seeking after them. It is easy for the content of courses to become frozen and considered magically indispensable and inviolable. Yet the content of any course was selected by human judgment on some basis.

As man's knowledge rapidly increases and conditions change, it is important to re-examine the curricular content to see if the priorities are appropriate in the light of current requirements. This does not mean that immediate utility is to be the criterion, but it does mean that with time a precious commodity preference must go to the subject matter which has promise of being of most significance in the present and future lives of the learners. It changes nothing to protest that knowledge should be acquired for its own sake rather than for pertinence in the contemporary scene because to do so immediately raises the further question of what knowledge is of most worth.

In addition to attention to objectives, other measures have been taken to improve subject teaching. These include (1) increased individualization, (2) emphasis on the concerns of students and of contemporary society, (3) correlation among subject areas, (4) use of group methods, and (5) organization into large units. Each of these tendencies has eliminated or diminished one or more of the short-comings associated with the subject approach.

Teachers and the Individualization of Subject Teaching

One of the limitations of subject teaching has been the practice of specifying in great detail and far in advance the content of courses. However justifiable such definitiveness and rigidity may be in special-ized courses for which students are to some extent selected with respect to interest and ability, it does not seem suitable in situations where this is not the case. Instead, it is necessary to recognize the possibility and indeed the inevitability that the conceptual levels at which students will operate will vary. To avoid freezing the level of conceptualization at some preconceived point, sufficient flexibility is necessary so that the same broad understandings can be developed by some students in rela-tively simple terms while others simultaneously probe far deeper and range far wider than is ever accomplished in the conventional situa-tion. A skillful teacher can make such provision within a single class and with any topic, whether it is Jacksonianism, the short story, or photosynthesis. When teachers feel unable to do so, it may be necessary to separate students into sections of narrower range, but the temptation must be resisted of then setting rigid prescriptions for each section. In some areas a dual-track approach has been used, such as with algebra and general mathematics—certainly preferable to providing nothing but highly academic algebra, yet perhaps if a broader view of algebra were adopted, it would serve all better still.

The idea of expecting, rather than deploring, differential achieve-ment is a difficult one for subject teachers to accept. The lure of high standards is strong, but it is a false notion that equates them with a single fixed standard for the latter is no standard at all for the most capable and it deprives the lesser able from any experience with academic subjects. Only as students are provided with experiences which possess *meaning* for *them* and as they pursue ideas to the limit of their abilities will standards really be high. The teachers who have done most to improve subject teaching are those who have found ways of making the important understandings of their fields available to more, not fewer, students.

Contemporary Concerns Emphasized

If a subject is important in today's curriculum, it is because it contributes to more intelligent behavior in today's world. Academic subjects need not be "academic" in the sense of being divorced from reality or so-called "real-life situations." Every facet of a student's life is affected by mathematical and scientific principles. The problems of community, nation, and world, daily impressed upon the minds of youth, are not something apart from the content of history, geography, political science, sociology, or economics. All literature in the English language or a foreign one, whether fantasy, biography or realistic fiction, deals with the wishes, fears, and problems which men share and of which students are aware. The subject curriculum is strengthened when it is planned so as to emphasize these implications rather than to ignore or overlook them.

The motivational value of relating subject matter to concerns perceived as significant by learners is too obvious to require elaboration. This is of course the epitome of interest. Another psychological justification may not be so apparent. Bright students usually recognize quite readily the bearing of generalizations upon specific personal and societal affairs and transfer what they have learned to these situations. Most students do not have this facility. For them it is necessary to make these connections explicit. When subject teaching is planned at the outset in terms of the lives of students and of the current scene, a major step in promoting transfer of learning has been taken.

Correlation of Subjects Promoted

A similar argument may be made with regard to transfer from one subject to another. One of the weaknesses attributed to the subject organization is the fragmentation of learning into discrete areas. Rich understanding results from weaving new learnings into the fabric of previous and simultaneous experiences. Some have felt that this can best be accomplished by actually combining the subjects themselves. Such fusions as general science, social studies, and even English are, as mentioned earlier in the chapter, efforts in this direction. Some forms of "core" represent further fusions of the language arts and social studies. Arrangements such as these are sometimes called integration of subjects. However, it is the integration of the learnings themselves, not of subjects, that is the primary concern. This may be facilitated by combining subjects but, as pointed out earlier, can be achieved without it, and in some cases the combination may be undesirable on other counts.

Subject teachers use three approaches to correlation. One is unilateral in which a teacher independently uses every opportunity to establish relationships. The chart suggested previously in this chapter is an aid in doing this. A second approach involves informed collaboration between two teachers for planning courses being studied by the same group of students in such a way that a close relationship results. Thus an art and an English teacher may explore ways of reinforcing learnings from the two areas. The third approach is a formal, systematic effort on the part of a faculty to arrange the program of studies in a manner which promotes correlation. Themes may be adopted for each grade level toward which much of the instruction will be directed. This approach is the most comprehensive, but it entails a greater danger of attempts to "force" artificial relationships than do the other two.

Group Methods More Fully Accepted

The discovery that the learner group can be an asset in learning is as relevant for the subject teacher as for other organizational arrangements. Teachers of English, social studies and science, in particular, have improved instruction by planning learning activities involving the whole class or subgroups in addition to those for individuals. A first step[5] in this direction often involves little more than substituting teacher-directed class discussion for individual recitations. A further step may consist of assigning small groups of students important subtopics to investigate more thoroughly and to report their findings to the class. Some go still further and encourage students to participate in identifying the topics of greatest interest or importance and to suggest ways of studying them. This becomes, in effect, a problem-solving experience in which gathering and organizing data, as well as drawing and reporting conclusions, are required. The question itself, stemming as it does from the subject matter of the course, may not be a problem for the students but finding an answer to it can be. There is no reason to believe that it is any less motivating for students to pursue matters about which they wonder or are curious than it is to work on their own "pressing problems" or those of the world.

Skills must for the most part be developed individually, but the establishment of principles and the elaboration of concepts are often enhanced by conjoint activity. Many attitudes of a social nature are best shaped through exploration in a group setting. Thus teachers promote the achievement of many important outcomes of subject instruction by including suitable cooperative learning activities.

Large Units Adopted

Implied in the foregoing is an organization of subjects into relatively large units of instruction although such units do not necessarily

---

[5] For excellent discussion of steps and stages, see Alice Miel *et al., Cooperative Procedures in Learning,* Bureau of Publications, Teachers College, 1954.

call for group activities. The value of the unit arrangement in focusing upon the more significant outcomes has been discussed in Chapter 7. Much subject teaching has profited from a shift from the day-to-day lesson approach to one which uses broad unifying themes as centers for extended periods of study. In biology these themes may be major functions of organisms; in social studies they may be phases of national development; in English they may be aspects of human endeavor around which literature, composition, and speaking can center.

In effect, unit organization does for the separate subject what correlation does for the subjects severally. Indeed, all of the tendencies cited in this chapter are aimed at preserving the virtue of a systematic approach to learning which the subject curriculum possesses, while at the same time creating conditions conducive to truly effective learning.

Questions for Discussion

1. Subject specialization and subject teachers have been harshly treated in many books and articles. Can anybody really teach anything worthwhile unless he knows his subject thoroughly?

2. Do thorough study and deep penetration into a subject actually interfere with effective teaching of relatively elementary knowledge and skill needed for ordinary living?

3. In this chapter it is proposed that a teacher have quite complete knowledge of various subject fields, of their content, and of the objectives sought by fellow teachers in other subjects and departments. Is this reasonable? Would it really make any difference to curriculum planning?

4. Are some subjects more respectable, more worthwhile, and more important than others? Are there "frill" subjects? What subjects would you eliminate?

5. What proposals have been made to increase the meaningfulness of content usually taught in the subject field you know best? Will they work? Will teachers use them? What changes have to come about to make your subject most appealing and effective?

6. Most subjects are said to serve a dual purpose. They provide the basic information for continuing growth in scholarship and specialism, and they contribute to general education. Which subjects do you think really fail in this dual role?

7. Suppose you were to begin from the bottom up, so to speak, and were given the task of creating an entirely new set of subjects for the high school, taking into consideration the needs of youth, rather than the needs of scholars in traditional subjects, current requirements of colleges, and so on. What subjects would you name? What content would you include?

8. What can you do to your subject to make it more palatable and useful without "watering" it down?

9. How should a department try to determine the effectiveness of its subject instruction and how should it proceed? What should it take into consideration in improving its members' subject teaching?
10. Content for subjects is generally selected by scholars and by teachers with acknowledged reputations. Is there anything wrong with this use of talent, particularly when many classroom teachers have little or no idea what should be taught?

Selected Bibliography

Burnett, R. Will, *Teaching Science in the Secondary School,* Rinehart, 1957.

Burton, William H., *The Guidance of Learning Activities,* D. Appleton-Century, 1944.

Crow, Lester, and Alice Crow, *High School Education,* Odyssey, 1951.

Douglass, Harl, ed., *The High School Curriculum,* second ed., Ronald, 1956.

Featherstone, William, *A Functional Curriculum for Youth,* American Book, 1950, chap. 5.

Gruhn, William, and Harl Douglass, *The Modern Junior High School,* second ed., Ronald, 1956.

Krug, Edward, *The Secondary School Curriculum,* Harper, 1960.

Leonard, J. Paul, *Developing the Secondary School Curriculum,* rev. ed., Rinehart, 1953, chap. 7.

National Council of Teachers of English, *The English Language Arts in the Secondary School,* Appleton-Century-Crofts, 1956.

New York State Education Department, *Design for Early Secondary Education,* The Department, 1954.

Venable, Tom C., *Patterns in Secondary School Curriculum,* Harper, 1958.

....

CHAPTER 11

Developing and Working
with the "Core" Program

Although most teachers, especially in the secondary school, will continue to teach the well-known subjects and to look for help in reviewing and revising the purposes and scope of their subjects and in developing the most meaningful experiences possible for their pupils, some subject teachers and specialists will be called upon to teach for the purpose of general education a kind of compromise course or one fitted to either the organized problems design or the freely emerging framework. More who are not asked to lend their personal resources directly may expect to participate with their colleagues in promoting, organizing, and developing such "core" courses. Teachers thus need to know what is involved, how the "core" can be explained and justified, how it can be managed and operated, what happens to students, how effective work can be carried out, what resources are used and how they are tapped, and what techniques and procedures are used in evaluation.

DEFINITION OF THE "CORE"

The word "core" has unfortunately been used so freely and so hazily both by uninformed neophytes and by informed experts that before we proceed to discuss the varied roles of the teacher in the "core" part of the total program, it is necessary to clarify further what we mean by "core."

The teacher has a right to assume that "core" is what "core" is, the central, basic, fundamental part of the curriculum. Should he believe that part to be certain required subjects, he has the traditional view. If he thinks of the "core" as a substitute or replacement for the most commonly taught subjects, he has the modern curriculum specialist's view.

Proponents of this approach to common or general education have categorized their ideas in various ways to make more vivid what they are talking about and what they call "core." The six types described by Alberty provide a useful reference for illustration. In the National Society yearbook, *Adapting the Secondary School Program To the Needs of Youth,*[1] he arranges the views as follows:

1. The core consists of a number of logically organized subjects or fields of knowledge each one of which is taught independently.
2. The core consists of a number of logically organized subjects or fields or knowledge, some or all of which are correlated.
3. The core consists of broad problems, units of work, or unifying themes which are chosen because they afford the means of teaching effectively the basic content of certain subjects or fields of knowledge. These subjects or fields retain their identity but the content is selected and taught with special reference to the unit.
4. The core consists of a number of subjects or fields of knowledge which are unified or fused. Usually one subject or field serves as a unifying center.
5. The core consists of broad, preplanned problem areas, or resource units from which are selected learning experiences in terms of the psychobiological and social needs, problems, and interests of students.
6. The core consists of broad teacher-student planned units of work, or activities, in terms of the expressed wishes or desires of the group. No basic curricular structure is set up.

The word "core" then is appropriately used for quite different arrangements for that part of the curriculum which is common. In this chapter we are using "core" to mean Type 5 in Alberty's list. Alberty's Types 1–4 are essentially subject-centered. Type 5 casts loose from subject dependence. It thus provides us with a chance to examine controlled problems in general education and to provide suggestions for moving toward it and carrying it out. At the same time, this discussion will make it possible to consider procedures quite as proper for a democratic teaching of the traditional subjects and for teaching in the "core" arrangements that are essentially subject-centered.

"Core" Emphasizes Process and Approach

"Core" is basically method. The essence of "core" Types 5 and 6 lies in the freedom permitted the teacher to plan with pupils the kinds of experience they will have. In the selected problems Type 5 the focus is on finding more manageable aspects of preidentified problems,

[1] N. B. Henry, ed., *Adapting the Secondary School Program to the Needs of Youth,* National Society for the Study of Education, 1956, pp. 119–120.

on determining objectives for groups and individuals, and on selecting activities that promise knowledge and skill useful in obtaining objectives. Much the same is true in Type 6 except that there is less restriction on problems and topics and even greater freedom to diagnose immediate personal and group needs and to plan learning experiences.

The most distinct element in Type 5 is the cooperative control involved, the determination of direction and action through an interaction process involving pupils and teachers. There are no external decisions made that specified content must be learned, nor that certain projects must be undertaken, nor that selected minimum essentials be attained.

A second characteristic of method in this type is dependence on internal and emerging evaluation to check progress toward immediate and broader goals and to provide for redirection and better cooperative group planning. Traditionally students have been under the obligation to master content and skills identified in advance by the teacher alone. The teacher has decided or has had decided for him whether progress has been accomplished. In the "core" the responsibility for reviewing growth and accomplishment and for diagnosing failure and need rests with the total group as they move from one stage to another.

Great emphasis is also put on large- and small-group teamwork for the purpose of defining, acquiring, and interpreting and presenting to others. With wholesome acknowledgement of the cultural place and motivational value of individual-to-individual competition, the central commitment is the development and use of group action skills.

Another aspect of method is pronounced dependence on survey, research, and investigation as the continuing technique for coming to grips with problems. True, modern teachers, particularly in the social studies and the humanities, resort to library assignments, community surveys, and reports, but they are not the major procedures in instruction. In the "core" they play a far more important role.

"Core" Includes Broader Functions

A major criticism of the secondary school has been that it has failed to take seriously into consideration the emotional and social concomitants of intellectual development. The "core" is thus set up as an arrangement to maintain and promote greater intimacy of the teacher with the child's personal development. Working with a wide range of topics and with emphasis on the pupil and his growth, the teacher can become a more effective guide and adjunct, relieving the special guidance officers and replacing the homeroom teacher.

"Core" Breaks the Traditional Time and Place Structure

To permit greater flexibility and to make possible a variety of activities, the "core" needs to be scheduled over several consecutive periods. Students are thus not interrupted in their work by the necessity of passing from class to class. Projects can be carried on in school and out of school. Movement of pupils from laboratory, to library, to shop, to music room, and to auditorium is then less rigidly governed.

TEACHER AS STAFF MEMBER AND THE "CORE"

We have said at the outset of this chapter that all teachers will not be personally assigned responsibility for "core." At the same time, it is not likely now that substantial alteration of the common program will be undertaken in many schools without prior thorough consideration on the part of those interested. Almost all teachers are concerned with the general foundation program and depend upon it not only for fundamental skills but for those attributes which constitute the basic elements of good citizenship. Thus they naturally must be interested.

Nowhere has the "core" been developed by simple and easy evolution. Those who have sought to dispense even in part with the old and familiar pattern of general education have found themselves faced with a variety of problems. Concept about the "core" itself has been difficult to develop. After that there have been the hard realities of theme selection, location of resources, development of diagnostic procedures, public relations, teacher anxiety, and a host of other details. Few "core" teachers themselves have been able to manage alone or even together with other "core" teachers. They have needed the resources, the support, and the active contribution of their fellow staff members.

This leads us to the conclusion that any teacher should have a picture of what he could do and probably ought to do to aid in the promotion and operation of a "core."

Clarification of the Place and Function of the "Core"

Most teachers in an ordinary school, regardless of assignment, are able to explain what the familiar required subjects are all about—to parents, to doubting Thomases amongst the student body, to occasional petulant fellow staff members who wonder at times why English and social studies "get so much time." In fact, even teachers of physics or accounting are usually quite conversant with the objectives of the general subjects.

On the contrary, in schools where there are "core" programs, even those types which are simply multiple-period arrangements for a teacher who is responsible for English one period and social studies another, it is possible to find teachers who wonder out loud, "What is this 'core' business all about?"

It could be argued that upon those who propose the "core" and upon those who manage it rests the major responsibility for clarifying and explaining what is being pursued. On the other hand, since general education and public relations are to a degree every teacher's responsibility, it is important that all teachers understand what a "core" is and why it might be employed.

Explanations for Use of "Core"

To a considerable extent, clarification depends upon the school situation and setting. Decisions to install "core" courses have come simply from the conviction of a teacher of required subjects that he can teach as much and more via a different pattern. Motivation has come from a realization that too many pupils are uninterested, discipline is exceedingly bad, retention is poor, or post-school citizenship is poor. Another starting point has been intensive review and appraisal of what the faculty wants its pupils to take with them from school.

Interestingly, few schools have a well-thought-through and useful statement on general education. It is easy to locate a short statement of philosophy or broad explanation of purpose, but there are few detailed analyses of cause and effect. We do, however, have several book-length treatments on general education and on what may be wisely included in it.[2]

Lacking their own statement of what they propose to do, it would seem that a faculty as a group might read one of these books together. In such a way, disagreements, questions, and confusions could be pointed up and thoroughly aired. Out of discussion and deliberation could come understanding if not agreement.

Far better, unquestionably, would be the writing of a clear statement about goals and purposes of the "core," followed by careful ex-

[2] B. Lamar Johnson, ed., *General Education in the American High School,* Scott Foresman and Company, 1942; Will French, ed. *Behavior Goals of General Education in High School,* Russell Sage Foundation, New York, 1957; Roland Faunce and Nelson Bossing, *Developing the Core Curriculum,* second ed., Prentice-Hall, 1958.

planation of its organization and programming. This could be followed by a discussion of procedures and techniques of teaching and a compilation of resource materials.

In New York City and in Minneapolis small pamphlets were prepared to give an overview for the "core" and to help clarify the purpose and define the idea. The New York City pamphlet lists as objectives:

1. To learn pupils' backgrounds, abilities, interests and problems and to win pupils' confidence
2. To help pupils understand their own abilities, strengths and weaknesses, face their own problems, make realistic plans and accept responsibility for their own actions
3. To help pupils to work together, and understand and get along with others
4. To look for and act upon opportunities to help pupils develop standards of judgment and standards of ethical conduct
5. To develop useful skills (Teachers aim to improve pupils' ability to read and develop their desire to read both for information and for pleasure; to help them to learn to use newspapers, magazines, pamphlets, textbooks, reference books, other books, the radio, motion pictures, and television; and to improve their ability to work with maps, graphs, charts, models, pictures, and cartoons)
6. To improve pupils' ability to listen and to communicate orally and in writing
7. To help pupils integrate the experiences they have elsewhere in school and outside the school with what they are learning in the core
8. To teach as much as possible of the subject matter commonly taught in the subjects that are combined in the core[3]

The Minneapolis *Primer for Common Learnings*[4] describes the three essential characteristics of a common learnings program to be:

1. Assistance to youth in solving their present problems thus giving them current success and furnishing them with techniques for future use. This purpose may be accomplished by
   a. Using the needs of youth as the basis for determining the content of the common learnings course; e.g., a unit in orientation
   b. Paying close attention to the studies of adolescent psychology to ascertain these needs and the nature of adolescence
   c. Counseling
2. Equipment of youth with those skills, attitudes, behaviors and bodies of information which should be common to all our youth in this present complex civilization. This purpose may be accomplished by
   a. Cutting across subject fields so that a complete picture can be developed; e.g., the social, economic, and cultural aspects of living in the air age as well as the scientific aspects

[3] *Suggestions to Teachers of Experimental Core Classes,* Board of Education, City of New York, 1951, p. 5.

[4] *A Primer for Common Learnings,* Board of Education, Minneapolis, 1948, pp. 9–14.

    b. Developing skills in democratic living by extensive participation in activities such as working together for the solution of common problems, pupil-teacher planning, and community projects

    c. Cultivating an articulate citizenry by varied experiences in communication in real situations

3. Use of the program to provide an effective teaching vehicle. This purpose may be accomplished by

    a. Recognizing that the more real the learning situations are, the more effective is the learning

    b. Utilizing the flexibility of the program to provide extensive use of community resources, field trips, the combined human resources of each school, and materials pertaining to problems of immediate concern

Of the now increasing bibliography on the "core," one of the best is Dorothy Mudd's review[5] of how the teachers of Harford County worked together to develop and extend their concepts before and while they produced materials and thought through details. Although the volume contains no list of objectives, the total report reveals clearly what emphasis came to be the concern of the group.

Location and Selection of Problems

With the subject curriculum the topics to be studied and the content to be covered remain nearly everywhere the province of the teacher to decide. Some teachers like lyric poetry more than they do précis writing. Some know more about mechanics than they do electricity. Some prefer foreign policy to the Westward Movement. The natural outcome, even in English, physics, and American history, is courses balanced to favor teacher interest, knowledge, and enthusiasm. Yet coverage in these subjects is generally restricted to a number of topics and follows to a pronounced extent the topics decided upon by the authors of textbooks.

In the "core," with emphasis on relating instruction to the problems and the needs of pupils, the burden of developing appropriate and flexible resources for the teacher looms much larger. So too does the matter of setting up some meaningful scope and structure to promote balance in pupil experience and to provide some organization and systematization which lead to efficiency.

Again, in both cases, the teachers assigned directly to the "core" may be expected to carry the major responsibility for working out diagnostic procedures, studying societal and student needs, and blocking out areas for cooperative planning and learning with pupils. But if the

---

[5] Dorothy Mudd, *A Core Program Grows,* Board of Education of Harford County (Maryland), 1949.

whole faculty and others are to pass on and approve as well as support this central portion of the general education program, it is better that all be involved in the basic decisions.

LARGE PROBLEM AREAS ALREADY IDENTIFIED

To date, considerable effort has gone into providing guidance on problem selection. The extensive studies of youth itself have given us the now well-known lists of developmental tasks. From numerous problem checklists and inventories of need and interest we can easily compile a priority summary. The Stratemeyer et al.[6] analysis of persistent problems of living defines scope and suggests more limited concerns for grade levels. We have mentioned the Wisconsin bulletin that relates problems to growth levels and characteristics. A number of school systems has published records of topic or problem titles covered or tentatively set for certain grades. In a chapter on "Designing the Core Program" Lurry and Alberty[7] have listed sixteen areas which they consider adequate and representative of the common needs of youth and appropriate for core Type 5. These are:

1. Problems of School Living
2.   "   " Self-Understanding
3.   "   " Finding Values by which we Live
4.   "   " Social Relationship
5.   "   " Employment and Vocation
6.   "   " Using and Conserving Natural Resources
7.   "   " Education in American Democracy
8.   "   " Constructive Use of Leisure
9.   "   " Family Living
10.   "   " Communication
11.   "   " Democratic Government
12.   "   " Community and Personal Health
13.   "   " Economic Relationship in a Democracy
14.   "   " Achieving World Peace in the Atomic Age
15.   "   " Intercultural Relations
16.   "   " Critical Thinking

GUIDES TO SUBPROBLEMS NEEDED

The numerous subproblems which are possible after the comprehensive questions or areas have been set down would stagger the imagination. What one could ask about family living or intercultural edu-

---

[6] Florence Stratemeyer et al., Developing a Curriculum for Modern Living, rev. ed., Bureau of Publications, Teachers College, 1957, chap. 6.

[7] Lucille Lurry and Elsie Alberty, Developing a High School Core Program, Macmillan Company, 1957, p. 60.

cation is endless. Similarly, a teacher responsive to questions from pupils could find himself invited to search out answers to a literal avalanche of queries about employment or self-adjustment. Whether individual or group bred, they could also be simple and trivial or substantive and instrumental in the study of further and more valuable matters.

We should at no point want to abridge the right and freedom of a teacher to decide with his pupils upon what to study. Even so the classroom teacher is not an entirely free agent. He is a delegate and, no matter how well trained, seldom so competent that he can not suffer the help and wisdom of his colleagues.

The listing of related and logical subproblems in any compendium of persistent life situations or continuing and appropriate areas for study is really a guide to what may and what might be chosen. Resource units containing many suggestions for learning units provide the same service.

At the same time "core" method requires that teachers select with pupils what it is timely and proper to study. "Core" teachers together or faculty groups as a whole can here provide a further reference help by including criteria for subproblem choice in each unit or by providing such a guide for all those developing possible learning units.

Reasons for taking up a specific question with a "core" group should, wherever proper, be the same as those for the selection of overall problem areas. Several of the books dealing with the "core" contain guides for topic selection which illustrate this. Faunce and Bossing[8] list six:

1. Knowledge of the topic should be useful now
2. Knowledge of the topic should be useful later
3. A topic should be interesting
4. Knowledge of topic should increase knowledge of the world around
5. Material should be available on the topic
6. It should be something not previously studied

Toops[9] includes five:

1. Is the area interesting and worthwhile to us?
2. Will it help us to live together better?
3. Will it call for many and varied experiences?
4. Can all of us participate and plan?
5. Is there material available?

[8] Faunce and Bossing, *op. cit.,* p. 144.
[9] Myrtle Toops, *Working in the Core Program in Burris Laboratory School,* Ball State Teachers College, 1955, p. 24.

Both of these touch on very pertinent matters, but there are other points that will be raised by teacher or staff. The five following are suggested additions. Together a staff should find more.

1. Is the problem one that is best studied and examined in school?
2. Is it one which permits questions important and significant to all as well as questions important and significant to individuals?
3. Is it one the study of which could develop significant values as well as contribute information worthy of retention?
4. Is it one of which difficulties of mastery are not beyond the competence of most of the group? Is it one better suited to a later level?
5. Is it one which can contribute richly to the broad range of objectives or which is unusually pertinent to limited goals?

Contributions to Preplanning

The bulk of planning for the "core" does not differ from good planning for curricular experience in any program. It involves identifying objectives, deciding on possible activities, and assembling resources for carrying those activities forward. But it should not be difficult to see that at the outset at least there will be considerable pressure on the "core" teacher to develop a fairly new set of units. If the spirit of the "core" is maintained in subsequent years, there will be continuing demand upon the teacher to produce.

Thus, we can anticipate that the burden of unit development in a new "core" program may be so great that the assigned teacher may need considerable help in addition to special provisions likely to be made for his independent production. Further, we do need to recognize that as the program moves along the "core" teacher will be looking for more and better ideas and for guidance about what should go into general education. The specialists on the staff can be of tremendous help as they are able to make suggestions and contributions with respect to areas for development, projects, and resources.

It would of course be foolhardy for the usual staff to embark on a Type 5 "core" without some transition steps involving modification of the subject organization. Carefully managed adaptations and experimentation should insure development of a number of units and plans which could serve as a backlog for the "core" teacher.

Some systems interested in "core" programs and in increasing resources have set aside funds for postschool and preschool workshops. Others have employed the summer workshop which provides a situation even more conducive to concentrated effort, increased faculty understanding, and unity. Through such an arrangement, special teachers can work on technical materials with their generalist colleagues without the distractions so common to regular session and after-school meetings. Activities appropriately pursued are:

1. Surveys of the community, its population, sociographic make-up, economic and political problems
2. Identification of citizens with special resources
3. Plans and instruments for evaluation
4. Outlines for autobiographies
5. Development of diagnostic instruments such as
   a. interest-finders
   b. basic skills tests
   c. attitude toward school
   d. pretests
6. Preparation of interview guides and reporting plans
7. Intensive study of special competence areas; science, art, drama, speech
8. Review of introduction and orientation techniques
9. Collection and reading-level assessment of resource materials
10. Production of guides for small group operation and function
11. Analysis of grouping procedures and purposes
12. Preparation of rating scales and check lists for
    a. teacher participation
    b. oral reports
    c. pupil teaching and telling efforts
13. Study of audio-visual materials
14. Organization of cumulative record file and logbook
15. Writing of basic material
16. Broad reading in problem areas
17. Determining broad policy on free materials, scheduling, research procedure

Service as Resource Person and Consultant

Every list of characteristics of the "core" includes the point that problems or topics taken up by the group should cut across subject lines. Activities and projects which students pursue to obtain information and develop attitudes should draw upon all the fields of content. The questions asked to extend, to clarify, and to obtain control of a major problem should relate to art, mathematics, shop, and so on. This means that the "core" teacher will be coordinating planning, deeper study, and reporting that at any one time may call upon knowledge from a half-dozen disciplines. He may be generally educated in all of them, but he will hardly be a specialist in more than one or two.

Consequently, the "core" teacher will need constantly to rely on the advice and help of those of his colleagues who have special training in limited subject areas. Even "core" teachers trained in a model program of preparation where they would use the problem-defining and problem-solving approach in their own education would inevitably face a similar responsibility.

The subject specialist can aid in the summer workshop or in regular continuing unit production. He may suggest activities that will build understanding, recommend reading material, and identify content that will serve to increase grasp and insight. While the "core" is actually in session, he will very likely be assigned to his own subject class; but in a well-ordered school, he will have some free time when he can meet with the "core." Also where the "core" program is effectively set up, arrangements can be made to have subject classes "covered" while the specialist meets for a period of time with the "core" group.

Facilitating contribution to the "core" program by specialists on the staff is very much a matter of good program planning. Usually the "core" meets during three or four typical class periods. If key teachers can be scheduled to be available to the "core" during one of these periods, from time to time, then they can easily meet with the whole group to

1. Present an organized lecture
2. Lead a large group discussion
3. Listen to, participate in reports drawing heavily on specific fields
4. Help them to see how a special activity would help total understanding
5. Provide balance and breadth in planning
6. Demonstrate how a specialist can be used as a consultant in an interactive situation
7. Check on their facts, understandings, evaluate their growth
8. Plan field trips, pointing out specifics for observation and consideration

Since the major work of a "core" program is accomplished in small group deliberation and research, with culmination of effort commonly taking the form of reports and presentations, the subject specialist can make his most telling contribution in suggestion and advice given to these small groups who wait upon him or send their delegate. In this more intimate relationship he can

1. Help define more sharply the subproblems involved
2. Help identify the scope of information worthwhile to a group
3. Promote broader and deeper special interests
4. Suggest novel and creative ways to communicate and to teach the larger group
5. Teach fundamental concepts and skills necessary to further study and to presentation
6. Read and review reports to be made
7. Aid in locating appropriate reading
8. Aid in locating and supplying material and equipment for construction activity, experiments, model making, recording, mural production, etc.

The teacher of the "core," too, will need advice on resources, projects, and personal reading. Casual meetings in the cafeteria, in the lounge, or in the halls will provide some opportunity for interchange. The "core" teacher should be assured of more help than this, however. Questions raised and information needed by the "core" teacher himself, related to his security as well as efficiency, do often demand more time in addition to scholarly depth. Here the subject teacher in a good cooperative atmosphere should be aware of the really valuable help he can render by being ready to augment the "core" teacher's personal skills and information. He can

1. Explain in a spirit of good colleagueship complex and difficult ideas in his special subject when asked
2. Locate and provide appropriate reading
3. Teach the "core" teachers basic skills, particularly art, music, speech

Participation in Evaluation

Should the subject specialist become as involved with the planning for and operation of the "core" as has been recommended above, he will come to pass judgment on both management and outcomes. Even were the "core" teacher alone responsible for the extent and quality of general education, the tendency for each teacher to evaluate would hardly be avoided. Participating teachers will just be more inclined to have and to express opinion. So, since each teacher ought to be both directly and indirectly engaged somewhere and somehow in the major part of the general education program and since each teacher will observe and react anyway, each should actively and systematically take part in evaluation.

EVALUATION A COOPERATIVE PROCEDURE

The first step for the faculty is to decide what it wants its generally educated pupils to be like. When this has been done, attention can be given to selecting and deciding on the instruments and the techniques which may be applied to ascertain to what extent growth has been accomplished. The next step involves determining when and how these instruments can be most effectively used with and for the classroom group.

Concern for student growth and development by all odds must be the foremost one. In addition to it, there are other matters which also need to be considered. The "core" is a departure which has implications for staff and community. Not only do adaptations seek pupil growth, they also are calculated to raise teacher morale, to promote more effective staff work, and to facilitate teacher growth. It may, too, be that "core" programs are aimed at obtaining more community participation, at increasing community support of schools, at directly affecting and improving community living. Assessment of pupil achievement in spelling, in oral presentation, in facility for doing independent research, for instance, will not provide much evidence on the achievement of these purposes. Thus, careful thought must be given to how to relate and to measure teacher attitude, how to gauge growth in philosophy and insight into children's needs and problems, and how to assess community reaction.

TEACHERS AND GATHERING OF DATA

Application of the available instruments, for the most part by the "core" teacher alone, should produce much of the information needed on growth in fundamental skills, in ability to use information, in attitudes, and in appreciation. Well-applied checklists, rating scales, observation forms, and intensive participation with students should help the "core" teacher see where his students are weak and how they have missed their objectives. But the best of "core" teachers and the most competent students probably always will be in need of as much corroboration as they can get of their best hunches and of their personal judgments. Here, other teachers, mainly specialists in speech, drama, music, and writing, can help by indicating their ideas of progress and need. Significant additions can be made by the specialists through interviewing, through observing student behavior in an all-school setting, through exercising personal judgments while participating cooperatively with students, and through noting relevant habits and ways pupils respond in special classes. Patrons should also be expected to help in the collection of evidence about how their children grow in school and particularly how they reflect school learnings in a variety of family and out-of-school situations.

One could raise a question about how so broad a participation might be expected to affect those doing the "core" teaching. It is not customary for physics teachers to get much involved in interpreting results from appraisals of students of English or home economics. Would not "core" teachers feel "on the spot" to have non- "core" teachers and others analyzing and interpreting appraisals of "core" work?

Doubtless this would be the case for some. At the same time, their reactions would depend on how "core" teaching has been conceived at the outset. We see the "core" teacher's job as that of helping guide the school staff's major trunk line to general education. Every teacher should be concerned about the gradual growth of students toward optimum development as a person and as a citizen. The "core" teacher is the staff's representative in this program. Faults in the program thus ought to be shared by all teachers, and proposals for inprovement ought to come from all teachers.[10] The "core" teacher should look to his colleagues as a guiding body as well as a resource group.

THE TEACHER AND THE PROBLEM-SOLVING GROUP

Attention to how the teacher can and should function in a democratic classroom or in a teacher-pupil planning situation has increased appreciably in the last ten years. There is now a considerable body of report and suggestion on how both the subject teacher and the "core" teacher may be most effective in his role. Much of what is recommended for one is equally appropriate for the other. In fact it is a common observation of proponents of better subject teaching that nearly all the procedures proposed for the "core" teacher can be employed by the up-to-date subject teacher.

No one would gain much from arguing the point. The subject specialists are essentially correct. Good subject teachers must take very many of the steps considered to be inherent elements in the "core" approach. At the same time we must admit that many do not do so. The subject structure and purpose, as we have pointed out, tend to work against the introduction of modern teaching methods.

The purpose of this section is not therefore to reveal an entirely novel set of procedures for teaching. It is rather to point up and to emphasize those aspects of "core" teaching which are particularly important, and to suggest some ways to carry them out effectively. Much of the resistance and apprehension connected with the "core" arises out of teacher uncertainty about how to work in the "core" and teach there. We hope that we can here explore enough of those aspects to encourage teachers to study more intensively several of the volumes[11] that focus for the most part on the teacher's roles in the "core" class.

Understanding the Group

The emphasis in the "core" is especially on the personal-social development of boys and girls. In the course of the year, it is the task of the "core" teacher to weld his students into a cooperative and cre-

[10] Faunce and Bossing, *op. cit.*, p. 357.

[11] Faunce and Bossing, *op. cit.;* Rosalind Zapf, *Democratic Processes in the Secondary Classroom,* Prentice-Hall, 1959; Louise Parrish and Yvonne Waskin, *Teacher-Pupil Planning for Better Classroom Learning,* Harper, 1958; Louise Hock and Thomas Hill, *The General Education Class in the Secondary School,* Holt, Rinehart, and Winston, 1960.

ative group. Through their unity the teacher should seek to increase their confidence and their power to handle more effectively the tasks they set for themselves within the broad guides laid down by others.

To promote this personal development and secure this unity, the teacher needs to be very well informed about the pupils with whom he works. He should know their concerns, their attitudes, and their attributes. He should know their background and experiences, their deficiencies as well as their accomplishments. He should know what to be cautious about and of what he may take advantage. To work most efficiently with his pupils he must know them.

RECORDS AS A STARTING POINT

Today the majority of schools, elementary or secondary, keep a fairly extensive file of information on each student. Some are much more complete than others because greater concern is felt for cumulating data or because resources and personnel are available. Occasionally, we may find students who arrive with no dossier at all, but they are exceptions.

The cumulative file thus constitutes a good initial resource in most instances for the teacher to begin finding out what his group is like—what its past record has been, where its weaknesses are.

Particularly significant to the "core" teacher are the materials on the background and on the personal and social development of members of the group. Insights here may be found in the anecdotal records, in attitude and interest inventories, in the health record, in reports of conferences held with parents, and in the family portrait. A good elementary school pupil folder will usually contain the results of some simple sociometric analysis, examples of student work, and analyses of some of the more pronounced characteristics of the child. It is likely a teacher will find included a social distance scale,[12] a type classification by teacher and pupil, an inventory of likes and dislikes, characteristics check sheets, work-habits form sheet, etc.

OBSERVATION AND STUDY NEXT STEP

Doubtless, the most useful approach to increased information and insight in the "core" is the opportunity given the teacher to work personally and closely with the student and to attend carefully to how pupils relate themselves to each other and to the tasks they have elected. Deep and searching discussion with pupils about themselves, about

[12] Ruth Cunningham, *Understanding Group Behavior of Boys and Girls*, Bureau of Publications, Teachers College 1951, pp. 401–406.

their ambitions, about their hurts and worries is not a customary part of the subject teacher's interaction with his pupils. A fair number make a try at it, and the expressed desire to do so is common, but subject teaching on the whole discourages it. For the "core" teacher the opportunity does exist, and the premium is on developing the intimacy so many youth in particular crave.

A truly effective teacher, concerned with broad and general behavior change, constantly and carefully observes the actions and the reactions of his students. He can learn much from signs of industry, from evidence of confusion and doubt, and from student work in isolation or at the center of things.

From time to time, prospective "core" teachers have asked what the teacher does when subgroups are meeting, when the class is broken up doing individual research, when half the students are elsewhere learning some special skill and they do not need the teacher. The answer in part lies here. The teacher should be engaged in intent observation and diagnosis, in putting two and two together, in checking out his hunches.

Guiding Pupil Experience and Insight

The goal of the "core" teacher is to develop his group into a unit which can select together significant and important matters to study and which can decide on effective ways to obtain knowledge and skill. Within the group he seeks to help individuals to perceive and accept worthy purposes for independent study as well. In a Type 5 "core," broad and general problems of social significance should provide the over-all scope and the many subissues should be identified in a variety of resource units. In each resource unit there should be numerous suggestions for ways to stimulate and to initiate special interest and action.

1. *Unified and confident groups should be secured first.* Those who have tried to elicit from classes what they are interested in and what they think they want and need to learn have soon discovered that the success of this technique depends very much upon there being a group rather than a collection of individuals. The teacher who plunges into a problem search before he knows how to increase the confidence of students in the teacher, in themselves, and in each other is doomed to failure. People young or old do not admit their failures and limitations because they are asked to do so. Serious deliberation and sharing of ideas and feelings do not come when there is uncertainty about others, particularly about teachers who so often in themselves are threats to self-respect. Penetrating self-examination, the searching of

motives, and the willingness to identify and accept hard tasks come only when the person is off the defensive and convinced of the support and common concern of those about him.

So, the first order of business with a "core" group is establishing interaction, developing warmth, creating an atmosphere of acceptance, and identifying the teacher as a resource guide. The problem is generally treated in most textbooks on method. Recently several books[13] have included chapters on means of getting launched and on the increasing of effective group function. Some attention is given to the latter point later in this chapter.

2. *Pupils should themselves take stock.* Pupils who have been in "core" groups before will have individual logs or notebooks containing records of their projects, ratings and checklists, analyses of objectives sought and opinions of progress made. If the members of the "core" group have been together for the last year, they should have a class log of units and topics covered, of reports made, of excursions, of visitors, etc. Recapitulation on these should lead easily and quickly to old and emergent problems known to the group and realized by individuals. Review of the final evaluations made in the last year's class should reveal leads to new work suggested there.

Many "core" groups of course will be made up of pupils new to each other, and for a long time to come in many secondary schools teachers and pupils who meet in a Type 5 "core" will be doing so for the first time. However, in the latter case there is still available a reasonable amount of reference for taking stock. Few children get through a year without knowing something of what they have failed to learn or to change. They have observed where their classmates have outdistanced them. They have heard from teachers, parents, and peers what they ought to do, and what they ought to know. Given a chance and encouraged, they can provide a substantial set of goals and objectives at the outset of any year.

3. *Personal problems and concerns should be explored.* Unfortunately, most schools still do not assemble data that will help a pupil look critically at his own growth in feelings, actions toward others, management of peer group interaction, and habits of dealing with problems that are personal. Part of this stems from lack of interest, despite much encouragement, of teachers in anything else but knowledge found in the subjects or in the mechanical skills taught in schools. Some

---

[13] William Alexander and Paul Halverson, *Effective Teaching in Secondary Schools,* Rinehart, 1957, chap. 5; Louise Parrish and Yvonne Waskin, *op. cit.,* chaps. 3, 7; Rosalind Zopf, *op. cit.*

reluctance has also derived from teachers' lack of know-how in apply-ing and interpreting instruments for diagnosis of personality growth and from widespread lack of both time and competence to reach an intimate level of give-and-take with students.

All definitions of the "core," however, call for a more decided ef-fort to help students with problems of personal development and of adjustment. In this proposal the "core" teacher is not cast into the role of a psychiatrist. Rather he is asked to serve more often as an interactor, as a listener to and a counselor on problems related to the students' struggle for self-enhancement.

Much of what we can do to help pupils see themselves better and to develop higher goals can be without fanfare or fancy techniques. The reading of simple vignettes relating human situations can precipi-tate personal reflection and accounts. Numerous human relations classes have demonstrated this. Autobiographies always encourage identification of past errors, of ambitions and vocational plans, of re-actions to events. Self-rating of roles and consideration of sociometric data should crystallize and pinpoint needs. Through sociodramas, ways of responding and their effects can be vivified. Subsequent discussion, particularly in the junior high, can elicit personal observations and re-quests for help. Creating small subgroups within the class, for examin-ing common worries of children, will facilitate self-reference through recognition of similar concerns in others. Planned interviews with older schoolmates can quickly reveal the normality of aches and aspira-tions and justify their existence.

Probably the best treatment of the need for a careful searching of personal problems is to be found in *The Emerging Self*[14] by Hopkins. In a chapter on "How is need-experience developed?" he examines how others must help the learner "to locate his need and differentiate more direct realistic, and meaningful behaviors."[15] Throughout the chapter he illustrates how questions can be used to encourage this more intensive self-study possible under the guidance of regular teachers.

4. *Social concerns and issues should be examined directly.* The center of the universe for most people is in themselves. As a man lives from day to day, he sees the problems of his community, or his society, or the world to the degree that those problems impinge upon him. The child who knows he ought to read more and to like his read-ing, but has trouble both reading and liking, seldom sees this personal difficulty as a part of the great problem of helping people with their

[14] L. Thomas Hopkins, *The Emerging Self,* Harper, New York, 1954.
[15] *Ibid.,* p. 149.

leisure or of helping them add to and enrich their experience. The needs for our citizens to be loyal, to have balanced patriotic sentiments, to understand our basic political ideas, for instance, do not somehow magically become concerns for young people. They are rather needs which are seen by, logically deduced by, adults, scholars, and social analysts. One of the greatest challenges of teaching is to expand the more intimate, personal, and immediate concerns of pupils into these more general problems and issues.

This progress from the minor and the immediate to the more comprehensive and remote can often be accomplished by beginning with the near at hand. A student's complaint that "there are no good books in this library" may in time lead to a study of how to evaluate literature or an investigation into the reading habits of the nation. Discussion of the discontinuance of bus transportation from homes close to a school may lead to a study of budgets and taxes. A good teacher likewise may parlay an innocently expressed doubt about the need to have a monitor on the landing into a unit on police protection, crime, and delinquency.

On the other hand, we can be assured that pupils in school know the adults are anticipating and expecting that attention be given in school to the study of problems that have a degree of unity in themselves and that offer opportunity for the development of skills and the acquisition of knowledge. Thus youth is not averse to being told what to study or be interested in.

Pupils also know the school faculty has ideas about the subjects they will grow in and to what extent during a school year. The "core" teacher can present in detail what the staff hopes the students will undertake. Teachers from later school years and of specialized subjects can always be counted on to have some ideas about the progress younger students should make in fundamentals and how to acquire information about past events and present community and group problems.

5. *The usual exploration techniques should be employed.* We all know that the alert teacher is constantly on the watch to arouse pupil interest in a great variety of learnings. The mathematics teacher relates his reactions at a concert; the physics teacher tells his students they will like a book he has just read; the business teacher clips an appropriate cartoon on today's youth for the corridor board. Television programs, local celebrations, radio round-tables are recommended daily. One teacher stops boys in the hall to quote lines from a play to arouse search for the source; another invites solution to a cryptogram. The value in such constant stimulation can be overlooked. It should not be.

More systematic plans though can be laid by the "core" teacher, without directly "loading the dice." Students can be sent to the library for general survey and reading of newspapers and journals. More precise direction can be given to investigate problems facing youth and young adults in our time. The community survey has long been advocated as a way of describing conditions as they exist and precipitating further examination of their cause and relationship to larger issues. A series of field trips to industry, to agricultural areas, to larger cities and smaller towns, to a university or a cultural center, to an exhibition or a fair may bring to the point of articulation questions, points of view, and observations that otherwise would never occur to a pupil.

Providing for Problem Census

The length and extent of exploratory study and the development of needs and interest must depend on the situation. Where cooperative problem-solving is being used for the first time, the teacher sensibly should keep things pretty well structured. After a personal acquaintanceship period and preliminary procedures in increasing group sensitivity, the teacher may actually direct students into a project with fairly precise limits. The orientation unit in seventh grade is regularly used for this purpose. Study of the school, the program offered, the objectives one can have, and the goals parents and teachers do have often provides a transition period and allows time for discussion periods on areas for investigation. It also provides for pupil self-appraisal and a chance for the teacher to appraise the group and the individuals in it.

By the time one or two well-structured units have been covered with a new group there should have developed the increased level of awareness and the rapport to make possible the recognition and the proposal of problems which might be considered by the group and by individual students. Out of this census of concerns, sharpened by skillful questioning and tightened up through good categorization and logical organizing, there should emerge the pattern for a semester's or a year's work by a group.

It ought to be clear that students' questions and specific problems proposed for study, when cumulated into more general categories, can easily turn out to be subproblems or dimensions of the continuing and persisting concerns from analysis of which broad resource units have been developed. In fact, one easy way of giving organization to problems as they are expressed by pupils is to list them under major headings selected to indicate scope; for instance, those from Lurry and Alberty listed earlier.

This does not mean then that the resource units and the subproblems should be thrust upon students nor that need-exploration should be a subterfuge to get pupils to study what one knows they will have to study anyway. The natural outcome is pointed out here rather to show the connection between honest examinations of interest and personal need and the materials likely to be produced in advance by any staff that seriously considers what the "core" may do. Knowing pupil problems, when organized, may be very similar to adult predicated problems, we still should utilize the deliberative, cooperative, problem-locating-and-defining process.

Actually no complete or final census of problems should be expected of any "core" group. Problems will never cease arising with any group for that matter, and some which emerge after a year is under way may prove to be far more meaningful and important than many of those considered significant at the beginning. Therefore the teacher should be sure that there is a plan for the group to review systematically its problem list and to add and subtract items from time to time.

ANALYSIS AND CLARIFICATION OF EACH PROBLEM REQUIRED

Although the problem census should produce general questions and logical and subsumable lesser inquiries, it should be obvious that the total possibilities in a study of an over-all concern like "What is propaganda and what can we do about it?" or "What is it important to believe?" will not emerge from the original enthusiastic cumulation of topics to study.

Much more careful specification of detail for each of the broad problems is necessary before extensive research and investigation can begin.

The resource unit, if there is one or a part of one dealing with the general problem, should provide a variety of questions, ideas of scope, and objectives that may be sought. The rather standard procedures for increasing specific concerns should be used. They are in the main the same as those identified earlier: small group discussion, directed library reading, help from consultants, movies and film strips.

Nothing should suggest, however, that at any time this problem extension and specification will prove to be any easy matter. Although some of the writing on cooperative and democratic classroom planning suggests it is, it isn't. The elicitation of appropriate and significant, of comprehensive and manageable questions requires real depth in the teacher and hard work on the part of students. What can be studied about a problem and what ought to be studied about it are matters both of scholarship and public policy. They ought not be considered lightly. Decisions about what should be included as subproblems in each topic area should be made with great care, and checked out from time to time with those outside the "core" group.

This point does raise the question of mistake-making as a way of learning. Obviously there should be freedom for error in a free planning situation. As long as adults are purposeful in permitting error, either in learning themselves or in causing others to learn, we could support mistake-making. But no one could long tolerate a skimming of the surface and a fiddling with the superficialities because a teacher and a group know no better and have no means to deeper and more significant matters.

RELATING PROBLEMS TO CONTINUING OBJECTIVES NECESSARY

Neither pupils nor adults can work purposefully on all things at once. Usually our effort has some focus. It must have if we are to learn new skills and ideas. Practice on partially acquired skills ought also at times to have formal dimensions and be concentrated.

At the beginning of any school year and periodically during the year a group should identify broad objectives upon which continuing application, study, and review are necessary. Most of these objectives will lend themselves at some point to direct approach. At the same time they should provide a constant orientation for group activities and projects in the various units undertaken. Objectives of this type include: to get along better with others, to plan more effectively, to extend use of resources, to report results more adequately, to increase vocabulary, and to think more clearly. At the outset of each unit they may well be restated and activities examined critically to determine if appreciable contribution is possible. The more these general objectives are served by the activity, the better.

Each unit and each specific project should also be directed toward narrower and more precise goals. Pupils and teacher should select activities together because they lead to the attainment of some knowledge or acquaintance with some event or because they provide personal satisfaction or increase in skill. During the time pupils work on these projects we should expect more growth to take place in the limited outcomes sought. Deficiencies and limitations identified in other knowledge and skills should be recorded by pupils and teacher for subsequent special attention, study, and direct teaching where appropriate.

The group should be conscious all the time that they are in pursuit of command of language, of ability to communicate, of fundamental knowledge for citizenship, or preliminary information useful in vocations, of ethical standards of behavior, of retention of data acquired, and so on.

The "core" teacher must seek, as must any teacher, constantly to make connections between present and remote goals. Present experience ought constantly be a diagnostic opportunity to see what is needed to move ahead against the broad objectives and the specific expectations for which adults have supported schools.

BALANCING OF PERSONAL GOALS AND GROUP GOALS
A RESULT

Failure to attend to individual differences in ability and interest can be as great in a "core" class, presumably democratically operated, as it is said to be in a subject class wholly teacher dominated. The democratic process can force individuals into compliance and obligate them to listen and "to participate" equally as ruthlessly as can authoritarianism and beneficent dictation.

The "core" teacher sets out to help the group to see by the process of careful interchange and deliberation what needs they all share, what they each can obtain from the work of others, what is commonly wanted or necessary to possess, and what similar goals there are.

At the same time the "core" teacher should be aware of and responsive to the more personal needs of individuals—needs both immediate and long range. Each unit should provide some real opportunity for the student to work purposefully against those needs and should make possible at the end some accounting of his progress. The student may be able to work on his own problems in some cases in small groups where others have similar problems or where he can get help because others know on what he is working. In a few cases, needs may be so intense and so personal that the student may require periodic opportunities or substantial time in one unit to focus his self-improvement efforts.

It can be anticipated that interest and enthusiasm may flag after a pupil has agreed to help a group. In such cases we may expect the group progressively to learn how to help the individual increasingly to mature in accepting group service roles. The teacher will always have to encourage, to promote, and to restore faith, nonetheless, as long as we have a cultural base which emphasizes self-serving and competition as much or more than it does cooperative effort.

Individual drives can be accommodated in scheduling. The class group should be able to set aside some portion of each day or a week for very personal activity by pupils. We all recognize that some needs can become so pressing that we cannot attend properly to anything else until they are resolved or until a program is arranged to move against them. There can and there should be in the "core" sufficient flexible time and conditions to make such shifts possible. One simple method is to reserve two or three hours a week for independent research and study, counseling, special reading, or some other personal activity.

Supervising Selection of Learning Activities

After problem identification, choices have to be made about what pupils actually will do to develop their insights, to acquire information, and to increase skills. All teachers have favorite exercises, and all have value judgments about what activities are most likely to provide for both specific and general objectives. A good resource unit will contain many suggestions about ways to approach a problem. Group deliberation ought to produce novel proposals and plans. Consultants should be able to add ideas.

When the list of possible individual, small groups, and class activities has been made, pupils and teacher together should decide what is appropriate and what is not. Pupil initiative and freedom should not be hamstrung, but it can not be completely unrestrained.

The teacher is never relieved of the responsibility to encourage the most efficient and rewarding means of learning and to discourage, in one way or another, those which require too much time, yield too little return, or cause too much frustration. It is incumbent upon the "core" teacher to guarantee through his tolerance and broad purpose planning that his group discover for themselves how investments in time and effort can render low interest. But again he does not do so by constant neglect. At the outset when activities or ways of learning more are nominated, he should raise questions related to time use, availability of sources, probability of easy arrangement, service to immediate and long-time objectives, availability of more practical alternatives, public relations significance, need for experience, etc. During the period of work, evaluation should be utilized; and at the end the group should ask, in addition to questions about what they learned, other questions about how they managed, where they had difficulty, what was necessary, etc. Their judgments and opinions should increase the wisdom of their future choices as well as provide information to add into the resource unit itself.

Planning Schedules Cooperatively

After organization, management of "working" time confronts the group. With each new unit we might anticipate a new schedule, but not necessarily. As with everything else, there is some pattern to "core" programs. Subgroups have to have time to work together, and in places where their resources and materials are. Along with provision for subgroups, there will often need to be arrangements for whole group meetings and for individual study. Most classes have found it helpful to have a daily planning period at the outset. Periodic progress reporting by subgroups helps prevent let-down and wandering. A steering committee can plan the rate of progress toward objectives, set aside time for individual and group research, schedule direct teaching periods, decide about deadlines, and arrange the order of culminating activities. Charts and records of progress can be kept on a chalkboard or on large posters to provide simple reference for teacher and pupils.

Supporting Group Self-Management

A *major* goal of the "core" is the growth of pupils in cooperating effectively in management. When objectives have been set up and learning activities selected, only the initial crucial steps in managing have been taken. When the subgroup has been chosen and committees meet to examine ways of working, or preparing, or presenting ideas and materials to the whole class, they will learn to plan and proceed by doing so. The culminating experience should give students a responsibility to decide what to include, mode of presentation, the means of review, and evaluation to use. Periodic lapses in enthusiasm, unexpected lack of resources, incompetence or unwillingness of members should lead to self-appraisal, to the development of alternatives, and to revision of plans. Through learning first to resolve fairly minor problems, the whole group and subunits of the group should become increasingly more capable of making good decisions on who will do what, how much time will be spent on listening and on highly focalized acquisition effort, when tests are appropriate, how special weaknesses can be eliminated, and what to do about discipline problems like inattention, failure to provide proper help, and so on.

However, when one visualizes a unit getting under way with four or five groups acting in school and out of school, with individuals studying alone, with periodic planning meetings, evaluations, and direct teaching activities taking place, one may be inclined to liken the enterprise to something far more confusing than a three-ring circus. A well-managed "core" is or should be at times like a three-ring circus. But obviously no one should expect to start with that amount of complexity or beautifully timed interrelationship. It will take time[16] to "train a group up to manage themselves." No overnight miracles should be anticipated or encouraged. A smart teacher will certainly not release the controls too soon or too fully.

Guiding Reporting

Individual and group reports are customary in most subject areas. Perhaps the major point to be made about "core" reports is that a greater premium is put on the culminating activity here and that quality of instruction depends more upon accomplished reporting. Actually, many students' research projects will have as their objective the pursuit of knowledge to be transmitted to fellow class members.

One goal of the "core" is to increase the power of students to communicate effectively with others and to take advantage of situations that will contribute to permanence of knowledge, because there is meaning. So reporting groups will need to consider ways and to set in motion procedures and actions which will cause retention. Much of the literature on the "core" glosses over this. It should be obvious that we can not be so remiss. Until there are excellent reports and presentations, until techniques for stimulation, repetition, and review are built in, we can not expect anything much in the way of retention.

The counterargument sometimes offered is that actually reporting is not a major concern since pupils work on different problems and activities, very often for themselves and out of their own interest. Others do not need to know the obtained facts; they are securing their own. To this we can agree in part. Activities should be chosen because they offer different routes, different information, and different insights to broad understandings. Yet activities also, very likely much more commonly, offer a chance for exploration of a facet of something whole that a group could well afford to know. Sharing is thus an essential ingredient and counterpart of delegated responsibility.

Leading Evaluation

No matter where we work we teachers are constantly involved in a single business—that of helping students to attach value to something, whether it be an idea or an attitude, a fact or a skill. We forever hope that pupils will move upward on the scale of values and that they will demonstrate their progress by knowing, remembering, and behaving.

The principal goal of the "core" is to help students move to higher and higher levels of self-management through their own in-

[16] Alice Miel, *Cooperative Procedures in Learning,* Bureau of Publications, Teachers College, 1954.

sights and efforts applied to successive experiences. This means that pupils must see clearly what they want; they must regularly pause to determine if their effort is leading toward accomplishment, and they must ascertain to what extent they achieved satisfaction and to what extent there remain or have emerged areas for extending growth. To do this, they must find means of measuring, but they must also review objectives, deliberate on alternatives, and revise procedures.

Evaluation, as we know, is not a one-shot affair; it is not an end point test, administered to threaten or to obtain a mark to pass judgment and to send home. It is a continuous process of review and retrospection. It is both a backward look and a forward look. It encompasses both results and plans.

Upon the "core" teacher, and every other teacher properly, rests the responsibility for working out with pupils the criteria to be utilized. The standardized tests speak for themselves. We know what they are. The questions to be asked and forms to be developed are different for reports, group procedures, class reactions, research approaches, log recordings, summarizations, planning steps, etc. They take time and must go through many stages, and they need to fit directly the activity out of which they grow.

In several volumes[17] there are examples of evaluation forms and procedures used. There seems to us little justification for adding illustrations. The more important issue is what criteria should govern evaluation. We propose that they are as follows:

1. Evaluation should be broad and comprehensive. It should include provisions for revealing progress against all objectives.
2. Evaluation should be focused on better planning and improved action. It should always be instrumental not consummating.
3. Evaluation should be managed by those who wish to develop values. Teachers must help and they dare not abrogate their adult evaluation, but they can not usefully set themselves up as external arbiters.
4. Evaluation should consider standards and common attainments whenever and wherever appropriate. Comparisons in competitive efforts against common objectives are useful when seen in the proper light and are a part of the self-testing which is necessary to an adequate concept of relative capacity.
5. Evaluation should include better evaluating as an important and estimable goal.
6. Evaluation should be continuous.
7. Evaluation should contribute wholesomely to motivation but should avoid being threatening and ego-diminishing.
8. Evaluation should be both personal and individual and cooperative.

[17] Ray H. Simpson, *Improving Teaching-Learning Processes,* Longmans, Green, 1953, chaps. 7, 8; Parrish and Waskin, *op. cit.,* Chap. 6; Faunce and Bossing, *op. cit.,* Chap. 15.

THE TEACHER AND THE DYNAMICS IN GROUPS

We have separated and left to the last in this chapter a discussion of some of the process considerations in group work. Throughout the foregoing pages there has been invoked, as a fundamental concomitant of effective objective setting, planning, and management of groups, the existence of a smoothly interacting unit of students. Such units, however, do not come about by magic; they are developed, and their development takes time.

A central function of the "core" program ought to be growth in understanding the psychological elements and the mechanical elements of the operation of groups. Throughout a long period we have had a format for conducting business democratically through elected officers, committees, and votes. Only since the mid-1940's have we given serious consideration to the deeper elements in the conduct and action of cooperative groups. There has been to date a minor transference of findings in this new area of research into public school classrooms. There is room and great need for its more rapid introduction. We can not avoid doing so if we are to achieve high level "core" curriculum programs.

We are aware even now though of the strong counterargument and general confusion over this point. Claim is made that the analysts of group action are seeking ways to produce conformity, to steal away individuality, and to adjust everyone to a mediocre normality. Some may be. It may be rather defensibly argued that fads and styles and mimicry are more pronounced today and are evidence of an unfortunate "sheeplike" behavior. The causes, if fairly examined however, are certainly numerous and far, far removed from the minor reduction of excessive competition in the schools. We need not attempt to examine that matter here. We pause only to say that mass media, threat in the modern world, and need for expressions of hostility are much more at the root of conformity than the occasional team efforts employed in the classroom.

Sharp clarification, on the other hand, is necessary for the "core" teacher. Group problem-solving skills and group analysis are a proper part of the school goal to increase respect for cooperative action, to secure recognition of its value, and to develop readiness to use it. We do not want the prospective American citizen to give up his individuality, nor reduce himself to a constant suppliant compromiser. There are place and need for strong, vigorously independent, competitive people. We want men to speak for the right as they see it, even when majorities are against them. We want them to persevere and prevail when their individually perceived way may and should become in time the view of the majority. At the same time, we should be foolhardy to protest so loudly as to seem to ignore the fact that we are social beings, living in convenient social arrangements. We are a society that believes that in unity there is strength. We know we must, if we would survive, find ways to use our combined resources in teamwork arrangements. It does seem apparent that we can not operate on any "either-or" basis. We must find ways to promote growth and strength in both independence and cooperation. As we encourage fierce individuality, we must foster national community.

The present contributions of the scholars in group research presage much more to come, particularly with reference to the power of groups to influence attitudes and behaviors which do not respond easily and quickly to verbal and logical presentation and to intelligent argument. As further study is undertaken, we may expect a real science of behavior change, but even now we have much of great value that can be used to increase group efficiency in many situations.[18]

Teachers and Training in Group Dynamics

It is not at all surprising that we teachers are little more than superficially informed about the research in group processes of operation. Courses in group dynamics have been offered for only a few years. With or without courses we have never been inclined to be overly analytical about why some groups have been responsive and productive and why others have been dead, if not downright hostile. The idea of our putting a searchlight into the deep recesses of interaction and of helping a group of pupils diagnose what makes a group experience not only satisfying but effective as a means of bringing about change in oneself and others has been outside our contemplation.

The study and improvement of group processes in action is not a simple matter. It is certainly something which requires good sound psychological background. Even with training and experience, a group's initial steps must be well planned and application must be slow and careful. Broad acquaintance with theory and research and substantial participation in group work ought unquestionably to be prerequisite to any serious experimentation in groups.

Until more teachers have become skilled in the psychology of group action, we can not expect and should not have much beyond

[18] N. B. Henry, ed., *The Dynamics of Instructional Groups,* National Society for the Study of Education, 1960.

rather simple analysis. The importance of attending to more than parliamentary mechanics, however, imposes the responsibility upon more and more teachers, particularly those in general education, to extend their understandings and resources in this area. Furthermore, the growth that takes place in each teacher will permit far more effective staff work and faculty deliberation.

Preliminary Exploration Appropriate

To begin improving the quality of interaction, to provide through groups more fruitful experience in communication, to increase participation and confidence, to promote respect, to create understanding of interdependence, and lessen conflict we do not have to delve deeply into motives, nor for that matter either study response and reaction or engage in penetrating evaluation of others' behavior. It is possible to focus attention and direct teaching on certain mechanics and skills and ways of acting that have always enhanced group effectiveness but have been identified more explicitly as a result of intensive group study.

Much has been made in recent books about the roles played by group members. These roles can be listed and their identification and description used to avoid or reduce divergence and confusion and to promote more positive contribution. Pupils can be assigned the jobs of observers and help trace the flow of thought and reaction as well as offer opinions on why the group sped along or faltered in its progress. Secretaries and recorders can be relied upon to a much greater extent to keep track of progress, to summarize, and to help redirect thinking. "Buzz" or subgroups can be set up to demonstrate how to stimulate communication and to provide opportunity for the practice of subgroup leadership. Small group demonstrations can provide opportunity to examine the effect of too much or too little talking, the consequence of failing to talk to the point, the price to be paid for poor definition, and the feelings people have for those who dominate, are not prepared, or argue endlessly. Panels give a pupil opportunity to examine how to promote and encourage thought in others while expressing his own ideas clearly and forcefully. Post-meeting reaction measures and typical evaluation questions can be used to emphasize everything from amount of participation to sense of, or feeling about, accomplishment.

In verbal communication itself, perhaps more than anywhere else, lies the key to good group action. We respond to gestures and postures but most often our cues to response come from how we are stimulated by others' words. The reason certain words come during moments of pressure, when we are tense or in sharp disagreement, must certainly be a matter for more than guesswork by the layman. But we do know that how we respond to others is not infrequently a matter of habit and pattern. There are ways to ask questions that reveal interest rather than nosiness. There are ways of expressing differences of opinion that invite further exploration. We can clarify by indicating what expressions and comments mean to us. We can reduce misinterpretation by listening to what others say instead of telling them what they have said.

Many aspects of group function can of course be selected out and discussed without reference to any one individual or situation. Most are commonly concerns of the teacher anywhere who wants good discussion, good student and class reaction. In few classes can we avoid examination of how to encourage the less interested pupil, what attitude to take toward the one whose contribution is honest but inadequate, how to stop unnecessary and unwanted fooling around, when to interrupt, how long to talk, and so on. Simple techniques for reducing anxiety and apprehension are usually needed by those who might only comment, as well as by those who must present and lead class deliberation. Demonstration of how to act out sociodramas and development of confidence to participate in them also ought to be considered. The sum total is that the teacher ought to draw upon an already voluminous literature on the simple attributes to be relied upon for getting along better with others. This ranges from Dale Carnegie[19] to R. F. Bales.[20]

Questions for Discussion

1. In the "core" program it can be expected that pupils will differ widely in the information and knowledge they possess. Are there not some facts, some poems, some dates we can not afford to let pupils pass through school without knowing? Would it not be possible to permit pupils to bypass certain knowledge by default or because they do not elect to commit it to memory?

2. Are method and process really more important than content?

3. Is it realistic to expect that a faculty will set itself up to become intimately involved in helping with the common learnings program? Will the staff in time not withdraw from responsibility, turn to their own onerous duties?

[19] Dale Carnegie, *How to Win Friends and Influence People,* Simon and Schuster, 1936.

[20] R. F. Bales, *Interaction Process Analysis,* Addison-Wesley, 1949.

Are there not difficulties and problems in an ordinary school program that would actually prevent the cooperative staff work suggested here? Could any of them be resolved?

4. Are activities included in resource units merely subterfuges to get pupils to acquire certain types of information considered by adults to be worthy of possession?

5. How will the "core" teacher maintain confidence in himself? He can not check his approvals and suggestions constantly with colleagues!

6. Will the "core" teacher ever direct and control the group? When and how often? How could control be justified in truly democratic situations?

7. Marking and reporting are very critical concerns in most schools. Will evaluation procedures eliminate reports to parents? How will parents be informed of growth? How will schools which require numerical marks of a competitive order be satisfied?

8. How should a "core" teacher handle a student who will not participate, will not cooperate?

9. Wouldn't a "core" program need highly intelligent pupils to function?

10. A teacher does not abdicate in a type 5 "core" program, but how can we call what he does teaching?

Selected Bibliography

Alexander, William, and Paul Halverson, *Effective Teaching in Secondary Schools,* Rinehart, 1957.

Association of Supervision and Curriculum Development, *Group Planning in Education,* The Association, 1945.

Cunningham, Ruth, *Understanding the Group Behavior of Boys and Girls,* Bureau of Publications, Teachers College, 1951.

Henry, N. B., ed., *The Dynamics of Instructional Groups,* National Society for the Study of Education, 1960.

Hock, Louise, and Thomas Hill, *The General Education Class in the Secondary School,* Holt, Rinehart, and Winston, 1960.

Hopkins, L. Thomas, *The Emerging Self,* Harper, 1954.

McConnell, Charles, Ernest Melby, C. O. Arndt, and Leslee Bishop, *New Schools for a New Culture,* rev. ed., Harper, 1953.

Miel, Alice, *Cooperative Procedures in Learning,* Bureau of Publications, Teachers College, 1952.

New York City Board of Education, *Suggestions to Teachers of Experimental Core Classes,* The Board, 1951.

Noar, Gertrude, *Freedom to Live and Learn,* Franklin, 1948.

Parrish, Louise, and Yvonne Waskin, *Teacher-Pupil Planning,* Harper, 1958.

Toops, Myrtle, *Working in the Core Program in Burris Laboratory School,* Ball State Teachers College, 1955.

Wiles, Kimball, *Teaching for Better Schools,* second ed., Prentice-Hall, 1959.

CHAPTER 12

....

Improving Extraclass Experiences

There are two groups of educators who would question the inclusion of a chapter on extraclass activities in a book dealing with the teacher and curriculum making. One of these groups consists of people who look upon these activities as lying outside of the curriculum altogether and therefore not relevant to the present discussion. The other is composed of those who feel that the goals of these activities ought to be incorporated into and indistinguishable from regular class work.

Each of these views has some justification. These activities do differ in several respects from the classroom instruction phase of the program, but they consist of planned learning experiences of a sort, and they do make contributions to and supplement objectives sought in the formal program. Furthermore, they make possible the pursuit of objectives often neglected but a proper province of the school.

From the other point of view, while it is true that some of the activities have already been given the status of formal courses and the goals and activities of others could well be more generally incorporated into the work of certain classes, the real values of most of them lie exactly in the fact that they are different and are not encumbered by prescribed outlines, marks, credits, and other features of the program of studies. Even if a "core" program should emerge, there are attributes of the elective activity which some feel would completely justify the existence of an activity period.

In any event two things seem certain. One is that these activities will remain a distinguishable part of the school program for a long time to come, and teachers will be expected to know what policies to support with regard to them, how to guide and direct them, and what to do to improve them. Secondly, these activities furnish teachers with an excellent laboratory, free of many restrictions and external expectations, in which they may try out, practice, and perfect techniques for developing learning experiences which they might hesitate to employ in the formal program of studies. In addition, it is not unlikely that many of the outcomes which are held desirable really can be achieved more readily through the activities program. The extraclass provides for the volume involvement most high school enthusiasts for a special interest area want. It makes possible many more breaks across age lines than even a well-managed "core" might. Despite sponsorship, there can be greater freedom and independence for students; attendance does need to be compulsory; advisors may only need to be guardians against wrongdoing.

Extraclass Activities in Historical Situations

Although it is true that education at one time was for the most part purely scholastic, there apparently have nearly always been some activities sponsored by the school that could be classified as extraclass activity. Back in the time of Greek formal education there was the Greek chorus; guilds were formed by Roman students (these could be compared to modern-day fraternities); in the training of knights such sports as riding and swimming were part of the curriculum; during the Renaissance, student governments became an activity in schools in Italy and Germany. In England, initiating students into the school was a regular activity and this practice was transplanted to the American schools of the colonial era.[1]

While organized activities outside the framework of the formal program of studies in American secondary schools are the product of the present century, there are isolated examples recorded from a century earlier. When students did try, however, their efforts were actively suppressed because school officials regarded them as dangerous to the educational program. Sponsorship of these activities was not considered suitable for a teacher. Boys were expelled for playing football. Learning was not to be lessened by irrelevant pastimes!

Activities came to be accepted by school officials as a necessary evil during the period from about 1900 to World War I. At that time school boards began to approve faculty members acting as coaches and sponsors. Few facilities were provided for the activities, but a general sympathy began to spread as both teachers and patrons began to see more clearly that something could be done for children which was not then being accomplished in the strait-laced academic program.

Following World War I, extraclass activities were finally accepted as a more integral part of the educational program. Educational officials began boosting the activities program through speeches, written

[1] Frederick C. Gruber, and Thomas B. Beatty, *Secondary School Activities,* McGraw-Hill, 1954, pp. 2, 3.

materials, and public relations programs. With the advent of World War II, the schools had the problem of continuing these activities in the face of such obstacles as shortages in transportation, materials, and equipment. The program, however, met the challenge and survived. Activities have now become even more prosperous and thriving.

Broad Scope of Extraclass Activities

Regardless of the richness of the subject-matter offerings of the school, there are many students whose interests and abilities have not been satisfied by the basic classroom curriculum, even a well-managed "core." The extraclass program thus has emerged to offer these boys and girls a means of pursuing avenues of special interest. Through it, native abilities and interests have been revealed when initiative has been encouraged and fostered.

A second broad purpose of activities has been to prepare the pupil for participation in the active life of democracy. In the program, students have learned to get along with others under conditions when fair play is required. The principles of democracy have been applied in practical and personal situations. Situations have been provided to develop a wholesome feeling for rules, regulations, and restrictions required in cooperative groups.

Activities also have sought to make the pupil increasingly self-directive. As students have been given responsibility, they have learned to think and to act on their own decisions to a greater extent than has been possible in the crowded classroom. The student council, through its consideration of major problems of school operation, has very nicely accomplished this.

Social cooperation growth and development is another objective that has been pursued in more informal gatherings. Working side by side for common goals has given students firsthand experience in the problems of meeting situations together. Profitable experiences here have shown the way to future successes, and mistakes have been turned into gains in the next participatory opportunities.[2]

The relaxed and happy atmosphere of the activities program also has been used to increase student morale. Through it, students have come to think of the school as an interesting place where important things are going on. Hitherto boring and tedious tasks have taken on a new meaning. Pride of accomplishment in the program has been transferred to pride of accomplishment in academic work as well.

[2] Kenneth J. Frasure, "The Council Cures a School Headache," *The Clearing House,* November, 1947, pp. 163–166.

Further, student activities have aided the student in discovering special qualities, interests, and abilities. Through club assignments, through sharing of experiences with others, and through many other activity opportunities, new vistas have been opened to the student. Successful accomplishment of projects has increased student sense of security and worthiness. At the junior high school level, especially, extraclass activities have been used to help students to explore themselves in various situations and to increase their self-understanding.

The extraclass program also has served to increase the teacher's avenues for study of his pupils in situations calling for total and integrated responses. Particularly is this so for teachers whose subjects are rather formally organized and taught, with limited opportunity for social interaction. With more of the administration of the group in the hands of student leaders, the teacher has been able to observe carefully over a longer period of time.

Opposition to Extraclass Activities Strong and Outspoken

Although these uses (and purposes) sound convincing to some and would be sufficient reason for continuing student activities within the official daily schedule, we know that vigorous spokesmen both within the profession and in the patron group are opposed. A few curriculum specialists visualize the "core" program as absorbing a very large part of the method of traditional extraclass offerings. These people would not argue with the continuance of special periods set aside for clubs, homerooms, and teams, however, if conditions do not permit integrating student council activities, group guidance, intramural competition and so on into a combined general education program. They would certainly much prefer to get rid of what they consider an odd splitting of the school offerings into what children want and what they are forced to do, but they would compromise.

More opposition is likely to come and does come from members of the teaching staff who see the extraclass program as essentially extracurricular. To them it is an unnecessary concession to pupils in an attempt to sugar-coat the hard realities of getting an education and in many ways is merely a subterfuge to keep reluctant and average pupils in attendance. Widespread overemphasis on competitive athletics at the expense of proper attention to academic studies has aroused considerable dissatisfaction. The pressure of administrators on teachers to sponsor student clubs is more than a little resented. Repeatedly teachers are confronted with "volunteered" groups, and occasionally by commandeered students who not only have no genuine interest but are actively antagonistic. Instead of pleasure, the extraclass assignment is simply another hour of cajoling, teasing, encouraging, suggesting, and controlling the difficult. Those who need the program do not want it, and those who want and dominate it do not need it.

Still more violent opposition is to be found among a fairly limited group of patrons who are appalled at the use of teacher time to supervise the practice of social dancing, the execution of finesses at the bridge table, and the discussion of the merits of various "drag" races and racers. It seems to this group that the serious and solid parts of the school program have been deluged with soda-pop specialties, all fizz and no body. These critics have no sympathy with pursuit of the broader objectives claimed and feel that any free time which might exist in the school schedule should be given over to an additional subject or well-supervised study halls.

Failure and Inadequacy—Not Uncommon

1. *Perhaps the commonest weakness of student activities is their failure to reach the students by whom their supplemental support is most needed.* Part of this has been because the activities until fairly lately have tended to follow the academic nature of the formal programs of study. Dramatics, debate, the newspaper, French Club, and orchestra have drawn from the more able who already possess a constellation of attributes of personal and social adjustment. Assembly programs put on by the homeroom or the science club have generally required advanced intellectual power and the responsiveness and interest so often associated with it and approved by teachers. Eligibility rules have been an all but complete barrier to the participation of those who are much in need of the recognition and of the attitude development which good, wholesome, physical competition can bring.

A number of studies has shown that another major reason why students do not participate is the cost associated with membership. A popular means of financing activities programs is the student fee: dues, admission charges, equipment charges, trip assessments, etc. Youths who encounter resistance to further school expenses from the home or who have learned to anticipate parental displeasure over "Ma, can I have five dollars for the bus trip to the stockyards?" withdraw gracefully with the excuse that they have other obligations or no interest. It does not take much imagination to guess who demurs first. It is not the youngster whose father is a dentist or a lawyer. Hand,[3] who has considered this problem more carefully than anyone else,

[3] Harold Hand, "Do School Costs Drive out the Youth of the Poor?" *Progressive Education,* January, 1951, p. 92.

has shown that the economically underprivileged (those most in need of supplemental efforts to arouse interest, to explore vocations, and to develop citizenship), experienced 40 percent less participation or representation than the average student had. Students from upper-income families, on the other hand, took part 35 percent more in the total activities program than did the average student.

We might say the curriculum specialist should not be concerned to do much about this problem. Schemes and arrangements for action might more properly be considered administrative matters. That point we should not care to argue. The point is that if the extraclass program has a legitimate role to play for all children, the community should find a way to support it as fully as it does any other aspect of its program. No legitimate educational activity should be hampered by fees, either for the participants or for audience or spectators invited to attend to provide color, reaction, or whatever. The curriculum maker, then, should be clear on what certain experiences can do for his students, and he should be prepared to insist before board of education and community that they are worthy of tax dollars.

2. *Too often activities get added out of whim or by happenstance.* An appreciably large number of schools appears to have very little in the way of a system for proposing, studying, and approving elements in this program. It seems that additions are made more often because a student group waits on the principal and is authorized to talk someone into being a sponsor. Or a teacher has only one special attribute or one burning interest and he prevails upon the principal who is usually all too willing to concede and to encourage the student council to authorize the offering of a new area for exploration. No clear goals are identified for the activity. They may exist vaguely in the mind of the sponsor or the original formation group, but they are not thought through carefully and little advance consideration is given to how everything is to be accomplished.

Some of this "open-endedness" is to be expected and probably even encouraged here and there. This is so particularly if we wish to carry to the extraclass program the whole idea of pupil involvement and planning. But surely, no charter should be issued nor should any longevity be guaranteed until the planning group has fairly well thought through where they are going and how they intend to get there. Purpose, direction and procedure naturally should be adapted after things get under way.

3. *Too many extraclass efforts are devoted to a fairly high level of pursuit, with limited attention both to multiple objectives and to the fairly sizable numbers of the unskilled and inept who turn out to par-*

ticipate. Perhaps best illustrative of this is the dramatics club which so often commences the year with a surprising number of hopefuls and all too soon settles down to a relatively tight core of the histrionic who already speak "trippingly on their tongues," who are adept at learning lines, and who can be counted on to render a good character portrayal.

In some communities it is the press club, in others the school annual, the science club, or the band that gets focused on quality production rather than general service at a lesser level of perfection. When this happens the socializing, democratizing, integrating, broadly supplementing values of the activity are lost.

With identification of this weakness in the extraclass program, we do not propose to argue that efforts to secure excellent products from student activities be abandoned. No school staff would be worth their salt who did not seek constantly to obtain the best possible level of performance from those under their tutelage. However, the point is made that the privilege of participating in culminating activities should be far more widespread than it is presently. Some less perfection can certainly be justified if the benefits can be more generally distributed.

4. *Most schools put their extraclass program on a take-it-or-leave-it basis.* If students find nothing of interest in the array of activities offered and if there arises no common interest which can be parlayed into an officially organized project, there are in many cases provisions for study halls where attention can be given to what the pupil has to do. Here and there participation is required of every student and each must make some choice. Needless to say, the whole concept of the extraclass movement is denied by such a policy. The sponsor winds up with a captive group; he is confronted with the same barriers he has with his formal classes, and invariably he fails. Luckily the practice of compulsion is not widespread.

At the same time, the pressure exerted fairly generally on students to join has some real proportions. Sponsors naturally encourage their best students; club membership is a common panacea of the guidance officer to increase interest, and social acceptance; the normal enthusiasm of club officers for bigger posts serving larger numbers adds to recruitment; activities assemblies, handbook promotion, homeroom evaluations and persuasions, point systems for school letters, references about employer, and college interest in well-roundedness and so on are used to get candidates to sign up. The effect of this is membership on the part of many who are not interested, insincere, wisely submissive but unmotivated. They serve as a pronounced drag on the more enthusiastic; they are inattentive and more than occasionally disorderly; they are unlikely to carry out assignments or contribute to plans and to projects. After several such imposed memberships and unsatisfying connections, many of these students become cynical about activities, claim they are run by the select, that "they" will not let you have any fun, that it is just another class filled with competitors looking for personal aggrandizement and supervised by teachers who expect the same thing in clubs as they do in regular classes.

In order to meet these criticisms and to accommodate a tremendous range of interests, as well as the drive to have real power within these groups, a number of schools has increased the roster of clubs to such an extent that to an outsider there seems to be a club for everything. Where there are too many for the faculty to cover, at times willing citizens from the community have come in to share the load. This expansion of the offerings usually helps; but it does not and apparently never will provide for the students who would enjoy opportunity to be together and work together yet have no urge to do so under the auspices of the arranged school program. Further, some of the activities certain groups of youth would engage in are relatively unacceptable to school officials: motor clubs and "drag" racing, secret societies, and gun clubs.

5. *Potential for diagnosis and the use of extraclass programs for helping the child in need is often overlooked.* Few schools have any systematic procedure for advisors and guidance officers to study the child with the purpose of helping him see in what aspects he could well afford to take active steps in order to develop more effectively. Homeroom programs or general assemblies wherein sponsors or student leaders speak sometimes help a student see what he can accomplish and how he can develop his personality or speed his social adjustment. Careful interviewing of teachers and students will reveal, however, that very little personal attention is given to explaining the relationship between an extraclass activity and a student's deficiencies and limitations. Rather the sponsors and leaders are looking for those with skills and powers already manifest.

In fairness, it must be said that there are sound but off-hand recommendations in many schools for better use of the extraclass program in diagnosis of youth needs. Increasingly the addition of guidance personnel makes more likely well-calculated encouragement of pupils to participate. But cooperative action by the pupil and dutiful application for membership can not be expected to bring excellent results automatically. The program must be adapted for the student and a decided effort made to provide (through his election of an activity) experience contributory to the ends sought. Where the sponsor is only interested in production, where student leaders are mostly concerned with their own political reputations, where in-groups run the show, the shy and unpoised student is more than likely to be simply flipped from the frying pan into the fire.

6. *Management details of the extraclass programs undermine success.* We are sure there are other factors present that might be explored in addition to these. Among them are monopolism of the program by school politicians, sabotage by parents and antagonists in the community, excessive limitation or number of activities, inadequate time assignment and improper scheduling, inconsistent parallel offering of credit and noncredit activities, and others. These ought to be considered by teachers who wish to improve the extraclass programs. They are not any less important than the ones included here for discussion.

DEVELOPING BETTER PROGRAMS

It is unlikely any school faculty can eliminate these or other causes for kinks and failures in a very short period of time. It also is unlikely any school will be so fortunate as to begin *de novo* a program of extraclass activities. We know of no school that does not have some noncredit provisions for its students. In a few places the clubs are clearly not a part of the official school day. They are distinctly set aside for after-school dismissal. This is quite unusual. In most systems now a period in the regular schedule (in some schools two periods) is set aside for the extraclass program. Student council, assemblies, intramurals, clubs, homeroom, group guidance, band and orchestra commonly share the period.

For the most part the scope of activities seems to have expanded without much careful thinking by the faculty about what to include and what should govern operations. The emergence of a new activity, as we have remarked, has often been on the order of happenstance or whim. Some enterprises have been shortlived and have quickly succumbed as the result of the departure of an enthusiastic sponsor or absence of student interest. Others have moved across the line into the credit structure and have been granted regular class dimensions.

No one should want to destroy the *esprit* that germinates fresh ventures, and surely for the sake of curriculum vigor we should protect the right of the outmoded and useless to wither away. The real strength of extraclass activities has been their flexibility.

We can expect for a long time to come to give school time, pay teachers and use school resources on extraclass activities. Yet, we can not allow activities to grow helter-skelter; we can not, as custodians of time and resources, permit undertakings which are substantially unsound educationally; we dare not continue to risk community distress and aggravation over elements which may be misunderstood or which may actually be of doubtful value; we certainly must avoid some of the failures and certainly all of the causes of failure identified above. This simply means much more attention to sound and careful planning and operation of the student activities program.

Basic Principles a Guide

In a chapter on extraclass activities Gruhn and Douglass have listed eight principles which could well be used to give direction to any planning efforts. Although they are general and inclusive, these could easily suffice at the outset to set the stage for discussion of local procedures and approaches. The guides also could serve as a basis for developing evaluation instruments and for setting up research studies and investigations to ascertain what conditions do actually prevail locally.

The principles set out are:

1. The activities should be planned and carried on in terms of well-formulated and accepted educational objectives.
2. There should be a sufficient variety of activities to meet the individual abilities, needs, and interests of every child in school.
3. The activities should be offered as far as possible during school hours and in the school building or on the school grounds.
4. Participation in the various activities should be possible at little or no expense to the individual pupil.
5. Participation in the various activities should not be contingent upon the pupil's achievement or conduct in other phases of the school program.
6. Competitive activities should be conducted largely or entirely on an intramural rather than on an interscholastic basis.
7. Audience activities, such as athletics, music, and dramatics, should be planned and conducted primarily for their contribution to the educational development of the students rather than to the entertainment of an adult audience.
8. The extraclass program should be closely integrated and articulated with all other phases of the educational program of the school.[4]

Parents and Pupils Helpful in Planning

Regardless of how thoroughly the staff explores the role of the extraclass program, they and their decisions will suffer if they deny

[4] William Gruhn and Harl Douglass, *The Modern Junior High School*, second ed., Ronald, 1956, p. 284.

themselves the help of parents and students. It is certainly more likely that teachers will involve students here than in their attempts to improve subjects and subject offerings. But involvement of parents is not so common nor so easy at any point. We are more inclined to postpone or to avoid that.

Yet general examination of the extraclass program offers a very healthy area for cooperative curriculum study. Changes are easier to make; syllabi and examinations provide no restrictions; criticism is easier because the sponsor is usually a helper not an expert; experiments may be made with both old and new activities.

The range of participation for adults probably ought have no limits. Parents ought, for instance, to think through with the faculty whether some similar objectives should be pursued in both credit and noncredit activities and whether there ought to be any charges or fees for clubs, teams, camp-outs, work projects, orchestra membership, and so on. They also ought to sit with the historical club or the modern language club on occasion to advise and help on projects. Representation and service on the total program advisory board with teachers and student council members ought to be easy to obtain. Through more intimate understanding, we can expect that citizens will be excellent ambassadors to the community and intelligent proponents before the board of education.

Much of the extraclass program is so arranged that students can hardly help but become appreciably involved in deciding how to carry on their activity. This is less true in athletics and in music, where the coaches are more often engaged in direct teaching and largely act independently in diagnosing need and in deciding what will be taught to whom and when. Perhaps, too, it is not always true in chess club or in bridge club where the goal is actually tutorial. Yet in the chess club and in the student council, in class groups and in homerooms, students do have much opportunity to share concerns, refine objectives, decide on ways to accomplish their growing and expanding purpose, evaluate their progress, and utilize local resources.

Development of Sponsorship Aids and Guides Useful

We should be able to cut down frustration by recognizing honestly the need of many teachers for help with sponsorship. Doubtless we can expect new teachers to have more general introduction to advisor skills. Methods courses in special subjects do include units on subject-allied special interest areas; and many colleges offer, usually at the graduate level, courses in extraclass activities. A number of books on principles of teaching includes a chapter on this topic; as do books on principles of secondary education.

Still the local school staff should undertake active effort in behalf of extending viewpoint on the part of new faculty, producing materials and resources for use by sponsors, and providing suggestions on ways and means of dealing with common problems.

All of these elements have been covered for some sponsors in one way or another over the years in conferences held to help high school editors and their advisors. More recently, similar meetings have been held for student council leaders and the faculty members who work with these pupils. Several school systems have a regular course in the credit program for student leaders, and there much attention is given to proper relationships with advisors, to roles and functions of the advisor, to ways leader and teacher can work together to promote interest, and so on.[5] Sponsors participate in and teach parts of these courses. However, we find no report of a handbook prepared by a local school district to give direction and support to the work of the sponsor, or of a local compendium of practical suggestions for consideration and possible use.

Several books on extraclass activities contain ideas on the projects which are good in a variety of clubs. There is a volume devoted to ways to handle commencement, and another on the home room; study council practices reports have described novel techniques. General help with discipline, lack of interest, dropping out, and pupil-teacher planning is to be found in a number of texts.

These resources ought to be made available. They ought to be on the teachers' library shelf. But we can anticipate they will only be most useful if rather decided effort is exercised to make teachers conscious of them and to encourage and promote their careful examination with application to the local situation. The most meaningful material will in the end be that which is produced through local people for local people and thoroughly discussed by local people.

We should expect to:

1. Prepare a clear statement of local philosophy of extraclass activities
2. Indicate the priority and focus in objectives for all activities
3. Organize the rules and general regulations which apply to teacher responsibility, student obligation, school and community use
4. Report and summarize special area successful techniques
5. Suggest ways to increase social interaction
6. Describe successful culminating activities

[5] Robert Frederick, *The Third Curriculum*, Appleton-Century-Crofts, 1959.

7. Recommend procedures for securing student leaders
8. Explain and illustrate roles of sponsors in exercising authority, vetoing proposals, and providing suggestions
9. Provide ideas on how to train student leaders
10. Research on pupil withdrawal, club failure, and student attitude
11. Identify special needs which should be considered: anxiety, extra enthusiasm, strident competition, freshness, impertinence, familiarity, etc.
12. Give advice and ideas on how to focus pupils' interests on broader and higher level objectives
13. Suggest how to break up groups, cliques, and in-groups which thrive in extraclass settings
14. List names of special resource people in the community
15. Identify locations for trips
16. Clarify rules on materials' use
17. Develop diagnostic instruments for personal problems, student attitudes, reaction to counsellor, etc.
18. Prepare forms for reporting observations, anectodes, analyses
19. Outline plans and cautions for writing regulations on conduct and behavior, attendance and participation
20. Show how problem and interest censuses are made

Faculty Observation of Pupils a Contribution

Under constant pressure to teach the child as well as the subject and with increasing encouragement from guidance departments to attend to the causes of student behavior, teachers have become more aware of the advantages of a warm personal relationship with pupils.

Despite this development, the subject-organized program continues to be oriented to its special content and the classroom remains a fairly formal arrangement. Even the subjectless "core" does not attain the pronounced casualness and easy interchange which thrive on the stage or at a camp. Although the extraclass program offers considerably more opportunity for intimate sharing of problems, for bringing up concerns seemingly not so acceptable in the credit program, a good share of its potential is still unused because it is not clearly seen as an important means to understanding and helping pupils in broad areas of personal development.

Much more attention should be given by faculties to better use of the extraclass program in diagnosing pupil needs, to the development of instruments useful in teacher observation and exploratory discussion, and to organized efforts to use information obtained in guiding both credit and noncredit experience.

Inspection of records in several schools with extensive extraclass programs has revealed that very little information is transmitted to any central agency that could be helpful to others in seeing more deeply into a child. Part of this lack comes naturally because it takes time to record and to report, and there are numerous other demands on the teacher. Another part, probably equally as large, derives from failure to pursue that deeper understanding and from the tendency to focus the activity on facts and subject skills rather than on personal feelings, attitudes, character traits, and human interaction problems. Another part comes from teacher lack of knowledge on what ought to be known about pupils.

When the extraclass activity is functioning properly, planned and managed by students and carried along by their enthusiasm, the sponsor should be expected to use his time very largely in conversation, in watching, in listening, to obtain information about and insights into matters like

Quality of home relationships
Anxieties and worries over growth
Peer interaction; acceptance and rejection, and reasons for each
Ambitions
Special attitudes and reactions toward selected adults
Concepts of self
Opinions on adolescent development matters
Unresolved questions and doubts
Past successes and discomforts
Common topics of interest and small talk
Reactions to credit course experience
Morale and sentiment about school
Failings and attitudes toward failure, criticism, frustration
Particular likes and dislikes, interests
Integration and use of credit course learnings

These items do not exhaust the list. They only suggest aspects which might be included. Any faculty can extend the list.

Organization and Administration Policies a Necessity

In the section on failures, attention was drawn to several conditions which frustrate the achievement of effective extraclass goals. When appreciable numbers of pupils do not or can not participate or do not profit from their participation, we ought to consider carefully ways in which the program can be organized so to serve more broadly and effectively. Only several aspects of concern to teachers who wish to improve management of the programs are mentioned here.

1. *Coordination is important.* The practice of having some staff member designated coordinator of student activities has been growing. Sometimes he is the advisor to the student council; sometimes he is an

administrative assistant to the principal. In small schools the principal may continue to coordinate or delegate the task part time to a staff member.

There are real advantages in having someone pay particular attention. Foremost is the fact that when someone has a job assigned, there is some possibility of active effort in examining the status quo, in stimulating consideration of means to improvement, and in carrying on with the details necessary to adjustment and improvement. Sponsors have someone to turn to for help and guidance. Vested with responsibility, a coordinator will ordinarily soon extend his knowledge about theory and practice elsewhere and provide a means for bringing in new ideas. Given authority, he can bring sponsors together to train them to work out policy, to establish regulations, and to serve as a cooperative guiding group for pupils and as a cabinet for advising the administration.

Staff members who want the extraclass program to improve could hardly do better than seek the appointment of some faculty member to provide supervision and leadership in this area.

2. *Credit recognition requires careful thought.*   We have noted that some educators believe that extraclass activities should as rapidly as possible be made part of the program of credit studies. The transition has taken place with dramatics, journalism, parliamentary practice, radio, public speaking, and others closely related to subject fields. The extraclass program thus has been a sort of apprenticeship. Movement on to the credit program has signaled respectability and guaranteed time in the schedule.

Certainly some extraclass activities should grow up. What can be learned in them is very useful information. On the other hand, pressure and precipitancy in turning the genuinely elective and personal interests of pupils into attendance-bound, mark-stimulated, and examination-controlled school subjects are unnecessary and unwise. Pupils want to pursue hobbies and interests as they, not someone else, see fit. Hobbies and interests are a legitimate part of growing up, of getting a full view of life, of developing as a citizen and as a person. There is no need for the school to infringe upon them as it promotes them.

3. *Limits on program should be established.*   Left to thrive on their own, however, extraclass activities have a way of multiplying that can easily raise doubts about the wisdom of not controlling them. We often hear teachers complain that pupils are so busy with "outside" activities that they do not attend properly to the academic courses that lead to graduation. Parents more than occasionally complain that their

youngsters are "in" too many things. When the same pupils have to be withdrawn from regular classes for string practice, for rehearsals, and for early departures to travel to "away" games, agitation on the faculty is not unlikely to reach some sort of climax. Better management and control of the extraclass program is thus sadly needed in many places.

The formal chartering of clubs and relatively involved regulations for securing sponsors can serve to limit excess enthusiasm. In many schools students themselves have taken initiative in setting up point systems to restrict both too numerous memberships and multiple officeholding. Some activities are designated as majors and others demanding less time as minors, with a student confined to one major and several minors. One can see immediately certain weaknesses in this, but some control seems better than none.

4. *Balance needs attention.* Some activities are exceedingly more appealing than others. The larger technical ones, as Frederick calls them, tend to overshadow and engulf the minor clubs. In many schools there is provision only for "big" activities with no consideration given to stamp club, basketry, camping, or camera. Prestige has come to be attached to membership in the "big" activities too. Pupils who have fewer or lesser skills and who can not compete on the field or on the stage discover that they are second-rate.

The consequence of this is that many clubs have a way of springing up and disappearing. They do not attract substantial numbers of pupils and they die off because they are small and are of secondary importance in securing for the adolescent what he wants.

Some are inclined to feel very strongly that this is the way it should be. The extraclass program should be "market-place operated" and the unsubscribed should be discontinued. We should not want to argue that point, obviously. But it does seem that attention ought to be given to examination locally of how to extend and expand the extraclass program so that students may have other opportunities than those guaranteed by tradition, power, spectator support, and gate receipts.

5. *Scheduling does make a difference.* The matter of time arrangement and the amount of time to be spent on activities[6] are particularly important. When a high percentage of activities is held after school, pupils who work part time or who live at considerable distance from the school in rural areas are unable to participate fully in the program. When activities are scheduled alternates to cafeteria sittings, the walkers suffer most, and exigencies of schedule rule out participa-

---

[6] For excellent discussion of scheduling see Robert Frederick, *The Third Curriculum,* Appleton-Century-Crofts, chap. 20.

tion of others. Some schools have eased this problem by holding a high percentage of meetings for groups within the regular school day, first or last period. Here and there the activity period comes just before or after lunch and occasionally as a complete schedule break to emphasize its proper place in the school day. It is really not possible to say one arrangement is better than another. Local conditions are particularly relevant, but we do know amount and enthusiasm of participation can be changed by finding the ideal time for any local school.

In any arrangement it is important to schedule the activities at regular intervals and often enough to maintain student interest. Seldom is anything much less than an hour satisfactory. With very many activities, at least two or three hours a week are nearly imperative, and with a number of the large technical undertakings, sports and dramatics, consecutive periods of time must be made available.

Another scheduling problem is concerned with the calendar of events. In large schools with many activities involving interscholastic competitions, others leading to periodic culminations, and a number depending on a variety of formal affairs, it is fairly easy for there to be heavy demand for assembly time, after school and evening hours. Encroachment on hours necessary for proper attention to minor activities and to study and do homework is often the case. Straightening this out is simply a management problem.

6. *Guidance in choices should be provided.*   Student handbooks now are more than likely to list the approved extraclass activities and to include a short description of an organization's purposes and general program. Assemblies, homeroom meetings, and student activities' days are also used to explain, and to recruit members. Students are usually encouraged to talk to sponsors, homeroom teachers, and club officers about membership. In practice, choice is probably most often determined out of the communication among pupils themselves.

Obviously we should not interfere with that, for the continuance and demise of activities should depend on the wishes and the evaluation of students. However, each teacher should know well what is the nature of each activity and the climate and atmosphere students set for it. Thus aware, he should be able to help pupils pick more wisely and to steer them into situations and experiences which he sees have potential value.

This means that much greater communication is necessary among staff about specific goals and that there should be increased sharing of information as to how student groups are functioning. In time, from more interchange among advisors and sponsors we should expect that new ideas may be offered with respect to what a club can and should do. More intensive discussion with pupils about what they want and think they may get should extend teacher information and insight into pupil concerns and needs.

7. *Constant exploration of additions and expansion will help.* One great advantage of the extraclass program is its freedom from the crystallization characteristic of the credit program. When activities lose their drawing appeal, they can easily be retired. When a new enthusiasm arises, it seldom takes lengthy deliberation to give it a place on the schedule unless it will involve a sizable expenditure. Some activities we know have become fairly well fixed and have remained over the years in some communities. It is seldom, for instance, that interest and support for sports have waned completely, although in many communities basketball has replaced baseball and here and there a school has failed to field a ball club. Orchestra in many schools has fallen on lean times while the marching band has thrived on the color and fanfare of football games. Debate and prize-speaking have been abandoned in a number of places because of lack of interest. On the other hand, student councils have continually increased and few schools do not have some form of student government even if the homeroom has had up and down success.

Whenever a fairly well-established activity loses status, we need to be alert to the factors which may be operating, as much as we need to be concerned when the registration in elective classes falls off. Causes may be shifting student needs, poor choice of experiences and projects provided, incompetent and inadequate leadership, uninterested and uninspiring sponsorship, changing prestige ideas in the student group, and so on. Regular study of activity rosters and effective and continuous student evaluation of their experiences ought to give us clues and promote adaptations where they are appropriate and necessary. Obviously we should not attempt to keep activities alive to satisfy particular faculty members nor to gratify a handful of pupils whose interest may be taking up staff time more wisely used to sponsor activities with larger drawing power. However, we should be constantly at work to develop insight into the demise of wholesome and formerly vigorous program elements.

Petitions for new activities may be expected to spring up spontaneously in any school. New staff members arrive with new and different hobbies; problems regularly come into the lives of students and arouse desire for a resource. At the same time, individuals and groups on the staff are constantly, or should be, looking at students critically to determine where there are deficiencies and limitations in total development. There may be casual reports in the lounge or remarks at a faculty meeting about the need for some provision for capturing the interests of certain students, for relieving pressure in study hall, for creating a sense of belonging in those who withdraw and seem to be compensating through excessive study. Or there may be, and we feel there ought to be, a systematic and continuing examination by faculty representatives of what adaptations and changes in the extraclass program will help students develop more effectively and attain more convincingly the major objectives and subgoals sought by the school as a whole.

Out of these spontaneous proposals and out of conclusions about what is needed and should be sponsored, the staff should be making its choices with respect to what it will advise approval of and promote.

What ought to be added and experimented with in behalf of extended and better experiences should be determined on the basis of some set of principles to which faculty, students, and patrons can give their support. In addition to those mentioned before, we would add

1. The activity should give real promise of helping students develop some skill or attribute not adequately provided for in the present program
2. The activity should have some potential for contributing to the objectives of general education
3. The activity should offer some possibility of making up for a lack of limitation considered significant in students
4. The activity should supplement and extend those steps already taken in behalf of goals appropriate for the school
5. The activity should provide for integration and functional use of learnings obtained in the credit program
6. The activity should lend itself to pupil management and operation

Evaluation an Important Means

It seems superfluous again especially to argue the need for checking on the effect and the attainments of purpose of the extraclass program. Any systematic effort at improvement must include its measure of progress. Yet evaluation is neglected and changes are often made or postponed on the basis of hunch and rather inadequate information.

The best evaluation any time is that which provides an accurate account of the extent to which the agreed-upon objectives have been obtained and reveals what other outcomes or concomitants there are which are not desired. Therefore, the staff should rely heavily upon its statements of what is to be accomplished in developing instruments useful in providing insights. In our opinion, as we have indicated several times, if those who are responsible work out their own devices and procedures for assessing, we are likely to get both a deeper insight into what objectives mean and more appreciation of how growth may be manifest.

The prepared instrument most commonly referred to is the section of the *Evaluative Criteria* devoted to "The Pupil Activity Program."[7] This is a collection of checklists which identifies elements in several parts of a good program, provides spaces for indicating their presence or absence, and sets out in each case questions which can be answered in terms of a rating scale. In the fourteen scales there is very full coverage in the fifty-five subitems listed. Without question, the scales, when used by a group of objective observers and raters, give good indication of breadth, focus, and nature of management. They do not actually give much evidence of success toward goals like increasing pupil morale, providing relaxation, developing social skills, and promoting peer interaction.

Miller, Moyer, and Patrick[8] have included their own questionnaires for parents, administrators, sponsors, and students. Although slightly more precise and personal than the *Evaluative Criteria,* these check lists do not get below the rather mechanical matters. These questions typify:

Are organizations conducted in a democratic manner?
Do you feel that you are profiting?
Do you have good advisors?
Which organization do you like best? Why?

We do not propose here to include anything in the way of an adequate discussion of what makes proper evaluative instruments for assessing the extraclass program as a whole or for judging any single activity. We would maintain though that little progress will be made in improving the quality of experiences in the extraclass program until far more penetrating studies and analyses are made than are possible with these two reported. The more detailed rating scales developed by McKown[9] point the direction in this as do the instruments prepared by Tyler[10] and his associates for the thirty schools' study. The Social Sensitivity Test, the Interests and Activities Questionnaire, the Interest Index, the Behavior Description Scale, and the like seem to us to

[7] Cooperative Study of Secondary School Standards, *Evaluative Criteria,* rev. ed., The Study, 1950, Section E., pp. 193.

[8] Franklin Miller, James Moyer, and Robert Patrick, *Planning Student Activities,* Prentice-Hall, 1956, pp. 606–607.

[9] Harry McKown, *Extracurricular Activities,* Macmillan, 1952.

[10] Ralph Tyler and Eugene Smith, *Appraising and Recording Student Progress,* McGraw-Hill, 1942.

offer more in getting useful data for determining what needs to be done internally in activities.

In closing his chapter on evaluation, Frederick[11] raises a caution about surrounding extraclass activities with too much formal and systematic evaluation. To this we can agree in part. Too much attention to introspection and too insistent application of measuring and observing might take some of the spirit out of youthful enterprise. On the other hand, living with the impression that we are doing very well indeed while we actually are doing very poorly would be the height of folly. We must not overwhelm, neither can we avoid nor fail at getting to the vital matters.

THE TEACHER AND SPONSORSHIP

In the end, the success or failure of the extraclass program rests most heavily upon each teacher who sponsors an activity. In any school enterprise the *esprit* of a group is hardly ever higher than the tone created by the most visible status figure. Enthusiasm and dedication may grow from intense interest of pupils, but it will not last for long if the teacher is not keen on his part. Loyal supporters of what a teacher stands for are always easy to find in any group of young people. When the attitude is positive, half the battle is won.

Just as in the more formal class, the teacher must not only release ideas and foster creativity, he must also be inventive and creative himself. The usual high school subject thrives on novelty, change of pace, and fresh approaches. The extraclass activity depends even more so on good timing, variety, and action.

Although it would seem unnecessary to say so, the teacher has to like children and be ready to go out of his way to bend to the dignified informality necessary in the club relationship. Even more so than in the regular subjects, the student is aware of how warm and friendly the sponsor is. There can be and should be reserve and expectations on the teacher's part, but students will soon detect the very impersonal and shy away. They want a setting where they can be themselves a little more, release their pent-up feelings, joke and jostle, and find out about the teacher's more private concerns and worries. They can be impertinent, but they would, as a whole, rather not be. They are usually content to stop short of being fresh.

Some teachers are just not cut out to be sponsors, either because

[11] Frederick, *op. cit.*, p. 141.

of outlook, style, nature of their interests, or their capacity for working informally. It is a mistake to force them into the extraclass program. They are better left to the more formal studies where they may, unannoyed, make excellent contributions and provide balance in approach to pupils. Unfortunately, many administrators do not or are unable to make such concessions. Either the demand for activities and advisors is so heavy that uncooperative people are forced to participate or the simple rule is "everybody must sponsor a club." With the formal and reluctant teacher, the club becomes simply another class and is managed like a class.

We know we can improve the extraclass program by organizing it better, by providing a sound financial arrangement, by scheduling adequately, by balancing the types and kinds of activities and so on, but it should be fairly clear that we can hardly expect to attain the greatest improvement until we have the most effective sponsors. The teacher curriculum maker then has to decide what needs to be improved in himself and others as sponsors. With that, he may proceed with positive steps to bring about needed changes.

Attitude and Personal Traits of Sponsors Important

Values and outlooks do not develop overnight. Neither does personality. In time most teachers can shift their style to meet the requirements if they try. A few are too rigid either to be helped or to help themselves. Nearly all of us, however, are helped by some picture of what to aim for. As with the credit program any staff can and should develop some sort of rating scale for pupils, teachers, and supervisors to use. Honest and frank discussion of self-ratings and ratings of others should help initiate and support efforts to change. Interestingly, the books on extraclass programs have far less to say on personal factors related to sponsor success than one might anticipate. The following advice from Frederick[12] may provide a starting point for developing a rating scale like the one included on page 360 and prepared by students in a course on extraclass activities.

The personal traits and characteristics of a sponsor greatly affect his success or failure. While an unattractive personality may hamper a teacher in the classroom, it will be even more damaging in the informality of a group meeting or a club activity.

Integrity, dependableness, trustworthiness, and good moral standards are so obviously necessary that one hesitates to stress them. The club sponsor has many opportunities to influence the lives of young people, and any weakness

[12] Frederick, *ibid.,* p. 221.

in these or other necessary personal qualities will result in serious damage to the organization, the school, and the students, in addition to the embarrassment and humiliation of the sponsor.

The sponsor must be able to get along with boys and girls, enjoy working with them and have an interest in and enthusiasm for the group's program. Patience, friendliness, a sense of humor, fair-mindedness, initiative, imagination, and self-confidence are all assets for the club advisor. His philosophy must be democratic, and he should be a good leader.

The informality which results from the closeness of association makes it even more essential that the advisor possess these qualities. Often the formality of the classroom can be used by teachers to cover up their inability to get along with boys or girls. Backstage in the preparation of scenery for the school play, or under pressure to meet the deadline for the school paper, a lack of patience, a hot temper, or a vulgar vocabulary becomes immediately apparent. The respect of students is easily lost in the informal setting of a club meeting, around a campfire, at a scout meeting, or at a square dance. These situations are conducive to the use of first names, wisecracks, or slightly off-color jokes which have no place in the sponsor-pupil relationship. This does not mean the advisor can not be friendly, genial, and a good sport, but he must retain that thin line of demarcation, the loss of which is bound to result in the deterioration of the student's respect for him.

SELF-RATING SCALE FOR SPONSORS

	VERY MUCH				VERY LITTLE
	5	4	3	2	1

1. I support the idea of extraclass activities.
2. I am happy and satisfied with my assignment.
3. I share wholeheartedly the goals set for the activity.
4. I look forward to and personally enjoy meetings.
5. I spend much time in considering ways to improve the activity.
6. I am asked regularly to sponsor other activities.
7. I encourage membership by the limited in ability as well as by the obviously skilled.
8. I can separate almost completely regular class experience and relations from club activity.
9. I like to chaperone young people at dances, at parties, and on trips.
10. I know what student body issues, concerns, present interests and emphases are.

	VERY MUCH				VERY LITTLE
	5	4	3	2	1

11. I find chitchat, student affairs discussions appealing and interesting.
12. Various students come to me often during regular hours to discuss our activity.
13. I attain close personal interaction with most students.
14. Boys and girls confide in me often.
15. I seek to help pupils with personal problems.
16. I systematically employ an observation and diagnosis process.
17. I regularly transmit helpful information about students to other teachers and guidance personnel.
18. I take an active part in helping club members have more success in regular classes.
19. I encourage and promote student planning and management.
20. I respond positively to student plans which require additional time and effort from me.
21. I anticipate good planning and am not upset by student ineptness and mistakes.
22. I seldom lose my temper, chastize students during activity meetings.
23. I avoid being annoyed when students do not carry out plans.
24. It is easy for me to stay in the background and listen.
25. I tolerate noise and commotion, fooling around.
26. I do not mind and appreciate student attempts at familiarity.
27. I can joke and kid easily with students.
28. Students control themselves with me and do not become "smart alecks" or impertinent.
29. I maintain and increase respect of students.
30. I find my chief satisfaction in student growth rather than in expressed appreciation of my effort.

Appropriate Skills and Approaches Derived from Careful Study and Try-out

We have noted that the good extraclass program now varies appreciably from the usual characteristics of the credit program and that it provides an ideal setting for trying out new teaching procedures. There is no threat from examinations. Little exists in the way of hierarchical content. The teacher is not obligated to cover factual materials and skills. The emphasis can be on adapting experiences to pupil concerns and interests, on developing objectives meaningful to participants, and on working out with students ways projects can be carried forward.

Students are aware of these freedoms, and on the whole expect to take a larger share in determining what to do and in managing the details necessary to success. In some clubs, they do not expect to go much farther than elect some officers and an official representative who will have few duties while the advisor is actually responsible for teaching and telling. In most cases, however, students are aware that the sponsor can share sovereignty and is really a guide, and that upon them may rest the responsibility for carrying out projects, locating and studying material, preparing reports and scripts and briefs, planning the use of time, and so on.

Nevertheless, cooperative and democratic management can be and is easily frustrated. This may be due to confirmed opinion on the sponsor's part that he should retain pronounced control or to his lack of confidence and know-how.

Thorough discussion of the purposes of extraclass activities may help change ideas about how a teacher should function as advisor. It is likely, though, that only active effort by the sponsor to adjust methods and to try out more democratic procedures will turn good theory into good practice. Two areas for exploration are discussed here.

1. *Objectives can be examined.* For the most part teachers can expect there to be officers and holdovers in most activities who know what was sought and done and what they wanted and got in the preceding year. Many clubs will have, and all ought to have a good statement of objectives. The teacher will usually have some idea of the goals of extraclass activities in general and the goals which might well be pursued in any one part of the program.

Statements of purposes and hunches will not, however, describe or reveal all that is possible to achieve or that students may wish to achieve from membership. Some of the deeper and more important motives or ulterior ones may not be represented, yet they do constitute a fair challenge to the teacher who would help the students select projects and manage their time in a way to provide for student personal needs.

We should not hope to unmask students completely, but we can penetrate somewhat deeper into reasons and help students see more clearly what is advantageous to them and what they may do to diminish anxieties, increase skills, develop ego, promote friendship, and so on. Where the more formal program leaves little time or place for thorough discussion of what an experience can do for a student, the extra-class situation sets no limits. A boy may say at the outset that he wants to know more about radio, ceramics, or public-speaking. Given the chance to interact and exchange with others, he may discover that he has other goals on which he can work.

To do this more thorough objective study, the teacher can try out "buzz" groups, make detailed interests and project censuses, establish criteria for choices, investigate possible overlap and need for improvement, develop inventories and employ other recommended steps to needs diagnosis, and plan novel ways to increase ideas and procedures to build up concerns and locate legitimate goals.

2. *Projects can be planned and selected.* What a group does may be directly related to and grow immediately out of objectives if they are stated precisely, or projects may be set up against long-view ambitions. Service clubs, for instance, have the broad goal of giving help in a variety of places in school and in a community. Many types and kinds of undertakings are available to them. Some are fitted to one set of students and not to another. Some provide experiences certain students need and others have already successfully met. Occasionally, requests or proposals are made that raise questions of propriety. They may be exploitative or nearly devoid of contributions to growth. Some may require too much time and effort while others give opportunity for useful preparation and skill acquisition.

An enthusiastic and ambitious service club can thus have many involved and difficult decisions to make in regard to allotting jobs while maintaining purposes and goals. Its members can give serious consideration to length of assignments, to ways of reporting on work done, to possibilities of participants bringing back information and teaching skills learned, to plans for evaluation, and so on.

The problem for the teacher is to make himself a significant part of the business of defining kind and breadth of service, of making contacts, and of determining rosters without setting the limits. There are times to stay on the sidelines, times to ask leading questions, times to suggest caution, and times to advise against or to make suggestions. There is the need for patience as students stumble, argue, and go the wrong way. There is the responsibility to build up better values and to obtain wiser choices slowly and by indirection.

Depth for Enrichment a Goal

Extraclass programs have grown so much in so many schools that most teachers have had some opportunity to participate as high school students. Further, the emphasis in schools and in society on hobbies has led many to extend themselves in independent study and application. The thriving business done by hobby centers alone is one indication of how many people use their leisure time for home projects. Even so, it is not at all uncommon to find teachers working with groups in areas where they have relatively limited skill and knowledge.

Shallow sponsor preparation ought to be a deterrent and a good argument against chartering certain clubs. On the other hand, we should be careful not to dampen ardor; and surely we do not want to discourage interest where staff members have fair preparation but not a great deal.[13]

We are fortunate when a staff member has had a long and intense identification with a good sound extraclass interest or when a prospective teacher has studied carefully what can be done in a particular activity. Ideas will come fast, and resources will be at the teacher's fingertips. Students will feel that their activity is well chosen and that their time is well spent.

Short of extensive acquaintance and rich background, the usual sponsor will need to build out his resources, multiply his ideas, and equip himself to provide sound guidance and correct information. This means study, development of personal skill, and individual hobby pursuit. Similar activities should be observed in other schools; courses should be taken in the area, and experts consulted for helpful materials and plans. Occasionally workshops or conferences should be scheduled to permit sharing of experiences and description and analysis of techniques.

---

[13] Sterner has reported that 96 percent of 323 beginning teachers in New Jersey sponsored pupil activities and that a substantial number of these teachers were less than fully prepared to carry on their assignment. See William Sterner, "Preparing Teachers to Sponsor Activities," *National Association of Secondary School Principals Bulletin,* February 1952, pp. 32–42.

Questions for Discussion

1. Why do some persons feel that the activities program should be operated completely outside the regular school day?
2. Should fees be charged for activities? If so, for which activities should fees be charged? What cautions should be observed in the charging of fees? How should the activities program be financed?
3. What qualities and qualifications should an activity sponsor possess? How do these differ from the qualities of the regular classroom teacher?
4. What should a teacher do to prepare for successful work in the activities program of the school?
5. What factors do you feel are most often overlooked in organizing activities programs? How can these oversights be prevented within an individual activity? Within the activities program as a whole?
6. What may be done to increase student participation in the program of activities? How may overparticipation be prevented?
7. Most adults remember that they obtained much personal profit and satisfaction from extraclass participation. What do they put the premium on?
8. The homeroom is one of the more pronounced failures in many schools, often being little more than an attendance period and a study hall. Why? How would you change the pattern?

Selected Bibliography

Frederick, Robert, *The Third Curriculum,* Appleton-Century-Crofts, 1959.

Gruber, Frederick, and Thomas Beatty, *Secondary School Activities,* McGraw-Hill, 1954.

Johnson, Edgar, and Roland Faunce, *Student Activities in Secondary Schools,* Ronald, 1952.

McKown, Harry, *Extracurricular Activities,* Macmillan, 1952.

Sterner, William, "Preparing Teachers to Sponsor Activities," *National Association of Secondary School Principals Bulletin,* February 1952, pp. 32–42

Strang, Ruth, *Group Activities in College and Secondary School,* Harper, 1946.

Trump, J. Lloyd, *High School Extracurriculum Activities,* University of Chicago Press, 1944.

Tompkins, Ellsworth, *Extra-class Activities for All Pupils,* U.S. Office of Education Bulletin, 1950, no. 4, Government Printing Office, 1950.

PART IV

WORKING WITH OTHERS FOR IMPROVEMENT

CHAPTER 13

••

Organization for Curriculum Change

The burden of the preceding chapters has been that the classroom teacher can make his greatest contribution to curriculum improvement in his close and personal planning with his immediate group. At the same time we have proposed that there are other areas in which his effort is needed and where his skills and his counsel are called upon. These include the specification of broad goals and purposes, the development of resources, deliberation upon policy, public relations, supervision of more formal activities, decision-making on structure and organization, and so on.

Effective function at these important tasks can not be secured unless each teacher has, in addition to conviction about their importance, some idea as to what is necessary in the way of organization to coordinate and release his competence and some know-how in working through organizational patterns. Procedures for local curriculum revision increasingly have emerged out of the ideas and suggestions derived from classroom teachers. Although more schools are adding curriculum directors and coordinators, the need for cooperative development of plans will not diminish. Awareness by the teaching staff of the administrative arrangements which can and do work and of those which create hostility and lead to confusion and limited results is quite necessary. Time and good will must not be wasted in uncoordinated ineffectual effort. They both can be saved when the staff is so informed as neither to be misled nor to be self-abused. The teacher who knows well only the immediate personal steps in curriculum improvement will soon find that he is partly equipped. To obtain what he needs and prefers to carry on effectively, he will have to work with, through, and for others. He can not escape the responsibility for bringing about the best organization possible.

The interdependence which makes this necessary has always existed. It is only recently, however, that we have come to emphasize that teacher morale and effect are related not alone to knowledge of how things have come about, but also to insight into what improvements are possible and to opportunity to affect the structure.

The movement toward more widespread participation has been gradual, and for this reason not noticeable to many people. The campaign to democratize school administration, underway for some time, has resulted in an occasional excessive dependence on the staff. Here and there complaint on the part of teachers that they have no time to teach has resulted. Still, most systems do not overtax their staffs, while everywhere there are patent signs of progress. Teachers pass on texts; they make out their own examinations; they decide agenda for faculty meetings; they cooperate in staff selection; they study to support a change in policy; they represent to the board, and so on. Faculties, in fact, have more responsibility than they think they have.

The Many Values of Good Organization

Few would argue against some formal means for managing these increasing areas of prerogative. We need clear understanding of who leads, who supports, who proposes, and who deliberates. Otherwise there is likely to be drift and inaction with periodic frantic scrambles to rectify mistakes. Accusation, recrimination, tension, and hasty substitutes may emerge to provide an uncomfortable legacy over ensuing years. Whereas, a good organization for curriculum change at state and local level has at least these advantages:

1. It clearly recognizes the need for improvement.
2. It paves the way for stimulation and motivation.
3. It designates and delegates responsibility.
4. It permits accounting.
5. It gives confidence to those who participate.
6. It saves time.

LEVELS OF ORGANIZATION

Regarding organization, the most pertinent concern of teachers is with the local situation they may affect easily and directly. For most of us this is in the building where we teach. In large cities the teacher may affect organization indirectly through opinions expressed to administrators and to representatives or through being a representative himself to some group drawn from the system at large. Impact upon the state's plan for curriculum development is possible for the classroom teacher, but usually only when the teacher is called upon to participate as an advisor by state officials. However, the classroom teacher can and should work at all levels wherever and whenever he can.

State Organization Plans

It is easy for the classroom teacher to be uninformed about the way the duly constituted state officers proceed in their efforts to secure better schools. To many of us, state superintendents and state supervisors are quite distant figures who occupy offices in the capital city. In many states one can teach for years without ever seeing a state supervisor. Bulletins and courses of study are more than occasionally not available. We know there are state laws but we do not know what they are. We may recall that county and city superintendents meet "up there"—but about what, we do not know.

Whatever we know, no state department has been completely neglectful of its responsibility to promote improvement. A department exists for improvement as much as it exists to establish, provide for, and control educational activity in the elementary and secondary schools. The situation is unquestionably better in some states than it is in others. In fact, it seems some state departments are a kind of excess baggage with nearly all planning for curriculum quality vested, by virtue of financial and personnel restrictions, in the local and county jurisdictions. In a few states the state education department is in effect a powerful, dominating, and demanding agency. It is said local action is virtually paralyzed by mandates, controls, checks, balances, and examinations. Neither extreme is defensible. Dominance robs a state of the genius of its teachers and saddles creativity with bureaucracy. Impotence makes a mockery of leadership and unity, and spawns both indolence and impudence. As usual, the happy medium is in between.

In every state someone is delegated the responsibility to oversee and to promote instructional improvement. Titles of such officers are unimportant really, but they include commissioners, superintendents, directors, bureau chiefs and supervisors who have, at one place or another, the power to issue regulations, arrange for the preparation of syllabi and courses of study, sponsor workshops and clinics, stimulate through letters and direct communications, issue examinations, approve local adaptations, accredit and register schools, and perform countless other tasks.

Most state departments have some division or department, variously subdivided, whose job it is to foster action in behalf of better instruction. The members of that part of the state agency act as consultants locally and to groups; they attend meetings of professional groups; their services are available to large and small working units; they produce bibliographies and plan publications. Research, promotion, evaluation, among other roles, are included on their job sheets.

In every state, classroom teachers are consulted and invited to participate in various aspects of curriculum improvement. The most common role is that of preparing and writing materials useful to teachers. To date perhaps a majority of state publications distributed to teachers has been nurtured through the planning and broad sketching stages and the final evaluation and approval steps by teachers. Actual writing in a very large percentage of cases has been done by teachers. For example, in the State of New York courses of study always grow out of the recommendations and suggestions of teachers, and the renowned and often abused Regents Examinations for scores of years have been the product of teacher deliberation in everything but the final and technical wording.

It may be said fairly that the plan in most states for improving the curriculum is to support and encourage every step that will bring active effort to bear. Membership in study councils is encouraged; inservice education courses are approved for credit; legislation is secured to permit district support of teacher study; grants are sought from the federal government and foundations to encourage testing; state universities and colleges are encouraged to develop field services and to adjust extension programs to emergent teacher needs. The specific acts of state agencies are seemingly endless.

Formal and special organization for curriculum improvement has also emerged from time to time. Most states have undertaken steps of one order or another that demonstrate much of a campaign nature. The purpose has been to stir up interest and to get more energy devoted to improvement. Alabama, Florida, Michigan, Kansas, Oklahoma, and more recently New York and Illinois, to mention a few, have treated themselves to special programs. For the most part, these have meant the appointment or designation of coordinators, the writing or rewriting of bulletins, sponsored workshops during the year and in the summer, increased consultantship to interested schools, reports of progress, and so on. General guiding or steering committees have been appointed and subcommittees chosen to investigate, promote, and report on numerous issues identified by the central group with the aid of teachers in every type of school.

PARTICIPATION STRESSED IN A RECENT PLAN

Over several years in New York State part of the State's plan has been promotion of more attention locally to the improvement of instruction and to development of organizations at the local level to facilitate curriculum development. Pilot workshops have been held in different geographic areas of the state and in several types of school districts. Mainly administrators and supervisory officers have attended some of the workshops. One brought together the teachers of a whole rural county, and others have served teachers and administrative officers together.

Each of the meetings has focused on the problems identified by local groups and subunits, and the topics for small group discussion have included examinations, discipline, personnel policy, materials and resources, recruitment and selection, in-service programs, staffing problems, concepts of the curriculum generalization and specialization, assignments, promotion, lay involvement, idea dissemination, and special education.

The major emphasis in presentations by top officers of the department has been on what is needed to move a local program forward. At each of the workshops and in a letter[1] to every chief school administrator in the state, Commissioner Walter Crewson identified and discussed ten areas in which sound growth and development need to take place. They are in

1. Effective practices in personnel selection
2. Adequate staffing to fix responsibility
3. Discernible staff organization for instructional improvement
4. Effective communication
5. Development of local curriculum materials
6. The involvement of key laymen
7. Budgeting for instructional improvement
8. In-service education geared to local needs
9. A well-understood concept of the curriculum
10. Periodic local evaluation in terms of locally established goals

TEACHERS AND KNOWLEDGE OF THE STATE PLAN

We would have to agree that the periodic new program approach has its merits. Perhaps the most important one is that as a result teachers are reminded that the state education department does exist and that it is anxious to fulfill its leadership role. A tub-thumping also probably encourages school superintendents to have a look at their

[1] Walter Crewson, *How to Use the Power*, New York State Education Department, 1958.

own efforts because the superintendent invariably is told generally what the state leadership desires. Nevertheless, we know that energetic campaigns have a way of not reaching as deeply as they should. During the height of most special state improvement programs we may find colleagues who are quite unaware of any ambitions to get something done.

Certainly it is better to have a well-conceived, well-staffed, broad, and continuing program for the improvement of the curriculum.

Whatever the case, we believe a classroom teacher should have a clear understanding of what his state's organization for curriculum leadership is. He should be able to criticize it, and be ready to propose alternatives. Great numbers of teachers in every state will in one way or another participate in the detailed operation of any plan. Ignorance creates suspicion; it also justifies compliance in place of genuine cooperation. Active interest and enthusiasm contrarily lead to better plans.

Delegate though we may, red-blooded people can really never become the willing pawns of those with more power and prestige. The alternative is to know what is better and what ought to be, even if our chance to bring it about seems remote. Good treatment of what a state's organized plan should include can be found in statements by Krug,[2] Alexander,[3] and Caswell.[4]

We cannot here spell out in great detail what the state plan should include. These characteristics are considered important.

1. Officers in the state department should be clearly designated as responsible for curriculum development.

2. Curriculum improvement should include at least development of resource materials, sponsorship of conferences and workshops, consultancy with local districts, establishment of criteria for minimum programs, stimulation and participation in experimentation, encouragement and support of voluntary professional organizations, accumulation of good practice illustration, visitation and observation in schools, preparation and interpretation of regulations, advice on local courses of study, evaluation of state school program effect, preparation of stimulus and report materials such as newsletters, intensive study of broad and of state issues in education, communication and cooperative examination with the public, promotion of in-service education and research.

3. State officers should be guided by committees and advisory groups drawn from the teaching group at large. An over-all group should constitute a

[2] Edward Krug *et al., Administering Curriculum Planning,* Harper, 1956, chap. 2.

[3] William Alexander, *State Leadership in Improving Instruction,* Bureau of Publications, Teachers College, 1940.

[4] Hollis L. Caswell *et al., Curriculum Improvement in Public School Systems,* Bureau of Publications, Teachers College, 1950, chaps. 13, 14.

curriculum council. There should be numerous advisory and planning sub-groups; some continuing with rotating members; some, *ad hoc*.

4. The major emphasis in the state's plan should be stimulation and en-couragement. Supervisors and curriculum workers should serve most directly and personally the needs of curriculum leaders in various districts in the state. Interest and action at the local level should be a paramount goal.

5. State regulations, mandates, controls, should be held at a minimum and constantly re-examined to determine their effect on local curriculum activity.

TEACHERS' CONTRIBUTIONS POSSIBLE

How can the classroom teacher exercise much influence? We should be naïve indeed to think a home economics teacher in an isolated community or in a city with a thousand or more teachers could straighten matters out with a twist of the wrist. The evolution of a good organizational structure and effective steps by the state agency must take time. It will come more rapidly, however, as the rank and file seek and support those arrangements which can be helpful to them. State officers are not inaccessible. They should be told directly what is needed, not so much perhaps to educate them or influence them, as to provide them with the knowledge for convincing superiors and law makers who hold the purse strings. Chief school officers in the districts certainly should be encouraged to exercise their influence. Resolutions from local teachers associations and the state organization representing teachers can have appreciable effect. Many complaining and "if I were running things" observations by teachers would be worthwhile if properly and carefully directed.

Organization in Local School Systems

Just as the state commissioner can not escape responsibility for attention to curriculum matters so the county or city superintendent or the supervising head of any large school district must not overlook his role. During the postwar building spree, tremendous amounts of time of the chief school administrators everywhere have been drawn away from instruction. The need for some effective delegation and organization of curriculum work has thus been sharply illuminated even in relatively small school systems. However, the value and importance of organization for curriculum work in the local districts have been recognized for a long time.

Curriculum leadership has thus come to be the delegated responsibility of an assistant superintendent in charge of instruction or a curriculum director or coordinator. Where very large systems are involved, there may be a whole curriculum division with appropriate titles for personnel with various leadership and administrative duties, the first-line resource person being called a consultant or a helping teacher.

The patterns of organization in local districts vary according to situation and to need. As with state programs, some districts have found it useful to have curriculum councils or central committees. Sometimes these councils are composed mainly of administrators. Most often, they are made up of representatives from the constituent schools and include teachers and laymen. Subcommittees are commonly set up to prepare guides, deliberate on policy, and establish better articulation among school units. In some districts special curriculum personnel are on call to provide help at behest of principal or department heads. In others, they are directly in charge of programs in subject fields and have great power to control and to impose.

Rarely will a teacher find himself in a school system in which someone can not specify who is in charge of the improvement of instruction and what provisions are made to make instruction better. In most cases the principal of the school in which we teach is mentioned first, then the many others may be identified: department heads, supervisors, curriculum coordinators, assistant superintendents. Before-and-after-school conferences, institutes, department meetings, curriculum councils, materials committees, visitation arrangements, in-service training courses, and supervisory visits are recognized as the media for deliberation, study and change.

TEACHER'S INFLUENCE GREATER AT THE SYSTEM LEVEL

Although the extent and complexity of some "local" school systems are so great that a teacher is far away from central office decision-making, remoteness is not a real penalty in most school districts. Usually a teacher does have reasonably easy access to the chief school administrator and many opportunities to express opinions to superiors who initiate change. Good ideas often do not get the hearing they deserve, yet everywhere there are superiors who *will* listen. In fact, one of the perennial topics of conversation at conclaves of school administrators concerns how to get more interest, more proposals and propositions from teachers.

Every school system has its committees on something. They may be on teacher recruitment, on athletics, or on the flower and welfare fund. Seldom is good deliberation on one school problem unrelated to another. In almost every good committee deliberation and report, there exists the chance to propose more attention to, better organization of

PLAN FOR LOCAL SYSTEM CURRICULUM IMPROVEMENT

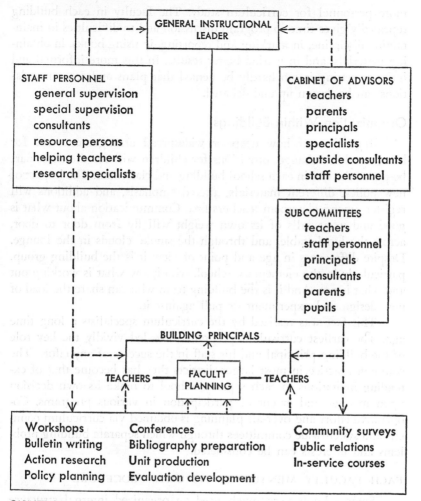

GENERAL INSTRUCTIONAL LEADER

STAFF PERSONNEL
general supervision
special supervision
consultants
resource persons
helping teachers
research specialists

CABINET OF ADVISORS
teachers
parents
principals
specialists
outside consultants
staff personnel

SUBCOMMITTEES
teachers
staff personnel
principals
consultants
parents
pupils

BUILDING PRINCIPALS

TEACHERS — **FACULTY PLANNING** — TEACHERS

Workshops	Conferences	Community surveys
Bulletin writing	Bibliography preparation	Public relations
Action research	Unit production	In-service courses
Policy planning	Evaluation development	

CABINET OF ADVISORS (Curriculum council)
1. Canvass needs
2. Define problems and projects
3. Recommend and plan procedures
4. Review and evaluate

STAFF PERSONNEL
1. Locate resources
2. Suggest projects
3. Develop materials
4. Provide ideas
5. Study literature
6. Plan studies
7. Manage details

SUGGESTED ROLES FOR GENERAL INSTRUCTIONAL LEADER
1. Coordinate activities
2. Propose & support policy
3. Encourage & stimulate
4. Report progress
5. Arrange meetings
6. Advise groups
7. Secure working conditions

SUBCOMMITTEE
1. Deliberate policy
2. Study problems
3. Cumulate data
4. Analyze literature
5. Evaluate progress
6. Consider proposals
7. Stimulate ideas

more personnel for curriculum study. The faculty in each building repeatedly gives time to program discussion and to difficulties in maintaining discipline, in marking and reporting, in using books, in obtaining materials, and in getting better results. In this more informal and intimate setting it can hardly be denied that plans and recommendations can be drawn up and debated.

Organization Within Buildings

Regardless of how deep or widespread arrangements are for bringing about change, provisions for children will for the most part be put to the test in each school building and classroom. The impact of new policy, different materials, altered emphasis, and additions will register among classroom teachers first. Communication about what is good and what falls of its own weight will fly from door to door, across the lunch table, and through the smoke clouds in the lounge. Despite differences in age and point of view it is the building group, particularly in the elementary school, who know what is working out and what is not. And it is the building team who can share the load of new design and experiment or pull against it.

This fact was realized by the curriculum specialists a long time ago. The earliest curriculum programs revealed vividly the key role of the building principal and his staff in the success of any effort. The common practice in most larger districts thus has become that of extending invitations to each separate school to make its own decision upon manner and extent of participation in various programs. Cooperative effort and over-all planning is obtained via curriculum councils and systemwide committees through which separate building problems and interests can be considered.

EACH FACULTY MENTOR OF ITS OWN PROCEDURE

Some schools very much need an organized internal structure even though they work as a single unit. They are so big that teachers can not meet easily together. When they do, communication is formal and intensive interaction is difficult if not impossible. As a result, division of the larger group into working units is necessary. For some concerns, departmental organization will serve best. For others, groups organized by grade level or by areas of personal interest will provide a good working arrangement. A building council may be helpful as a screening device and for purposes of administration and more intensive deliberation on general policy. A vice-principal for program or a curriculum assistant may be needed to "head up" activities.

However, in most of our schools the faculty is not so large and unwieldy as to necessitate a very involved plan for curriculum study. Departments are usually small and can study their own problems easily. More general issues needing fairly thorough investigation can be assigned to committees of the staff.

Problems upon which the faculty may need or desire to work arise quite naturally in periodic faculty meetings. These days no school large or small can escape from suggestions made in educational journals, from ideas brought in from conventions and professional meetings, from the dreams of teachers, and so on. Daily the desks of principals are flooded with inventories, evaluative devices, descriptions of what good schools do, invitations to try new books and materials. Parents constantly ask questions and protest. Pupils refuse to or can not read and can not do their arithmetic. Someone wants to introduce French, or typewriting, or establish a point system for extraclass activities. The agenda can soon become filled with curriculum concerns.

The upshot of the continual emergence of problems ought to be the appointment of committees to study these matters and to recommend action. Occasionally the whole faculty should deliberate.

So we can ask, "Isn't this enough?" An ordinary live faculty in a typical small school can not really help itself. If at all conscious of pressures and appeals, of exhortations from state leaders and professional reformers, it will perforce have to ask questions, add to or subtract from what it is doing. What more than correct use of proper resources in the face of recognized problems is necessary?

We probably could agree a written-down plan or set of steps is not necessary if significant issues are regularly coming to faculty attention and their resolution is accomplished by wise and timely faculty choice on how to investigate thoroughly and what to do in the end. But we know faculty meetings in many, many schools are few and far between. Curriculum improvement projects too often get postponed by details of administration and by lengthy debates on minor matters.

Even in a small school, then, we should expect that certain steps would be taken in behalf of organized curriculum study. A wise faculty will go so far as to decide who will take initiative or have responsibility and will agree on the time, and perhaps on the way, the steps should be taken. As a beginning list, we suggest that a local school plan should include

A periodic problem census of local curriculum concerns
Regular and systematic evaluation by teachers of their individual success
Follow-up study of graduates

Cooperative teacher-parent identification of problems
Systematic examination of professional journals
Official representation at study council and professional meetings
Participation in in-service programs
Arranged visits to other schools
Periodic review of courses of study
Released time arrangements for group study
Utilization of consultants to pinpoint problems and to help plan approaches
Standing committees on meeting agenda, evaluation, and other areas of constant concern
Ad hoc groups to explore deeply and thoroughly in areas of temporary or special interest

REAL INITIATIVE FOR TEACHER

As has been pointed out, the intimate interactions in any building or small system provide open sesame for the individual who accepts his responsibility to bring about more and better plans. Direct appeal can be made to colleagues to study problems; motions to create committees can be made in faculty meetings; requests for help on personally initiated projects can be presented to others.

With this freedom, it is doubtless easy for one to become a busybody or so active in sketching the plans for curriculum improvement that he usurps the prerogatives of the principal. He also may earn the distrust of older staff members who fancy themselves the sources of suggestion or who have actually earned some chevrons on the sleeve of prestige. Thus, suggestions and proposals may wisely come at times only as innocent questions and casually but appropriately expressed wishes.

It takes time to develop a set of steps that includes comfortable lifts from one level to another. Because we know what can be done, we may be anxious to get there too fast. Because the local level is where we as teachers can have most influence, we must be watchful that what we propose may be happily received for the most part and may work out well.

CAREFUL CONSIDERATION OF COMMITTEE DYNAMICS
A NECESSITY

Faculty members contemplating a plan for local organization for curriculum improvement should be aware that there are numerous problems which subgroups may encounter. Some of the problems are common to individuals too. First, participation is time consuming. Provision must be made for meeting-time as a part of the regular schedule. Otherwise the work may be considered as extra and unimportant by some of the faculty members. Second, certain faculty members may become overloaded with committee work. Faculties and their administrators often turn to a few for leadership on any problem that arises. Certain willing souls are too cooperative to resist. Unless careful attention is given to balanced assignment and to arrangements of work load, some members may become so overburdened that their teaching suffers. Third, it is not uncommon for the administrator to decide the present structure does not provide for the particular problems facing the staff and to appoint another committee to execute the new function. This practice leads to discomfort and a feeling of frustration among those on already existent committees. To guard against this, the functions of all committees should be carefully defined to include what they should consider and how long they should exist. Fourth, action often does not follow on proposals. This produces frustration which can be relieved only as administrators actively seek implementation. Fifth, no group lives by itself. Its effectiveness is determined by the relationship and the working arrangements within the group. Great care should be exercised to see that those who can work together well are assigned to groups. Although we may hope to improve faculty interaction, understanding, and mutual respect through small group function, we should be unwise to staff committees with teachers who are uncongenial.

The following list[5] of principles for committee operation suggests some cautions for those who would organize the staff into smaller working units.

1. A committee should understand clearly what it is to do and what its powers are. A commission or specification should be prepared in writing for the committee, stating its objectives, functions, and authority.
2. The committee should concern itself with real problems. It should not be put in the position of merely giving its approval to policies that have already been put into effect. The agenda for each meeting should be based on the problems the committee considers important. An agenda that is developed from a problem census of the committee will receive more responsible consideration than one that is prepared in advance by the chairman or staff members. (The problems that are of concern to the chairman and the staff will, of course, be included in the problem census.)
3. The outcomes of the committee's work should be continually interpreted to it. Activity leaders may be invited to committee meetings to describe outstanding achievements, exhibits may be arranged, and reports may be presented. The committee should emphasize the significance of its work.
4. Committee members should be given firsthand experiences with the pro-

[5] Malcolm S. Knowles, *Informal Adult Education*, Association Press, 1951, pp. 174–175.

gram by appearing at ceremonial events, inspecting activities, and otherwise taking an active part in the program.

5. The administrative work involved in efficient committee operation should be handled smoothly. Notices of meetings should be sent well in advance, materials of value in preparing for discussion should be distributed, minutes should be reproduced and distributed, and appropriate action should be taken on decisions made by the committee.

6. The committee should evaluate its work periodically.

7. Responsibilities accepted by committee members should be clear, specific, and definite. Provision should be made by the committee for some method of following up on committee assignments.

LOCAL INITIATIVE AND PLANS

We could very easily belabor the generalization that good first steps do not guarantee a finished product. We know there is much more to good building than getting a start. We may have the curriculum council, planned meetings, good problems, money for resources, arrangements with consultants and with college professors for courses, and a good staff available, but all must mesh smoothly in operation or our plans will bring little profit.

1. *Plans must come from those who will carry them out.* The disease of many new principals appears to be to get "something under way." Granted, new administrators are often employed by the board or the superintendent to give strong leadership. They frequently come to new posts with a fair amount of recent training and conviction about stimulating the staff. And often their advent is accompanied by the expectation that "we will now get out of the rut." At the same time we know that there will be colleagues who will see the new principal as a threat. Some on the faculty with power will lose it. The line-up of those who will hear first, who will be "in the know," who will gather prestige from recognition will change. More work will be demanded. New skills or the demonstration of ones long put to rest will be required. Those who are threatened will not respond positively at all. If they do, it may more often be in self-defense and in a manner to protect themselves rather than to make a genuine contribution.

For instance, in a small city high school a relatively new principal, anxious to exercise his leadership, secured from his board a thousand dollars to have a semester-long workshop on instructional improvement. His move grew from representations to him by several enthusiastic members of the local teachers' association who said the teachers would support the step. His confirmation with the group at a regular faculty meeting drew no protest. When the time for registration came, a third of the staff presented excuses. After several unhappy and unproductive planning sessions, the workshop leader undertook intensive interviews with members of the staff. To his consternation he discovered that over 50 percent of those attending did not want to give the time; they were resentful over being parlayed into acquiescence; they wanted college credit only; and they did not want to do any work. What could have been worse?

Such reluctance is surely not alone the desert for new principals. Many well-seasoned school heads have found their nicely laid plans stirring up resentment and stimulating evasion and escapism. Why?

At best the move to improve someone else is a ticklish business. Even most blandly put it is an insult to many. This is a point administrators and classroom teachers who want cooperative effort ought to be careful to remember. "We ought to have a program to improve instruction," invariably means to some, "You are not so hot and you need help."

Teacher leaders and teacher proponents of programs to develop the curriculum must be keenly aware of this obligation to get widespread and genuine conviction about the need to do something. After that, every step in the organizational structure for keeping up the stimulation and for facilitating action should be evolved by a process which has some chance of getting full participation and real consensus.

Most really professional people do not work well on other people's plans. They want to "call their own shots." We teachers certainly should know this. We must then be ever vigilant to remind our leaders that ideas and proposals that come from or are heartily and widely approved by the staff, after they have been given a chance to measure the personal and human cost, will more often succeed because they will get support.

2. *Action must be nourished.* Involvement in setting up plans, opportunity to propose and discuss alternatives will in themselves, we know, build ego. When we have agreed that something can and ought to be done, there is gnawing need in many of us to see that it is done, whether by ourselves or others. We gain self-satisfaction and strength from something accomplished. We develop interest in the success of our project.

Involvement in deciding what to do and in action will not, despite their effect, build all the gumption we need for continuing positive curriculum work. Agreement to write units or to experiment, acquiescence to workshop participation, or a vote for intensive study of the frustration levels of children will not necessarily release energy and get production. The world is filled with people who see what needs to be done and want to make changes but do not.

Therefore, there should be built along with every set of plans for curriculum improvement, arrangements to provide exhortation and encouragement. Periodic evaluation will do so, for the deadline to report will get most of us off our well-known resting spots. Enthusiastic challenges by "visiting firemen" will restore our resolution. Promises to ourselves and deadlines will help screw some courage to the sticking point. Reasonable goals and regularly planned sessions for work will set up possibilities and routines to get them accomplished. And of course success is a breeder apparently unsurpassed in the promotion of production.

3. *Leadership resides in all of us.* We can agree easily that the man who gets paid to lead, to stimulate, to help should do so. But, we not he, are more than seldom our brother's keeper. In any crowd you and I decide for ourselves, and from moment to moment, who will stir us, who will earn our loyal devotion. Few of us are really "sent" by our leader. More often than not we take our cue from those with whom we identify, at our own level.

Each teacher has the responsibility to keep up the spirit in his colleagues. Each of us knows whom we attract and whom we influence. With whom do we eat, to whom do we report our little embarrassments, on whom do we depend for consolation, in whom do we have faith that snide comments are safe? When we have answered, we know whom we can bring along, whom we have a chance to convince, whose antagonisms, self-doubts, and lethargies we can dispel. In essence this means that each teacher can be a leader in curriculum improvement.

4. *Cooperative skill is imperative.* We have remarked before on the competitive training of most teachers, and upon the suspicion it has created of any procedures that require sharing for the common welfare. We do admit that much verbalization about cooperation has taken place, but it has not developed much skill or comfort in cooperation for most of us. In adulthood most of us have continued in our independent ways, periodically fortified in them or driven back to them by waves of sentiment among administrators and laymen for rating our merit and rewarding it, by a study of comparisons. Cooperation is an intellectual and contemplative matter for most of us. It is hardly an emotional or motivational matter.

The next chapter focuses on the detailed conditions and skills necessary to good group production. In presenting the ideas and cautions there, we recognize fully that all curriculum improvement does not come through the efforts of groups. However, a great many changes can not come unless groups agree to them.

The curriculum movement has been scorned particularly for being "groupy." It may fairly be said that great excitement about process in groups did sweep the ranks of curriculum specialists after World War II. However, a wholesome correction set in after several years. The truth of the revelations about groups was not thereby disproved. The fact that the dynamics of group interaction are potent factors in what people, formally or informally assembled, can produce together was well established and remains clear. He who ignores the process simply entertains blissfully the prospect of partial success. He who flails about denouncing groups altogether, in some mistaken defense of individualism, merely denies himself the advantage of cumulative wisdom.

Upon the classroom teacher who will increasingly be asked to work with others on many problems there rests an obligation to know what gives a group power. How can loyalty and unity be developed? What creates hostility and what removes it? What is the role of a leader? Who are the leaders and how should they work? What causes one to make free contribution? How can redirection be obtained?

We all have served on a committee one time or another. Some of the committees have moved along beautifully; the secretary has kept good notes and written an able report; the outcome has been useful, and we look back upon it with a sense of accomplishment. Other committees have floundered and flopped; there have been confusion and frustration; ill-feeling has arisen; the end result has been only recrimination and regret. These contrasting experiences ought to be enough to spur us on to seek an "understanding of groups."

PRINCIPLES OF GROUP PLANNING

Everyone is in on it. The planning gives opportunity and encourages all members of the group who will be directly affected by the results of the planning to participate and share in the thinking.

Planning should grow out of the expressed needs and interests of the members who compose the group. The basis for planning should be the group goals rather than those imposed by one.

Planning gives scope to individual interests and an opportunity to "belong." The final determination of the problem is broad enough to include the real interests of all the members of the group so that each may "belong," that is, have status in and recognition by the group.

The most effective plans come out of a process which combines continuous planning and evaluation. As the work progresses changes are made as the actual work proves them necessary. The planning leads to continuity, to more seeking, learning, and evaluating, to changing behavior continuously to meet new situations.

The planning itself and the things planned are flexible and "open-ended." There is provision for the group to rethink its purposes and procedures and to state new ideas frankly. The sequence of events in group planning is *not* Herbartian, not seriatim. Goals change and ends and means change as experience direct.

Group planning results in "collective self-control" for the sake of group goals; it does not inevitably result in someone's telling someone else what to do.

The most effective plans grow out of a process that is often slow and seemingly drawn out. Group members are patient with the process. Those who cry "action not more paper plans" can speed up the realization of plans without planning to do so. The "doer" must be the planner.

The planning uses all available resources of the environment which are pertinent to the problem. Furthermore planning makes use of existing plans and resources rather than starting from scratch with every new problem. We build on what we have, provided it is useful and furnishes a foundation for the problem.

Planning requires documentation and record-keeping. The results of group thinking, discussing, planning, deciding, acting, and evaluating must be preserved to provide continuity and direction. Records must be available for purposes of summary and evaluation.

Planning provides means for recognizing the contributions of all to group goals. Each individual grows with self-confidence in his ability to contribute. Hence group members should receive recognition for their help.

Planning gives order and shape to group experiences. It enables the group to do things in an orderly way, to think before action, and to act in the light of facts rather than guesses.

Group planning is not power based. The group does not plan under the influence of the majority or minority in the group or outside the group. It plans in terms of cooperative action and the mutual acceptance by all of the group goals.

Leadership Emphasis Necessary

Ideas about leadership have been undergoing considerable re-vamping with intensive study of how leaders function best in various fields. In but a few years the belief that "once a leader always a leader" has given way on a broad front to the conviction that leaders grow out of situations. One who is actually a leader at one moment or one place may not be the leader at all at a subsequent time and location. A person may retain his title and he may give certain formal signals and orders, but he is not necessarily a leader thereby. Neither do combinations of height and brains or gold braid and peaked caps always make leaders.

Recent research has it that leaders are those who are sensitive to the needs of others and can muster the resources to serve those needs. They are also people who can create genuine needs in others as they command the wherewithal to provide satisfactions.

Out of these asseverations has now grown a new body of literature on what must be known as a status figure or as an appointed or legal head to secure the most from a group. Whether all that the new expositors on leadership say will hold up under continued examination remains to be seen. We do not choose to argue the merits of their case here. The contention that real leadership is situational seems at present sound enough.

Every school has its authorized head. And in every case, picked by a board, recommended and approved by a faculty, or designated by a superior officer, his duty is to lead the staff and to help them find ways to the fullest contribution they can make. Curriculum responsibility may be delegated to another, but then the mantle is merely shifted. The leader is there. Whether he can lead or not remains to be seen. The fact that leadership is situational does not relieve us of locating the leaders.

The situation, of course, is many things. It is for the most part the staff, their past experiences, their expectations, their established ways of acting, their internal tensions, and so on. If the head—the principal, the supervisor—has been chosen by staff members, we may anticipate that he is felt to have the attitudes, the style, and the power his advocates want. At least there will be a honeymoon until they discover he is a counterfeit. If he is dropped unheralded into the driver's seat, he will naturally need to demonstrate his value as soon as possible. He will be looked to in time as acceptable and useful, or else subordinates will come to submit where he has immediate power and directive control while looking to others for their signals.

We are indeed fortunate when our authorized heads are also people whom we admire, whose suggestions we happily accept, and whose requests we work upon because we see them as crystallizations of our own desire and means to our own satisfaction. It is unnecessary to say that all too few teachers find themselves so blessed.

We do, though, regularly find that there are among our colleagues many who can be our guides, our stimulators, our sovereigns. The next-door teacher who interests us in sponsoring a club, the social scientist who catches our fancy about the faculty play, and the mathematician who invariably summarizes sentiment sufficiently to clarify how we should vote on social security or health insurance particpation demonstrate leadership when it is needed. In group deliberation we find it is Mary who says what is needed to reduce tension; it is John who volunteers to read a report; it is Harry who gets us back on the track. The principal or the department head may be there, but he is not leading. We are.

What has been said here simply is that when you need "it" and someone has "it," he is your leader. Does this mean then that everyone should struggle manfully to become the leader or that we should be grateful for those who are our leaders and abandon those who aspire but fail?

Obviously neither extreme is an adequate answer. We know we must, as good professionals, offer our best to our colleagues. In other sections of this book we have argued that each teacher should be ready to propose to others, ready to raise questions and point out directions, ready to take initiative, ready to recruit helpers. Here the position is that a classroom teacher should undertake actively to secure and develop the most competent heads. We can not really, despite our self-sufficiency, do well when there is weakness at the apex. Indifference will stifle initiative. Ineptness and incompetence will kill it.

1. *Obtaining leaders.* A staff may go years before it may have the pleasure of a new principal or an added officer to promote curriculum study. When the opportunity occurs, any faculty which does not make its wants known defaults on its responsibilities. Specifications should be clearly written first for the job, as it applies to instructional improvement, and next for the kind of person to fill it. If there is no means for formal faculty action, the teachers' association should be employed.

2. *Helping leaders grow.* Regardless how clever or how ingratiating a superior officer is, he can not go far if he is not aided in doing what he ought to do. Successful curriculum directors are those who share their thoughts, seek to know our sentiments, help us lift our

concerns above the humdrum, and eliminate the petty annoyances. If we do not listen, will not reveal feelings, and magnify the unimportant to outlandish proportions, however, we may hopelessly block a sincere leader's efforts to move toward us.

Curriculum directors may more likely be unsuccessful because they make what seem obvious mistakes. They are not alert to petty jealousy; they do not recognize a widespread need to be close to papa; they talk instead of listen; they forget how our hard work builds *their* reputations; they do not build us up to others; they do not really give us the concrete help we want; they dream too much and expect too much; they never let us rest; they have too many prerogatives, secretaries, and freedoms; they attend too many conventions; they blame us because we are so dull; they fumble meetings; and they issue memoranda "From the Desk Of."

A trained man ought to know better, but many do not. Very many others who would lead us to instructional uplands actually are not trained or very poorly trained. Their ineptitude may not be as exasperating as oblivious mismanagement, but their plight and ours usually leaves us no alternative other than to bridge the gap. "Pulling out the chestnuts" for a boss may not set well, and the issue may be argued. There are times when an honest appraisal and moves to unseat the driver are justified. However, most of the time, something short of that is necessary and advisable.

3. *Helping leaders lead.* How may we help leaders move curriculum improvement ahead? First, we can exercise all the subtlety in ourselves to tell him how his behavior aggravates and irritates people. We can tell him—in the hall, at a picnic, in a conference on a discipline problem—what we need. We can encourage him to put items on the faculty meeting agenda or to invite a committee to plan faculty meetings, and thus get at least some open discussion of grievances. We can offer to make a problem census, or a follow-up study, or a teacher perception inventory for a course paper at a local college, and in such manner show him where his unrecognized problems with people and with the curriculum lie. We can invite him to help us study our students and to teach while we watch.

On nearly every faculty there are those who dislike the head, those who can undermine confidence, those who scoff and criticize, those who pull back. When we too recognize these dynamics and want to minimize them, there are many moves that will help. Pointing out the strong attributes in the leader can change attitudes; scotching rumors and exposing inquiries, hunches, and comments that arouse suspicion will help diminish gossip and incipient disloyalty. Helping colleagues to produce should aid them in reducing their fear of the leader's annoyance due to their inactivity.

Some of our heads will have to be taught how to lead groups too. Courses, reminders from human relations experts, or books on group dynamics will not make sensitive and artful chairmen for faculty meetings and local committee groups. Neither will knowledge that there can be expert chairmen guarantee swift response to our proposals. We can surmount the obstacle only by confronting it. We should analyze the occasional good meeting, import films, demonstrate in our own classes, invite the head to work out process with subgroups in a "core class," relate examples of success in other schools, review the evaluations of student council or student senate meetings, chart the failure of a student leader . . . to show how real leadership is exercised.

4. *Helping leaders keep up spirit.* We all know that a man who has no vision and no urge to achieve himself or see others achieve will seldom attain great things. But passing along verve to a leader is not easy. Some spirit can be aroused by vigorous presentation and youthful exhuberance. Acceptance and active support should provide encouragement. Selfless contribution of ideas with expectation of their later appearance as novel proposals from the boss may be helpful. Providing an administrator or supervisor with signs of loyalty and interest can also help promote initiative. Contrarily, cold reception to ideas, complaints about the time involved or difficulty of work will soon dim the bright beacon in any front office.

As with youngsters, our ace in the hole probably is his problems. If we can discover what concerns are paramount, what will serve the needs of the supervisor, what will lighten his load at the same time that it improves the lot of teachers, we have some good chance of getting unlimbered a drive to stimulate teachers. Searching out those needs takes leadership . . . in teachers.

Clarification of Goals Required

Desire to improve instruction or to get a report written or just to be active is sufficient reason for some to spend time in committee meetings and to deliberate endlessly. Occasionally, the opportunity to meet with colleagues merely to share and discuss things is given as the reason for having meetings. Those familiar with the study council movement and efforts to sponsor local sessions of similarly assigned personnel have heard this upon a number of occasions. Whether it is people who have nothing else to do or who have great insecurity in working along by themselves who act like this one can not tell.

Most teachers are not so minded. They want to see where they are going. They want to know, moreover, why they do not go faster and finish sooner. Where it all fits in is important; and how the product may be useful personally is a persisting question. Much curriculum study has borne little fruit and aroused much antagonism not because it was unorganized, unsupported, or unstaffed, but because groups have lost both their way and their zeal.

Somehow it seems quite easy for curriculum study to get so fuzzy or involved that a teacher can justifiably ask, "What are we trying to do anyway?" Part of the reason for this is that much of the real and meaningful identification of problems to investigate has been the work of some individual or central planning group. The topic is "opened-up" (silly pedagese!) by some expert, consultant, or supervisor who wants progress. He never does clarify for the group how much or what is required.

The widespread reluctance of teachers to "write it down" and the support so often indirectly given by curriculum theorists who counsel against premature decisions cause much uncertainty. Thus, the sooner a committee can "pound" out on the blackboard and then into notes what it exists for, what it expected to do, how long it will take, how it will approach its goals, and when it will report and to whom, the better.

Resource Help Important

The use of consultants from within a school system and from outside has increased over the years. A few central office administrators who at one time directed and chaired meetings have been replaced by a corps of "on-call" resource workers in a number of larger administrative units. The employment of specialists from universities and of state department supervisors to keynote meetings, to help plan action research, to counsel periodically with working groups has become fairly common.

However, many teachers and school systems do not get as much from these curriculum consultants and resource personnel as they might. Too often we are still inclined to anticipate what we need to know. We are likely to sit back and wait for their "pearls of wisdom."

Consultants and curriculum leaders themselves have tried to break this pattern. Recently trained supervisors and resource personnel have been taught to exercise restraint in seeming to know all the answers and to promote growth of the staff to the point where they are more likely to see "experts" as catalysts, diagnosticians, fellow explorers, and participating workers.[6]

As teachers, we ought to see that we can use consultants for helping us to get problems well defined and to advise us on the preliminary stages of projects we want to do. We can use them later to review progress. From their stories and reviews about programs elsewhere, we can develop background. We also can ask directly for answers to precise questions we have fashioned. We can call upon them for references to new materials and alternate plans. Through their suggestions and guidance we can avoid errors that will consume time and produce few long-term results. Actually, the burden is on us if we are to profit from the visit of a consultant or the employment of a resource person. As we know what we want, we can increase the efficiency of those who work for us.

IMMEDIATE SUPERVISOR MOST IMPORTANT

Classroom teachers most often will find their curriculum needs served by a local supervisor whose cooperation can be obtained on request. The burden of proper use here thus lies squarely on the teachers. There certainly do remain old-time autocrats, and in far too many places supervisors and curriculum specialists are expected to merit-rate teachers; we know this makes them *personae non grata* even though they sometimes delude themselves into believing teachers do not mind or do not notice or, worse yet, like to be rated. On the other hand, wholesome development in supervision has made approach much easier. The modern supervisor does not want to come unless he can really help and unless his help is really wanted. At their conventions and in self-evaluations with colleagues and superiors, supervisors often wonder how they can become more in demand and what they can do to gain access on a sound basis. One often asks another, "How can I show teachers where I can help them and what I can do?"

We have to recognize that sometimes we do not perceive our weaknesses or admit we need help with timing and tempo, introducing material, testing more subtle goals and objectives, and use of the resources in children. Polite questions, a request from the supervisor to

---

[6] See Marcella Lawler, *Curriculum Consultants At Work,* Bureau of Publications, Teachers College, 1958; Oregon Association for Supervision and Curriculum Development, *Being a Curriculum Consultant,* State Department of Education, 1960; and *Using a Curriculum Consultant,* same source, 1958.

help another teacher, a timely suggestion to visit one who startles us by excellence in our weak area may wake us up so we begin working on shortcomings. It is nice to have a supervisor who is a past master at creating confidence and at insinuating friendship and acceptance upon us. At the same time, it is much better if we can decide for ourselves at the outset that there is still a real value in having colleagues with proven competence and excellent resources near at hand. Once we have decided good teaching can be a team enterprise, our own goal can easily become increased attention to the aspects of that teaching where the counsel of supervisors will be worthwhile.

OUTSIDE SPECIALISTS USEFUL TOO

Although this growth in concept ought to take place in more teachers, it should also take place in principals and chief school officers. Many school systems never take advantage of the benefits of free service from the state agency because the school head would rather "leave well enough alone." In areas where study councils have been developed there are always systems that do not belong. No university professor ever gets into some communities.

There is much to be said for such self-sufficiency. A few school systems have enough depth in their own personnel not to need outside help. Perhaps we should have more so stalwart and independent. Yet it seems hardly likely that communication and interaction with others will fail to bring some profit.

Teachers can have a great deal to do with the progress of a school system in using consultative service and with a building principal's obtaining appropriate service from outside personnel. Properly presented, knowledge of the competencies of specialists, understanding of local needs and information on who can help, and good ideas on how and where to use outside resources encourage action. Active participation in area study council meetings with effective back home reporting will help prove the value of membership in councils and justify the substitute's pay. Wise planning of faculty meetings and occasional workshops and conferences sponsored by the teachers' association with good use of carefully selected visitors can often be convincing.

MODEST EXPECTATIONS WISE

It does seem unnecessary to comment that we ought not expect too much of system resource personnel or a once-a-month brand of consultant. Nonetheless, overexpectation is exactly one of the pitfalls. Part of it comes naturally from the "you-gotta-show-me" attitude. If people are experts, get more money, or have more status, they ought to show their colors with a real flourish—such is frequently the attitude of those resentful of prestige and titles. Even the expert away from home can be accused of saying the obvious!

If we are fair and reasonable, we know we should not call for help on simple matters. Neither should we request conferences and workshops on perennial problems that have no pat solutions or for which radical and nearly impossible changes are required. But if we do, we should expect the well-known mitigations and face up to the major surgery sure to be suggested.

Few problems in education are solved easily and quickly. The importation of a supervisor or a university expert will not add the magic ingredient which relieves a staff or a teacher of hard work and frustration. Consultants can at times raise our sight levels, add to confidence, bring a fresh viewpoint, save us from some unnecessary legwork, or ineffective scheme of operations. It is seldom possible for them to have a blueprint that will solve all problems.

Orientation of New Staff Necessary

Operation of any good school ought to provide for the introduction of new staff members to what is going on in the school system. This should include a thorough examination of curriculum activities against an historical background. Failure to do so can hamper continuous forward movement in curriculum planning. In many cases teacher turnover has resulted in complete standstills and occasionally in reversal of direction. Alert administrators have thus scheduled meetings for the purpose of explaining school philosophy, school procedures for dealing with problems, and recent progress on basic issues. These meetings are often included in preschool workshops or at new-teacher conferences. Here and there the general, helping teacher may have the responsibility for indoctrination. An older-teacher guide system can be similarly employed. Teacher handbooks, containing everything from statements of philosophy to procedure on sick leave, have now become standard and contribute in this area.

Informal and unorganized efforts also are used to supplement and improve orientation. In fact, this unplanned indoctrination is at times more useful and more important than any series of lectures and presentations by a supervisor and a selected panel of teachers. The esprit that moves many a school system along is not manufactured in recounts of "how we do it here." It is rather developed from the nods, smiles, and smirks that speak in place of and louder than words.

It would be very nice if every new and young teacher could

catch up to the most positive outlook and interpretation and move forward from there. It must be said, "It would be nice," for there are many who never do catch on, who join the ranks of the "Doubting Thomases," and attend upon the unpublicized ceremonials that put the latest curriculum effort to rest.

Continuous committee work will offer some opportunity for the new staff member to be brought along slowly. A gradual build-up of understanding will result from references to past decisions and agreements and from explanations of why certain steps were necessary. The greatest help, though, should come from the teacher who wants his colleagues to have a positive attitude and an interest in carrying on basic work reaching back a number of years. It thus rests upon the teacher to contribute useful information, insight, explanation, and an objective record of events through day-to-day contacts with those who have recently become staff members.

Materials an Imperative

We have mentioned before the fate of many reports, courses of study, and bulletins. We have cautioned against concentrating curriculum work in the hands of a few able writers. Change of viewpoint does not come as often as we would like through providing material on what ought to be done.

Nonetheless, the alternative hardly seems to be no writing and no paper production at all. Deliberations at the state level and intensive examination at area workshops sponsored by the state do produce valuable ideas and suggestions. The easiest and simplest way to make those results available is through well-written reports. Careful local group review of these reports should precipitate further thinking and refinement. The burden of proper use naturally lies on the shoulders of local leaders who know how to use reports for initiation, for resource purposes, for comparison, for evaluation, and for guidance.

The actual writing of reports locally does have distinct advantages. It provides a record and a reference against which remembrance about agreements can be checked. It calls for refinement of statement and balance in expression. It forces the authors to think about the wider audience and the variety of attitude and reaction. Putting ideas, arguments, positions down on paper forces more exacting definitions and decisions than we can get by any other means. It provides something concrete and specific to be examined, reviewed, and revised when changes can be agreed upon. It gives evidence of accomplishment and denotes some culmination.

The facts that a report has to be written by fewer people than can contribute to it, and that in order to have unity and good style it needs a single editor, hardly constitute good arguments against production. All the members of a staff of fairly good size can participate in the sketching process to produce scope; all can confer upon basic ideas and point of view; all can contribute to illustrations and examples of successful approaches and activities. When they do, the product is not some abstraction but a tangible entity and end point to give both pride and satisfaction.

There may be a few teachers who prefer to keep secret the special arts and skills which make them successful. Pretty generally we have matured beyond that stage. On the other hand, the willingness to share does not release a veritable flood of contributions. Those who have searched for practice and ideas for study council publications testify quickly that most teachers are pretty modest about themselves. They are not inclined to "toot their own horns" through telling about or writing out their most effective techniques. They think most teachers do something similar, and they consider their own very questionable ways rather "usual stuff." This attitude is further enforced by the inclusion in many publications by both official and voluntary groups of exceedingly obvious and quite elemental ideas, often with little proper screening of the suggestions.

Yet we are all hot on the trail of the practical as well as the novel. Neither comes for the asking. Both emerge out of hard work and as gems from many discards. When we have discovered them, however, we must of course pass them along for the sake of our students.

Questions for Discussion

1. Why is the problem of organizing for curriculum change currently so difficult in school systems?
2. How do intermediate, state, and national efforts at curriculum modification create curricular problems for local school systems?
3. Why is the participatory approach to curricular change being encouraged by curriculum makers?
4. Why is it important for the classroom teacher to be involved in local efforts to change learning experiences offered by the school?
5. Curriculum change can be opportunistic, directed, or participatory. How could you determine what actually is the case in a school system?
6. As a classroom teacher would you prefer to have supervisors free to visit you only "on call?" What safeguards would you want in your relationships with supervisors?
7. School systems are increasingly appointing curriculum directors, curriculum coordinators, curriculum consultants, curriculum resource workers. Do we need them?
8. Will helping the status person compromise a teacher with his colleagues?

Selected Bibliography

Alexander, William S., *State Leadership in Improving Instruction,* Bureau of Publications, Teachers College, 1941.

Association for Supervision and Curriculum Development, *Action for Curriculum Improvement,* The Association, 1951.

Association for Supervision and Curriculum Development, *Group Processes in Supervision,* The Association, 1948.

Association for Supervision and Curriculum Development, *Leadership in Improving Instruction,* The Association, 1960.

Caswell, Hollis, *et al., Curriculum Improvement in Public School Systems,* Bureau of Publications, Teachers College, 1950.

Doll, Ronald, A. Harry Passow, and Stephen Corey, *Organizing for Curriculum Improvement,* Bureau of Publications, Teachers College, 1953.

Henry, N. B., ed., *In-Service Education,* National Society for the Study of Education, 1957.

Kelley, Earl, *The Workshop Way of Learning,* Harper, 1951.

McNally, Harold, and A. Harry Passow, *Improving the Quality of Public School Programs,* Bureau of Publications, Teachers College, 1960.

Spears, Harold, *Curriculum Planning Through In-Service Programs,* Prentice-Hall, 1957, chaps. 4, 8.

Wanamaker, Pearl A., *Planning for Effective Education,* Office of the State Superintendent of Public Instruction, State of Washington, 1955.

Yauch, Wilbur, *Helping Teachers Understand Principals,* Appleton-Century-Crofts, 1957.

....

CHAPTER 14

Cooperative Procedures with the Staff

The application of local faculty study to curriculum modification is relatively new. A quarter of a century ago there was little emphasis upon faculty involvement in the solution of educational problems. Rather the question of what to do and how to do it was conceived to be the area of the well-trained specialist. The distinction between administration and teaching was quite clear. The administrator regarded his job as that of supervisor and director of all activities. Teachers, still rather poorly trained, were expected to follow the plans and outlines provided for them. The administrator installed the program and the teachers carried it out.

In the intervening time, the subservient position of the teacher has been appreciably altered. Increasingly, as administrators have come to understand more what democracy in education means, teachers have been invited to exercise greater freedom. The prerogatives of participation in decision-making about a variety of matters have been extended to them. The need for a teacher to possess the skills by which to interact effectively and to plan and produce cooperatively with administrators and with colleagues is now pronounced.

It is not appropriate here to examine in detail the many influences which have contributed to this trend. The improved preparation of teachers has had a great deal to do with it. So has the recognition by administrators that true professionals will not willingly act as automatons. Intensive study by the psychologists on change in perception, attitudes, and habits has undermined old concepts of leadership. The new science of human relationship has fostered enthusiastic exploration of how small groups and committees can function best to facilitate change.

Research from this movement has fairly convinced a great portion of those who have exercised leadership that change can be wrought only from the involvement of those expected to make the change. Additional support has come from the conclusions that through cooperative and group approaches

1. There is a greater volume of better ideas.
2. Wider responsibility and participation lead to increased morale.
3. Harder work and increased effort are released in pursuit of democratically determined goals.
4. More teachers find personal friendship and a sense of importance and reason to be professional.
5. Decisions are sounder and more defensible.
6. The burdens of office are spread more widely and decisions are more balanced and enlightened.
7. There is opportunity for personal therapy and the release of feeling.
8. Identification with other persons facilitates reorientation of position and brings about changes in one's own way of responding and acting.
9. Self-understanding is enhanced.
10. Others can be helped to change through group support and through clearer definition of what is permitted and approved.

As we have said before, there are teachers and administrators who are not in accord with this trend and who are unhappy because it has come about. The underlying reasons for their outlook are not easily fathomed. Some of their reluctance no doubt comes from personal concepts and convictions and deeply engrained habits, some from lack of careful thought about the matter, some from a fear of democratic power, some from a wholesome reluctance to be carried away by the most recent tub-thumpers who are excitedly convinced that "groupiness" will solve everything. However, it seems but a matter of time until even the dedicated opponents of cooperative effort will find some use, if not a great deal, for group deliberation upon a very wide scope of problems.

Difference of Groups in Size, Purpose, and Definition

There are of course a number of types of local professional groups which may affect thinking about the curriculum. They range from mere collections of fairly disinterested and casual onlookers to highly intimate and purposeful units. In between those groups who assemble by chance and those who come together for the specific objective of interacting vigorously with each other, there are many possible arrangements of person-to-person relationship which may contribute to curriculum change.

In the school setting there are commonly several formal and official arrangements within which personnel assemble. The faculty as a whole is one kind of group. Departments represent operational subdivisions. Small continuing and *ad hoc* committees are examples of the usual ways to bring people together for special purposes. The larger formal groups like faculties, regularly serve as audiences, as receivers of presentations and announcements, and as deliberating and voting agencies. By contrast, small groups more often are called upon to obtain intensive examination of ideas, to work out the details in broad plans, and to produce specific materials.

When we speak of cooperative action and group participation in curriculum development we may have reference either to large and fairly unwieldly numbers or we may be thinking of these small committees set down to explore some issue or concern. We may be thinking of voting groups or we may be thinking of several teachers who have undertaken to plan a research project or to produce a report.

Since the recent emphasis on small group function, however, there has grown up the idea that a collection or an assemblage is not really a "group." The word *group* has come to have special meaning. It is considered to be something more than a roster of people and names, more than a listening or voting agency of quite impersonal nature. It is an entity quite beyond its components and has a quality produced by the interaction and interdependence of the members. It is a kind of a unity to which the members give their allegiance, to which they have subtle ties, and in whose welfare they are personally involved. The difference between a good group and a poor group lies in the variance in identification and in individual self-effacement. In keeping with this more recent definition, it is generally held that good groups grow; they become, emerge out of the physical and psychological presence of individuals.

Group Processes

Regardless of whether one wants to accept this special usage, the purposes for which people are assembled or are called together determine pretty largely what procedures will be used. If the object is to transmit information or to secure information from an expert, those assembled will listen while an individual talks, a panel discusses, films are shown, recordings are played, or demonstrations are held. From time to time questions may be raised, comments may be invited, and attention may be stimulated. The control of the meeting will rest with the chairman or the lecturer; time and duration of the session will be determined arbitrarily or by acquiescence of the listeners to a suggestion.

If the meeting is large, the interaction among members, if permitted, will usually be fairly formal. The well-established rules for maintaining order may be resorted to, and a quite objective and impersonal atmosphere may be created and promoted. The amount of communication will perforce be limited and extensive exploration will be obtained only with the breakup of the group into smaller units.

When the group is small, six or eight members, most of the formality may be dispensed with. Members can arrange themselves in a circle; there need be no highly organized presentations. If reports are to be rendered, interruptions may take place easily, even during a pause of breath. Interaction can be much more intimate, and personal reactions and observations may be permitted and arranged for. In so small a group everyone can participate and active effort may be undertaken by the more secure to get the less vocal to contribute. Leaders may precipitate more active thinking and expression.

LESS FORMAL PROCESSES IN SCHOOL FACULTIES

In the usual faculty meeting there may be a compromise with respect to procedures used. More staff members may participate and communication may be less formal and more personal. Reactions to the way things are handled and proposals for novel means of clarifying issues may be quite in order. Comment and expression by members may be for the purposes of reflecting feelings, of encouraging response from the timid, or of summarizing contributions. The faculty may break up into smaller groups for producing ideas, for more intense discussion of certain points, or for suggesting better organization to deal with selected problems. Individual faculty members may present the reports of committees; there may be panel discussions; the principal may easily turn over the meeting to program chairmen or to the faculty group who have made the agenda.

Since most faculties get their work done through committees the most common processes used are doubtless familiar to nearly everybody. The problem assigned is more clearly defined and expressed through members' arguing out what can and should be done. Experts or resource people are brought in to suggest the dimensions of more lucid statement and to increase understanding. Through volunteering, tacit understanding, or group persuasion and pressure, teachers are assigned various subaspects for investigation. Ideas and preliminary drafts are brought in at a later date. Progress reports may be prepared for the whole faculty. Eventually the committees' proposals are presented, orally or in a dittoed or mimeographed form, for further reaction.

PROCESS THE KEY TO SUCCESS

Whether meetings are big or small, parliamentary or informal; whether they are for the purpose of transmitting information or of securing reaction, whether they are set up to raise morale or change opinion—they often fail. They fail in reaching conclusions, and they regularly fail in becoming the "groups" the specialists would have develop. The sorry records of some congresses, the occasional explosive adjournments of annual school meetings, and the final unhappy dissolution of endless numbers of committees stand as testimony that all that begins well does not necessarily end well.

Over many years there has been study of how meetings may be run most effectively, how time can be saved, how satisfaction can be obtained. We know that exasperation and hostility develop when we do not start on time; lack of interest and nonparticipation accompany overtime sessions; lack of an agenda leads to disorganization; inadequate chairmen permit digression; weak voices drown with their ideas against a sea of faces; improperly kept minutes misinterpret agreement. There are numerous volumes on how the processes used in a single meeting or in a series of meetings can lead to survival and accomplishment or to impotence and eventual bankruptcy.

Most of us are familiar to a degree with the ideas mentioned above. They have been taught to us in one way or another, through first-hand experience or in high school and college courses in parliamentary practice. We are not so familiar with some of the ideas on what is involved in promoting the growth of a group into an effective interacting unity. Most people are more likely to be acquainted with the precedence of motions than with the interpersonal elements that generate confidence. The means useful to and important in intensely deliberative groups have only recently been sought out for examination.

TEACHERS' NEED FOR THESE NEWER PROCESS SKILLS

Since there seems little likelihood that anyone will be successful in turning back the clock, it must be anticipated that more and more of the efforts devoted to improving the curriculum will be expended in intensely deliberative groups. In the medium-sized schools the entire faculty will more often explore more thoroughly and define more sharply what must be done to produce quality experience. In the large systems representative committees will have to be relied upon for general planning and the proposition of projects. Production activity and subsequent or accompanying reaction and participation will have to be secured in building units and in special work groups.

The teacher has practically no chance of escaping from involvement with others. Thus, the extent of progress and the quality of product will depend very much on the extent to which the teacher understands the dynamics of curriculum making groups and on his skill in helping to promote the unity and power of those groups.

Characteristics of a Good Group

Because there are many kinds of groups, one is at the outset at some disadvantage in trying to cast a framework large enough to include the numerous qualities found desirable when such varied groups are faced with different tasks. The easiest thing to do then is to focus on what ought to be the characteristics of the group with which teachers are most familiar, the building faculty. In the following paragraphs fifteen attributes of a good group are set forth. Obviously it is not proposed that the list is exhaustive. It will, however, provide some picture of what teachers and administrators should work toward if they hope to facilitate curriculum change by the power in groups to alter conditions which prevent growth.

1. Individuals feel comfortable and accepted as an important part of the group.
2. Individuals have a sense of responsibility for the group's success.
3. Each person respects the membership of every other person and sees him as a contributor and valuable resource.
4. Individual opinion and position are expressed and presented for objective valuation.
5. Each person feels committed to adjust and adapt in the direction of acceptable common agreement.
6. All members respect the individual's privilege of personal exception.
7. Decisions are arrived at after full ventilation and exploration. Methods of short-circuiting thorough deliberation are not acceptable.
8. Assignments and service tasks are willingly accepted.
9. Leadership is a function of tasks and leaders are valued and appreciated by participants.
10. Individuals are able to give up their purposes or see their purposes in the more general goals of the group. The purposes of the group are cooperatively set.
11. Interaction promotes broad participation and communication seeks levels of objectivity and unemotionality.
12. A warm, personal relationship and identification permits acknowledgment and analysis of tension points.
13. Evaluation of progress and of the factors related to it is continuous and has the purpose of improving the conditions out of which progress comes.
14. External impositions and frustrations are understood and do not fractionate and dissolve the strands of loyalty and unity. Recrimination and blame are controlled as directed inwardly and outwardly.

15. Deeper analyses of personal problems of participation and response emerge as confidence and respect for the group's power to help a man grow individually are increased.

Teachers Responsible for Developing and Maintaining Good Groups

We have already said that mature groups do not come automatically into being; neither do they grow because some curriculum director wants them to develop. They grow rather out of insight into the importance and value of intimate and personal democratic procedures, out of commitment to make groups function effectively, out of competent leadership, out of excellent and improving member skills, and in settings which permit and provide fertile conditions.

It takes determined effort on the part of many to bring about group unity and solidarity. The enthusiasm of the leader and the dedication of one or two is not enough. Unless the inclination to participate actively spreads to all members and each accepts responsibility, it is not at all likely that strong cooperative groups will emerge.

Promotion of Cooperative Democratic Procedures

With all our talk about democracy and our dedication to the ways of democracy and with increased numbers of administrators and supervisors encouraging cooperation, it would seem there ought be no problem in the schools about getting fellow teachers to accept a real share in decision-making. Such is not the case unfortunately. The search for enthusiastic volunteers on the high school faculty is often amazingly unrewarding. Nearly every staff finds itself with teachers who never make a contribution and vigorously protest either opportunity or obligation to attend meetings. Reasons offered are usually that meetings are cut and dried, dominated by the principal, limited to announcement-making, or fruitless with respect to discussion and suggestion.

More frank and revealing excuses can be elicited when some effort is devoted to closer examination. An appreciable number of teachers do not want to be bothered with deliberation. They do not, despite administrative theory or natural rights, see their job as that of advising on policy, even when it affects themselves. They do not accept the idea that subordination requires them to present their best ideas and thoughts to superiors. Satisfied to be dissatisfied, they would rather protest against than contest with discomfiting conditions.

At this point, too, not a few faculty members have already been fairly well abused by some pseudo-democrat or thoroughly convinced of the needlessness of democratic action by some benign administrator with whom they invariably found themselves in agreement.

It must be recognized also that although there is great turnover and replacement in staffs, a fair number of any faculty will have been around for years. Much too often, they have been "burned." They have deliberated and investigated, perspired and prepared only to find their reports filed, their advice ignored, their exploration of critical elements deflected or sabotaged, and their proposals vetoed. Cooperation to them is the well-known expectancy that they "coo" and the legal powers, principal and supervisors, "operate."

One cause of reluctance—among others that could be mentioned —is the well-understood or vaguely felt power relationships which exist within any group which is not truly democratic. With regard to power, teachers are no different from boy scouts or politicians. They soon learn whose opinion is respected by whom, who are the first to know the thoughts of the mighty, who obtains favor and recognition. On any faculty but a brand-new one, and even there because the chief invariably assembles his lieutenants out of past acquaintance and loyalty, there exists an informal status system. Any radical adjustment of patterns always threatens these vested interests and comfortable arrangements whether they be of the "kitchen-cabinet" type or some other variety of compromise. Thorough cooperative interaction will disturb old communication systems, introduce threats to established symbols of status, and create new alignments and relationships.

Antidemocracy is discouraging and exasperating. People ought to know better and rise to the challenge to implement what we believe in. That they do not is a sad commentary on the effect of our teaching. At the same time, it is a test both of our own conviction and our power as teachers to increase insight and to stimulate growth.

Exhortation and argument, coffee-klatsch discussion, and personal campaigning will produce agreement to make a better try on the part of a few. An in-service course which carefully explores cooperative selection of problems and management by the class members may restore the optimism of some. Fairly full ventilation of what is democratic and what is not, of what makes for group success and failure as an academic question, with several colleagues in the teachers' lounge may lead to good preliminary clarification. Even a speaker who tells an assembled faculty why curriculum improvement must and can be attained through high-quality group deliberation has a chance of stirring a few. But we dare not be too optimistic.

It is to be expected in most cases that a single teacher can neither be the initiating agent nor the sole agent in increasing regard for democratic techniques. Yet, where the status leadership is so inclined, in short time a nucleus of the like-minded can be recruited. Some plan or hope for a plan to develop group activity can be developed.[1] On most faculties one should be able to find some colleagues who see the importance of mature, deliberative groups and are willing to join forces to get administrative support directly or through wider faculty understanding. Here and there we can expect to find human relations experts or special staff members who throughly understand the dynamics in groups and have as an assignment the job of creating better human interaction.

Once there is an organization or a cadre for promotion, a great variety of steps consistent with the situation may be undertaken to obtain attention, response, conviction, and finally personal identification. These may include some of the following:

1. Invitation to selected staff members to compile agenda for the year's faculty meetings
2. Use of faculty committees to do manageable jobs; e.g., deciding on preschool workshop, planning of workshops, deciding on school calendar
3. Opportunity given teachers to react to faculty meetings and to offer suggestions for improvement
4. Subgroup analyses of perceptions of the principal's role after teacher evaluation of him
5. Intensive study of individual pupils as a case group
6. Utilization of the interest and devotion of those who wish to participate. Avoidance of forcing engagement upon the doubtful
7. Priority emphasis on working on the perceived and expressed problems of the reluctant
8. Careful reporting of the further action taken on recommendations and proposals. Participation by those concerned in further steps in administration
9. Scheduled discussion of some of the common techniques and procedures used in small groups. Better still is slow and casual introduction of them in committee meetings of routine nature
10. Demonstration by an accomplished small team of highly effective group interaction with subsequent evaluation

IMPROVEMENT OF DELIBERATIVE GROUP ACTION

Even though we may be committed in our own minds to exercising our democratic responsibilities, we should know that a great deal is involved in getting improved interaction and thinking. At the outset

[1] See Matthew Miles, *Learning to Work in Groups,* Bureau of Publications, Teachers College, 1959, for unusually fine treatment of how to plan and carry out training programs.

there is our own impatience with those who simply have lesser capacity and seem never to produce anything worthwhile. Also, there is our honest recognition of our own limitations with the realization that our betters see things more clearly than we do. There are the pouters, the intransigent, and the excessively argumentative who block agreement and raise tension to impossible levels. Conversely, there are those who work to rush everything to a conclusion, who are forever "moving the previous question," and who constantly wonder out loud if they are getting anywhere. Into nearly every group at some time or other come those who do not know the meaning of compromise, those who cannot examine an issue objectively, and who are intensely anxious to be given credit for any successes there are.

Group interaction is, at its best, costly of time. Short on sophistication, participants can easily prolong what ought to be done more quickly. Digression and extraneous comment come easily in groups. Repetition and re-argument of the same topics occur very often. At the same time issues are considered closed and abandoned before there have been understanding and consensus. They come alive at subsequent sessions, or, remaining unresolved in the minds of several, they impede later thinking and action.

Personalities Often a Block

Personal animosities and hostilities interfere seriously with any arrangement to get cooperative thinking. Despite our desire to make education a cooperative affair, there are on every faculty fiercely competitive people. Aware or unaware of their drives, they are intense in efforts to be recognized, to gain preference, and if possible to gain control. To these people groups are but a means by which they may support their own well-fixed perceptions and gain their own ends. Actually unresponsive to objective examination, they regularly hide their true purposes or are unwilling to examine very thoroughly what they are or may be.

Committees Often Viewed Cynically

Unfortunately, a great many groups are appointed or organized to do someone else's bidding, to work on problems and projects in which there is limited interest. Status personnel may head such groups. Members have no consuming desire to help. They may until the end complain good-naturedly or bitterly, dependent on personal conception of use and abuse, that they do not see what has to be done or why the task is important.

Related to this is the widespread idea of what a committee is. More accurately than facetiously committees have been defined as "the unwilling appointed by the incompetent to do the unnecessary." In not a few communities the faculty has been "committeed" to virtual revolt. The result is adequate enough attendance not to be accused of insubordination or lack of professional responsibility. The chairman thus inherits the task of getting out some kind of report. Committee members are quite willing to approve his effort, amazingly often without very much examination of the text before consent. They see their roles as that of playing along with a somewhat necessary evil and not being too disturbed by obligation of membership.

Lack of Ideas and Energy a Discouragement

Even when a purposeful group has been assembled, all too often there is breakdown because as bright as the members are, when combined they are not bright enough. They may see clearly what to do, but they can find no solution through exchange of opinion. They can not obtain good concrete plans from each other. No one has the energy or the brains to produce a format upon which there can be agreement. The outcome is rather endless and painful sessions, likely to involve recrimination and avoidance of blame through identification of scapegoats.

Perhaps as much the cause for group ineffectiveness as anything else is plain laziness, hidden behind a variety of dodges which protect against the direct challenge. Some laziness surely arises from dispiritedness from exploitations. Some comes from low morale resulting from inadequate salaries, dishonest practices of administrators, attacks on the schools, lack of opportunity for advancement, and from inadequate recognition and approval by supervisors. We should be less than honest, nevertheless, if we did not acknowledge that teachers are as subject to the desire to escape from toil as are their so often berated students and as are a great many more who have not grown out of childhood. Hardly anyone chafes at the bit to spend tedious hours at developing new courses, pushing better objectives and generalizations, or even producing a book of new-type examination questions. The verve so characteristic of the first-year teacher dissipates all too quickly across the years, whether we like it or not. The jobs of adopting a new book, changing assignments, preparing new tests, arranging different trips, or previewing films get postponed simply because they take time. Committees too fail to produce because there is work involved. Numerous suggestions for breaking curriculum log jams are vetoed because key teachers see the cost in hours they would prefer to spend in doing the many more pleasurable things nearly everyone now claims he has no time to do.

Improvement Necessary on a Wide Front

What to know and do for improving group work thus covers a very large number of considerations. Earlier, attention was given to some aspects of simply getting more than a cynical kind of support for the democratic process itself. In the several preceding paragraphs we have indicated that other efforts could well include study of the various personality problems of teachers and training in rather simple means of therapy and rehabilitation. Interest could extend to the tangible and easily understood elements involved in providing appropriate physical arrangements. It should appropriately encompass examination of mechanical operations and techniques.

The items discussed in the following pages are considered with no pretense that they include all there is for improving small group interaction. There are a number of books which give far more adequate consideration to what is involved. He who is very interested in being an excellent group participant and leader should certainly consult them.

Legitimate Use of Groups a Prerequisite

As we have said, many groups fail because they are brought together unnecessarily or for indefensible reasons. It is not at all unusual for teachers to be asked to do what a competent specialist should do or decide what someone constituted with authority and responsibility ought to determine independently. Regularly, teacher committees are set up by planning groups, more often by supervisors and administrators, because a faculty should be active, because creativity is a most recent "problem," or because the administrator does not know what to do and he wants some one to tell him. The volunteer method is used widely to get local faculty members to staff projects dreamed up by study council executives, graduate students, and professors. It is used to obtain research workers and "grass-roots" participants on high powered state-sponsored-and-directed workshops and clinics and experimental programs. It is employed everywhere to secure brains for report card investigation, follow-up studies, and surveys of resources. Reinforced by tenure threats, merit pay scales, and re-assignment practices, this volunteer method produces in wholesale amount committees which have something less than honest interest and certainly anything but unanimity of positive purpose.

As long as administrators or even well-intentioned faculty or system steering and planning committees conjure up jobs for others to do or seize upon the protestations of a few who object and so write job tickets for "volunteers" or appointees, we can expect low-level group work. This revelation should come as early as possible to the legally designated heads in schools and to their satellites and helping agents. We can hope that the training courses for administrators and the literature written for curriculum leaders will help them understand the point.

Again, the classroom teacher cannot afford to sit back complacently or petulantly until enlightenment is conferred upon or manifests itself to those in power. The obligation to help the high and mighty as well as the well-meaning but unfit devolves up all of us.

IDENTIFICATION OF TEACHERS' OWN PROBLEMS

The alternative to working always on someone else's purpose requires little genius for discovery. Group work can and should be organized around the needs and problems genuinely significant to the participants. It ought to grow out of identification and specification by teachers of what they want to study. Seldom should committees be set up if they do not, out of interest and need, all but create themselves. They should come about most often because the faculty really wants them.

It should take no very profound argument to convince all teachers that they are entitled as well as obligated to express personal choices. The demand that administrators and supervisors listen to and recognize teachers' problems is one refrain that teachers ought to repeat. The concerns of teachers may not always be appealing to administrators, but teachers who do not want to work on others' choices should in time get their own on the program. Independently and together the teaching group should without fear identify on what they want to work.

PROMOTION OF COHESION

When all genuinely come to want the same thing, we might expect a unified front and unreserved output in its behalf. If six teachers want to work out a better schedule for small ensemble groups so as not to interfere so much with regular classes, if they want to offer a whole-school approach for health improvement, if they want to lay out a plan for teaching world-mindedness, we might anticipate that they will pull together and contribute individually, freely, and enthusiastically. Such hopes are of course often realized, and six who want something very much do attain their ends because each gives and takes easily; each applies himself fully; each helps the others think through proposing, listening, questioning, criticizing, and so on. But small groups of teachers who set out toward common goals get sidetracked too and end up in sharp disagreement, with less than adequate results, and resolved not to get involved again.

Very often even a small committee of the faculty is composed of a few who want something very much and of others who represent various levels of intensity of interest. Their relationship, we know, is all too likely one of strained relations, uneven participation and uncertain progress. Whether the purpose is a plan or a resulting series of personal behaviors in the classroom, the warmth of sincere, common purpose does not develop, and whatever the outcome, it is limited by the absence of strong positive interaction and unity in the group.

Much has been made in conventions, in classes, and in workshops of introducing people, of having participants hear their voices by discussing their problems and so on. No one would deny the value of such procedures to get a chance group warmed up. But such a simple approach would hardly have much impact or be appropriate for a deliberative group whose members know each other well. In fact, the amount of knowledge faculty members have of each other and the experiences they have had in the past are easily the source for apprehension, distaste, and defensiveness. For that reason, it is important that there be as much cohesion as possible in the faculty as a whole before much attempt is made to produce more unity in a deliberative subgroup.

FACULTY SUCCESS CONDUCIVE TO GROUP SOLIDARITY

We know that people belong voluntarily to agencies that get them what they want and with which they can identify. Respect for and support of an organization increases as it proves effective. If we rely on this principle, it seems only sensible that the first order of business is building up in a faculty a sense of power and adequacy by the successful resolution of problems which brings rewards to the whole group. Admittedly, location of issues so fruitful is not easy. However, until most or all the faculty can report, "We had this or that problem and we were able to get relief by————," there is little likelihood that teachers will perceive the wholesome roles useful to unity in a group.

Projects to raise morale may need at first to be minor and fairly removed from the curriculum. They might include provisions for a faculty lounge, board financial support for an in-service course, or an altered distribution method for books and supplies. But as teachers come to see the faculty as a powerful instrument in obtaining what each wants on a less complex level, they should increase confidence in it as a means of approach to less obvious, more subtle, and difficult problems.

We cannot expect that an ordinary classroom teacher will carry all the weight in developing a "we" feeling in the faculty. At the same time good spirit and loyalty can be conveyed to others. The constant reference to "we" and "us," inclusive of administrators, in a reasonably sized school (fifty to sixty teachers) can have some impact. Initiative in proposing items for the agenda can bring attention to topics out of which there might arise a sense of accomplishment. Proposals to evaluate faculty influence and effect can lead to insights about meeting times, attitudes, and procedures used.

Teachers who have prestige and are respected should be encouraged to make proposals and set expectations. Group behavior norms, we know, are set by those who hold positions in the hierarchy of status. Teachers who, because of recent membership or because of absence of appeal, do not rate high with others must obviously win over to their causes those with more stimulus value.

PARTICIPATION A SOURCE OF IDENTIFICATION

Although gaining ends that count through group study and action will afford the most satisfaction, studies[2] on group function show that, short of accomplishment, good feeling and liking for a group are increased by group-centered leadership. The democratic approach by status individuals and increased participation by faculty members themselves produce support and loyalty. Part of this doubtless arises from the fact that we all preach democracy and jealously guard our rights to be heard. When the situation encourages us to exercise those prerogatives by which we set store so vigorously, we can not help but approve. Our self-respect is enhanced; we have evidence that we are wanted and that our ideas are worthwhile.

The more people interact with each other the more they can come to share ideas, ideals, sentiments, anxieties, and worries. Per-

---

[2] M. G. Preston and R. K. Heintz, "Effect of Participatory vs. Supervisory Leadership on Group Judgment," *Journal of Abnormal and Social Psychology,* vol. 44(1949), pp. 345–355.

haps some kinds of familiarity breed contempt, but the research on groups shows clearly as the song says, "the more we get together the happier we'll be." The more regular and the fuller the communication, the more adequately we can gauge the capacity of others to respond and to reflect in ways that will promote our well-being. The result is friendship. Friendship within a group is the critical factor in its morale. Wherever possible, then, we must increase the opportunity for faculty to meet in many places and in many combinations.

Mastery of Interaction Skills

Both in status leaders and in positively inclined participants there may be the proper spirit but at the same time there may also be a woeful lack of the skill and habit necessary to smooth function. We cannot expect that groups ever will come to have a real unity until members have developed those skills. We can not "teach" skills in a book, and there is not room here to present a lengthy transcript and analysis of a group in action to illustrate the timing, the use of resource persons, the pattern of questions and responses, the resorts to techniques for emotion relief, the helpful and hindrance roles of members, etc. Detailed records can be found in several books[3] on the group process. Even they can not reveal the most subtle of the skills which include gesture, posture, cast of the face in expression or reaction, and tone quality, and tempo of the voice. These can be identified and related to smooth function, consensus, rising conflict, or exasperation only in the very process itself and corrected for the most part only through exact reflection and demonstration by the offended, the aggravated, or the displeased. The best we can do here is to identify some of the skills which, when performed adequately, will facilitate communication, create good feeling, keep destructive emotion low, promote thinking, and so on.

Before we identify the skills that should contribute to cohesion, it may be helpful to make note of several other points. We must be sensible enough to accept the protest that all can not be "process." A good part of the doldrums which assailed group process after the first waves of excited support in the late 1940's was simply rebellion against the emphasis on technique and procedure. Very harsh opinions were expressed and rightly so. The enthusiastic got so carried away in

[3] Norman Maier, *Principles of Human Relations,* Wiley, 1952; Ronald Lippitt, *Training in Community Relations,* Harper, 1949; Franklyn S. Haiman, *Group Leadership and Democratic Action,* Houghton Mifflin, 1951; Herbert Thelen, *Dynamics of Groups at Work,* University of Chicago, 1954; A. Harry Passow *et al., Training Curriculum Leaders for Cooperative Research,* Bureau of Publications, Teachers College, 1955.

some quarters that those who wanted answers to problems only discovered that they were feeling guilty about their personality limitations and their antiquated parliamentary procedure.

Since then there has been a more sober view of how to proceed. Some schools have had training sessions with a team from a university to demonstrate good and bad technique. Others have agreed to improve their faculty meetings and committee meetings by calling in a process observer or by appointing one. Curriculum leaders and administrators have been increasingly using post-meeting evaluation, cooperative agenda-making, case-study analyses, and role-playing. More teachers have taken courses in small group function and know what they can do to help others. The idea that we have to turn people into process specialists overnight has disappeared. The emphasis now is on gradual change and improvement.

The four types of skill discussed below are useful ones in which any staff should expect to improve slowly. They surely are not examples of radical procedures. Rather, each is common yet important to the total function of any cohesive group.

1. *Objective and impersonal expression.* Probably more than anything else, what people say to each other draws them closer together or builds insurmountable barriers between them. We have always known of the power of words to soothe or to stir a veritable cyclone of feeling. Only recently has there been real study of the semantics involved in improving our relations. The volume of analysis has now grown to sizable proportions, and no teacher should have failed to study intensively something[4] on the use of language in thought. Words which evaluate others repeatedly enter our expression. We tell others what "they" have said rather than indicate what "we" have heard from the meanings their words have for us. We jump to conclusions based on our abstractions and generalizations and regularly fail at the quest for definition that will help us each say the same thing.

Some mocking has accompanied the effort of specialists to work through the rhetoric jungle, fun being directed at certain phrases which have come to be second nature to group dynamicists. Nevertheless, the teacher who says, "*I* hear you saying," "What *I* get from you is this," "Am I correct when I gather that?" has a much better chance of getting a complete translation and of keeping ideas straight than is the case

---

[4] S. I. Hayakawa, *Language in Action,* Harcourt, Brace, 1941; Stuart Chase, *The Tyranny of Words,* Harcourt, Brace, 1938; Wendell Johnson, *People in Quandaries,* Harper, 1946.

when he responds "You do not believe," "I think you are wrong because," or "You are unfair and unjust."

2. *Attentive and purposeful listening.* It is the height of simplicity to remind anyone that a person does not enjoy talking when no one is listening. Yet careful examination of transcripts shows repeatedly that people neither listen nor know how to listen. One example will suffice. In a presumably mature group a faculty member said what he was there for and wanted to know in what way he could improve pupil morale. The next three spokesmen gave him suggestions and comments and the general discussion for the next fifteen minutes was on that problem. But he was so busy recovering from his pointed, emotional, and accusatory expression of need that in effect he was in another world, reflecting on how he had told them, how he could have said it better, and how he could have been more explicit. Thirty minutes later when he gained the floor again, he announced, "Half an hour ago I asked. . . . I haven't got an answer yet."

We can laugh at this, but it happens repeatedly. Unaccustomed as they are to public-speaking, our colleagues everywhere are hardly aware of being present while they experience stomach butterflies and muster up sufficient courage to speak, while they are speaking and often not hearing what they are saying, while they are recovering, noting their perspiration, and moistening their lips back to normal.

Even though they do not speak, others are thinking up answers and disagreeing before they have heard a proponent out. Maybe the first measure of words clearly signifies an old refrain after we have known people for some time, but it does not always have to be so. Watch a group carefully, see how many are formulating a response before they have heard out the previous speaker, see how many are prepared to make their own comment unaffected by and unrelated to what the man on the floor has said or is to say. Repeatedly people ask for recognition before they know what addition, contribution, or exception has been made. Little wonder meetings get sidetracked, the issue gets blurred, and hours are wasted in digression.

3. *Purposeful contribution.* No one ought to be in a group unless he can help the group do something. That covers a lot of ground to be sure. For one can help a group by being hard to convince, by manufacturing gems of wisdom even if they are dropped with explosive overtones, by comforting others distraught when they need to concede, by tactfully adding support at the right time, by avoiding reacting when to do so immediately after certain others is to propose conflict, and so on. What we have reference to here, however, is in the

nature of the much reiterated role-functions which a participant may perform. At many points in group discussion there arise opportunities for one to summarize or call for a summary, for one to step in and de-emotionalize an interchange between two who are at odds, for one to help another accept a good point made by someone whom he really can not recognize as helpful or bright. By so doing we move thought along, keep conflict down, promote respect, make life together toler-able, reduce frustration and prevent the search for scapegoats in peo-ple or method.

Knowing when the crisis points or the gaps are at hand, perceiv-ing the need for initiative or for a corrective move is in itself a type of skill. The words used, the questions asked, or the proposals and sugges-tions made are important, but sensitivity to what is needed at a partic-ular moment is the crux of the matter. Much comes, of course, with knowing what can be done and has worked out. When it becomes clear that there is not enough information on a topic, a member who pro-vides or proposes a way to get it prevents wrangling over opinions. When the topic is too vague and ill-defined to permit concrete sugges-tion, he who steps to the board and writes down an outline or breaks the matter into logical parts restores focus and stimulates direct action.

Benne and Sheats[5] in their analysis of functional roles identified seven actors who can build and maintain a group. They are:

1. The encourager who praises, agrees with and accepts the contribution of others. He indicates warmth and solidarity in his attitude toward other group members, offers commendation and praise and in various ways in-dicates understanding and acceptance of other points of view, ideas and suggestions.
2. The harmonizer who mediates the differences between other members, at-tempts to reconcile disagreements, relieves tension in conflict situations through jesting or pouring oil on the troubled waters.
3. The compromiser who operates from within a conflict in which his idea or position is involved. He may offer compromise by yielding status, admitting his error, by disciplining himself to maintain group harmony, or by "com-ing half-way" in moving along with the group.
4. The gatekeeper and expediter who attempts to keep communication chan-nels open by encouraging or facilitating the participation of others ("we haven't got the ideas of Mr. X yet," etc.) or by proposing regulation of the flow of communication ("why don't we limit the length of our contribu-tions so that everyone will have a chance to contribute?", etc.)
5. The standard setter or ego ideal who expresses standards for the group to attempt to achieve in its functioning or applies standards in evaluating the quality of group processes.

[5] Kenneth Benne and Bozidar Muntyan, *Human Relations in Curriculum Change,* Dryden, 1951, pp. 100–101.

6. The group-observer and commentator who keeps records of various aspects of group-process and feeds such data with proposed interpretations into the group's evaluation of its own procedures.
7. The follower who goes along with the movement of the group, more or less passively accepting the ideas of others, serving as an audience in group discussion and decision.

Any classroom teacher can play one or all of these roles whether his faculty is trying to use the "group process" or not. As we have pointed out, when the faculty is together and verbal exchange is taking place, there is a process. It can be improved and the group made to feel better and more like a unit as someone expresses combined feelings, dismantles confusion, and restores direction and confidence.

4. *Effective performance of group maturing activities.* People can come to like their company on a superficial level pretty soon. What happens when they get down to serious business is the test of how well-knit they are. Such is the case with groups. Their strength is really tested when there comes the time for intensive examination of the process and the re-education of those who deflect, block, and paralyze good group production. Here no end of tact is required to reveal to participants their weaknesses, their limitations, and their failures. Disintegration of a group can come about quickly when faults are directly or indirectly pointed out. It is less likely to come about when the group has purpose and has had some success in achieving certain goals. Even so, criticism, veiled as evaluation and helpful suggestion or anything else and presented without rancor or recrimination, has to be handled with extreme care. It can destroy in a trice what it has taken months to attain.

Participation charts, interpretation, interaction analyses, feedback, and motive search need to be used as groups mature. They help push interaction to a higher and more effective plane, but they do require considerable skill. Even hypothesizing and wondering if this or that meant anything may be enough to touch off reaction in the insightful and resentful. Too fast movement into the business of locating deeper, more involved factors related to production success will threaten security and safety. However, real group cohesion will come and be evident only when rigorous analysis is possible. Knowledge of and final mastery over the subtle and detailed interferences are necessary to a group's sense of both existence and well-being.

Personal Adjustment an Objective

Groups can not develop or survive when members are beset individually by problems of personal adjustment. The excessively competitive person who must prevail and dominate and is made miserable by compromise or concession will constantly fractionate a faculty. He will invariably be in search of cohorts, more likely sycophants, to outvote and outmaneuver the remainder of the staff. Likewise, the hostile and resentful who rankle under any subordination and perceive others as out to reduce their self-esteem and to attack them, will divide to conquer, search for manifestations of injustice, and withdraw with their marbles like the petulant child in the springtime. We can not build a cohesive group without helping these people and those who are pursued by deep-set anxieties. We must locate and support those who are yet so childish as to be uncertain whether they want to be directed by others or direct themselves, and who thus teeter between accusing their leaders of neglecting them and fretting because they have been told what to do.

We can not describe or try to type here the variety of personality cases that might be found in a faculty. Unfortunately, there are people so badly adjusted that the normal range of skills available to the usual curriculum leader and ordinary teachers is not enough to handle their condition. If a really unified group is to be obtained, these people have to be counted out or the group has to be turned first into an instrument for psychotherapy directed by a clinician. Happily, the worst most faculties have are prima donnas—lazy people who would protect themselves by honest or feigned lack of interest, anxious men and women who do not want to expose themselves too much, envious folks who are fearful their colleagues will get notice or salary, and so on.

What these people need is respect for their human weaknesses. They need opportunity to see themselves fairly and to know they are not degraded by colleagues for their limitations. They need help with overcoming their self-doubt, their inclination to defend their ideas too eagerly, and their quickness to exasperation and anger. They need freedom to tell their difficulties and to confess their desire to abandon behaviors they know are not highly regarded by others. They need to be sure the faculty or the group is a family, ready to lend support and to defend against the prying of others outside.

To presume to be so mature as to have capacity as a regular teacher to be any or all of these resources to colleagues is to presume a lot, but certainly not too much. Life for all of us is filled with one confusion or another, and we find our way out more often than not through what we administer to ourselves with the help of those around us. We can be of service to our fellows by simply extending understanding to them just as they render help to us with their compassion.

EMPLOYING "PROCESS" TECHNIQUES

We know that a faculty assembled after school will talk, freely and animatedly in small eddies, about last Saturday's game, the expulsion of Joe Smith, or the new shoe styles. Called together by the principal they regularly pack away their enthusiasm and their ideas. Sometimes this grows from obeisance to recorded authority, sometimes because announcements are the order of the day, sometimes because of seating arrangements that isolate the individual or groups or interfere with communication, sometimes because no one has known what is to happen and no one is prepared to question, to respond, or to propose.

We have already pointed out that genuine deliberation can come when there is something to deliberate about and when the topic to be examined is of interest and real importance to the group. At the same time, well-oriented and positively inclined groups can and do lose momentum and succumb to confusion and anarchy because they need to know better some simple matters of interactive group operation and management. Despite the attention given to these quite uninvolved techniques and conditions, it is surprising how many teachers are unacquainted with "group procedures" and, more important, resistant to the use of several of the steps considered most critical to success according to the "process" students.

Physical Arrangements an Aid to Communication

Sitting in a circle, in an elliptical pattern, or in some other manner to make possible direct face-to-face communication is recommended in all the literature on group function. Nevertheless, constant pressure seems necessary to keep people so seated. Even in classes where group process is practiced and analyzed, students too often slip back into comforting row on row audience tiers unless the leader is vigilant. What a hitching and halfhearted shuffling of chairs usually accompanies any request to form a circle!

Still groups can be too large for circle arrangement. When they are, there is no use and not much common sense in forcing a faculty to it. We are wiser to reserve face-to-face settings, where unity and interaction build fast, to more manageable numbers, and in the long run perhaps most often to groups of not more than twenty.[6]

---

[6] The number chosen here is not proposed as any contention with those who feel that five to seven constitute the best-sized unit for intensive cooperative thinking. It merely proposes that groups over twenty in number become quite unwieldly.

Better Understanding of Leader Roles Needed

More than a minor amount of the reluctance to break out and stay out of the audience habit lies in an inadequate notion on the part of participants of what is the proper role of the leader, statuswise or otherwise, and of the functional roles of each member. We have heretofore noted that at some time or other all persons may expect to be leaders because they are sought out and followed for the resources they can render. Even so, we err if we use that idea to ignore the fact that nearly every group has in it at the outset and usually all the time someone who carries appointed or elected responsibility to exercise certain parliamentary prerogatives of chairmanship. Circled, squared, tiered, or tongue-tied, every group internally demonstrates a verbal deference and regularly manifests a spatial deference to such a person, more so if the group meets often. Mature old hands at group participation break down this subtle barrier, but the half trained will not. Neither will those who find themselves officially led by strong and dominating people. And certainly it will remain where participants have the traditional concept of a chairman.

Each teacher must again turn to the "group process" books[7] for an extended characterization of the proper leader. No list is sufficient to provide an adequate picture of what this accomplished catalyst can do. Myra Woodruff suggested the following duties for one selected to "lead" discussion groups in workshops on the improvement of instruction.

Sets an informal and comfortable atmosphere in which people feel free to participate
Helps the group to locate its major mutual problems within the broad areas of the topic
Helps the discussion to keep to the point on the topic of mutual concern to the group—rather than to slide off into tangents of concern to individuals
Helps the group to become familiar with resource materials in the areas of major group concern
In addition, the *leader* has the following responsibilities:
Provides optimum physical setting for the group
Helps group to get acquainted
States the purpose of its discussion and the broad area in which it is to work
Helps the group to find its major interest within the topic
Gets the discussion started
Makes it possible for all group members to share ideas and experiences toward solutions
Releases resources of the group

[7] See p. 413.

Encourages all members to participate by:
    recognizing minority points of view
    helping group members to find areas of agreement and disagreement
    suggesting at times that an articulate member "hold his ideas" a moment
        in order for the group to hear from the others
    utilizing contributions of each member
Helps group to come to some conclusions
Before discussion begins—makes some plan for summary so team understands who will be responsible
Allows time at the end of the discussion for a summary[8]

Similar suggestions are made in a leaflet distributed by the U.S. Department of Agriculture.

SUGGESTIONS FOR DISCUSSION LEADERS
GETTING READY

1. Arrange group in circle, so each person can see every other person.

2. Provide table space, if convenience, for leader and entire group, as e.g.:

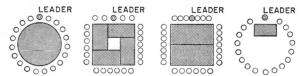

Source: *Suggestions for Discussion Leaders,* Extension Service, United States Department of Agriculture, n.d.

3. Let all stay seated during discussion, including leader. Keep it informal.

4. Start by making everybody comfortable. Check ventilation and lighting.

5. See that everybody knows everybody else. At first gathering go around the circle, each introducing himself. As a newcomer joins group later, introduce yourself to him and him to the group.

6. Learn names of all as soon as you can.

7. Have blackboard, chalk, and eraser ready for use in case of need. Appoint a blackboard secretary if the subject matter and occasion make it desirable.

8. Start on time, and close at prearranged time.

[8] Myra deH. Woodruff, *Suggestions to Leadership Teams for Discussion Groups,* New York State Education Department, 1957.

9. In opening, emphasize: *Everyone* is to take part. If one single member's view fails to get out in the open, to that extent the discussion falls short.

10. Toward this, emphasize: *No speeches* by leader or group member. No monopoly. After opening statement, limit individual contributions to a minute or so.

CARRYING ON

1. Make your own preparation for the discussion. Think the question through in advance. Aim to establish connections between ideas of background materials, and experience and ideas of group members.

2. Aim at outset to get a sharply defined question before the group. Have three or four alternatives put on board if you think this will help: "Which do you want to start with?" "Is this question clear?"

3. In general, don't put questions to particular group members, unless you see that an idea is trying to find words there anyway: "Mrs. Brown, you were about to say something." Otherwise: "Let's have some discussion of this question . . ." "What do some of the rest of you think about this?" "We've been hearing from the men. Now how do you women feel about this?" "What's been the experience of you folks up in the northern part of the state in this connection?" Etc.

4. Interrupt the "speech-maker" as tactfully as possible: "While we're on this point, let's hear from some of the others. Can we save your other point till later?"

5. Keep discussion on the track; keep it always directed, but let the group lay its own track to a large extent. Don't groove it narrowly yourself. Try to have it

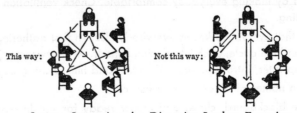

This way: Not this way:

Source: *Suggestions for Discussion Leaders,* Extension Service, United States Department of Agriculture, n.d.

6. Remember: The leader's opinion doesn't count in the discussion. Keep your own view out of it. Your job is to get the ideas of others out for an airing.

7. If you see that some important angle is being neglected, point

it out: "Bill Jones was telling me last week that he thinks. . . . What do you think of that?"

8. Keep the spirits high. Encourage ease, informality, good humor. Let everybody have a good time. Foster friendly disagreement. Listen with respect and appreciation to all ideas, but stress what is important, and turn discussion away from what is not.

9. Take time every ten minutes or so to draw the loose ends together: "Let's see where we've been going." Be as fair and accurate in summary as possible. Close discussion with summary —your own or the secretary's.

10. Call attention to unanswered questions for future study or for reference back to speakers. Nourish a desire in group members for continuing study and discussion through skillful closing summary.[9]

Varied Roles For Group Members

These criteria naturally will not produce moment-to-moment skills or change habits. Yet knowledge that leaders will be "up" to these ought to help each teacher perform his responsibilities or his group task roles.[10]

1. The *initator-contributor* suggests or proposes to the group new ideas or a changed way of regarding the group problem or goal. The novelty proposed may take the form of suggestions of a new group goal or a new definition of the problem. It may take the form of a suggested solution or some way of handling a difficulty that the group has encountered. Or it may take the form of a proposed new procedure for the group, a new way of organizing the group for the task ahead.

2. The *information-seeker* asks for clarification of suggestions made in terms of their factual adequacy, for authoritative information and facts pertinent to the problems being discussed.

3. The *opinion-seeker* asks not primarily for the facts of the case but for a clarification of the values pertinent to what the group is undertaking or of values involved in a suggestion made or in alternative suggestions.

4. The *information-giver* offers facts or generalizations which are "authoritative" or relates his own experience pertinently to the group problem.

5. The *opinion-giver* states his belief or opinion pertinently to a suggestion made or to alternative suggestions. The emphasis is on his proposal of

---

[9] *Suggestions for Discussion Leaders*, Extension Service, U.S. Department of Agriculture, n.d.
[10] Benne and Muntyan, *op. cit.*, pp. 99–100.

what should become the group's view of pertinent values, not primarily upon relevant facts or information.

6. The *elaborator* spells out suggestions in terms of examples or developed meanings, offers a rationale for suggestions previously made and tries to deduce how an idea or suggestion would work out if adopted by the group.

7. The *coordinator* shows or clarifies the relationships among various ideas and suggestions, tries to pull ideas and suggestions together or tries to coordinate the activities of various members or subgroups.

8. The *orienter* defines the position of the group with respect to its goals by

DISCUSSION IS SHARED LEARNING

| *Leader's Responsibility* | *Group Member's Responsibility* | *Everybody's Responsibility* |

Describe clearly the purpose of discussion, introduce topic, and define issues

Participate but don't try to dominate

Be friendly

Be honest

Encourage participation

Contribute ideas

Be fair

Summarize occasionally

Keep to the topic

Be yourself

Keep discussion "on the beam"

Ask for clarification when needed

Watch for signs of boredom

START ON TIME

Possible timetable for meeting

| Introduction 10 minutes | Film Showing 20 minutes | Presentation by panel or leader 10-20 minutes | Group Discussion 40-50 minutes | Summary 10 minutes |

Clear up confusion

Conclude before "meeting runs down"

END ON TIME

Source: *Suggestions for Discussion Leaders,* Extension Service, United States Department of Agriculture, n.d.

summarizing what has occurred, points to departures from agreed upon directions or goals, or raises questions about the direction which the group discussion is taking.

9. The *evaluator-critic* subjects the accomplishment of the group to some standard or set of standards of group functioning in the context of the group task. Thus he may evaluate or question the "practicality," the "logic," the "facts" or the "procedure" of a suggestion or of some unit or group discussion.

10. The *energizer* prods the group to action or decision, attempts to stimulate or arouse the group to "greater" or "higher quality" activity.

11. The *procedural technician* expedites group movement by doing things for the group—performing routine tasks, distributing materials, or manipulating objects for the group, e.g., rearranging the seating or running the recording machine.

12. The *recorder* writes down suggestions, makes a record of group decisions, or writes down the product of discussion. The recorder role is the "group memory."

Recorders and Consultants a Help

In addition to the leader, to function well each group needs someone to keep track of ideas and to make a record of its progress. Also most groups can profit substantially from a picture of how they have operated and functioned. And more than occasionally groups need help from resources which are not present in the members and must be obtained from outside, i.e., consultants. These service agents to the group, along with the chairman, have come to be called, in group dynamics parlance, the leadership team. A leaflet[11] prepared for an Association for Supervision and Curriculum Development convention in 1955 and subsequently revised indicates that the recorder should try to

Record major topics and issues
Select and record important contributions to the issues
Contribute to the group, using the discussion record as a guide and resource
Summarize the content
Assist the leader

The consultant or the resource person should

Contribute needed help *as requested*
Volunteer information when he or she senses the need
Encourage the use of all members' resources
Assist the leader and recorder in other appropriate ways

Miss Woodruff[12] puts it much the same in saying that he

---

[11] Fred P. Barnes, and Vernon L. Replogle, *Approaching Your Study Group Creatively,* Association for Supervision and Curriculum Development, 1956.

[12] Woodruff, *op. cit.,* p. 2.

Sits in the group as a group member, participating informally
Helps uncover and sharpen problems
Contributes specific information where needed
Raises pertinent questions or alternative points of view for group consideration
Refers to relevant material
Uses illustrations to clarify a point if group doesn't supply same
May emphasize or amplify important points in the discussion
Assists the leader by helping the group to stay on the subject

Usefulness of the Process Observer

During the letdown on group dynamics there has been decided de-emphasis on the functions and use of the process observer or analyst. Some of his duties can be and have been taken over by the consultant. Some originally promoted have been dropped along the way because these members take too much time away from production or because they were too threatening. Indeed, it does seem in retrospect that the "psychologizing" involved in analyzing the interactions in groups produced both guilt and cold feet to such an extent that teachers, and even early enthusiastic supporters, withdrew. Yet we can not really expect to improve groups unless we look at them critically (after they have become unified and can stand the shocks from external or their own objective appraisal). Mature groups certainly can profit from process observers. Developing groups ought to profit from some of the more mechanical and descriptive jobs an insightful spectator can do. These are

Secure a participation chart, revealing—
    number and types of contributions given by whom
    supportive responses given by whom, for whom, for what
    challenges and disagreements expressed by whom and after whom
Judge and evaluate the emotional tone
Assess length and nature of frustration to problem solution
Chart idea manufacture
Search for motives and blocks
Analyze the semantics
Appraise influence and effect of position, gesture, posture

ACCEPTANCE OF NEW ROLES A LENGTHY PROCESS

None of these servants of better function can do much for a group, however, if a faculty is not ready to have him act in the ways suggested here. Again, no genius is required to secure that insight. We can rest assured that these roles will have to be introduced to more than a few. It will take a long time to change the common mental map of a chairman, an expert, and a secretary—and their functions.

For us who are convinced that these roles are necessary, there exists, as usual, no simple formula for installing them. We can introduce these ideas by talking about them, by encouraging demonstrations, by promoting faculty member attendance at conventions and meetings organized into small groups, by posting simple explanations, and by supporting professors in operating in-service courses this way. Our influence will be greater if the administrator knows what we are talking about; it will be surer if we are modest and patient; it will pay if we respect apprehension and the tenacious grasp of habit. But what we can do will always be a product of the situation in which we find ourselves.

Questions for Discussion

1. What may a group leader do to help the participants feel at ease in a group discussion in a school faculty meeting?
2. What factors are important in the assignment of a committee to short-term functions or tasks?
3. Why do long-term committees seem to function with less difficulty than short-term committees with a special assignment?
4. What do you think are the major strengths of such processes as "brainstorming" and "buzz" sessions?
5. What positive effects does group participation have upon the individual? Are there also negative effects that may come from group participation? Identify some negative effects and tell how these may be prevented from occurring.
6. Why do some school faculty members become uncooperative and inattentive in large group meetings?
7. How would you differentiate between the status leader and the process leader? Are both of these needed? Why or why not?
8. How may groups make the best use of consultants? What cautions should be used in selecting consultants?

Selected Bibliography

Association for Supervision and Curriculum Development, *Group Processes in Supervision,* The Association, 1948.

Auer, J. Jeffrey, and Henry Lee Ewbank, *Handbook for Discussion Leaders,* Harper, rev. ed., 1954.

Bales, Robert F., *Interaction Process Analysis,* Addison-Wesley, 1949.

Benne, Kenneth, and Bozidar Muntyan, *Human Relations in Curriculum Change,* Dryden, 1956.

Bonner, Hubert, *Group Dynamics,* Ronald, 1959.

Hayakawa, S. I., *Language In Action,* Harcourt, Brace, 1940.

Haiman, Franklyn, *Group Leadership and Democratic Action,* Houghton Mifflin, 1951.

Henry, N. B., ed., *The Dynamics of Instructional Groups,* National Society for the Study of Education, 1960.

Kelley, Earl C., *The Workshop Way of Learning,* Harper, 1951.

Maier, Norman, *Principles of Human Relations,* Wiley, 1953.

Miles, Mathew B., *Learning to Work in Groups,* Bureau of Publications, Teachers College, 1959.

Thelen, Herbert, *Dynamics of Groups at Work,* University of Chicago, 1954, chap. 3.

CHAPTER 15

∙∙∙

Community Participation

In the comparatively rural and sparsely settled land of our fathers, the members of the local school committees selected the teacher, prescribed the curriculum, and set forth the policy related to the activities for which the teacher was to be responsible. The program of the school was evaluated in terms of how quiet the teacher was able to keep the pupils and how well the students could read, write, and cipher. Parents came with their children on the first day of school to meet the new teacher and to arrange for necessary books and supplies. On this first day parents talked over living arrangements for the teacher and usually it was set up so that the teacher would live a few weeks or days with each family. Later there were pie and box suppers in which the adults participated with enthusiasm. Every girl wanted her pie or box to bring the highest price and the men spent as freely as their purse would permit. The amount spent was a matter of pride and was considered a community contribution to education. As the year wore on, there were spelling bees, geography matches, debating contests, ciphering contests, and community sings in which old and young alike participated. The teacher was sometimes challenged by the most able adults at spelling or ciphering. A victory by the teacher was looked upon as a measure of teaching success or as a predictor of competence.

With the church, the school was the center of community life. Every hamlet had its school to make the offspring literate. It also had its school as a meeting place and as a hall where many of the serious problems of community improvement could be discussed. But few were confused about the role or function of the school. The simple charge to the master was not difficult for any citizen to understand. Teacher was not priest. Neither was he parent nor master-craftsman. He had his job to do, and the patrons soon knew whether he did it or not. Furthermore, in nearly every community there were citizens who knew more than the teacher. They were not threatened by him. He transmitted what he knew, and he did not explore too deeply ideas foreign to those found in the community and supported vigorously by those in power. He taught the familiar, the traditional, and the sacred: poems they too had learned by heart, quotations from the great orators and writers, selections from the basic documents, aphorisms bound up in special readers, and so on.

Communities and the Loss of Intimate Teaching Power

We know recent social and economic conditions have changed all this. The truly educational activities carried on by children outside the school have given way before the onslaught of the machine and its counterpart, urban living. The "chores" done by the children in the rural economy of that day have largely been replaced.

Their gradual disappearance has led to extension and expansion of the school's functions. At the same time the professionalization of education and the growth in size of schools and communities have broken the intimacy which existed when the school's functions were sharp and clear. Although citizens still attend school activities, although they may still meet in school buildings to discuss problems, what children experience and what occurs in school has come to be less and less understood by the patrons. The school has come to be "run by someone else." The citizen as likely as not may think "they" do or do not know what they are doing. There may be a board of education and there may be an administrator to approach and assail, but "they" are pretty distant figures.

The Citizens' Understanding of Transitions

In an earlier chapter we have argued that the program of secondary education must be conceived in the light of these changes and their effects if it is to be truly an instrument of national policy in transmitting our heritage and in guaranteeing our future. It has become imperative that schools offer not merely an opportunity to study the traditional matters. The society must permit them to have a far more comprehensive area of operation to make up for the gaps a different way of life has created. At the same time, we must recognize that the schools belong to the people. It is their prerogative and responsibility to decide what the role of the school should be. Although the citizens have delegated much of their intimacy and vigilance to boards of education and to highly trained and accomplished administrators and their staffs, they have not given up nor should they be denied by bureaucracy their basic task of defining and broadly directing the activity of the school.

A world torn with strife and rumors is dependent upon a people that is able to exchange services and information in an effective and easy manner and which has the character and quality to deal with the frightening problems of the atomic age. Recent inventions and discoveries have so decreased distances and increased possible destruction that a policy of "muddle through" is certain to produce too little effective cooperation too late to stem the tide of fear and defeatism. The only source of safety stems from the kind of people that live in the world. In such a scene, the American people again have placed great faith in educational institutions. If education is to be effective under these circumstances, it must be viewed as the responsibility not only of children and youth but of adults as well. Adults may not rest lightly on their years and pass judgment on the basis of their memories. They must secure the insight which will insure decisions about the school that will lead to an ever more adequate program for our time.

The necessity for a still more vital educational system has been brought to our attention with considerable force as a result of the rapid Russian advances in the fields of science and mathematics and of their challenge to overcome and surpass us in all fields. In a democracy, the problem of meeting an educational challenge of this type can be hindered or aided by the attitude of parents and other community adults and by their understanding of action and purpose. If the adults of the nation are alerted, informed, and helped to participate in making appropriate decisions for our schools, the immediate as well as the long term results can be dramatic and constructive and we shall have nothing to fear, either from the disappearance of our character and basic skills, or from the training or boasts and dedication of our world competitors.

Conversely, an ill-informed adult population may make anything approaching adequate educational opportunities all but impossible.

Teachers and Development of Adult Understanding

We in the teaching profession can not escape the import of this simple message. Our job is to make the schools more effective in obtaining and protecting the ends valued by our society. We must show those who have clear perception what needs to be done; we must help those who are confused or unconcerned and inactive to see what alternatives there are and what they must do to make a decision. At the same time, we as a profession must listen. If the public does not speak, we must ask them to do so—for the schools are theirs. Despite our custodianship, we may not run the schools without public approval and support. Despite our professional training and insight, we can not deny ourselves the great wisdom and creative power of the citizens. We now have known this for several decades.

Even so, the ideas in modern philosophies of education, carefully studied and examined, and the meanings for us in these varied social changes have led to an increasing gap between our concepts about the public schools and those widely held by the citizens at large. The scientific movement in education, which gained added emphasis after World War I, has also helped give the professional educator insights into the problems of education that are not commonly possessed by the general public. As a result, the public in most cases has lagged far behind. They are not only out of cadence; they are in large part confused and to an appreciable degree in disagreement about what is good and proper for the school to do. They are also petulant and resentful over the power the professionals have come to have through regulations, rules, and laws.

Changes made in educational offerings and methods, unfamiliar to parents, have led to a feeling of isolation. Some of the attacks discussed in Chapter 2 have grown directly from the fact that John Q. Citizen has suddenly awakened to find the schools different, and he knows neither how nor why the changes came to be. He suspects the dish has been too fancy with the spoon. Little wonder he has been cantankerous and will be more so unless we bring him up to date.

Our historical idea about public education has been to consider the objectives and purposes of education in the full light of public discussion and scrutiny. At the same time, it has been generally agreed that the professional should determine the methods by which these objectives should be accomplished. There is more than a little difficulty in this division. It arises from the futility of trying to discuss objectives in a meaningful manner without dealing with real school situations and problems. Thus, there is a need somehow to bring general considerations to a meaningful level with examination of situations in detail. The public has not had the time to do this; neither have they seized the opportunity nor responded to coaxing to do enough of it to relieve themselves of a gnawing discomfort as to the competency of their employees to work out the details.

CLOSE INTERACTION AND INVOLVEMENT A NECESSITY

Something more solid and something more intimate and personal than a custodial report is necessary. A good hard core of competent and well-informed citizens who know personally and thoroughly what must be secured and why. That can come only as many citizens are closely involved in a wide variety of the aspects related to the development and carrying out of a good program. This means study of such problems as school goals, housing, salaries, finance, redistricting, and evaluation. It means also closer citizen efforts to get the objectives of the school accomplished through involvement in the planning of learning activities and in teaching.

The teacher and the parent must enter into a partnership much beyond the casual interaction now commonly practiced. Somehow they must recapture or substitute for the warmth of relationship that characterized the traditional little red schoolhouse. Citizens must re-establish a sharp and clear understanding of what the school should do. Teachers must again communicate visibly and vividly how effective the school is in pursuit of its approved goals. Parents must work on many tasks along with the teacher because, despite their loss of the natural tools (side-by-side chores, long evenings together, home teaching of cooking, sewing, etc.), parents have not really given up distilling their own experience and teaching values and sentiments as well as transmitting knowledge and skill.

JUSTIFICATION OF COOPERATIVE EFFORTS

This is a pretty big order, and it raises several serious questions. Should teachers spend hours of their time explaining the need of certain operations to citizens? Doctors do not. Is not the teachers' place in the classroom—planning, aiding, correcting, stimulating, and so on? Administrators should clarify matters if anybody should. Should the public not trust its competent, professionally trained people to carry out properly those steps appropriate to the publicly valued objectives? They trust lawyers and pharmacists. Will not familiarity and partnership breed contempt and promote widespread discontent on otherwise unnoticed matters? Even carpenters are allowed to cover up their mistakes. Should teacher-scholars in special subject areas rely on uninitiated and uninformed parents? Who has not heard the old saw, "Speak some of that there algebra for me, son." Should we not at some point "fish or cut bait?" What is everybody's job is often nobody's job. Is there really enough profit to spend all the time and effort? Should teachers not "stick to their knitting"?

If we have any idea or hope of getting our colleagues—and ourselves—out of isolation and on the way to greater involvement with citizens than has been the case, there had better be a relatively strong reply to each of these questions. The desire to escape from prying eyes and explaining why, and to be free to do as each chooses is not at all uncommon in teachers. Home visits are widely denounced as useless and not worthwhile. Parent interviews are granted reluctantly by many teachers. And although most teachers will tolerate parents underfoot during National Education Week or a special visitation to go through the daily program, it is well known that a teacher does not want anyone to cramp his style by wondering why he teaches what he does in the way he does. We might as well be realistic about this.

The Broad Effect of Minor Changes by Teachers

Probably what the teacher does in school produces more home discomfort than any other source. If there is homework, there may be trouble over the T.V., over a place to do the work, over quality of work done, and over inability of the parents to do the assignments. If there is no homework, the parent wants to know why, berates the child for "having it easy," and complains against the school for neglect. When report cards as clear as cryptograms arrive, there is irritation over inability to explain this C or that D. Absence from English to practice baton twirling raises questions about what really counts even if it is obvious what children want. A year ended without *Old Ironsides* or *Barbara Frietchie* learned raises real doubts about what has been taught. Especially is this so when the parent knows his child visited the baseball museum, made a street survey about who drinks milk and how much, cut pictures out of every magazine that carried the mystery serial but does not know the capital of New Hampshire or the major river in New England.

In the examples cited here some of the trouble lies in basic disagreement over what ought to be taught and what ought to be learned to the point of good use and retention. Citizens may not object to the discontinuance by a teacher or by an English department of memorization of Hamlet's "To be or not to be" soliloquy if they know why the choice was made and if they know what replaced it and why.

Perhaps some day we shall be so correct in diagnosing what is needed and so wise in deciding what is valuable and can be valued that we shall escape the need to explain. Until this time, however, we dare not tamper with the righteous indignation of a citizenry who come to the point of discovering their employees have done away with their treasures. It is exactly some of this that has brought us to much of the confusion discussed in Chapter 2. In the last several decades we have ruthlessly cast out some signs of an education which many of the public could recognize. Without these familiar marks, we have cut them adrift. Little wonder they suspect us of either irresponsibility or irrationality.

Teachers and Explanations of Details

The changes in content and in approaches to teaching are so vast that we could not hope that a few individuals or a small staff working with an administrator could explain them. There is so much to be told that the only hope of keeping anywhere near up to date is reliance on the whole teaching staff.

Here each teacher must take hold. If he does not, in time the lack of understanding will grow into a mountain of disillusion. We have vivid testimony of this in the picayune aggravations that have tumbled out of those citizens who have finally become "fed up." Once one tries to reply to their barbs, he discovers the complainants are veritable porcupines of discontent. Blunt one spine and there are four more beside it. There is no access to understanding because there is such a mass with which to deal.

This means simply that curriculum developments need to be engineered, explained, and re-explained from the broadest possible base by all those who are involved in changes in order to provide the most complete explanation. There is no substitute for the teacher.

The Public and Exercise of Power

As extensively and properly trained persons, teachers would be a little more odd than they are *if* they did not bridle at the lack of confidence shown in them by the public. We have said before that the attacks on public education's adequacy have bitten deeply into the self-regard and morale of the profession. We know colleagues, some of long tenure, have departed in disgust at the abuse they have suffered from all-wise columnists. Teachers are on the whole sincere and dedicated. Their actions have always been in what they have thought the best interest of children. Mistakes have admittedly been made and over the years there have been wild-eyed if not false prophets who have gathered for a time a mesmerized following, but those who have cast aside common sense or responsibility are hard to find. Whoever accuses, we have an honest record, and we are hurt by those who say we do not.

An honest record, however, does not absolve one completely when he is a public servant. Neither does long and arduous toil at low pay entitle him to freedom from criticism and censure. Nor does special competence endow him with the right to decide alone what is right and proper and what is not. The fate of the public servant is to be exposed from top to bottom.

The crucial question is what should the public know and how much should they be told. Give an inch and thus perforce render up a mile? Or tell anything and everything and trust that nakedness will be blessedness? That we can not do the latter is obvious. We would have to make everybody who was interested a teacher. Impossible! But we do have to be less esoteric than we have been. Teaching is a profession but much of teaching is not as mysterious as operating on heart valves nor even as involved as producing esters in a laboratory. Anyway, when the public comes to decide whether we have made the grade, they need to know what we did in failing.

We can not resolve the issue here. But there is no reason why patrons should not know when phonics is taught and how, how the fractious and disorderly are restrained and reprimanded and why, what the new method of multiplication is and what supports it, how free art expression develops a more natural flow in later drawing and painting, how geographical facts are obtained through project study, what pupil-teacher planning accomplishes and how it is done, what muscles and skills are developed on a trampoline, and so on. Every teacher and certainly every faculty should sit down to think seriously about what ought to be told to patrons.

The Public a Help

Teachers are surely not perfect, and they need not think they need to be. However, tradition has it, despite low salaries and ridicule of the profession,[1] that teachers should be above reproach, paragons of virtue, and always correct. Who could expect else when we have made so much of the last item? The result is a deep-rooted fear in many of us that we shall be discovered, revealed to be merely humans.

But citizens know better and are more sensible. They share knowingly with all teachers the offhand but accurate admission that many teachers are but a page ahead in the book. They know we make mistakes, champion the wrong causes, violate all the basic principles of good educational psychology, yet we are forgiven and applauded for our effort and for our more numerous moments of superb maneuver and success.

It is to be seriously doubted that revealing a number of our problems to the public, asking their advice how to make up for inade-

[1] Washington Irving's Ichabod Crane.

quacies, inviting and using their resources will in any way lower our esteem. In fact, honest admission will get us farther.

To look at it from another angle, it is always better to "have it out" than to permit half-truth and error to fulminate into broad scale infection. As we have noted above, no parent can have a child in school long before he is caused to wonder if the teacher is anything but an ogre, an addlepate, or a sloth. Reports at home are regularly something less than complimentary. Anything that will represent the teacher in his true light and explain to parents reason and right in assignments, projects, detention hall, investigations into family finance and other secrets of connubial bliss would be all to the good.

One other point. Disrespect does not come from honesty when dignity and mature deference are maintained. No teacher who works closely with parents is under any obligation to yield his professional self-respect. All who have taught, even a short time, have discovered that one can come to have not only extensive knowledge of a pupil but real affection for him without yielding to excessive familiarity. It is just as possible with parents.

Citizens Competent to Aid in Curriculum Planning

How much citizens can contribute to planning within the special subject areas depends naturally on the kind of community in which the school is. In a university town where there are many excellent linguists, in an industrial community where there are engineers and physicists, in a rural area where there are top-flight farmers we should expect that those specialists would have much to offer. A teacher should be able to call on them with no loss of pride and with every expectation that their contributions will serve to make courses more functional and to bring them more quickly up to date. Technical schools over a long time have had their trade and vocational advisory committees. The participation of local farmers in appraising and planning agriculture courses is well established.

Less often have there been created citizen groups to work along with teachers on the general education courses. Social studies and English teachers, in particular, have not been inclined to employ members of the community to review and revise their courses of study with them, yet in these areas there are more likely to be people who have good background.

There may be communities where nobody knows as much as the teacher, but they are few and far between. Several people in almost every community are able to help. Their questions alone, their attempts to understand why changes are in order, their observations about approach should drive us back on our resources.

No Sacrifice of Prerogatives

Any conclusion that involvement of citizens means abdication by the professional staff is absurd. We are hired by the citizens to plan for and with their children and so to teach them. Responsibility for a class and for its success is clearly the teacher's. He must in the end reserve the right to make an independent decision and live with the consequences.

In general, the advice given with respect to defining the proper provinces for citizens and for teachers is that citizens limit themselves to deciding *what* should be taught and that teachers preside over *when and how.* This would mean parents could insist that schools teach about tooth decay, seek an enthusiasm for books, and obtain pupil knowledge of the events leading to the Civil War. Teachers would decide whether to employ tooth models, require colored drawings of tooth structure, have a visit from the local dentist, and in what grades to emphasize tooth care and protection and how often.

But we can see immediately *what* and *how* are not so discrete as they might at first seem. Whenever we start talking about something we want taught we can quickly get involved in *how* we are to teach something more abstract or higher up the scale. For instance, is sentence diagramming a *how* or a *what* if at a more complex level we are seeking good sentence structure? Are written book reports a *how* or a *what,* when at another level we are seeking appreciation of and interest in good reading? Is teaching the function of various parts of the digestive process a *how* or *what,* when we may be in pursuit of good eating habits, control of constipation, or general rules of good health?

We should be remiss if we did not recognize this ticklish matter. Some things are clearly *how* and some are not. We can not expect to separate all the *how* and *what* sharply and completely. The more detailed we get with *what* the more we are apt to infringe on *how.*

Patrons should be encouraged to tell us what they set store by, what they would like to see taught, what they think makes a difference on matters large and small. It remains for us to decide when they have begun to dictate method at our expense.

Citizens' Committees a Proof

In the discussion above, we have touched in general on what closer relationship between community and teaching staff ought to contribute to curriculum improvement. We have said it should aid more citizens in understanding what the teaching profession thinks the schools ought to do, it should increase insight into what is required in the way of resources and finances to accomplish goals people hold as important, it should reveal to the community that the staff have not taken nor do they intend to take their school away from them, it should strengthen the teacher's hand and provide him local supplementation with real competence, and it should serve to make the teaching profession more and more aware of what citizens feel their children and youth need to learn.

From explaining to and planning with the citizen we may also expect that there will be increased appreciation of our teaching problems and difficulties. We know that some of our most trenchant critics are all but ignorant of what now goes on in the classroom, in pupil scheduling, in counselling and advising, and in student activities. Even young graduates of public schools are inclined to fuzzy memories about topics covered, about discipline problems, about the volume of papers, and about the innumerable duties of the teacher. Honest citizens everywhere have acknowledged their experience tantamount to a revelation when they have taken the time really to get into the detail of an elementary or a secondary school teacher's day. Much less carping criticism follows. Much more interest in better pupil-teacher ratios, in higher salaries, in helpers and resources is forthcoming. The numerous citizen committee reports available from the National Citizens Commission for the Public Schools[2] reveal this vividly.

AREAS FOR COOPERATIVE EFFORT

The readiness and attitude of both community and staff will determine how general and how broad citizen participation will be in efforts to improve the curriculum. If no one has ever asked members in the community to prepare a monthly exhibit for the library and to provide a film series on serious social problems, requests for help may go unanswered. Even invitation of parents to a meeting to discuss the possibility might be rejected if the school has never been willing to ask for help. Anyway, the problem of getting citizen participation under way on any wide scale is not simple. It may well be years before we will find ourselves working extensively with citizens in the areas suggested below. Some of these problems of setting up and working with such groups are discussed in the next section. But first, in what areas should we anticipate working with citizens?

[2] National Citizens Commission for the Public Schools, New York, New York.

In Diagnosis of Community Needs and Problems

Most communities today inherit their school programs. The boards of education approve dibs and dabs because of occasional pressures or because they are forced to make additions under state regulations or as a result of college admission specifications. Witness the juggling of courses and the adjustments to suit the gifted. No community begins *de novo*. Even Oak Ridge, Tennessee, which sprang out of nowhere in World War II, although it challenged its staff with building a fresh and model program, was forced to accept a fairly restrictive model. It couldn't buck the system.

The fact, however, that each community is tied into a larger structure and must be responsive to the needs of state and nation translated into state educational requirements should not relieve it of the obligation to look at itself critically, to examine its strengths and weaknesses, to assess its lacks and emerging needs and thus to consider ways to improvement. A number of communities have done exactly that and their successes and problems are reported in several volumes.[3]

SCHOOLS IN THE LEAD

Sometimes the moving force in such a "look-see" is the local governmental unit, sometimes a voluntary group sponsored by the Chamber of Commerce or the League of Women Voters, or sometimes the board of education. Regardless of the impetus or the management of such a project, the effectiveness and the role of the school in bringing improvement or in contesting with varied conditions are soon under serious consideration. Members of the school staff, if not on the original committee, are called upon to suggest how the school can help attract industry, decrease delinquency, contribute to clean-up efforts, increase percent of those voting, obtain more adequate understanding of the need for slum clearance, retain youth in school longer, provide more suitable clerks and typists, work with disorderly pupils from blighted areas, and so on.

Few teachers or prospective teachers are now unaware of the "community school" argument. We know too that enthusiasm for it on the part of proponents has not swept American education like wildfire. Yet we should realize we as teachers can not build a good curriculum nor do proper justice to a community until we ask ourselves more often and determine more scientifically what the community needs.

But we do not propose to argue here the pros and cons of the

[3] Elsie R. Clapp, *Community Schools In Action*, Viking, 1939; Nelson B. Henry, ed., *The Community School*, National Society for the Study of Education, 1953.

community school. It should be obvious to all that schools exist to improve the life and lot of the people. The staff are hired not only to do the jobs a board of education and the citizens who elect them see as needing to be done, they are by nature of the contract expected to diagnose, suggest, and encourage. Thus, they can not justifiably long avoid examining both the influence and effect of education and the possibilities and potentials.

TEACHERS AND USE OF NUMEROUS APPROACHES

The teacher can proceed with diagnosis as a member of quite a large survey and investigation group, or he can contribute directly by working with students and parents within the scope of the "core" program or through a special subject. The English teacher and his committee can ascertain what the reading preferences and habits of the people are; the guidance officer with his advisory group can explore the personality successes and failures of graduates; the "core" teacher with selected adults can investigate the attitudes toward education; the business department can work closely with representatives from local industry and commercial establishments to determine what skills are needed and what practices will attract and hold young local graduates.

On Broad Goals and Objectives

Perhaps this is where citizens have worked most often and effectively during recent years, and it is a natural next step after diagnosis. It has become more or less the usual thing now for the board of education, particularly when contemplating building additions, to appoint citizens to study intensively what the local school is obligated to do. Such groups in some places have made very thorough canvasses of the schools' offerings, considered their adequacy for pupils who are in attendance, examined follow-up and success data, interviewed parents, and so on. Many of the reports submitted as a basis for planning buildings and for deciding on staff and equipment needs have been superb. It is quite often the case to have the committees recommend broader and more comprehensive functions for the school and to go quite beyond teacher hopes in proposing additions.

Many documents,[4] checklists, books, and pamphlets are now available to help citizen groups in this area. The National Citizens' Commission Working Guide No. 5 was produced to this end. The

[4] National Citizens' Commission for the Public Schools, *What Should Our Schools Accomplish?* The Commission, 1955; National Education Association, *How Good Are Your Schools?* The Association, 1959; New York State Education Department, *Teachers for Today's Schools,* The Department, 1948; James B. Conant, *The American High School,* McGraw-Hill, 1959.

NEA publication *How Good Are Your Schools* combines goals with evaluation. An early booklet of the New York State Education Department entitled *Teachers for Today's Schools* sought to clarify relationship between good education and good teaching. Dr. Conant's investigation into the American high school added another item to the list.

Committees that attend to school purposes and objectives soon run head-on into the question of what are the proper roles and prerogatives of other agencies in the community. On a correctly balanced committee there should be spokesmen for and loyal representatives of the church, the home, the recreation commission, and so on.

The thorough ventilation of relationship between school and other agencies may clarify how much of their functions the school should acquire, supplement, or avoid undertaking. But again we should not be too optimistic. We must be aware that who ought to do what is a question laden with explosives. Eventually citizens have to decide whether their schools will teach modesty, table manners, the use of prayer, respect for authority, fly-casting, joy in work or not. If they can not decide precisely, they will have to give strong emphasis to direction. In the tension which accompanies the formulation, teachers need be prepared to explain why they think the school should or should not extend itself in specific areas.

On Explanations of Learning and Teaching

It is a fact that everybody has learned and everybody has taught. Each may at the outset say he was not so good at either, but deep down most people have their ideas how learning and teaching could be improved. Citizens too on the whole pretty well agree with professionals on some of the most basic aspects of the teacher's work. They believe teachers should be patient, should "not get above a kid's head," should provide practical illustrations, and should create learning situations where pupils can work out their own answers (learn by doing!). They also agree that sarcasm and continued public abuse are injurious, that better learning takes place when children are really interested and happy, and that analyses of the causes of error must accompany attempts to learn.

We also know the school's patrons have some outmoded ideas about the teacher's roles in the classroom, about motivation and discipline, about drill and retention, and so on. Much of our tribulation comes because the citizens are much more supportive of atomistic psychology than they are of Gestalt psychology.

This does not mean one should set out to make the local butcher into an educational psychologist. But it does mean we will have little success in convincing him of the sense of a "core" program, the advisability of teacher-pupil planning, or the need for trips, projects or even unfamiliarly titled units until he can manage in his own words the basic concepts derived from our prodigious research.

P.T.A. meetings offer some opportunity to explain how we teach and why. Occasional reports to civic clubs and to preschool parents, careful explanations in parent interviews and committee meetings on report cards and reporting procedures provide fairly easy channels for instrumental explanation. A great many schools have a parents' night now in which teachers explain what they hope to do and how.

Long experience with public schools and their relations with parents has convinced us, the authors, that for years much much less explanation has taken place than ought to have been the case. When a wrathful citizenry rises up in annual meeting to jeer at the guidance department, to ridicule a developmental reading program, and to cheer when someone cries in anger that "we ought to put the teacher back in the driver's seat," we should know something is out of kilter and more than a few are hopelessly uninformed. Still, school after school can report little systematic effort to help the public get enough insight to approve and support the changes the staff would like and ought to make. Every teacher sincerely interested in curriculum improvement should insist that he and his colleagues decide "what they know and can explain about learning" and that a plan be developed for raising the community's level of understanding.

On Broad Framework Changes

How the public school and its curriculum are organized and what the structure for educating children will be does not change very often or very radically. Yet even minor changes are commonly known to arouse protest and resentment. Much of the hurricane which has struck the "educationists" gathered force over the years because bit by bit additions and deletions were made without sufficient notice to those who could be concerned.

If we have any hope of accomplishing some of the major surgery curriculum specialists encourage us to undertake (items like a subjectless "core," community school techniques in learning, ungraded primary units, functional subject approaches, and broad scale teacher-pupil-parent planning) we have no alternative but to share our hopes and fears through all the years with more than the usually quite inarticulate and unconvincing members of the board of education. Board members seldom have a good constituency to report to, and it is seldom one finds them actively engaged in testing community sentiment widely or well or engaged in reporting in anything like sufficient detail what they support. The administration and the teachers in most schools have got to get out beyond the board, not to play both ends against the middle, but to guarantee the generous public enlightenment, detailed argument, and explanation even the best newsletters and periodic public statements will not produce.

In the Study of Boys and Girls

Although the teacher develops many fine skills and transmits precious items of knowledge, he hardly begins to approach the parent in his scope or critical function. Yet the parent for the most part is a rank amateur, perennially asking the plaintive questions, "Am I doing right? Is there not a better way? If I only knew what children are really able to be like?" Teachers may need to know more about children in order to educate them, but how much better equipped they still are than "Ma" and "Pa." Parents everywhere envy teachers their courses in child development and adolescent psychology even though in their exasperation they regularly abjure the recommendations of the common newspaper advisor while half-heartedly trying them.

The modern parent wants to know more about his children— "What makes them tick, what their current problems and worries are, how to get to them." He wants help wherever he can get it. The resounding success of books on bringing up children ought to clinch this point if nothing else would.

Of course, we as teachers are nowhere near as confident of our knowledge of children as those amateurs are of it. A good taste of the abstract cross-sectional data stuffed into psychology books and a few ineffectual encounters with one of mother's little demons are enough to remind us we have but scratched the surface. The fact that each child is an individual and has his own reasons for behaving dawns on us with a thump after a few days in the classroom if we have been a little evasive about it before that.

Where could there be a better situation? We invariably need and want to know more and so do parents. Cooperative study will relieve some of our headaches over lack of knowledge about pupils. It should also reveal increasingly plainly to both parents and teachers what the evolving and emerging needs of children are, what experience is pertinent to their progress toward maturity, and what curricular adaptations will serve best.

In Planning and Carrying on Instruction

At all times we may be sure the parent is most interested in what is happening to his own child in the classes he elects or is forced to attend. Few teachers have escaped with a teaching career free of some parents who have offered advice on how John should be taught, of some who have asked, "Why in the name of goodness should you teach the subjunctive of *to be* now?" or of some who have "heard" lessons at home or who have done the homework. We hear anguished protests that "they" are unresponsive, but a little pressure and some direct encouragement rouses most adults out of any exhaustion parenthood has created in them.

There are so many ways a teacher can use citizens that it will not do to discuss each of them. We shall content ourselves rather with indicating some of the more common bridges teachers have used independently in search of close cooperation with the community.

As with most other activities, good bridges can be planned long in advance and a ready store of ideas is helpful. On the other hand, we must admit no canned list could ever be complete or adequate. First it would get out of date. Most important, dependence upon it would steal away from a teacher his birthright as a professional to be inventive, creative, and individual in carrying out general principles with which he is in agreement.

These practices are ones which have been reported in the authors' classes or observed in communities with which we have worked. Interesting summaries of a more detailed nature can be found in Helen Storen's pamphlet,[5] in a chapter by Gertrude Fitzwater in the National Society yearbook,[6] and elsewhere.[7]

Citizens have

1. Read compositions for the English teacher
2. Made a roster of specialists in any number of areas
3. Given reports of trips and personal experiences

[5] F. Helen Storen, *Laymen Help Plan the Curriculum*, Association for Supervision and Curriculum Development, 1946.

[6] Gertrude Fitzwater, "Cooperation Helps Individual Classrooms," in *Citizen Cooperation for Better Public Schools*, Nelson B. Henry, ed., National Society for the Study of Education, 1954.

[7] Association for Supervision and Curriculum Development, *Toward Better Teaching*, The Association, 1949; Nelson B. Henry, ed., *The Community School*, *op. cit.*; Association for Supervision and Curriculum Development, *Building Public Confidence in the Schools*, The Association, Washington, 1949; United States Office of Education, *Working with Parents, A Handbook*, Government Printing Office, Washington, 1949; Edward G. Olsen, *et al.*, *School and Community*, Prentice-Hall, New York, 1945.

4. Acted as teachers' aides in supervision on playground, in cafeteria
5. Planned and participated in culminating activities; festivals, recitals, plays, debates, forums
6. Helped investigate local historical matters: anti-rent wars, first settlements, family geneaology, famous murders and ghost stories, folk tales
7. Constructed equipment
8. Explored and agreed on what to teach about labor-management relations, sex, comparative religion, communism, political party positions
9. Tabulated and analyzed results from local and standardized tests
10. Guided trips and chaperoned parties
11. Interviewed graduates, businessmen, and fellow citizens
12. Studied what a course of study ought to include
13. Decorated rooms and arranged parties
14. Examined the effect and impact of trips and excursions
15. Made with pupils prior investigation and arrangements for trips and field studies
16. Studied industrial shifts and developments to identify areas of instructional need
17. Read professional books on method, the "core," and helped teachers perfect skills
18. Prepared evaluation forms
19. Regularly prepared a bulletin board
20. Accumulated information about practical use of subject knowledge
21. Worked on mutually agreed upon objectives at home and reported degree and kind of progress
22. Thoroughly studied the subject's place in a liberal education
23. Taught special subgroups in the evening or on Saturday, contributed special talents too numerous to list
24. Helped explain courses to lay groups
25. Explained their work or the function of agency, or the problems of the community
26. Investigated what other institutions teach and should teach, and sought ways to relieve the teacher of these obligations
27. Prepared bulletins on discipline, on homework supervision, on how to study
28. Examined supplementary books, prepared bibliographies, and appraised difficulty level of books
29. Made a problem census with a class and helped them diagnose their needs through adult complaints and criticisms
30. Supervised student work experience in voluntary agencies

In Cooperation on Evaluation

None of the areas discussed above could be explored without suitable plans for evaluation. Diagnosis is evaluation; planning is evaluation, study is really evaluation; for evaluation is locating something, determining its nature and amount, and putting a value on it. If we do not have enough of something, or it is not complete enough, or we can not manage it, we undertake to acquire more, see more, control more, and so on. Evaluation is and ought to be an integral and continuous part of doing anything and thus in part relatively informal. However, there are times and places for quite formal investigations and accounting, and we can separate such testing and appraisal periods in a fairly definitive way.

On the whole, school systems have not gone in for systematic studies of their success in relation to the objectives they have accepted or the needs of the community. Although the school survey carried on independently by a university or cooperatively with the community under the direction of university professors or state education department personnel has been used generally around the country, actually only a comparatively few school systems have been touched. The *Evaluative Criteria*[8] and evaluation instruments[9] developed in several states and by other agencies have been used more widely, but still citizens have been sparingly involved. In some communities rather good publicity has followed on the final report, and various citizens groups have been presented the recommendations and given opportunity to read and discuss the printed or mimeographed copy. It is generally agreed, however, that there ought to be more involvement, more often. The sentiments of the people are critical, and we should have more accurate estimates of them than we customarily do. Barbers, grocers, and garagemen talk and vote. Seldom do teachers really know what they think or what they know and have to think with.

The compilation of details of a more formal and organized study of the extent and adequacy of the school program should be led by the administrators. Every classroom teacher should have his proper part in advising on the areas for consideration and the approaches and instruments to be used. Constantly he should also encourage invitation to competent citizens to provide reactions and to share in interpreting the results of inventories,[10] questionnaires, and interviews.

GUIDES FOR WORKING WITH THE COMMUNITY AND CITIZENS GROUPS

In any community a misspoken word, impatience with those who are opposed or slow to understand, neglect of the niceties of good human relations can easily tip the precarious balance which means

[8] Cooperative Study of Secondary School Standards, *Evaluative Criteria,* 1950.

[9] Southern Association, *Evaluating the Elementary School,* The Association, 1949; Texas Education Agency, *Evaluating the Elementary School,* The Agency, 1949; New York State Education Department, *Teachers in Today's Schools, op. cit.*

[10] Harold C. Hand, *What People Think About Their Schools,* World Book, 1948.

good will and good support. Siding with one group or appearing to may quickly alienate another; few communities are immune to animosities and struggles for power. Overeagerness to reveal all and to lay bare the bones of discontent will more likely than not lead to gossip, to lack of confidence and in the end to diminished respect. The business of working directly and regularly with citizens is not as easy as "falling off a log." Rather it is an enterprise requiring much good sense, tact, a deep insight into people, and an understanding and sensitivity in depth to the dynamics common to community life.

We must admit many teachers have had little opportunity to examine seriously the nature of communities and their processes. Not many training institutions require courses in educational sociology or sociology. Very few school orientation programs include any adequate introduction to and analysis of community forces for new teachers. It is not at all surprising to find teachers with ten years' tenure in a system who are quite unaware of who really talks to whom, who entertains whom, who one sees to get things done, what roles and responsibilities are coveted in the community, and so on. The larger the population center, the more involved and invisible the lines of relationship. So much so is this true that in larger cities the classroom teacher is seldom concerned and leaves community dynamics and their diagnosis to the superintendent and his staff.

But such escape or ignorance should neither be necessary nor justified. In suburban, rural, and small village systems the teacher should find it fairly easy to become informed. In the city the most important unit for curriculum study and improvement is the building staff and the local area of the city they serve. With the elementary group, except in a special school for the gifted or the handicapped, the service areas for each school are nearly always well defined. In some cities there may be more difficulty at the high school level. But in most school systems teachers could and should attend more to what forces are at work in the community.

This point made, we propose that each teacher extend his perception about what to look at, where, and how to look at his community. Several references are listed below.[11]

We would turn our attention then in the remainder of this chapter

[11] Edward G. Olsen, *op. cit.,* chap. 3; Lloyd Cook, *Community Backgrounds of Education,* McGraw-Hill, 1958; Robert J. Havighurst, and Bernice L. Neugarten, *Society and Education,* Allyn and Bacon, 1957; William O. Stanley, *Social Foundations of Education,* Dryden, 1956; August B. Hollingshead, *Elmtown's Youth,* 1949.

to examination of some of the more common problems likely to be encountered by teachers in working more closely with citizens and to some suggestions on how to make cooperative work more effective. The following guides in each case do not apply equally to general study and policy committees, production groups, or instrumental arrangements made by a classroom teacher. The short discussions, however, emphasize the application.

1. *Cooperation should be an approved policy.* Every teacher will come to meet and work somehow with citizens in the community. Churches are always anxious to have them as members of the choir, Sunday School teachers, and leaders of their youth groups. The civic clubs seldom overlook the prospects of a new member. Someone from the school regularly makes a good addition to the fire company, the Legion, or fraternal organizations. Likewise, the alert teacher can hardly help but explore and make his own way. We have all been taught to locate the spots for good field trips, encouraged to invite parents to chaperone, and advised to enlist speakers and resource persons into our classes.

These natural interactions and communications should lay the groundwork everywhere, but on the whole they are too casual and individual. The total influence is usually all to the good; we earn respect, have numerous opportunities to explain and champion causes, smooth ruffled feelings and earn supporters. But the steps taken should be "official."

Thus, the teacher should expect the board of education to adopt a resolution indicating its desire to have broad-scale teacher interaction in behalf of curriculum improvement with citizens in the community. This will clarify both for the citizens and the administrators the responsibilities the board sees them as having. It should at the same time define the prerogatives of the committees and groups which may be created and specify the steps and procedures to be used in setting up cooperative arrangements.

This statement[12] issued by the Battle Creek, Michigan, board is illustrative:

"Recognizing the growing importance of public education in American democracy and being in complete agreement with the point of view that the schools should remain close to the people and that they should maintain constant contact with all elements in the community; and accepting the principle that all concerned with the work of public education—the pupils, parents, and

[12] Association for Supervision and Curriculum Development, *Building Public Confidence in the Schools,* The Association, p. 24.

teachers—should have a part in developing the educational policy in the schools; we, the members of the Board of Education of Battle Creek, hereby go on record endorsing the instruments of democratic cooperation now functioning in our educational program, including the Parent-Teachers Association, Educational Advisory Council, the Teachers' Association, the Engineer-Custodian's Association, the Secretaries Association, and the City-Wide Student Council.

"As a Board, we wish to encourage study, discussion, and active participation by all concerned through their several organizations in the promotion of the best possible program of education for our community. We believe that effective education for democratic living takes place only when edequate provision is made for actual practice in democratic action.

"In recognizing the above mentioned cooperating organizations in the educational program of the Battle Creek public schools, and by encouraging their active participation in educational policy-making, we wish to make it clear that in no way does the Board wish to escape its responsibility to the citizens of the community as the official governing body responsible to the people for a final decision on all matters of policy and educational programs.

"Under the statutes of the State of Michigan, the Board assumes its full responsibility in all matters relating to the program of public education in the City of Battle Creek, and invites fullest cooperation from all groups through suggestion, discussion, and recommendations, reserving to itself the right and the obligation to make final decisions based upon available evidence on all matters affecting the educational program carried on in the public schools of Battle Creek."

2. *Citizen cooperation should be coordinated.* It is easy to see that such general encouragement could produce a rush of activity well out of hand. So much could get underway in a good-sized community and so many could become involved that responsible school officials might lose track. In any community, citizens with good intentions or with ulterior purposes can assemble to talk about and plan for the schools. They do not need the sanction of the board nor the services of any one connected with the local schools.

But where activities are undertaken in behalf of the board and by its official representatives the "horse is of another color." As teachers, we should certainly insist upon the right to make free professional choices in behalf of better education. But in cases when we do have better communication and more detailed description of curriculum building efforts in the hands of some coordinating, guiding, and evaluating agency we may avoid numerous pitfalls: overlapping, partial coverage with consequent protest, teacher-teacher disputes, retrial of earlier failures and so on.

In connection with this point, it is worth mention that it is not impossible to saturate a community or some parts of it to exasperation with requests for help. The likelihood is diminished if citizens, banks, industries, lawyers, and other sources are indoctrinated slowly. However, we must admit that the common expectation is that pupils will be taught in school by teachers. We can ask too often for the same explanation or demonstration. Also we can frequently err in utilizing community resources already fairly well explored by pupils. We might talk our way out of the situation described below, but we must recognize the potential danger in overuse.

The manager of a large local dairy maintaining a "Public View" milking operation asked a visiting first grade how many present on a trip to the milking barn had not seen "bossy" do her business through that particular plate glass before. Everyone present allowed as how his daddy had brought him there to see the sights. The manager, Chicken Little that he was, told the custodian of the nearby conservation department maintained game farm what he had found out, at the local barber shop. Lo and behold, when the first grade bussed over the hilltop to squeal at the raccoons and offend the captive bear, the proper query revealed a fateful answer! Every first grader had been to the game farm with his daddy too.

The properly trained teachers, who have learned all about planning with children, will doubtless snort at this ineptness or respond with poise that we can learn many different things from the same experience, with a parent, with a teacher, or with another teacher. Agreed and happily supported! But members of the public who do not know that or do not accept it are apt to wonder where our common sense is and how respectful we are of the time of children when we take them where they have been before.

3. *We should state clearly and simply the job to be done.* Here seems another rather obvious point. Would any reasonable person enlist citizens if he did not know what for? Probably not, but there are several in this world who provide groups with assignments vague enough or "sweet talk" camouflaged sufficiently that they accept without knowing "what they are in for" and quite at a loss to know what to do after they are assembled. Membership on such committees has surely been the dubious pleasure of thousands of teachers!

Not only should the task to be undertaken be well defined, the charge also ought to indicate a time for completion of deliberation and the nature of the product anticipated. The time of citizens these days has become more and more heavily committed. Assemble any group, relatively small as working units should be, and you soon discover how impossible it is to set a day and hour for meeting. Experience with lay advisory committees shows attendance not to be better than 50 percent. Long drawn-out assignments, requiring good communication and interaction, are simply out of the question.

4. *A balance of focus is imperative.* When we begin to identify people to help us, to constitute the room committee, to plan a year-end culmination, to advise on the content of a course, to work with our faculty appointees on grouping, we can pull the switches that blow the fuses or that light our way to progress. Some people say they do not want to be consulted or involved, but there is little evidence that they abound in numbers.

This is where knowledge of community and awareness of attitudes, of differences of opinion, of diverse commitments among patrons are important. There are those who "expect" to be on one type of committee and would resent being degraded to another. There are those whose service on a vocational committee would only be in behalf of disruption. There are some who want "in" but are discomfited in the presence of the "wheels." There are the anxious and the determined who want their way and the quiet and inarticulate who save their disagreement and disavowal for the safety rendered by cliques and intimates. There are those who are in contention over the success of their offspring, over family status, and over popularity in aspects of community life. The types and varieties are endless.

We cannot expect to know all the motives, hopes, prejudices, and other traits and states of mind and personality of those we enlist and of those whom we do not enlist, but who can and do react. Yet we cannot ignore the fact that groups whom we ask to help us make better curricula must attain some unity themselves and must enjoy the support and approval of those who will be affected by their decisions. We can cite only a few examples.

A grade teacher's mothers' committee brought together to discuss reading groups exploded in heated controversy because one member secretly "represented" a parent resentful over her child's limited ability.

A ninth-grade mathematics teacher promoted continuing criticism of his program because he failed to consult all the insurance men when obtaining help on a unit. He played a favorite and lost.

A sixth-grade dramatics project was "spiked" through vigorous protest by several parents who saw the Junior League "running the teacher."

Proposal and support of participation in a writing contest by an academically minded group seriously increased parent aggravation about pupil exploitation and neglect of basic study.

A committee on the gifted, composed of volunteers, obtained introduction of earth science and the movement of general science to the eighth grade. Parents complained bitterly at the neglect of the concerns of others, agreed the school was for the elite.

There are no sure-fire methods of getting good and effective representation on a citizens' committee. Much of our selection will depend on the purposes of the group assembled. Sometimes every point of view is necessary, sometimes not. We should not be much concerned over who is picked to help with construction or decoration. We certainly want the college-trained, the local businessman, the labor representative, the selective-minded, the guidance-oriented, the practical-versed to deliberate with us on the breadth and nature of offerings in distributive education.

Probably the best we can do is ask:

Who ought to be on this kind of committee?

Whose interest is at stake? Who has special resources? Who will want to know directly what transpires?

What questions will be raised and by whom if he is appointed?

What is his style and approach? What axes may he have to grind?

Who will counteract and steady his influence?

Who will give us different ideas and points of view?

5. *Expectations should be modest.* Citizen groups have turned out some startlingly good material. Educators who fairly appraise lay reports can easily wonder at times who the professionals really are. Be that as it may, the burden of work for great numbers of "citizen" contributions has been by educators. And there are numbers of laymen efforts that cause one to blush for their brevity and complete avoidance of the deeper matters that have to do with quality. Yet who could expect volumes or products representing full time attention.

The simple lesson is to seek modesty and restraint in what is requested and to make an extremely wise choice on whom to ask for research and highly creative effort, and on whom to ask for expression of opinion and relatively unprepared contribution. The emphasis in this chapter and the promotion in other writings might cause one to assert, "Why, they want to have parents do everything." Nothing could be further from the position taken. Laymen should be involved far more extensively than they are, really more in the interest of understanding than anything else, but we must be aware that their participation may cost us more in time for a fair number of products we get than we might at first wish or anticipate. Like everything else, our prospects will have to be gauged in terms of the resources and conditions with which we have to work.

6. *Citizens should be chairmen; teachers, act as resources.* The deference paid to teachers is amazing. They are more articulate, tend to fill in the gaps, volunteer to arrange chairs, know how to pose mo-

tions, step with ease to the board, have a great many of the answers, and can so easily manage things in general. Participation charts prepared in three teacher-help groups revealed teachers were holding the floor over 70 percent of the time. Part of this difficulty came from teachers trying to explain what they wanted, from teacher apprehension that matters would go in the wrong direction, from impatience with the slow emergence of ideas, from reiteration born of the feeling that participants did not understand, from teacher familiarity with the setting, and from members' discomfort.

It is miraculously easy for a teacher to become chairman by default unless he is adamant, gets strong people on the group at the outset, stays in the background, parries a reasonable number of requests with suggestions on how to get a better answer, shifts questions to others for their opinion, and so on. But citizen groups are not free and independent when they parrot teachers' ideas or get dominated into teacher preconceptions.

This raises the question as to whether community curriculum committees ought to function quite free of professionals once they know their assignment and have agreed to it. Surprisingly they arrive at conclusions and productions which are most pleasing and acceptable. What could be better for morale or public confidence?

7. *Provisions for good meeting should be studied.* The misery in which many volunteers meet is enough to kill off any support. Witness the skirt-creeping struggles of mamas in third-grade chairs, note the wasteland of empty seats in audience-arranged rooms, watch the struggles to keep awake at after-dinner meetings, observe the sessions without pads and pencils, and you have a start. Usually committee chairmen need a simple guide to their role even though they may have some experience. Help with reproduction of notes and reports, with mailing out reminders, and with arranging for meeting places and resources are far more important than we often realize. Agendas are critical and so are precise explanations to those we or our representatives may visit. Most people need to get prepared, and a telephone call, well timed in advance, will save lots of embarrassment.

Our experience has been that there are far too many offhand and inadequate preparations for the involvement of citizens. Competent teacher curriculum workers ought to know we just do not simply assemble any more. We know who is coming, what seating arrangements will facilitate communication, what locations will reduce tension and be free of noise and confusion, what questions may be uppermost, what proposals will move things along. He who invites and thinks up what to do on the spur of the moment often moves into trouble and deserves it.

8. *Groups should be trained in the interactive process.* If we are to encourage and rely on cooperative lay-teacher action in the future, the skills of citizens for working together ought to improve as we have proposed should be the case with faculties. Even if we get less production, as long as public power to deliberate in groups grows and spreads, we shall have made a great contribution. But as with faculties, there must be care to see that process does not overwhelm product or that citizens do not lose patience with psychologizing. We can employ recorders and observers and hold occasional evaluation sessions. We dare not, however, encourage too quickly any deep probing of prejudices, obstructive behaviors, or petty motives.

Groups who produce well may be asked to review and reflect on the causes of and factors associated with success. Several of the handbooks[13] now available for lay groups should be put at each committee's disposal. Occasionally it may be useful to bring people together to present and to analyze a group in action.

9. *Consensus should be the goal in policy groups.* A proper introduction of a problem to citizens assembled to consider change and alterations and new proposals will include the fact that lay cooperation seeks above anything else the surveying and understanding of common thought, and not the imposition of the will of those more powerful over those with fewer supporters. The drive to early votes and the approval of far-reaching motions too often leave bitter sentiment and create faction among the adherents and followers of those out-balloted. Citizens ought to be advised to put the too often improperly used "motion on the previous question" to sleep for the duration. Half of those who are trapped by it forever resent it, and the rest come to figure you can not win anyway. Few maneuvers exasperate the sincere exponent of full ventilation and sharing of thoughts any more than those of the self-important parliamentarian who unbinds his less literal-minded and sometimes wrangling peers with a cathartic from Robert's *Rules of Order.*

For the most part, citizens are quite unskilled at the steps helpful in getting changed perception. Short on training, they often fall victim to trying to convince by out-talking. We must encourage them, instead, to assemble their facts first, to develop the art of getting full expression from the reluctant and opposed, to enlist acceptable status

[13] D. M. Hall, *Dynamics of Group Discussion,* Interstate Printers and Publishers, 1950.

figures in bringing about identification and change, and to provide time for compromise and for revision or abandonment of values. This does not mean minority reports are unacceptable or that the man with exceptions in his heart should be worried and harried until he comes to agree out of exhaustion or out of a conscience-stricken conformity. It begs simply for less violent contention where such need not be.

10. *Reports should be prepared and distributed to those concerned.* There is something to writing a thing down that pushes one toward excellence. It may be the permanence of words or the fact that saying what one really means is not at all a simple matter even for the best of authors. No matter, we seldom have anything worthwhile unless we get it recorded somehow, and the better organized and the more succinct the rendition, the more useful it always is. People who palaver may help each other get some better idea of things, but they do not have much that is concrete upon which they can agree. Also documents, even not so good ones, somehow convey a sense of accomplishment and a degree of completion.

We thus should expect some report for a large portion of our work. The job will sharpen thinking, and it will tell the group and others where they have gone and what they have done.

11. *We should expect conservatism and caution.* Well-selected and well-piloted lay groups have a real wisdom. Seldom do they go off the deep end, "buy a pig in a poke," or fall in behind the starry-eyed idealist. Although once given a chance, likely to risk more than we might anticipate, the layman resists dispensing with things he has known and grown up with. For instance, bring a citizen group in to look over the literature offering or the content of American history or the required subjects. They do not jump with alacrity to shearing and shucking even what they, in lighter and in less responsible moments, may have belabored with abandon as useless.

Part of the status quo tendency admittedly does arise because volunteers are so often those who did well in school. Those who jump at assignments are usually more than partly educated. In fact, it is not at all difficult to get the academic tradition represented pretty quickly. Some rather good field work is necessary then to enlist those who may not have been so comfortable with the past. There is a fair nucleus of the well-educated in this category. What we have to do is inveigle them in and support them with some others who may at first feel like strangers.

11. *Varied images and stereotypes should be anticipated.* The nonacademic often will have the idea that they do not count for much

in these matters. They may feel they do not belong. The more eager on the other hand may think the citizen group a heaven-sent opportunity. They see teachers as souls in need of a little straightening out and a citizens' report as a way to do it. To some, still, the school is a forbidding place, teachers are vindictive if one throws his weight around too much, hard work done for a public agency is merely carrying the load of someone who is getting paid but not producing, and so on.

We can expect thus to have some reformers cool down; others will demur but leave us uncomfortable with their explanations; requests for help will signify lack of scholarship and too much educationism to some, while it will mean a half-hearted attempt to make up for past neglect to others.

Thus the bitter with the sweet. The only way to smash false images and break down stereotypes is to wade right in and demonstrate that purpose is genuine and old perceptions are inaccurate. Where citizens have a chance to work with us, discover we respect and trust them and value their contributions, and see for themselves our competence and capacity to deal with their fears, criticisms, and penetrating questions we can break down the fragile facades that separate us.

12. *Deep personal commitments should be respected.* In every community there are people who find it next to impossible to change their ideas about how some things should be done. When everybody around them has altered his view, they are unmoved. More often than we should, we find such persisting souls ostracized or made the symbols of general reaction. Some perhaps deserve demonstration of impatience, but on the whole it is necessary to recognize that not everybody "can go along."

In educators who think they are right or could be right there will spring continual hope that persuasion, cooperative effort, more penetrating questions, and better data will bring change acceptable to almost all. There is nevertheless usually a point at which more effort is too exasperating and without reward. It seems hardly sensible that time and resources at such junctures should not be more profitably used. Graceful recognition of the complete obdurateness of a person on a point and discontinuance of any effort to persuade him may well assure later cooperation in an area where the individual is accessible. Hardly anyone is impervious to all good ideas. Therefore, we should be alert to discover what people set store by and to invite their participation when we anticipate their interest will be high and their contribution will be positive. Our goal should be to enlist people where they can and do want to work and on matters where they do not expose themselves if they take new positions. Outright and fierce contention with laymen and colleagues is unavoidable from time to time. The strong and righteous very often do want their say and will not be throttled or bypassed. Baiting the confirmed, however, is silly.

Notwithstanding, we have to raise questions about dearly held values. Should we not invite the faithful and unyielding opposition, say, to discussions aimed to replace numerical reports in subjects with interviews and conferences, to discontinue required memorization of *Il Penseroso,* to change civics to citizenship education, or to introduce certain elements of sex education?

They should be told when matters of deep concern to them are to be examined. They should be told what decisions have been made by a group, if they do not choose to participate. They should be permitted after-the-fact rebuttal and given the right of appeal even though they have absented themselves during the deliberations. Their existent and continued opposition and discomfort need neither be appreciated nor respected in the literal sense of the words, but rather should be objectively lived with, avoided as a source of recrimination, and not considered a reason against good, wholesome, and helpful meeting of the minds on other matters.

13. *Lay participation should be evaluated.* Working as extensively with laymen as this chapter suggests will take away at one point the teacher's precious time for his independent and personal activity. It ought to restore time at other points because some of his tasks will be taken over by laymen; and a broader, required and presently neglected scope, not even possible without laymen, will be covered. Still, whether time will be saved or whether hoped-for results will be obtained cannot really be determined in advance. How matters work out is actually what counts. With lay participation, like everything else, the teacher cannot afford to allow the "educationist" to talk him into activities that dissipate his energies and that in the end do not really lead to more learning by children. Therefore, efforts to work more closely with the community should not be undertaken without attention at the outset to the outcomes which are contemplated. We embark on too many projects on curriculum improvement without knowing what we expect to get as results and without having any respectable and adequate means of demonstrating both that we obtained our goal and that it was worth our effort.

In Chapter 16 this point is further emphasized and suggestions are given for checking on plans and procedures utilized to get things done better. It is sufficient to say here that specification of the goal is usually very inadequate. Everywhere most inadequate data are collected to provide any concrete evidence. The most common situation is the report of vague impressions by the principal when he is asked for a statement on outcomes.

In the National Society Yearbook on Citizen Cooperation, Chapter 11 is devoted to appraisal. Hand and Hamlin[14] have included there a number of guides to judging the impact of closer school and community interaction. The following list gives some indication of how comprehensive evaluation can be.

1. How was the arrangement effected?
   a. Were all who might be affected by the arrangement (or their representatives) consulted?
   b. Were the specific needs for the arrangement and the purposes to be accomplished by it determined before the arrangement was made?
   c. Were the relationships to existing organizations determined?
   d. Were competent consultants used in planning an over-all structure of school and community relationships?
   e. Was the arrangement chosen because of its adaptability to the community or was it copied from another and different community?
   f. Did the board of education initiate or approve the arrangement in an adequate statement of policy?
   g. Did the organized school staff concur in the arrangement?
   h. Were those included as representatives of the people really representative of them? If not, has there been real effort to include more representative persons?
   i. Is each person participating in the arrangement a free individual or is he responsible to a group or an individual?
   j. Is there a charter, constitution, or other document which indicates clearly the field in which this particular kind of cooperation is to function, its purposes, its restrictions, and its relationships?
2. What are the purposes of the participants?
   a. Are the participants "pure in heart," seeking only the best education for the children, youth, and adults of the district?
   b. Do the participants see their central task clearly and work consistently upon it?
   c. Are adequate time and thought given to refining the particular purposes and goals to be sought?
   d. Do all participants understand and accept the stated purpose? Are new participants inducted into an understanding of them?
   e. Are the purposes feasible?
   f. Is there frequent appraisal of progress toward accepted goals?
   g. Do the purposes have to do with the major goals or objectives of public education or are they confined to details of conducting a traditionally conceived school systems?

[14] Nelson B. Henry, ed., *Citizen Cooperation for Better Public Schools*, National Society for the Study of Education. 1954, pp. 270–272.

3. How is the arrangement operated?
   a. Do the participants continuously and systematically appraise their work: have appraisals improved their work?
   b. Is the work of the participants planned as far in advance as is feasible?
   c. Is the planning carried out democratically?
   d. Is the work of the group planned in relation to the work of other groups which are responsible for or interested in the schools?
   e. Are democratic discussion procedures principally used in meetings? Are minority groups and individuals protected in their rights to self-expression?
   f. Has the group become a study group, which marshalls facts and considerations before announcing its conclusions?
   g. Are the interests and abilities of all participants well utilized?
   h. Do participants attend meetings regularly?
   i. Is there adequate use of consultants?
   j. Are adequate records kept? Is the work of the group properly reported to those who should know about it?
   k. Does the group stay within its prescribed field?
   l. Does the group always recognize the rights and responsibilities of lay citizens, the board of education, administrators, teachers, and non-academic employees?
4. What have been the effects of the arrangement upon the participants?
   a. Have the participants developed an increased interest in those who are served or might be served by the schools, in the schools, and in the work of the particular groups?
   b. Is there more widespread and more active participation in the work of the group?
   c. Do the members of the group feel increasingly that their work is necessary, perhaps indispensable?
   d. Do the members increasingly appreciate the privilege of membership in the group?
   e. Do the members increasingly enjoy working together?
   f. Are the members learning? Are their visions widening? Are they becoming more accurate and objective in their thinking about school affairs?
   g. Do laymen and schoolmen appreciate each other more and like each other better? increasingly enjoy being and working together?
   h. Are the leadership tasks being better performed? Is new leadership developing?
   i. Do the members contribute new and fresh ideas about the schools and education?
   j. Do the members want to communicate their new ideas and radiate their new enthusiasms to their fellow laymen and teachers?
   k. Has the group developed the courage of its convictions?
5. What have been the effects of the arrangement upon education in the district?
   a. Have some of the possible gains or goals proposed for the school program been attained?

b. Are the group and its work increasingly understood and supported by professional workers and citizens in the district?

c. Is the group helping to develop closer relationships between the schools and the organizations and institutions of the district?

d. Has the group helped to develop in the people of the district and in the professional staff a less complacent attitude toward the schools, caused them to become more constructively critical, made the schools seem more important to them, and made them more appreciative of the good things the schools do?

e. Has the group helped the people of the district to become able to do what they can for themselves in school matters and to rely less upon outside agencies?

f. Has long-range planning for the schools been promoted?

g. Have new needs for education been discovered in the district and related to the program of the schools? Have any activities been discovered which are no longer needed?

Questions for Discussion

1. How would you go about promoting and precipitating cooperative community-school curriculum improvement where there is none now?

2. As a new teacher in a community, what basic guides should you employ in locating local resources to supplement your classroom teaching?

3. What are some curricular additions or subtractions you think might stir up community discontent? How should they be decided upon to minimize community reaction? How would you insure against a suspended reaction?

4. How would you prevent the bossy and the aggressive from taking over the group you assemble to help with curriculum tasks?

5. If people will default on their obligations, they will surely overlook their opportunities. Can we ever really hope to get involvement from those who are most reluctant? How?

6. Should some teachers extensively utilize and interact with the community when others do not?

7. Should we ever hope to have the contentious and vital effect on the community envisioned in writings on the community school?

8. Can we ever obtain the public respect the European teacher enjoys with similar problems on what should be taught and how?

Selected Bibliography

Association for Supervision and Curriculum Development, *Building Public Confidence in the Schools,* The Association, 1949.

Clapp, Elsie, *Community Schools in Action,* Viking, 1939.

Gabbard, Hazel, *Working With Parents,* Government Printing Office, 1948.

Henry, Nelson B., ed., *The Community School,* National Society for the Study of Education, 1953.

Henry, Nelson B., ed., *Citizen Cooperation for Better Public Schools,* National Society for the Study of Education, 1954.

Hopkins, L. Thomas, *The Emerging Self,* Harper, 1954.

Michigan Department of Public Instruction, *The Community Is Your Classroom,* The Department, 1954.

New York State Education Department, *Citizens Advisory Committees: Avenues to Better Schools,* The Department, 1952.

Pillard, Matthew, ed., *Administrative Leadership in Community Planning for Education,* CASDA, College of Education, State University of New York, 1951.

Storen, Helen, *Laymen Help Plan the Curriculum,* Association for Supervision and Curriculum Development, 1946.

CHAPTER 16

....

The Teacher and Curriculum Research

_____

The main trend of American education in the twentieth century has been the persistent attempt to ground the art of teaching in the results of scientific research. In part, this attempt has consisted of efforts to apply the findings reported by students of society and of individual behavior; in part, it has involved an endeavor to apply the methods of science to the direct study of educational problems in the school setting.

Despite the appeal which the prospect of scientifically sound educational practices has in this age of science, the results have fallen far short of expectations. Much of what is known is not being applied and no science of education worthy of the name has developed. Changes in practice have occurred, but often without the benefit of carefully conducted research. Yet the quest continues.

That the quest has not been as fruitful as might be hoped does not mean it is futile. The dedication to research, persistent as it has been, has not been strong on the part of a large proportion of the profession. A few so-called leaders—"educationists," perhaps—have been zealous proponents, but many members of the profession, often ironically priding themselves on being "practical people," have had little enthusiasm for research. Yet it must be assumed that all of them desire to improve teaching and to do so on as sound a basis as possible.

If teachers possess this determination to modify the art of teaching in accordance with scientifically derived knowledge and if they accept as valid the central thesis of this book—that curriculum making is an important part of the art of teaching—then it is apparent that they must expect and be expected to act as consumers and producers of curriculum research. Unfortunately, many have little understanding of research techniques and principles and indeed some appear fearful of them. Others confuse any venture new to them with research. Teachers do "experiment" with different approaches to instruction in the hope of getting better results. Some say they "never teach the same way twice." On the surface, this experimental attitude seems admirable. But the trouble with it is that after one year or two there are only vague impressions concerning results and little, if anything, concrete to demonstrate to others or even to convince themselves. Yet when it is suggested that these efforts need to be planned more systematically and that careful records need to be kept, these teachers profess ignorance of the concept of controls or even shy away from the thought of accumulating data. Thus the experimentation, which with a little care could be so valuable, often is so unsatisfying that the teachers comfortably slip back to earlier ways with very little notion of what is best. This state of affairs is not necessary, for the basic ideas of research are neither complicated nor mysterious. In this chapter some of the rudiments of research are presented in the belief that with a little effort any teacher can become a skillful user of research findings and a helpful, competent partner in research activities.

THE MEANING OF RESEARCH

Essentially, research involves an attempt to solve a problem[1] by testing hunches as to a solution. In the process, data are obtained, organized, and interpreted but they are only means, not the central features. The elements of greatest importance are (1) the problem, (2) the hunches or hypotheses, and (3) the conclusion. Statistical tools are often but not always used to increase confidence in the conclusion.

Definition of the Problems

It is peculiar how many students fail to recognize that one must first have a problem before one can engage in research. The explanation probably lies in the fact that they have been required to write papers as assignments and have had to hunt around for a topic on which to write. But one does not do research on a *topic* nor does one do research unless one needs to: that is, unless one has a problem to solve. A problem exists, therefore ways of solving it through research are sought; one does not first decide to do research and then seek a problem. However justifiable violation of this principle may be in the academic setting, there is no reason for it in the actual school situation.

[1] Some would define research more broadly as any attempt to get information together to help one do a better job. We do not reject this idea, but we would rather here confine the discussion to a narrower and more precise view.

There the problems are real and numerous and the only incentive for engaging in research is the hope of solving some of them.

Problems vary, of course, in complexity, importance, and generality. Simple problems involve fewer interrelated complicating factors than do complex ones and require fewer data, obtainable by more straightforward means in a shorter time. One problem is of greater importance than another if its solution will affect more people over a greater length of time and effect a greater reduction of difficulty in practice. A complex problem may not be as important as a simpler one. The question of generality is still another matter and refers to the extent to which the solution is applicable in other schools or in situations other than the one in which it originated. A problem may be both complex and locally important and yet its solution may have little general value. A teacher or faculty would be well advised to focus first on problems of greatest importance and to begin with the simpler of these.

DRAFTING OF A GENERAL PROBLEM LIST

It is doubtful if any teacher or school is without curriculum problems, although we know some seem unaware of them or unwilling to admit their existence. These people are obviously not ready for nor interested in a research approach. But in most situations the individuals involved are vaguely if not acutely aware of the existence of problems. Often, however, no attempt has been made to see what agreement exists as to the priority of these problems. This can, of course, readily be accomplished by means of a problem census in which all members of the staff submit in writing a list of problems considered by each to be most pressing. When this is done, it may be expected that many will seem trivial and the actual meaning of most will be very unclear. To illustrate this, a list is presented here of the suggestions proposed in forty-five minutes by thirty members of a staff of two hundred. They are listed exactly as they were recorded on a blackboard and were suggested, not as problems bothering teachers most, but specifically as proposals for formal, state-subsidized research.

1. How to teach disciplines in various categories.
2. Uses of school day plus Saturday.
3. Eleven-month school.
4. Math taught at rate of high level group.
5. Accelerated fourth to sixth grade science program.
6. Harvard University testing program—reading.
7. Early identification of artistic.
8. Visual aids lab.

9. Develop units or kits for perception in science.
10. Novel or restructuring, re-perception training.
11. Group of teachers to improve curriculum in depth.
12. Kinesthetic approach.
13. Further exploration of readiness.
14. Lab approach to math.
15. Plan for enrichment of content background of teacher.
16. Parental involement. Training parents.
17. Eighteen months of science on Senior high level.
18. New courses—logic, philosophy, psychology.
19. Newspapers as sole teaching aid.
20. Examination of over–under achieving.
21. Workshops to coordinate better arithmetic program.
22. Summer camp with special purpose—science.
23. Special orientation and improvement in service program for substitutes.
24. A self-study of the gifted.
25. Concepts rather than facts in science.
26. Fusion of citizenship education to treat broader concepts.
27. Seminars to emphasize an area.
28. Space age courses cutting across content lines.
29. Move classrooms to outside area.
30. Outside specialists for gifted.
31. Flexibility of content and treatment in all content areas.
32. Kgd.—on through: foreign language for the able.
33. Blocks of time to be devoted to one area in high school.
34. Acceleration at junior high.
35. Physical fitness program (study of effect).
36. More T.V. courses for the able.
37. Pressure limits of the able (how much frustration).
38. Study of creativity in able.
39. How build self-confidence, a sense of self, ego strength.

Later, subgroups considered each suggestion in terms of certain criteria, but in the usual school situation it is more customary to conduct a resurvey in the form of a checklist containing all of the original suggestions. This furnishes an index of the seriousness with which they are viewed. The entire procedure can also be carried out in a meeting through discussion. When collective action is not contemplated, the individual teacher simply needs to record the problems he himself senses and determine which he has the greatest likelihood of being able to do something about.

Staffs which regularly study the characteristics and needs of students, follow up school leavers and graduates, meet with community members, conduct standardized achievement testing programs or which in any other way are actively assessing the effectiveness of the school program are constantly made aware of problems demanding study.

In point of fact, it appears to many observers that the more effective teachers are, the more aware they are of shortcomings and the more inclined to seek ways of improving both themselves and their programs.

SELECTION AND ANALYSIS AS A FOLLOW-UP

A problem, once decided upon for study, must be carefully analyzed and defined. When a practical problem is involved, this process consists mainly of being explicit about terms. The statement of the problem must be sufficiently precise that anyone would understand exactly what it was. For example, item 34 on the list above reads "Acceleration at junior high." As it stands, it is meaningless as a problem, What about acceleration at junior high? What is the problem? Is it a question of who should be accelerated, whether anyone should be accelerated, what the effect of present acceleration is, or what form acceleration should take? What is meant by acceleration—"skipping a grade," doing the work of three years in two, or merely considering topics ordinarily encountered in later grades? What effect of acceleration is of interest here—academic achievement, social repercussions, or emotional reactions? If it is academic achievement, how measured? In other words, before this can become a problem for research it is necessary to state what one wishes to find out about acceleration, what one means by acceleration and in what form the effects will occur.

Often subproblems are recognized and the identification of these constitutes the analysis. Usually, preliminary facts surrounding the problem must be obtained in order to complete the definition and call attention to the component problems.

For example, the problem of improving reading ability among ninth graders may be analyzed into subproblems involving vocabulary, comprehension, rate, and other aspects. Examination of standardized test results may indicate that the problem is primarily one relating to "study-type" reading. Thus the initial broad problem can be refined into something quite specific.

THEORETICAL PROBLEMS DISTINGUISHED FROM PRACTICAL

Theoretical problems differ from practical ones in that they stem from unexplained phenomena or unverified logical consequences of a theory. The researcher's goal is not to discover a better way of doing things but to explain and predict better. To carry out such research, it is necessary first to make logical deductions from theory and translate these into terms relating to actual operations. This is difficult both to do and to explain. It is as if the theoretical and the practical were two distinct and separate realms. The rules of one do not hold for the other. In the realm of theory there are statements—some of them assumptions, and from sets of these statements necessary conclusions may be drawn or deduced. But the fact that such conclusions are "true" in the sense of being correctly arrived at does not mean they are "true" in fact. Nor may their correspondence to reality be directly checked since they are not in the realm of reality. To test them, a bridge must be built by relating the theoretical statements to the world of things and events. The technical term of this process is "epistemic correlation," but the important point is that theory must be expressed in operational terms before it can be checked. In view of the looseness of educational theory, this is difficult but all the more essential for the progress of the profession. School people are of course more likely to be concerned with practical problems, but it should be realized that when a theoretical investigation can be carried out, the results will have greater general value.

In a recent study it was desired to determine whether social acceptability of pupils was related to their success in learning to read. No attempt to change practices used in teaching reading was immediately envisioned. Later, perhaps, new approaches could be tried out if the initial findings suggested that it would be worthwhile. But at the outset the only goal was to test the theoretical hypothesis that success in reading was associated with social acceptability. To test it, the hypothesis must be expressed in operational terms. The researcher must define "reading success" and he must define it in terms of the operations to be used in detecting its presence or absence or in measuring its degree. Likewise "social acceptability" must be given a specific meaning with reference to what kind of observation will be made.

Thus, this inevitably involves some movement toward quantification—or at least classification which permits counting. Some research is apparently purely qualitative and some people decry the emphasis on reducing complex matters to numbers. But even "more" and "less" imply quantity, and every conclusion or generalization suggests that in more cases or more often something is true than it is not. In the situation described here, reading success was defined as a score on a specified standardized reading test; social acceptability was considered to be the number of classmates naming a given pupil as the person he liked best in the group. When these two scores—one based on measurements, the other on counting—were available, the hypothesis could easily be tested.

HYPOTHESES AS DIRECTION INDICATORS

The very idea of hypotheses seems to frighten some students and teachers. Yet it is so crucial in research that unless it is understood and correctly applied, worthwhile inquiries cannot be conducted. For research implies that data will be collected to aid in solving a problem and, without an hypothesis as a guide, there is no way of knowing what data to gather. It is a ridiculous waste of time to go about acquiring information at random. It is essential to have a good hunch as to what information is needed.

The hunch or hypothesis is in effect an idea, an inspiration. Imagination and creativity are almost indispensable to the formulation of hypotheses, although in many cases good ones have been hit upon almost by chance. As indicated in the preceding section, the theoretical researcher relies heavily upon deduction from theory for clues to hypotheses worth testing; teachers will be guided partly by their own observations from experience and by implications for practice perceived in theory, for by reflecting about his work the teacher notices things which set him wondering. Certain results *seem* to follow from certain conditions. He wonders if they really do. Or going beyond what he has actually done, he wonders what would happen if he were to use a particular approach or type of material. Usually, we leave it with that— just wondering. But when we can bestir ourselves to do something about it, we can put some of our hunches to the test.

Preliminary fact-gathering in connection with the analysis and definition of the problem may also provide leads to hypotheses. In analyzing the problem relating to "study-type" reading, for example, it may be suspected that pupils with certain characteristics or who have had certain experiences tend to do better than others. These apparent facts are then, in effect, hypotheses which bear careful checking. But whatever its origin, some sort of reasonable guess is necessary before further systematic collection of data is possible. If there is nothing to test, there can be no test.

Specification of Population in the Sample

Once there is an idea to test or a procedure to try out, it is necessary to decide upon whom or what to test it or try it out. This is implicit in the problem and should be explicit in the hypothesis. If some effect is the subject of inquiry, this effect must have reference to some particular group or population of people or things. Any characteristic which may come under study must be an attribute of a specified group of people, objects, or processes, which is known as the *population*. There is no such thing as research on a procedure or quality in the abstract.

Teachers need not be afraid of the term "population." It is not a difficult concept but it is extremely important. It simply indicates for whom or what the results are applicable. In most cases the population will consist of pupils, but it may also be comprised of books, instructional units, or any other group of entities concerned with curriculum. Sometimes the entire population can be studied. Individual teachers may, for example, study a class or several sections with the knowledge that the results apply only to those groups. When the interaction among members of a group is under study, it is almost essential that the whole group be studied. But when the population involves large numbers it is not always possible, or even desirable, to include all. For purposes of instruction it is obviously necessary to include all pupils, but not for research; for good public relations it is desirable to reach all of the public, but for research it is not necessary.

A SAMPLE AS SYMBOL OF THE POPULATION

Thus when the population is too large, it is often necessary to deal with only a portion of it which may be considered representative of the whole. This is known as a sample and it must be selected properly if conclusions applicable on a large scale are to be drawn. The theory of sampling is complex and when a nationwide public opinion poll or the quality control procedure for a large manufacturing concern is involved, careful and elaborate measures must be taken. In the school situation this is not possible nor is it necessary. A few precautions are sufficient. If possible, one should probably avoid any sample of less than thirty-five cases. It is well not to have a sample of less than one in ten nor more than one in four. Thus, if the population is less than 140, the entire group should be used rather than a sample. However, how a sample is drawn is more important than its size.

A *random sample* is usually preferable since this is one in which each member of the population has an equal chance of being selected. If each component of the population is numbered, the numbers for the sample can be determined from a list of random numbers or by using the order in which the last digits of telephone numbers appear on any page in the directory. A random selection can also be made from each of various subgroups into which the population is organized, taking a number from each proportional to the size of the subgroup compared with the total. This assures both randomness and representation of important categories and is called a *stratified random sample.* A *systematic sample* is also satisfactory if the cards representing the items are well shuffled or if their order is clearly irrelevant. Before drawing every tenth or eighth item or whatever fraction is desired, the starting point can be determined by a chance process thus giving everyone an equal chance of being selected.

Often some facts are known about the total group and if these same facts are ascertained about the sample and the two sets do not deviate significantly, confidence is increased that whatever else is found to be true of the sample would also be true of the total population. For example, if the sample were one of pupils, information might be available on sex, age, and intelligence quotient, and it should have a composition in these respects similar to that of the total group which it represents. This is only a check on a valid procedure, however, for just because comparability exists, an invalid procedure does not become satisfactory.

It is a common error to assume, when information about a group of pupils is incomplete, that the unknown data would probably follow the same pattern as the known. The reason for the lack of data must be considered. If it is due to the failure of some of the sample to respond, there may be a reason for this failure which is based on an important difference between the respondents and nonrespondents. When the nonrespondents are in the majority, it is obviously hazardous to draw conclusions about the sample and certainly about the population from which it was drawn. This should be kept in mind whenever a school uses the questionnaire technique for getting information.

The Value of Careful Experimentation

There are four ways of getting information on which to base practical decisions. The most frequently used is to consult the literature for reports of research already done which bears upon the problem. A second approach, and probably next in frequency, is to canvass the opinions or practices of informed people regarding various solutions under the assumption, often fallacious, that what the majority thinks or does is indicative of what is best. The third method is to engage in research of a descriptive type in which firsthand information is obtained and relationships are ascertained. As a result, attempts may be made to draw certain comparisons and to speculate regarding causal factors.

The highest level of research activity involves prediction and requires experimentation. This is difficult to do properly in the school situation. Many seem to think that trying anything new is experimentation, and of course it is in one sense of the word but not in the research sense. This does not mean that it is not useful and desirable for teachers or the school as a whole to try new approaches which in their judgment seem promising. Much curriculum improvement has come about from experimentation of such informal nature. But many innovations have been accepted without any conclusive evidence of their effectiveness. The injection of more carefully designed research techniques into school experimentation might engender increased confidence in the wisdom of changes on the part of both professional and lay people.

CONTROL OF EXTRANEOUS FACTORS

Sound experimentation requires, rather, careful control of groups and conditions in order to avoid misdirection by effects not really due to the factor being studied. That is, if two groups are used, they should be formed and treated as much alike as possible, except of course for the matter under study. It is possible, however, to permit several factors to vary if a person sufficiently well informed about statistics is available.

Schools usually find it possible to establish control groups sufficiently equivalent to groups selected for a given experimental treatment to permit useful comparisons with established practices. While pairing of individuals is extremely difficult, satisfactory equation of groups can be achieved by assuring that they have similar means and distributions in regard to a number of variables which are considered relevant. These might include age, sex, intelligence, and specific aptitude. Groups formed by chance methods, by which each individual has equal probability of being assigned to an experimental or a control group, usually exhibit satisfactory equivalence. When this does not prove to be the case because of small numbers, a few judicious shifts can rectify chance imbalance.

The selection of teachers for each approach should also, theoretically, be accomplished by chance means. However, in the practical school situation this is not always possible and some compromise is necessary. It is desirable that teachers be favorable to the approach they use and this may not be the case when they are assigned randomly. Therefore, their preferences in this regard should be considered if the experiment is to be successful. Furthermore, public acceptance of experimentation might easily be jeopardized by teachers' airing of their dissatisfaction with unwanted assignments. Differences in teacher ability, if marked, will bias results, but more often than not pairs of teachers of comparable skillfulness are available.

Before commencing an experiment, it is important to specify as completely as possible the nature of the experimental treatment or untried procedure, and also that of the control situation. It is also essential that the claims for the two practices and the proposed method of verifying them be stated. This usually involves measures of some sort and a schedule for taking these measures must be formulated and followed. Sometimes this calls for testing at both the beginning and conclusion of the experiment so that changes may be noted.

For instance, a test in arithmetic might be given to some pupils and then two groups formed which are as near alike as possible in arithmetic scores and perhaps other attributes. If these matched groups were then taught more arithmetic by two different methods or with different content or materials, they would have to be tested again to determine which group gained most. But suppose it were desired to see whether a given approach was more effective with two groups, one of which was better at arithmetic than the other. Again initial and final tests would be necessary and the percentage of improvement of each group might be noted. This would also be necessary, if for some reason the groups had to be taken "as is" without matching.

Statistical methods are usually necessary to determine the probability that any differences in the extent of change might have occurred through chance alone. On each school staff there is undoubtedly at least one person who understands the calculation and interpretation of "Critical Ratio" and if not, the concept and formulas are treated in any elementary book on statistics.

THE "NULL HYPOTHESIS" IN TESTING

But statistics are of little value if there is no well-defined hypothesis to test. The researcher must "claim" that certain results will be forthcoming, but it is not necessary for him to expect them. His hypothesis is usually a claim of superiority or at least difference of effect for one procedure as against another. However, it is not possible statistically to prove directly that a difference in results is not due to chance. What is done instead is to rephrase the hypothesis as a "null hypothesis," which asserts that there *is* no difference between the two procedures in terms of their effects. This null hypothesis cannot be proved either, but it can be rejected under certain circumstances, and when it is rejected, the original hypothesis receives support. For example, if we are comparing the effectiveness of method "A" and method "B" in improving grammatical ability, we hypothesize that one, let us say "A," will bring about more improvement than the other. When the results are in, there will be a difference. If it favors "B," our hypothesis obviously is not supported. If it favors "A," we must still consider that it may have occurred by chance. This we can check statistically. If the difference is so small that it is probable it arose from chance, we reject our original hypothesis. If, however, it is highly improbable that the difference could have resulted from chance, we reject the null hypothesis of chance occurrence and accept our original one.

In general, when a new curriculum approach is being tried experimentally, it is necessary not only to have a similar group as a control, but also to insure that insofar as possible the two groups are being treated alike in all respects except the factor being tested. Obviously identical conditions are impossible to achieve, but with certain precautions unnecessary discrepancies can be avoided and other deviations can at least be noted and considered in the interpretation of results. Repetition of the experiment in the same school and duplication of it in other schools help cancel out the effects of unavoidable situational differences and add to confidence in the results. Regional school study councils make possible such replication in member schools and, further, can often make expert research advice available. If a competent research person is associated with the study and the treatment is replicated under several kinds of circumstances, he can apply an analysis (covariance) which will mathematically take into account some of the uncontrolled factors.

MODEST CONCLUSIONS CAUTIONED

After data have been collected, analyzed, and interpreted, it remains to draw conclusions from the study as a basis for determining the advisability of adopting certain curriculum changes. Two cautions should be observed in this regard.

If an experimental technique did not prove superior to the existing practice, one must seek whether sufficient time was allowed for it to exhibit any superiority, whether its failure to do so might be attributed to teachers' lack of skill with the new method, and whether the measures taken really dealt with the areas in which superiority was expected. Sometimes it is of value to know that in certain respects a new approach at least does not produce lower results because then other advantages are in the nature of added gains.

Second, it is important to recognize that a difference may be statistically significant yet practically inconsequential. Statistical tests only show the probability of a difference arising by chance alone, not whether it would be worthwhile to change current practice. In agriculture a 10 percent increase in effectiveness is usually demanded before the adoption of a new technique will be recommended. In education, perhaps the equivalent of a 5 percent gain may justify a change. However, it is always necessary to consider the gain in the light of any additional time, energy, and money required, and even more important, any undesirable side effects which might more than cancel the advantages attained.

Research conclusions do not by themselves determine what *should* be done. To determine this involves value judgments. Facts can aid in knowing how to achieve what is valued and values themselves are modified as understanding based on facts increases. But if experimentation shows that more desirable attitudes are acquired and better skill in solving problems is developed when pupils engage in group problem-solving activities than when the teacher develops concepts and principles with them, this will not lead to a decision to use the group method if teachers do not place very high value on attitude formation or problem-solving ability. Furthermore, conclusions from research may support several practices. For example, if method A produces better problem-solving ability but less factual knowledge than method B, the value judgment as to which of these two results is most desired will determine which method is adopted. All that research shows is that under certain specified conditions, if this is done, that will result.

Sometimes there are inconsistencies in the total situation which militate against acting upon research conclusions. Thus the faculty may verbally place high value upon a certain kind of outcome and may indeed sincerely value it highly. But then the whole evaluation system of the school may ignore this outcome entirely and stress others which are really considered less important. If the work of the teacher or the effectiveness of the school is judged on this basis, no amount of research findings will persuade teachers to adopt different practices. Then, too, even if changes would be rewarding, teachers might feel so uncertain and insecure with them that they hesitate to attempt a departure from familiar, though inferior, ways. So research results must be interpreted in the light of the whole situation. And in this regard, it must be remembered that each situation is different, and therefore what was found to be true in one by the most meticulous research may not apply in another. However, unless there is strong reason to believe that the circumstances are quite dissimilar, it is desirable to profit from the experience and research of others and to spread the application of results as rapidly and widely as possible.

TYPES OF RESEARCH

Research can be classified along several dimensions. In the previous section four types based on methods of obtaining data were mentioned. A classification on the basis of area of school operation might identify research in administration, finance, school organization, guidance, and curriculum—the last being the area under consideration here. Even this category could be broken down into research in various subjects, in extraclass activities, in methodology, in materials, in evaluation and, indeed, in means of effecting curriculum change.

Action Research

It is also possible to view research in respect to originators. Thus researchers may be scholars, concerned to a greater or lesser degree with the application of their findings but not responsible for the application; or in contrast, practitioners may be doing research to improve their own practice. The latter type has come to be known as "action research," and was first employed by sociologists who initiated programs of social change among groups who themselves were persuaded to participate in the research process of testing the effects of various practices. It was readily adapted to educational situations as university representatives joined with school people in approaching the practical problems of the latter through the scientific methods of the former.

Action research of this sort has several advantages. It assures that the problems investigated are real and significant. It aids scholars in obtaining necessary data from schools since, instead of obliging an outsider, school personnel are furthering their own interests and hence are more inclined to expend additional time and energy in this often laborious process. Further, of course, it reduces the lag between research and practice by making them one. Finally, it has become not only an avenue for program improvement but also a means of professional growth on the part of school staff members.

Desirable as participation in research by practitioners is, it also is the source of the major weaknesses of action research. Involvement in the program being studied increases the difficulty of remaining objective and may bias results. If excessive, it may also interfere with the effective performance of the basic educational functions of staff members. But the principal weakness has been that, because of the widespread encouragement of action research, much that has been done in its name has not been research or at least not good research. To some extent this was due to the fact that schools attempted research without the assistance of someone who understood research design. This is not to say that staffs or even individual teachers cannot do worthwhile research without the aid of university people; but if they do it alone, at least one of the staff members must understand the research process.

The in-service education of teachers might well provide for learning research procedures, whether in formal university classes, in local instruction by a competent staff member or in the course of actual guided experience in research. Smallenburg has recommended that teachers be able to use such basic research tools and skills as:

1. Observing and recording significant pupil behavior.
2. Using group tests and inventories.
3. Interviewing and counseling.
4. Using and interpreting cumulative records.
5. Utilizing questionnaires, autobiographies, etc., to get information about children.
6. Participating in case studies.
7. Handling simple statistical procedures.[2]

These are of course valuable abilities, but they all pertain to the carrying out of a research design not to the formulation of such a design. It is by the absence of a good design that most action research seems to suffer. One reason for this appears to lie in the interpretation of cooperative research which has developed.

Cooperative Research

A further classification of research on the basis of who does it distinguishes between individual and cooperative research. Action research is not necessarily cooperative nor is cooperative research necessarily of the action variety. Either a scholar or a practitioner can individually set up and carry out a research project, although he may require the cooperation of many people in obtaining the necessary data. Similarly, an entire project might be the cooperative endeavor of a team of scholars or of a group of school staff members. It may even involve a number of school systems, as in the case of studies by school study councils.

The idea of cooperative research on a continuing basis is, it should be clear, the logical result of the evaluation of curriculum development during this century. In the early days authorities remote from the school decided many curriculum details on the basis of tradition, experience,

[2] Harry Smallenburg, "Research Tools for Elementary and Secondary Teachers," *Growing Points in Educational Research,* American Educational Research Association, 1949, pp. 58–61.

and their best judgment. Then scientific means were employed and efforts were made to convince teachers of the worth of recommendations and to instruct them in how to implement the new ideas. External groups with checklists came into schools to conduct surveys and sent the schools the results of their evaluations after they had departed. Later, this procedure was modified so that school staffs first evaluated themselves and then were visited. Eventually it was recognized that if any real changes were to result from such evaluations, the external group had the responsibility to remain to help effect improvements.

At the same time administrators were beginning to realize that changes could not be imposed and that teachers should have a say in the process. Under this democratic approach one person's opinion was as good as another's, regardless of the basis for it. Meanwhile, the professional literature tended more and more to report so-called "successful practices" invented by various schools, and people on other faculties could cite these to introduce new ideas and support opinions. Curriculum leaders and supervisors, recognizing that changing teacher behavior was a learning process, began to focus on the problems faced by teachers as a starting point for improvement. A scientific approach to problems was favored and, when used in a group situation where mutual support and pooling of talent was possible, developed into cooperative action research.

In faculty study-group situations, research has been bound up with the group dynamics process. Two of the basic assumptions in this process are (1) that those who are to carry out decisions ought to participate in making them, and (2) that decisions should be made on the basis of facts insofar as possible. Hence, when in the course of deliberating on possible curriculum improvements a faculty group reaches the stage of proposing various alternatives or hypotheses, it has become common practice to decide tentatively on one of them with the idea of "trying it out" and noting its effectiveness before adopting it or trying another alternative. This "trying out" has come to be considered by many as experimentation and, thus, one kind of research. Seldom have any controls or even objective methods of evaluation been used. Indeed, frequently the fact that some books or periodicals were read to get suggestions as to alternative approaches has been enough to lead some to believe they were conducting curriculum research.

PROBLEM-SOLVING AS DISTINGUISHED FROM RESEARCH

There is much to commend a cooperative attack on common problems, but it is necessary not to confuse deliberation with research.

There is often an excellent opportunity to conduct research in connection with such group deliberation, but if it is done, it should be carefully designed and executed. Compared with the total time in which an experimental technique is applied, the amount of time required to establish an acceptable research situation is small and usually makes the difference between meaningful results and wasted effort. But other kinds of research besides experimentation can be conducted cooperatively—such as evaluating the program or some aspect of it; studying the community or community opinion; discovering characteristics, needs and problems of pupils or at least certain groups of pupils; and following up graduates and early school leavers.

CONDITIONS SUITABLE TO COOPERATIVE RESEARCH

The advantages of cooperative research lie in the greater number of ideas made available as to both hypotheses and procedural matters, the opportunity to check one another's thinking and the sharing of the load of gathering data and tabulating results, although with the last mentioned maximum use should be made of machines and clerks to avoid wasting professional time on routines. The over-all direction and coordination of a cooperative study should rest with one person. In large systems it may be both initiated and coordinated by a director of research or of curriculum. In smaller systems, curriculum study may be proposed by any member of the staff, but the coordination of a particular research effort might well rest with a designated teacher, competent and interested in managing the details. It may be necessary to provide not only this person, but the other participants also, with some time during the school day to carry out such a project properly. If it is not considered worthwhile enough for this, time should not be wasted on it. Administrators should view activities of this type not only as means of improving the school program but as valuable in-service training experiences and as stimulants for staff morale and alertness.

FORMAL REPORTS A NECESSITY

The results of research by staff groups should be set down in written form and also discussed by the staff. A written report provides a basis for later reference and permits sharing results with other interested parties. Discussion of the outcomes is essential to determine what, if any, change in program should be made on the basis of them. As stated earlier, no research study ever decides anything; it may provide factual information and even predict the consequences of certain actions, but it cannot provide value judgments regarding what course of action should be and will be taken. It must take its proper place in the cycle of making decisions, taking action, and surveying results which characterizes intelligent curriculum improvement.

IMPROVEMENT AND EXTENSION OF COOPERATIVE RESEARCH NEEDED

It has not been the intention here to disparage the idea of cooperative action research. If its shortcomings have been stressed, it is only because their elimination is desirable in order that the process may be more effective. There is no doubt but that participation in such activities helps teachers develop valuable insights and skills which will permit them to do better research individually with regard to their own problems. Certainly, having followed the course of an inquiry from beginning to end, they are more likely to understand and accept the conclusions and defend practice which is based on them. Working with others in this way contributes to a teacher's self-confidence and a staff's sense of unity. It enhances the professional status of teachers to be acknowledged as the ones most fitted to resolve school problems and it encourages them to be creative rather than plodding technicians. As the practice becomes more widespread, the resulting interchange of views and findings for the purpose of mutual reinforcement rather than uncritical imitation should strengthen the invisible bonds of the profession. Similarly, as college specialists and school faculties work together in such research the needed rapprochement of theory and practice should be accelerated.

That such claims are not extravagant can be concluded from reading descriptions of action research projects. In a mimeographed report of "A Qualitative Study of the School Day" which several elementary schools in Minneapolis carried out in 1951, one reads such comments as the following from various schools:

"The staff indicated some changes in themselves, such as a deeper understanding of children's growth processes and needs, a broader concept of behavior, an increased awareness of suitable techniques, and the importance of a teacher's mental health."

"Because the study was chosen by the staff, their interest and desire for worthwhile outcomes was greater than had the study been imposed upon them. The broad scope of the study and the limited time to grow in familiarity with the new techniques were deterrents. But the desire for growth and achievement on the part of the majority of the staff gave real purpose to the study. The staff showed interest in concentrating on specific aspects of the larger problem another school year. . . ."

"At times there was a feeling of dissatisfaction with their own progress, but this was directed toward constructive planning for another year. As plans were made to continue the study, suggestions were made to work intensively in one area, to define in detail their problem and method of attack, to plan for some total staff activities, and to ask for more specialized help. This seems to indicate that the group developed considerable insight into the problem they faced."

Reading the account of an extensive project as that reported by Foshay and Wann in the book entitled *Children's Social Values* impresses one with the worthwhileness of both the process and the results of action research. In addition, the authors of the book express their convictions as follows:

1. The quality of experience for learners, that is, the curriculum for learners, is dependent to a large degree on the teacher's conception (understanding) of the curriculum.
2. Curriculum change is therefore a consequence of change in the teacher's conception of the curriculum.
3. Changes in the teacher's conception of the curriculum result from involvement of the teacher in a process of re-education which consists of actual testing of educational theory in practice.
4. Cooperative action research is an excellent way to involve the teacher in the process of re-education.[3]

Accounts of other action research projects have appeared in books and magazine articles. An excellent description and summary has been written by Marie Hughes for an issue of *Educational Leadership*.[4]

EXPERIMENTATION BY THE CLASSROOM TEACHER

Curriculum problems vary in their extensiveness. Some are so extensive that they can only be attacked through the cooperative efforts of many people within a school or even of many schools. Others can be investigated by a single interested individual. Establishing the conditions necessary for cooperative research requires a combination of leadership skill and faculty attitudes which is not easily attained and not yet present in many schools. But despite the absence of such joint research activities, each teacher, as an individual, always has an opportunity to carry out investigations within the context of his own work. Even when group projects are underway, it is still possible to carry on additional study in individual classrooms.

All teachers continually make certain observations and to varying

---

[3] Arthur Foshay and Kenneth Wann, *Chidren's Social Values,* Bureau of Publications, Teachers College, 1954, pp. 276–277.

[4] Marie Hughes *et al.,* "Iron County Teachers Study Their Problems Scientifically," *Educational Leadership,* May, 1955, pp. 489–495.

degrees try different approaches in the course of their teaching. This does not mean that they are engaged in research, but both of these activities are basic to descriptive and experimental research. The point is that by making them somewhat more systematic their value can be increased. Being performed by a practitioner for the primary purpose of improving his own practice—this is action research and several values can be ascribed to it.

Values of Individual Action Research

The chief benefit must of course lie in the results insofar as they serve to improve instruction. Innovation does not necessarily result in improvement, but without innovation there can be no improvement. One reason for a research approach is to provide a better basis for determining whether or not an innovation does improve instruction.

But the process of research, as well as the results, has values. It provides an added dimension of interest to the teaching process. It frees the teacher from complete dependence upon outside authorities on the one hand and upon subjective impressions on the other. Such research is scholarly activity in which any teacher can engage even if he has little opportunity to contribute new knowledge to his subject field or its parent discipline. Every teacher can have the feeling of growing expertness in one aspect of the curriculum, that is to say, the content and learning process in his subject field.

The extent of individual research activity and its success depend in large measure upon the climate of the institutional setting. Seldom, perhaps, is it actually repressed or even discouraged, but often there is not the encouragement needed by those who lack sufficient confidence or inclination to incorporate a research approach in their work. All teachers can contribute by lending their support and encouragement to those of their colleagues who wish to engage in such activity, even if they themselves do not. But one of the values of actually undertaking to study problems of one's own is that it frequently inspires colleagues to do likewise. It becomes, therefore, an important factor in staff morale as well as a focal point for personal professional growth.

Types of Problems

It seems futile to attempt to list the problems which teachers might study. Some lists of this sort are available in the literature, but teachers will not wish to work on problems other than their own and it is inconceivable that any teacher lacks problems or is unaware of them. To inventory these, four questions may be asked.

First, what is the teacher now noticing, casually but continually, about the characteristics of pupils or their behavior in certain situations? What does he frequently wonder about in regard to the type of pupil most likely to react in a certain way? Does he, in other words, have hunches about the differences and similarities among his students? If so, can he state one of these hunches explicitly and then arrange to record systematically his observations with respect to it? After a suitable period of time these data can be examined and studied to note whether they support or refute the teacher's original impression. This is a form of descriptive research.

Various characteristics may be the object of study—students' interests, problems, errors or whatever. Also, various categories may be studied—boys compared with girls, brighter with slower, more mature with less mature, those with a given previous experience and those without, those from high socioeconomic homes with those from low, and the like. None of this involves experimentation yet many valuable insights can come out of it.

A second question might concern a change in method and its effect. Every teacher has tried various ways of teaching different topics, but no one can have considered all the alternatives. It should be possible to try some new ideas out each year in a carefully prepared experimental situation. If the teacher has a record of how previous classes performed on a given topic, and he has reason to believe (or better, evidence to show) that his present class is not greatly unlike the previous ones, he can use the new technique and note whether different results obtain. If he has, concurrently, two sections which are similar, he can use the old method with one and the new with the other. He can in some cases divide a single section into two parts and treat each differently. It may be possible to use the new approach with the entire class for some units and the former one for other units. In each instance it is, of course, necessary to have some way of measuring the effects, and sometimes the teacher may have to devise a new test or a questionnaire or a way of recording observations, but often regular classroom testing techniques are all applicable. It depends upon what is to be measured.

A third question the teacher might ask relates to the materials used in teaching. One textbook compared with another, a single textbook compared with a variety of source materials, teacher-made exercises compared with a workbook, an audio-visual aid compared with another mode of presentation—all these suggest experiments teachers can perform with instructional materials. Again, attention to matching of groups and of conditions and to objective measurement is, of course, necessary.

The fourth question concerns ways of administering the classroom situation. Teachers frequently have ideas for new ways of grouping pupils in a class, new physical arrangements of the classroom itself, and new distribution of time for various activities. These, too, suggest the possibility of experimentation to determine whether the difference proposed makes any difference in results.

It should be recognized that problems differ not only in content and in the research technique required, but also in the length of time involved in solving them. Some may be completed in a day or two, others may continue for a full year or more. Some call for repetition at various times to note changes or confirm earlier findings. Others may be longitudinal and trace certain pupils over a period of several years. A teacher with a particularly strong interest may carefully and systematically collect data over a period of ten years on succeeding groups and then have overwhelming evidence to support a given hypothesis or to demonstrate unmistakable trends. On the other hand, data may already be present in cumulative records or a class register which may be analyzed in a single evening and yield a valuable insight into some relationship. It is important to think of problems as coming in many shapes and sizes.

Thus, problems for research lie all around a teacher—in the facts and figures already in his records, in the observations he is already making but not recording systematically and examining analytically, in the new ways he is trying but not objectively noting the effects of, in the ideas he has but never does anything about, in all the things about his work that perplex him and make him wonder. No doubt there are teachers who would not enjoy submitting these problems and ideas to research study, but most would find excitement and enjoyment in the process and from the results gain a little more confidence in the practice of their profession.

Importance of Reporting Results

While much of the value of a teacher's research activities lies in the process itself and in the knowledge gained by the individual himself, the value can be increased by sharing the results with others, both within and without the system. Colleagues can be informed through informal conversation, through more formal written reports, or oral presentations in staff meetings. No teacher should hesitate to distribute a report of such activity through the faculty mail nor to ask an administrator if he feels there would be faculty interest in hearing a summary.

Externally, the results of a study can be submitted to a professional journal, reported formally at a meeting of an appropriate association, or referred to in the course of discussion at a conference or workshop. It is well to prepare a written summary which can be furnished to interested parties upon request. The ever-increasing number of school study councils, each with its own publications, provides a suitable avenue of communication to teachers in a given region.

It is not with the thought that others will be able to apply the findings of a study that a report on it is urged. Indeed, it is often dangerous to generalize beyond the particular situation in which the research was done. But by reporting it the teacher may encourage others to (1) undertake a closely related study, (2) duplicate the study in a different setting, or (3) use some of the same approaches on a completely different problem. Furthermore, the original researcher depended on the reports of others to know what had already been done on a problem, and he owes it to others to report his efforts so they will also know.

However, even more subtle than these effects of reporting is the possibility that the knowledge of such activity by some teachers will encourage other hesitant teachers to try it themselves. Ignorance of research methods is not the chief barrier—this can be overcome by reading, inquiring, and practicing. Lack of time is a genuine limitation but then, too, the extent of research must be tailored to the time available and much of it uses no more time than conventional practice. The greatest obstacle appears to be *fear*—fear of admitting to having problems, fear of making mistakes, fear of departing from familiar ways. Teachers should provide their colleagues with support, encouragement, and assistance in their research efforts and in turn be able to expect the same. This kind of professional spirit and activity bodes well for improving curriculum, up-grading teachers, adding zest to teaching, and increasing lay confidence and respect. It begins with one person.

PROMOTING RESEARCH

It should be apparent to the reader that research does not take place unless the right conditions are present. The willingness to work for those conditions is evidence of true professional determination to improve service to society on a sound basis. Professionalism begins with an attitude and is expressed through positive actions consistent with that attitude. Favorableness toward research efforts is a part of the attitude and its expression is found both in the application of their results and participation in the process.

Encouragement of Consumership

In the academic disciplines, research and scholarly activity can be justified solely on the basis of extending knowledge. There need be no other purpose. In the field of education there are people who, like their academic colleagues, are driven to conduct research simply because they wish to know the unknown. But this is not sufficient reason for educational research. It must improve practice or it can not be defended. Therefore when research is done and the bulk of the profession is ignorant of it or fails to apply it, there is that much less encouragement for researchers to continue. Put positively, when research results are applied, further research is encouraged and support for it is more likely to be forthcoming.

Three conditions are necessary for research findings to be applied: (1) desire, (2) awareness, and (3) freedom. The desire to apply, or for that matter to produce, research must stem from some conviction of its value. Whether this is in terms of saving time and money, deciding issues intelligently, having a basis for defense against critics, or enhancing one's own professional self-regard and security is immaterial. The important thing is that its value be recognized and associated with the improvement of educational practice.

Regardless of desire, one cannot apply that which one does not know. How awareness is brought about is not important. Individual initiative in seeking reports of research or well-organized administrative efforts to disseminate them to a staff can increase awareness. But where teachers do not care and there is no leadership, conditions for application obviously are not favorable.

Finally, there must be freedom—to try things on one's own and to meet together to decide what should be tried collectively. This "trying" can take three forms. It may be a matter of putting into practice a recommendation based on research findings, trying to duplicate a research study to verify the results, or of attempting a new variation of a study. None of these is possible in a situation in which morale is low, restrictions are many, help is withheld, or freedom is in other ways curtailed.

Establishment of Conditions for Production

It is clear that the conditions which favor the consumption or application of research are basic to conducting it in the school situation.

In addition, however, there must be a certain tendency to wonder and want to find out, a willingness to make and record careful observations, a disposition to defer decisions until the results are in. Of course, along with these qualities there must be a degree of confidence derived from knowledge of how to proceed.

Individual teachers who possess these characteristics will, if the situation is not entirely impossible, find a way to engage in some sort of research. But to encourage this attitude more widely, a group approach is almost essential. If leadership is forthcoming to bring teachers together to discuss the curriculum of the school and to identify and clarify problems, it is almost inevitable that the suggestion will arise that further study requires additional facts. At the moment a group ceases pitting one opinion against another and suggests putting them to the test, research is in the offing.

We should welcome such opportunities for group discussion, not because the group situation necessarily produces better ideas, but because it provides an opportunity to propose research activity. Any project which goes beyond the single classroom must have group cooperation to succeed. In some instances active participation of a number of people is needed, but it is the nonparticipant who is a threat if he does not understand or approve the study. For this reason, when all members of the staff sponsor and initiate studies of such scope, even if they have nothing to do with their conduct, we are pepped up. With such moral support plus tangible administrative facilitation, research aimed at program improvement is possible in schools.

Questions for Discussion

1. Is it realistic to expect a teacher to engage in research as part of his job? Should physicians be expected to carry on medical research? Consider what value there might be in a physician having kept an accurate record of his cases, the action he took, and the results. Would this be more valuable than to rely on his impressions of what was effective as a treatment?
2. What limitations do you see in "action research" as compared with so-called "pure research"? Is there such a thing as pure research in education?
3. What in your opinion are the reasons why research findings in education do not affect practice more than they do? What steps might be taken to rectify the situation?
4. Is there any moral question in your mind regarding the use of experimental procedures in teaching other people's children? How do you resolve this question if there is one?
5. Research can tell what did happen, what does happen, and even what will happen, but not what should happen. What relation is there, then, between the value judgments involving the curriculum and the findings of curriculum research?
6. Much has been made of the desirability of using good "group process" in

discussing curriculum problems. Yet good discussion is not good research. Do you see any conflict between the two or how do they relate to each other? Do you believe that discussion amounts to little more than the "pooling of ignorance?"

Selected Bibliography

Association for Supervision and Curriculum Development, *Research for Curriculum Improvement,* The Association, 1957.

Best, John W., *Research in Education,* Prentice-Hall, 1959.

Corey, Stephen, *Action Research to Improve School Practices,* Bureau of Publications, Teachers College, 1953.

Foshay, Arthur, and Kenneth Wann, *Children's Social Values: An Action Research Study,* Bureau of Publications, Teachers College, 1954.

Hovet, Kenneth, *What Shall The High Schools Teach?,* Association for Supervision and Curriculum Development, 1956, chap. 7.

Rummel, J. Francis, *An Introduction to Research Procedures in Education,* Harper, 1958.

Shumsky, Abraham, *Action Research Way of Learning: An Approach to In-Service Education,* Bureau of Publications, Teachers College, 1958.

Stratemeyer, Florence, *et al., Developing a Curriculum for Modern Living,* Bureau of Publications, Teachers College, 1957.

Taba, Hilda, and Elizabeth Noel, *Action Research: A Case Study,* Association for Supervision and Curriculum Development, 1957.

Index

Index

Action research, 476
Activities, development of, 339
  evaluation of, 356
  improvement of, 346–347
  objectives and purposes of, 338, 362
  opposition to, 341–342
  organization and administration of, 351–356
  parent participation in, 348
  principles for, 347, 356
  projects in, 363–364
  pupil participation in, 348
  scheduling of, 329–330, 353–354
  scope of, 340–341
  selection and organization of, 329
  sponsorship of, 348–350, 358, 360–361, 364
  weaknesses of, 342–346
Adult education, 431
Alabama, 372
Alabama State Board of Education, 108 n.
Alberty, Elsie, 312
Alexander, William, 51 n., 107 n., 145, 322 n., 374
American Association of School Administrators, 234 n.
American Textbook Publishers, 249
Anderson, Vernon, 172 n.
Angell, R. C., 101 n.
Anshen, R. W., 101 n.
Association for Supervision and Curriculum Development, 50, 193, 234 n., 256, 392, 449 n.
Audio-visual, film evaluation, 263
  film sources, 261
  uses of film, 261
Ayer, Fred, 93 n.

Bales, R. F., 336
Barge, Jean, 32 n.
Barton, George, 122
Basic commitments, 106
Battle Creek, Michigan, Board of Education, 449
Benjamin, Harold, 34
Benne, Kenneth, 63 n., 93, 416, 423 n.

Bernard, Jessie, 102 n.
Board of education, 3
Bobbitt, Franklyn, 36
Bossing, Nelson, 309 n., 313, 319 n., 332 n.
Bowles, Governor, 22
Broad fields, 285
Brunner, Edmund, 102 n.
Buffalo, New York Public Schools, 32
Burgess, E. W., 101 n.

Campbell, Doak, 172 n.
Capital Area School Development Association, 245 n.
Carnegie Corporation, 23
Carnegie, Dale, 336
Caswell, H. L., 26 n., 36, 55, 133, 134, 172 n., 374
Chall, Jeanne S., 248
Church, 102
Citizens participation, 433
  background of, 430
  competence for, 437
  effects of, 438
  guiding principles for, 447–461
  justification for, 433
  problems of, 431
  topics for, 439–447
Clapp, Elsie, 440 n.
College students, 106–107
Commission on Reorganization of Secondary Education, 123 n.
Committee operation, 381–382
Community changes, 101–102
Community school, 440
Conant, James B., 23, 24, 441 n., 442
Consultants, 391
Content, 44, 185, 209
  choice of, 47
  re-examination of, 299
  selection of, 28–29, 33, 171–175, 312–314
Cook, Lloyd, 448 n.
Cooperative research, 477
Cooperative Study of Secondary School Standards, 77 n., 357, 447 n.

"Core" curriculum, characteristics of, 306
  common learnings in, 310–311
  data gathering for, 318–319
  definition of, 305
  difficulties of, 308
  evaluation of, 317–318, 331–332
  function of, 308–309
  guiding pupils in, 321–324
  initiation of, 314
  needs of students in, 312, 319–321
  objectives or purposes of, 307, 309–311, 327–328
  planning for, 314–315
  problem census in, 325–326
  report groups in, 331
  resource people for, 315–317
  subject specialists in, 316–317
  topic selection for, 313
  types of, 306
  understanding of, 305
Corey, Stephen, 54 n., 63, 93
Correlation, 301
Course of study, 42, 183–189
  content of, 185–186
  definition of, 183
  objectives of, 184–185
  outline for, 188–189
Crewson, Walter, 373
Criticism of education, reaction to, 435–436
Cronbach, Lee, 47 n.
Cumulative records, 320
Cunningham, Ruth, 320 n.
Curriculum, coordinator of, 54
  definition of, 3–4, 35
  evaluations of, 26
  framework of, 130
  guides to, 9, 44–45
  models, 30
  national control of, 97
  organization of, 34, 130–133
  scope of, 18, 146–150
  specialists in, 30–31
Curriculum bureaus, 239
Curriculum change, broad fields in, 285
  committees in, 380–382
  complexity of, 86–87
  consultants in, 391–392
  correlation in, 301–302
  fusion in, 287
  insight into, 99–100
  integration in, 288–291

Curriculum change (*Continued*)
  lay participation in, 16–17
  leadership in, 384–385, 387–390
  local groups in, 399–400
  methods of, 8–9
  need for action in, 9
  objectives or purposes in, 390–391
  organization for, 370, 382–384
  procedure in, 378–379
  report writing for, 395–396
  resistance to, 84–85
  state leadership in, 371–372
  student learning as a measure of, 11
  study councils in, 393
  supervision of, 392–393
  survey of, 88–91
  teacher participation in, 375, 398–399
  trends in, 370, 373
Curriculum committees, problems with, 380
  principles for operation, 381
Curriculum framework, controlled problems explanation, 145
  subject approach, 137
  teacher contribution to, 133
  unrestricted, 155
Curriculum improvement, approaches, 8 ff.
  clarification of goals, 390
  cooperation in, 56
  initiation of, 4
  local action for, 382
  process of, 36
  teaching as a part of, 10
Curriculum leaders, 388
Curriculum planning, activities in, 53
  application of, 50
  approaches to, 7–8
  community analysis in, 126
  complexity of, 70–71
  controlled problems in, 144–155
  cooperative nature of, 10, 11–12
  democracy in, 56
  difficulty in, 37
  experience approach to, 4
  frustration in, 71–72, 85–86
  history of, 36
  implementation of, 30
  improvement of, 48–50, 81–82
  influence on, 132–133
  initiation of, 6, 29
  lay participation in, 30, 39, 51, 436, 438–439, 442–446, 447–461
  leadership in, 92–93

Curriculum planning (*Continued*)
  local aspects of, 98
  local unit in, 375–378, 379–380
  national control of, 97–98
  organization of, 52–53
  orientation in, 394–395
  pupil participation in, 25–26
  purpose and scope in, 32–33
  recommendations for, 23–24
  research in, 64, 463
  sequence in, 178–179
  social policy in, 96–98
  subject framework in, 137–144
  supervision in, 43
  syllabus in, 178
  teacher participation in, 3, 10–11,
    26–27, 39–41, 55, 57, 53–56, 73–
    74, 95–96, 133
  unrestricted framework in, 155–163
  values in, 7, 19, 73

Dade County, Florida, Public Schools,
    47
Dahlke, Otto, 104 n.
Dale, Edgar, 248
Davis, Calvin O., 36
DeBernardis, Amo, 239 n.
Denver Board of Education, 187
Denver Senior High School, 55
Dewey, John, 109
Diedrich, Paul B., 176 n.
Diplomas, 284
Doane, Donald, 25
Douglass, Harl, 347
Drop-outs, 24

Education, dependence on, 105
Educational Policies Commission, 42,
    103, 109, 123 n., 292
Elementary schools, 28
Evaluation, 317
  criteria for, 332
  lay participation in, 458–461
  procedures in, 212
Experience, 4
  quality of, 48
Experience curriculum, 156
Experimentation, 50, 471, 481
Extraclass activities, administration of,
    351–356
  evaluation of, 356
  guides for, 347

Extraclass activities (*Continued*)
  history of, 339
  opposition to, 341–346
  scope of, 340
  sponsorship, 348, 358

Faunce, Roland, 309 n., 313, 319 n.,
    332 n.
Featherstone, William, 125, 126 n.
Fitzwater, Gertrude, 445
Flesch, Rudolph, 248
Florida, 372
Foshay, Arthur, 481
Frederick, Robert, 349 n., 353 n., 358,
    359–360
French, Will, 122, 124, 309 n.
Fugitive materials, 254
Functionalization, 288
Fusion, 287

Garrett County, Maryland, Public
    Schools, 47
General education, 27–28, 306
Gestalt psychology, 188
Goals of education, *see* Objectives or
    purposes
Governor's Fact Finding Committee on
    Education in Connecticut, 22
Group cohesion, 410
Group process, 330, 333–336
  advantages of, 302
  attitudes in, 408
  characteristics, 403–404
  committees in, 401
  consultant in, 425–426
  definition of, 400–401
  difficulties in, 406–409
  evaluation of, 459–461
  leadership in, 420–423
  observer in, 426
  personalities in, 417–418
  physical arrangements for, 419
  principles of, 385–386, 406
  promotion of, 404–406
  recorder in, 425
  roles in, 416–417, 423–425
  skill in, 402–403
  teacher knowledge of, 56, 413–417
  teacher training for, 334
  use of, 409–413
Group work, 56
Gruber, Frederick C., 339 n.
Gruhn, William, 347

Haiman, Franklyn S., 413 n.
Hall, D. M., 455 n.
Hallenbeck, W. C., 102 n.
Halverson, Paul, 51 n., 322 n.
Hamlin, H. M., 459
Hand, Harold, 342, 447 n., 459
Havighurst, Robert J., 104, 448 n.
Hayakawa, S. I., 414 n.
Heintz, R. H., 412 n.
Henry, J. D., 24 n.
Henry, N. B., 25 n., 306 n., 334 n., 440 n., 459 n.
Hill, Clyde, 20 n.
Hill, Thomas, 319 n.
Hock, Louise, 319 n.
Hollingshead, August, 104, 448 n.
Home, 101
Homework, 434–435
Hopkins, L. T., 26 n., 107 n., 155, 162, 173, 323
Horney, Karen, 72 n.
Hughes, Marie, 481
Hulstrunk, A., 240 n.

Illinois, 147, 372
Individualism, 103
Individualization, 200, 207
In-service education, 100
Instructional materials, audio-visual, 258–264
  classification of, 241
  community resources, 264–266
  location of, 231–245
  science, 256–257
  selection of, 251–264
  sources of, 236–245
  teacher development of, 240–245
  types of, 245–264
Irving, Washington, 436

Johnson, B. Lamar, 107 n., 309 n.
Johnson, F. Ernest, 102 n.

Kansas, 372
Kansas Improvement Program, 45
Kansas State Education Department, 146 n., 151 n.
Kideney, Isabel, 21 n.
Knowles, Malcolm, 381
Krug, Edward, 35 n., 40, 53, 374
Krutch, Joseph Wood, 19

Latin Grammar School, 279, 281
Lawler, Marcella, 392 n.

Learning, 28
  activities in, 175, 210, 329
  classification of activities, 211
  experiences in, 4, 48, 49, 58
  functionality of, 275
  materials for, 210, 230
  organization of, 176–185
  reinforcement of, 273
  skills in, 273–275
Leonard, J. Paul, 48 n., 145, 172 n.
Linderman, James A., 219
Lippitt, Ronald, 413 n.
Lonely Crowd, The, 19
Lurry, Lucille, 312

Mackenzie, Gordon, 54 n., 63, 93
Maier, Norman, 413 n.
Mann, Horace, 109
Marschner, Ruth, 92
Methods, teaching, 36–37, 42–43
McKown, Harry, 357
Michigan, 372
Miel, Alice, 63 n., 204 n., 302 n., 330 n.
Miles, Matthew, 406 n.
Miller, Franklin, 357
Milne School, Albany, New York, 242
Minneapolis Board of Education, 310 n.
Minneapolis Public Schools, 480–481
Mossman, Lois, 175
Motivation, 35–36
Moyer, James, 357
Mudd, Dorothy, 311
Muntyan, Bozidar, 63 n., 93 n., 416 n., 423 n.

National Council of Teachers of English, 42
National Citizens Commission for the Public Schools, 439, 441 n.
National Education Association, 441 n.
National Industrial Conference Board, 255
National Society for the Study of Education, 25, 36, 459
Needs of the nation, 126
Needs of pupils, 125–126
Needs of youth, 25, 312
Neugarten, Bernice, 448 n.
Newark, New Jersey, Public Schools, 32
New York City Board of Education, 310 n.
New York State, 27, 284, 256, 372, 373

New York State Board of Regents, 21, 31
New York State Education Department, 45, 55, 278, 441 n., 447 n.
New York State Teachers Association, 237 n.

Oak Ridge, Tennessee, 440
Objectives or purposes, guides to, 109, 122–125
  implementation of, 43–44
  in core curriculum, 327–328
  lay understanding of, 14, 22, 441–447
  priorities for, 42–43
  selection of, 168–171
  through subject fields, 291–299
Ohio School Survey, 22
Oklahoma, 372
Olsen, Edward G., 445 n., 448 n.
Oswego, New York, College of Education, 230
Oregon, 392
Overstreet, H. A., 72 n.

Parrish, Louise, 319 n., 322 n., 332 n.
Passow, A. Harry, 413 n.
Patrick, Robert, 357
Pennsylvania Department of Public Instruction, 187
Planning, activities, 175
  kinds of, 167
  objectives in, 168
Prescott, Daniel, 292
Preston, M. G., 412 n.
Progressive education, 18–19
Progressive Education Association, 47
Psychology, basic generalizations, 110–120
  teacher knowledge of, 107
Public relations, the teacher in, 53
Pupils, needs of, 25–26
Pupil-teacher planning, 40, 202–205
Purdue University Opinion Poll, 32

Regents Council on Readjustment of High School Education, 21
Rendell, J. W., 239 n.
Research, applied to teaching, 110–121
  conditions conducive to, 479
  consumption of, 486
  definition of, 464
  methods of, 469

Research (*Continued*)
  problem approach to, 464
  problem, examples of, 465–467
  problem, selection of, 467, 482–484
  problem, types of, 467–468
  production of, 486–487
  promotion of, 485–486
  reporting of, 479–480, 484–485
  skills in, 477
  teacher responsibility for, 463
  types of, 476–478
  value of, 471–472, 482
Resource persons, 315–317
Resource units, 47–48, 313, 326
  characteristics of, 208–212
  construction of, 212–216
  definition of, 206
  evaluation of, 217–219
  illustration of, 219–227
  learning activities in, 209–210
  materials in, 211–212
  outcomes of, 208–209
  purposes of, 47
  use of, 48, 227–228
  value of, 206–207
Replogle, Vernon L., 79, 80 n.
Riesman, David, 19
Roberts, Kenneth, 242
Russell Sage Foundation, 42
Romine, Stephen, 124, 174
Russia, 431

St. Louis, Missouri, Public Schools Survey, 31 n.
Santa Barbara, California, City Schools, 148–150
Saylor, J. Galen, 40, 107 n., 145
Schenectady, New York, Public Schools, 240
School programs, criticisms of, 6–7, 17–20, 24
  religion in, 19
  resolution of, 15–16
Scope and sequence, 146
Scott, Winfield, 20 n.
Sharp, George, 63, 76
Sheldon, Edward, 230
Shores, J. Harlan, 135, 145, 155, 173
Simpson, Ray, 332
Smallenberg, Harry, 477
Smith, B. O., 135, 145, 155, 173
Smith, Eugene, 357
Smith-Hughes Act, 282

Society, changes in, 100–106, 429–432
industrialization of, 102–103
values in, 104
Southern Association, 447 n.
Spaulding, Francis, 31 n.
Spears, Harold, 33
Special education, 27–28
Specialists, 393
Specialization, 268–270
Staff, cooperation, 398
orientation, 398
Stanley, William O., 102 n., 135, 145, 155, 173, 448 n.
State departments of education, 371–372
Sterner, William, 364 n.
Storen, Helen F., 445
Stratemeyer, Florence, 155, 179 n., 312
Study contract, 242–244
Study councils, 393
Subjects, functionalization of, 288
goals of, 278
merger of, 287
proliferation of, 283
Subject-centered approach to curriculum, 46
Subject fields, 34–35, 274
art, 274
biology, 268, 271–272
civic responsibility in, 297–299
commerce, 283, 441
constants, 284
economic efficiency in, 296–297
electives, 284–285
English, 272–263, 274, 279–280, 289, 441
enrichment of, 275
foreign language, 282, 290
home economics, 274
human relationships in, 295–296
improved teaching of, 299–303
knowledge of, 270–271
mathematics, 274, 281
music, 282
objectives or purposes of, 278
practical arts, 282–283, 290
self-realization in, 292–295
social studies, 219–227, 272–273, 274, 280, 289
trends in, 278
units in, 302–303
physical education, 283
science, 256–257, 285, 290

Subject framework, 137
faults in, 138
supports for, 141
Supervision, 55
Supervision in curriculum planning, 43
Supervisors, duties of, 78–79
Supplementary books, 251
Survey courses, 286
Symonds, H. A., 72 n.
Symonds, P. M., 107 n.

Taba, Hilda, 104 n.
Teacher planning, 167–168, 172, 329–330
Teachers, anxiety, 71
attitudes of, 80–84
attitudes toward authority, 78
behavior in classroom teaching, 324
behavior in activities, 358–359
decisions of, 42
evaluation of, 77–78, 83–84
function of, 75
frustration of, 85
growth of, 69–75
improvement of, 299
leadership of, 92
modern, 65–69
perceptions, 72
preparation of, 29
qualities of, 69–70, 75–77
relationships, 71, 291, 319–320, 350–351, 3 69–370, 380, 433
roles, 39, 53, 88–91
scholarship of, 127
self-evaluation of, 77
status ideas of, 73
supervision needs of, 79
traditional, 64–65
values of, 73, 127
work load of, 57
Teaching aids, 45
Teaching, improvement of, 299
individualization of, 300
Texas Education Agency, 447 n.
Textbooks, 46–47, 171–172
evaluation of, 251–254
selection of, 249–251
uses of, 245–248
Thelen, Herbert, 413 n.
Theory, resistance to, 84
Toops, Myrtle, 313
Transfer, 301
Tyler, Ralph, 123, 357

United States Department of Agriculture, 421, 422 n., 423 n.
United States Office of Education, 97, 445 n.
Units, definition of, 189–190
examples of, 150, 151
planning of, 187, 193–201
structure of, 200–201
student planning for, 202
systematic approach to, 198
teaching of, 206
types of, 191–193
value of, 188

Values, 7, 19, 104
Virginia, 133

Wann, Kenneth, 481
Waskin, Yvonne, 319 n., 322 n., 332 n.
Wesley, Edgar, 169 n.
Wilhelms, Fred, 68–69
Wisconsin, 47, 147
Witt, P. W., 239 n.
Woodruff, Myra, 420–421

Yoakum, Gerald A., 248

Zapf, Rosalind, 319 n., 322 n.